SHONEN JUMP GRAPHIC NOVEL

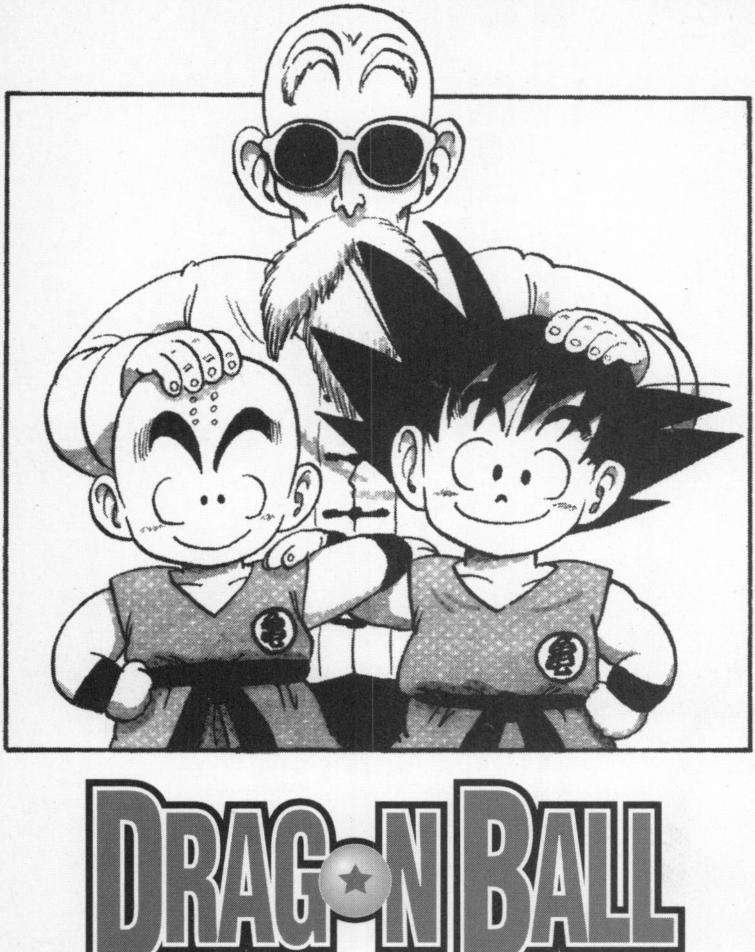

DRAGON BALL

Vol. 3

DB: 3 of 42

STORY AND ART BY
AKIRA TORIYAMA

THE MAIN CHARACTERS

Son Goku
Young Goku learned kung-fu and inherited the magic *nyoibô* staff from his grandfather. He once had a monkey's tail, but he lost it under strange circumstances in Vol. 2.

Yamcha
A martial artist and bandit, Yamcha initially wanted to steal the Dragon Balls, but he went to the city to be Bulma's boyfriend instead.

Bulma
A genius inventor, Bulma met Goku on her quest for the seven magical Dragon Balls.

Pu'ar
Yamcha's shapeshifting friend.

Oolong
Immature, shapeshifting Oolong was originally a villain that Goku and Bulma defeated.

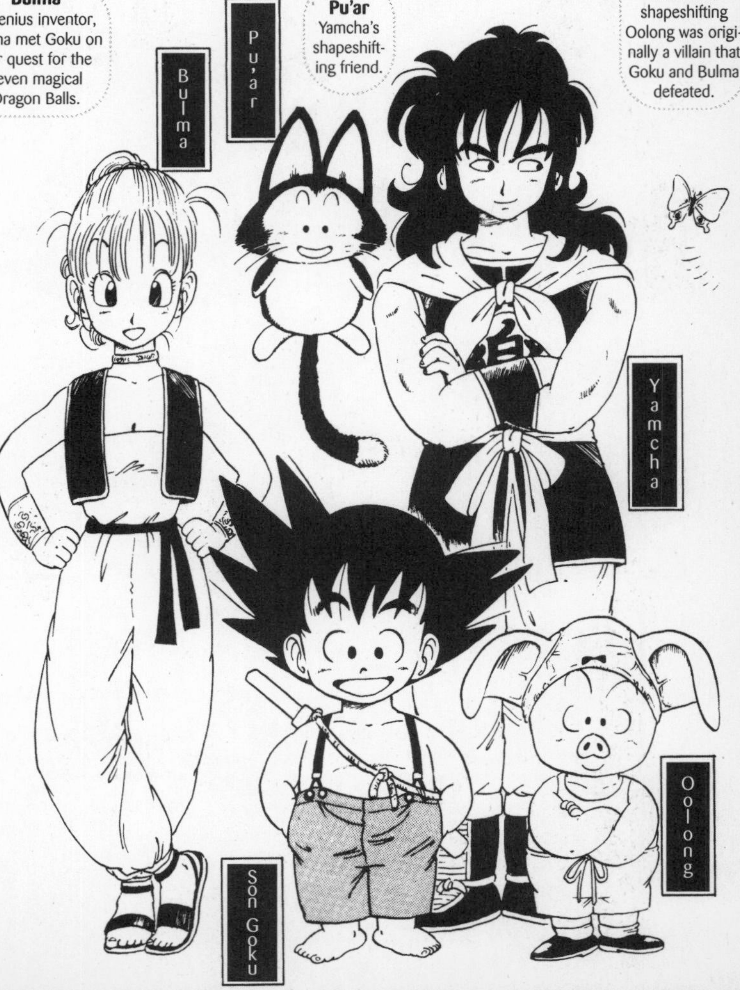
Pu'ar
Bulma
Yamcha
Oolong
Son Goku

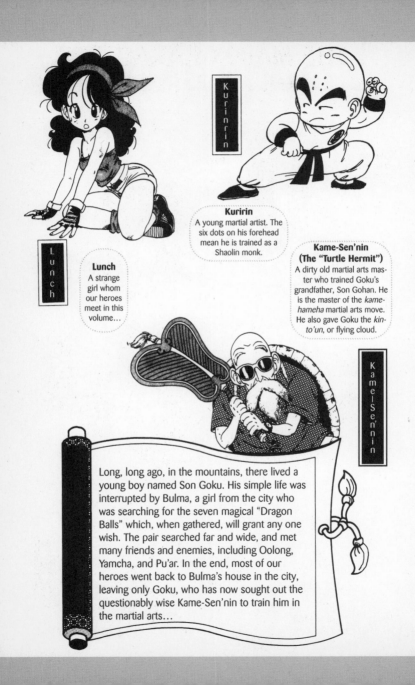

Kuririn

Kuririn
A young martial artist. The six dots on his forehead mean he is trained as a Shaolin monk.

Lunch

Lunch
A strange girl whom our heroes meet in this volume…

Kame-Sen'nin (The "Turtle Hermit")
A dirty old martial arts master who trained Goku's grandfather, Son Gohan. He is the master of the *kame-hameha* martial arts move. He also gave Goku the *kin-to'un*, or flying cloud.

Kame Sen'nin

Long, long ago, in the mountains, there lived a young boy named Son Goku. His simple life was interrupted by Bulma, a girl from the city who was searching for the seven magical "Dragon Balls" which, when gathered, will grant any one wish. The pair searched far and wide, and met many friends and enemies, including Oolong, Yamcha, and Pu'ar. In the end, most of our heroes went back to Bulma's house in the city, leaving only Goku, who has now sought out the questionably wise Kame-Sen'nin to train him in the martial arts…

DRAGON BALL 3

CON- TENTS

ドラゴンボール

DRAGON BALL

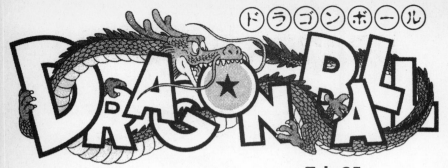

Tale 25
A Rival Arrives!!

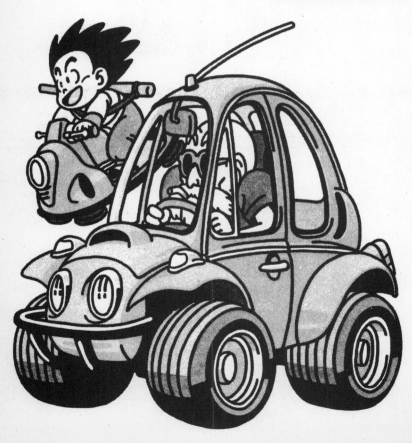

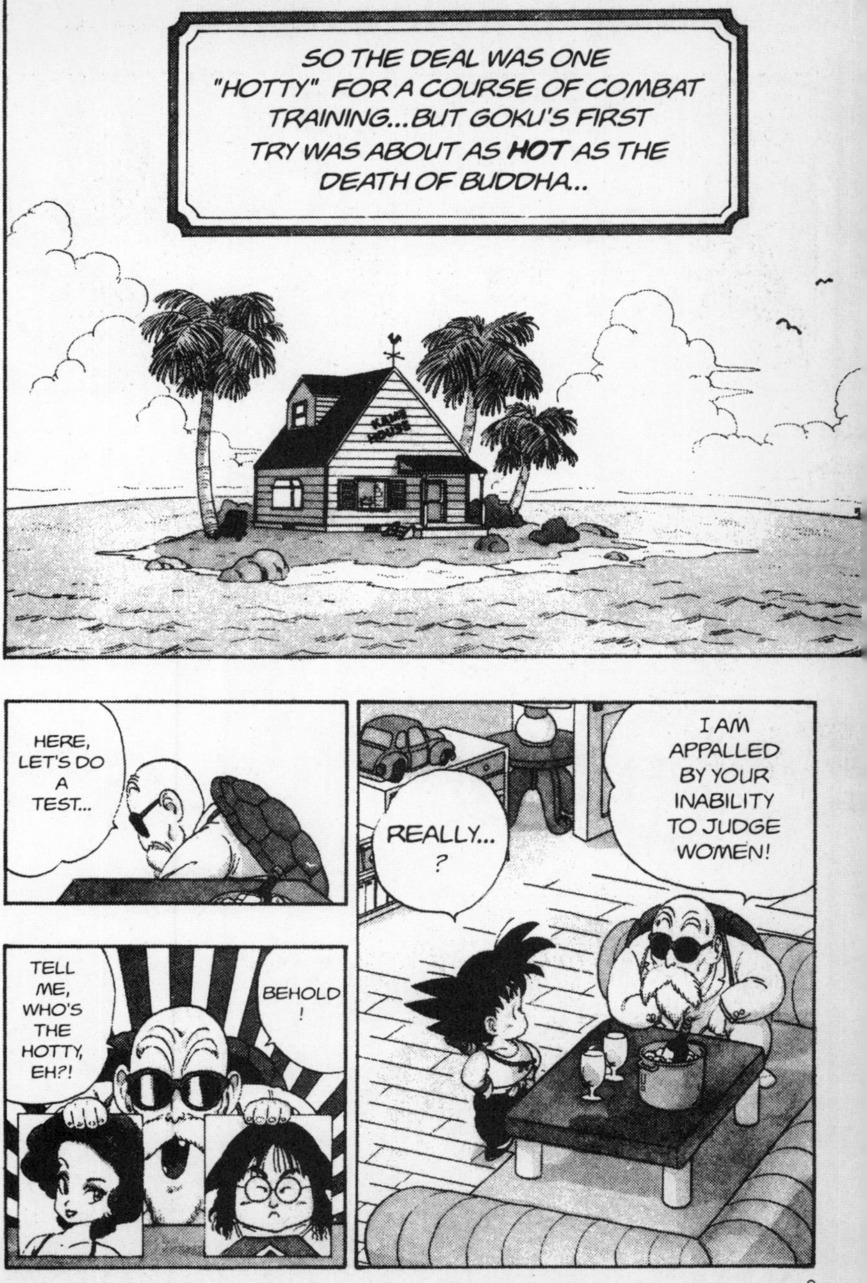
SO THE DEAL WAS ONE "HOTTY" FOR A COURSE OF COMBAT TRAINING...BUT GOKU'S FIRST TRY WAS ABOUT AS **HOT** AS THE DEATH OF BUDDHA...
I AM APPALLED BY YOUR INABILITY TO JUDGE WOMEN!
REALLY... ?
HERE, LET'S DO A TEST...
TELL ME, WHO'S THE HOTTY, EH?!
BEHOLD !

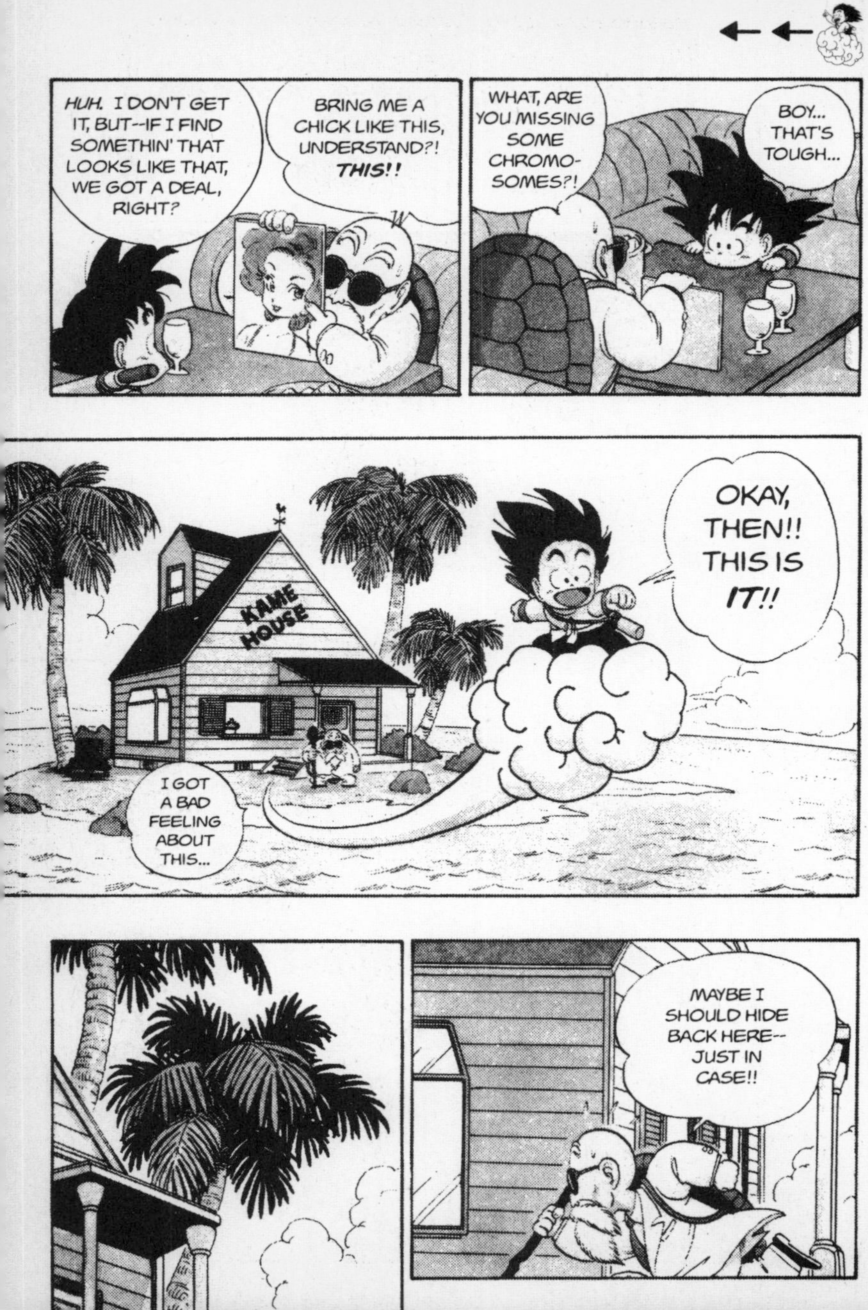
BOY... THAT'S TOUGH...
WHAT, ARE YOU MISSING SOME CHROMO-SOMES?!
BRING ME A CHICK LIKE THIS, UNDERSTAND?! **THIS!!**
HUH. I DON'T GET IT, BUT--IF I FIND SOMETHIN' THAT LOOKS LIKE THAT, WE GOT A DEAL, RIGHT?
OKAY, THEN!! THIS IS *IT!!*
KAME HOUSE
I GOT A BAD FEELING ABOUT THIS...
MAYBE I SHOULD HIDE BACK HERE-- JUST IN CASE!!

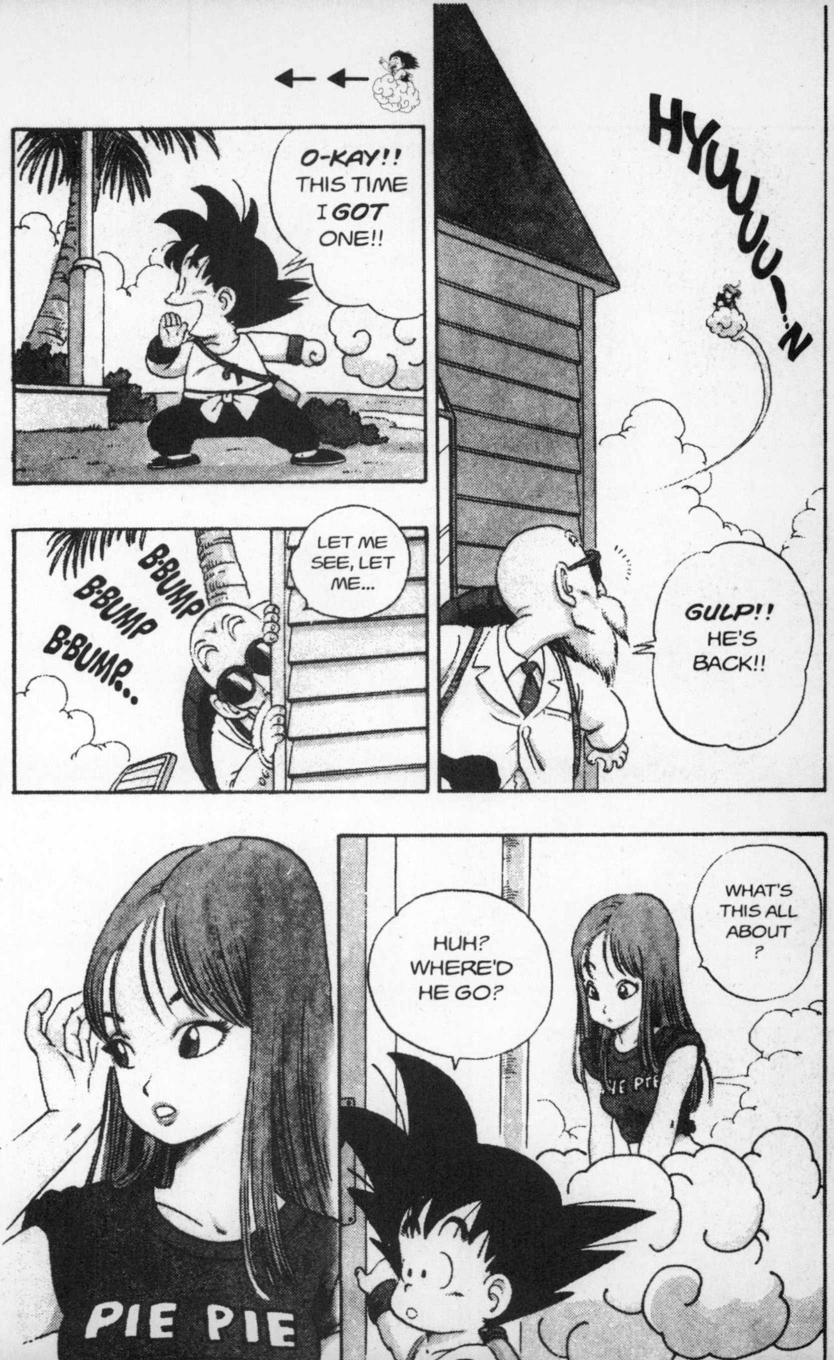
HYUUUU–N
GULP!! HE'S BACK!!
O-KAY!! THIS TIME I GOT ONE!!
LET ME SEE, LET ME...
B-BUMP B-BUMP B-BUMP...
WHAT'S THIS ALL ABOUT?
HUH? WHERE'D HE GO?
PIE PIE

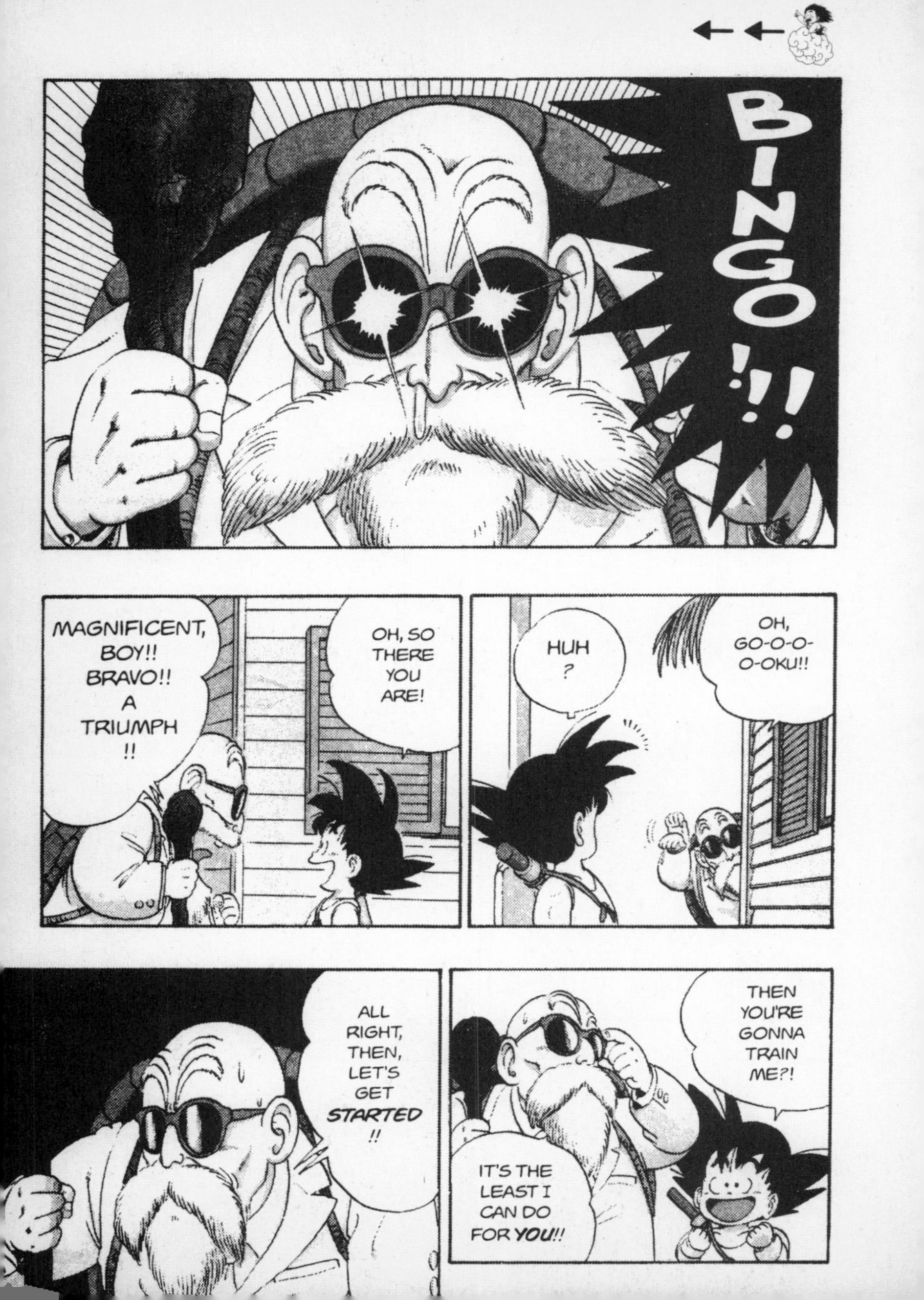
BINGO!!!
OH, GO-O-O-O-OKU!!
HUH ?
OH, SO THERE YOU ARE!
MAGNIFICENT, BOY!! BRAVO!! A TRIUMPH !!
THEN YOU'RE GONNA TRAIN ME?!
IT'S THE LEAST I CAN DO FOR YOU!!
ALL RIGHT, THEN, LET'S GET STARTED !!

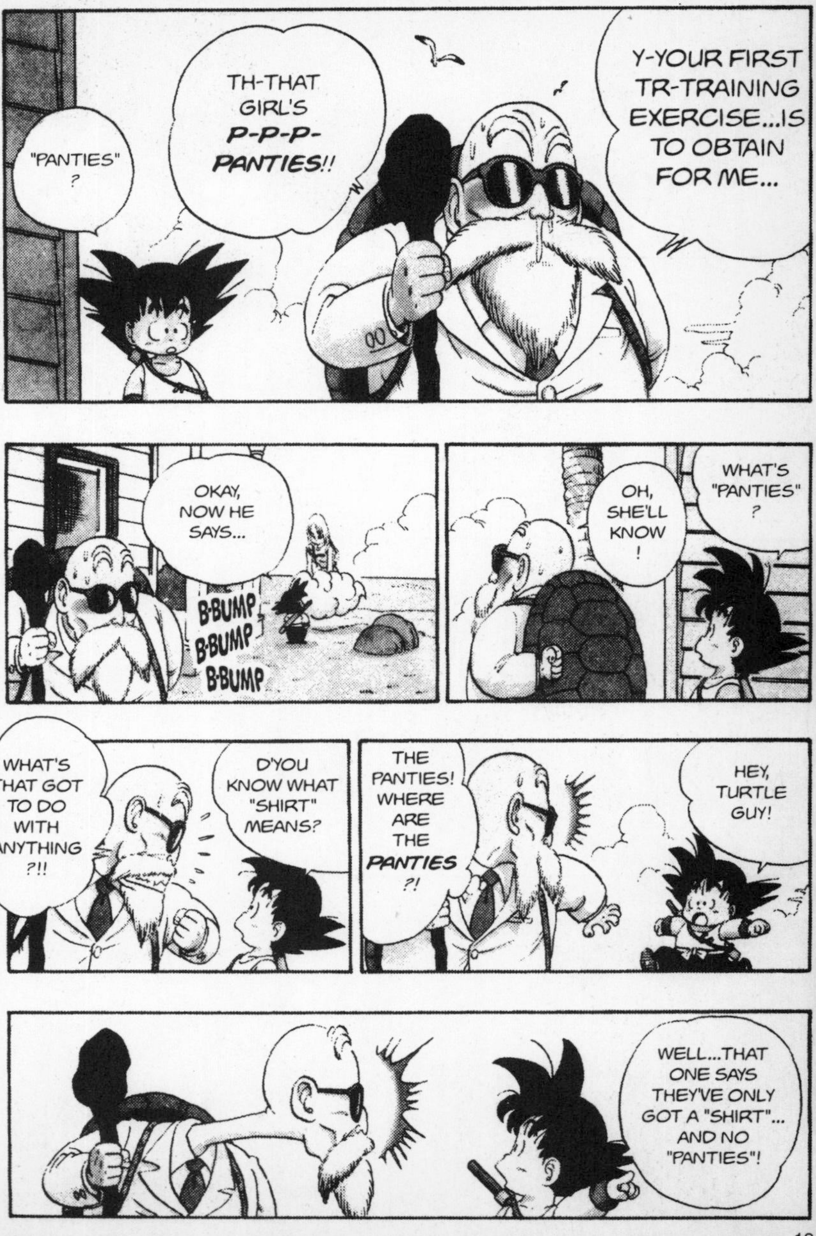
Y-YOUR FIRST TR-TRAINING EXERCISE...IS TO OBTAIN FOR ME...
TH-THAT GIRL'S P-P-P-PANTIES!!
"PANTIES"?
WHAT'S "PANTIES"?
OH, SHE'LL KNOW!
OKAY, NOW HE SAYS...
B-BUMP
B-BUMP
B-BUMP
HEY, TURTLE GUY!
THE PANTIES! WHERE ARE THE PANTIES?!
D'YOU KNOW WHAT "SHIRT" MEANS?
WHAT'S THAT GOT TO DO WITH ANYTHING?!!
WELL...THAT ONE SAYS THEY'VE ONLY GOT A "SHIRT"... AND NO "PANTIES"!

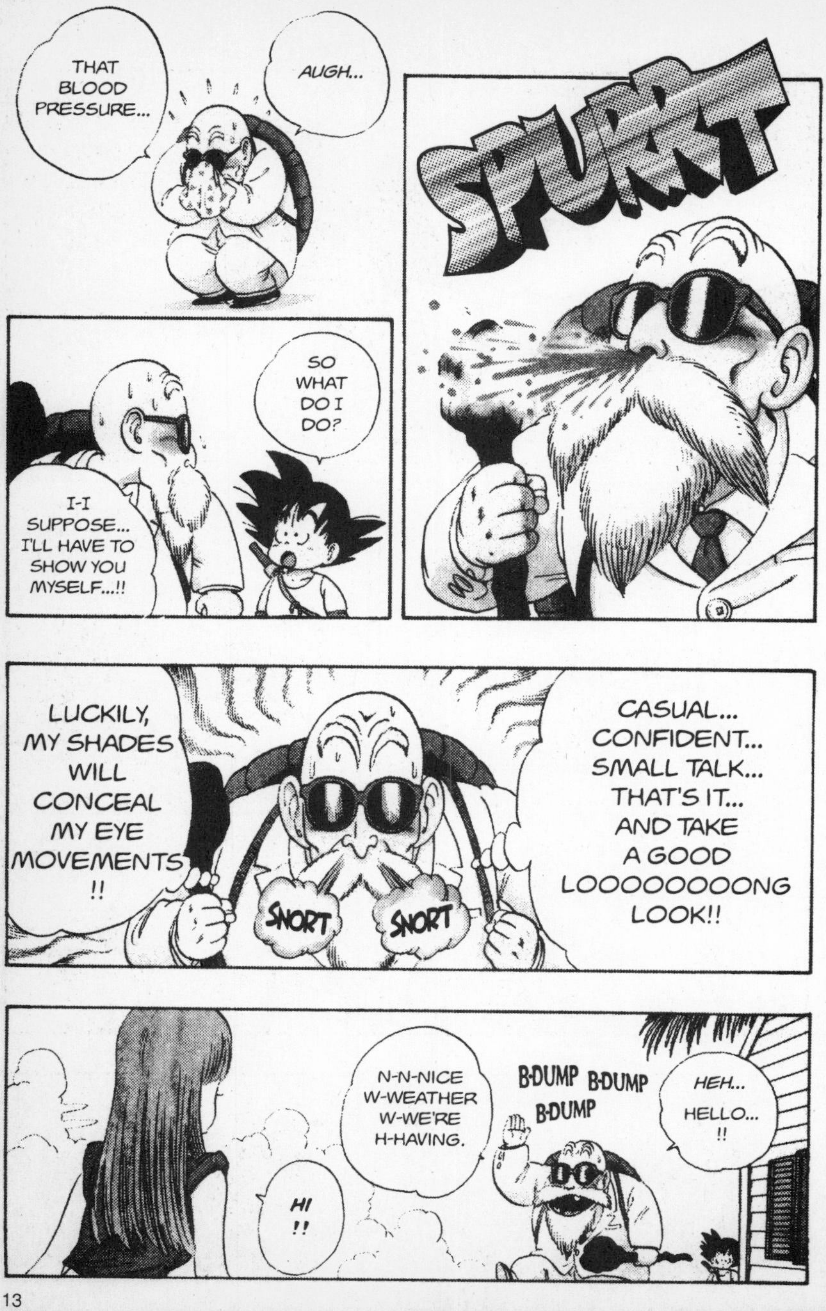
SPURRT
AUGH...
THAT BLOOD PRESSURE...
SO WHAT DO I DO?
I-I SUPPOSE... I'LL HAVE TO SHOW YOU MYSELF...!!
CASUAL... CONFIDENT... SMALL TALK... THAT'S IT... AND TAKE A GOOD LOOOOOOOONG LOOK!!
LUCKILY, MY SHADES WILL CONCEAL MY EYE MOVEMENTS !!
SNORT
SNORT
HEH... HELLO... !!
B-DUMP B-DUMP
B-DUMP
N-N-NICE W-WEATHER W-WE'RE H-HAVING.
HI !!

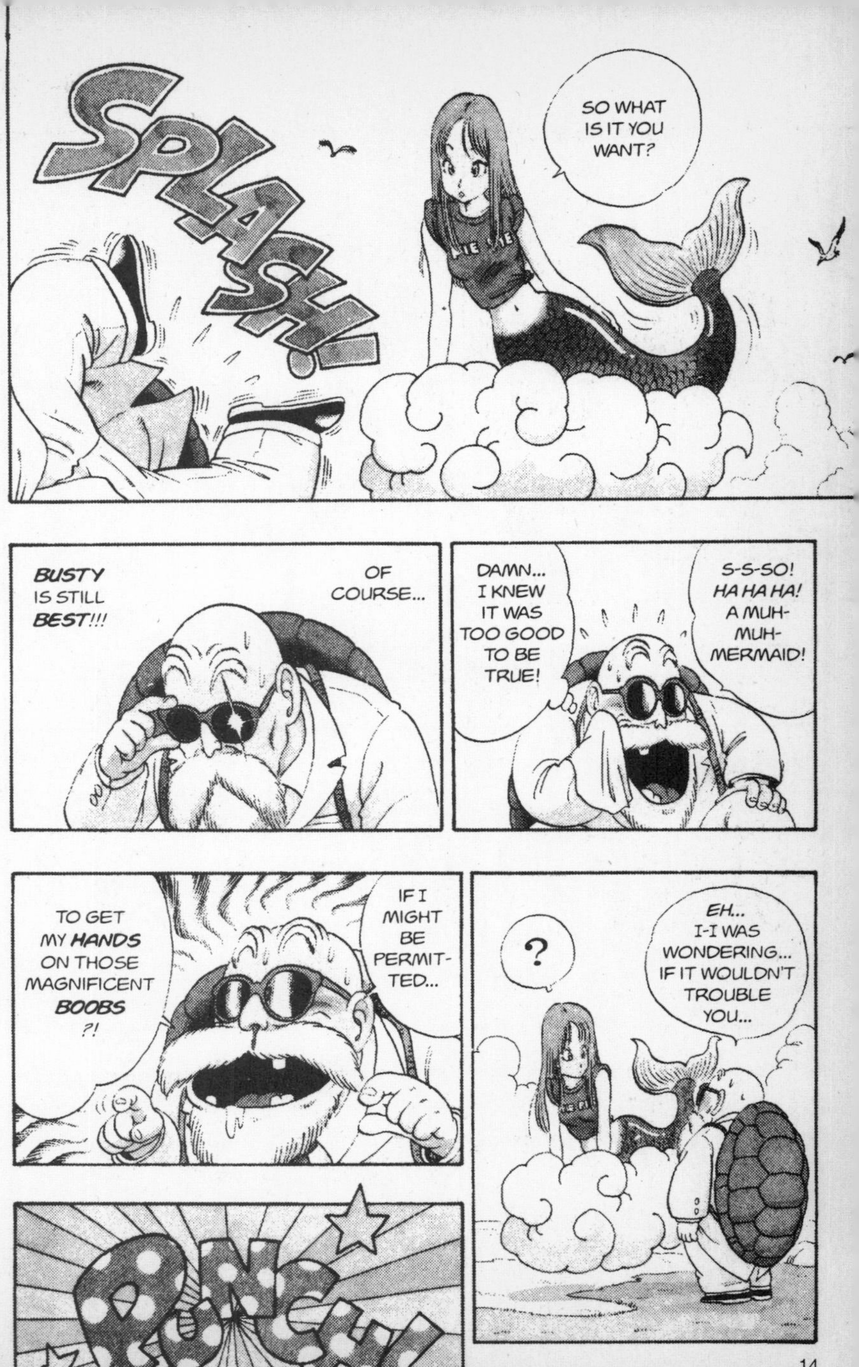
SO WHAT IS IT YOU WANT?
SPLASH!!
S-S-SO! HA HA HA! A MUH-MUH-MERMAID!
DAMN... I KNEW IT WAS TOO GOOD TO BE TRUE!
OF COURSE...
BUSTY IS STILL BEST!!!
EH... I-I WAS WONDERING... IF IT WOULDN'T TROUBLE YOU...
?
IF I MIGHT BE PERMIT-TED...
TO GET MY HANDS ON THOSE MAGNIFICENT BOOBS ?!
PUNCH!

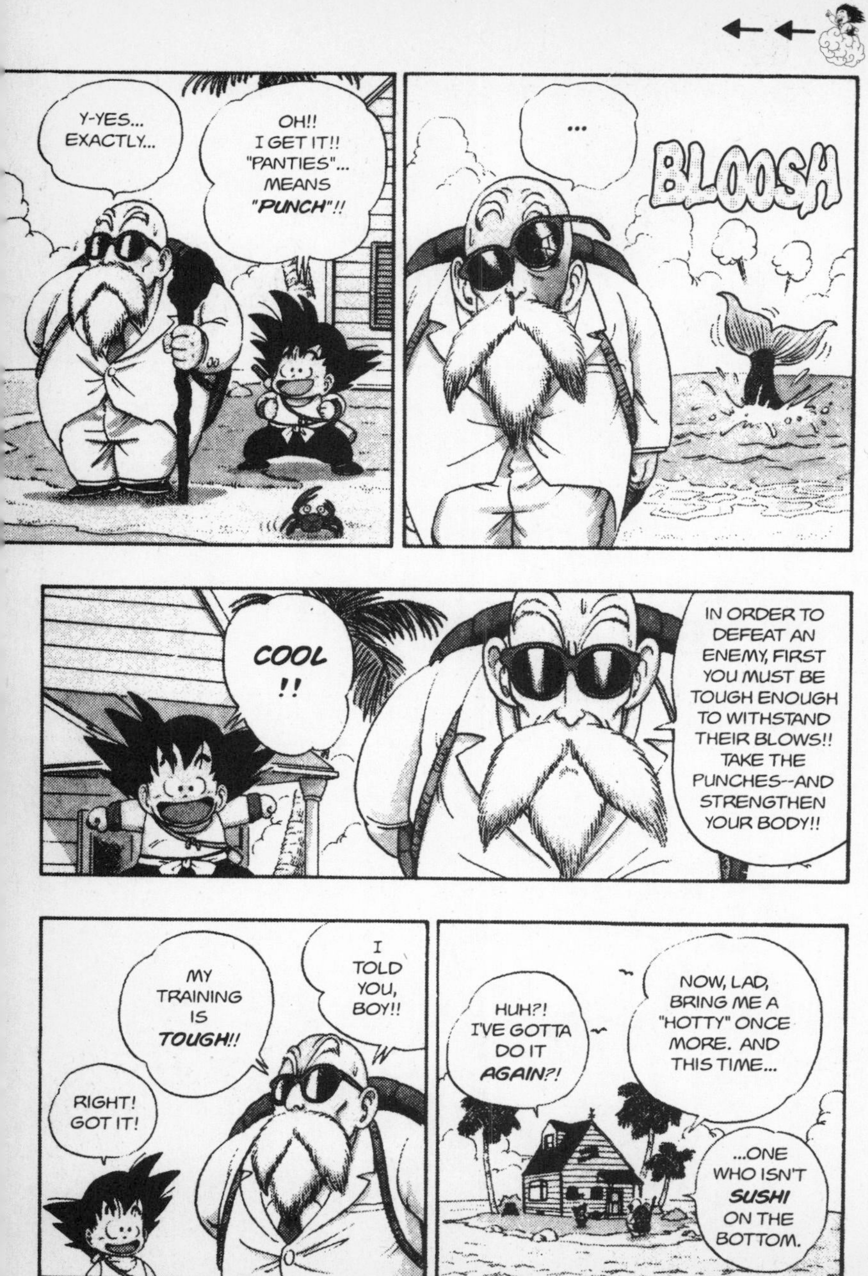
...
BLOOSH
OH!! I GET IT!! "PANTIES"... MEANS "PUNCH"!!
Y-YES... EXACTLY...
IN ORDER TO DEFEAT AN ENEMY, FIRST YOU MUST BE TOUGH ENOUGH TO WITHSTAND THEIR BLOWS!! TAKE THE PUNCHES--AND STRENGTHEN YOUR BODY!!
COOL !!
NOW, LAD, BRING ME A "HOTTY" ONCE MORE. AND THIS TIME...
...ONE WHO ISN'T SUSHI ON THE BOTTOM.
HUH?! I'VE GOTTA DO IT AGAIN?!
I TOLD YOU, BOY!!
MY TRAINING IS TOUGH!!
RIGHT! GOT IT!

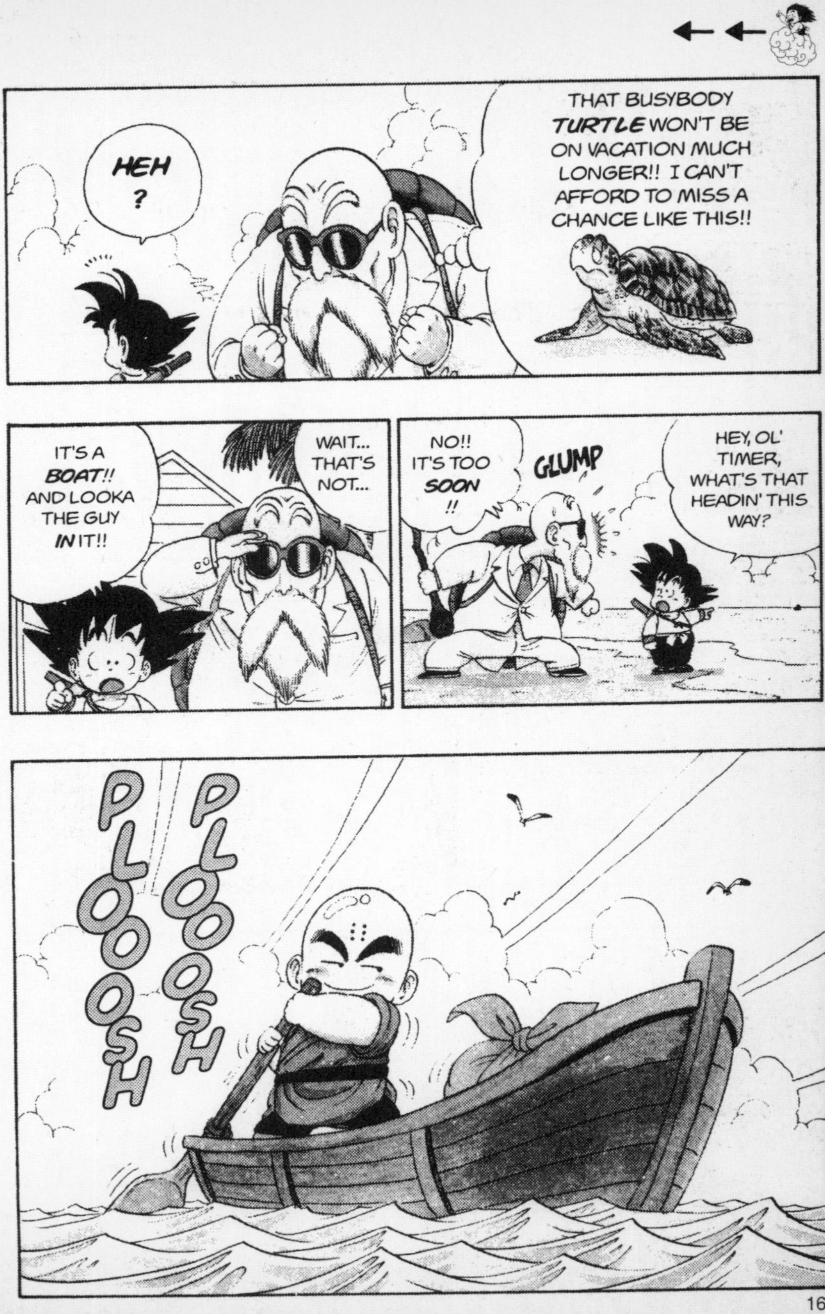
THAT BUSYBODY TURTLE WON'T BE ON VACATION MUCH LONGER!! I CAN'T AFFORD TO MISS A CHANCE LIKE THIS!!
HEH ?
HEY, OL' TIMER, WHAT'S THAT HEADIN' THIS WAY?
GLUMP
NO!! IT'S TOO SOON !!
WAIT... THAT'S NOT...
IT'S A BOAT!! AND LOOKA THE GUY IN IT!!
PLOOOSH
PLOOOOSH

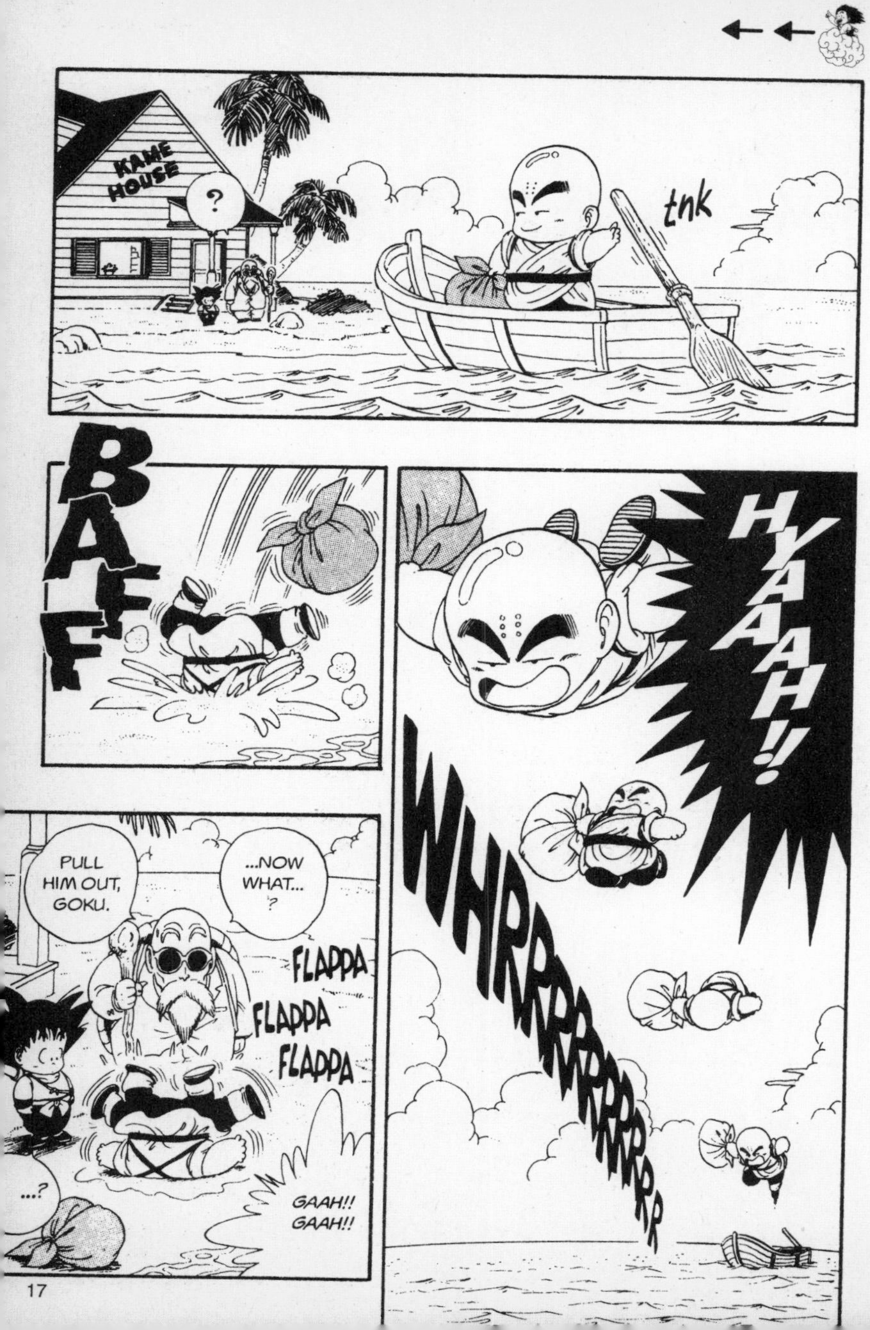
KAME HOUSE
?
tnk
HYAAAAH!!
WHRRRRRRRRRRRRRRR
BAFF
...NOW WHAT... ?
PULL HIM OUT, GOKU.
FLAPPA FLAPPA FLAPPA
GAAH!! GAAH!!
...?

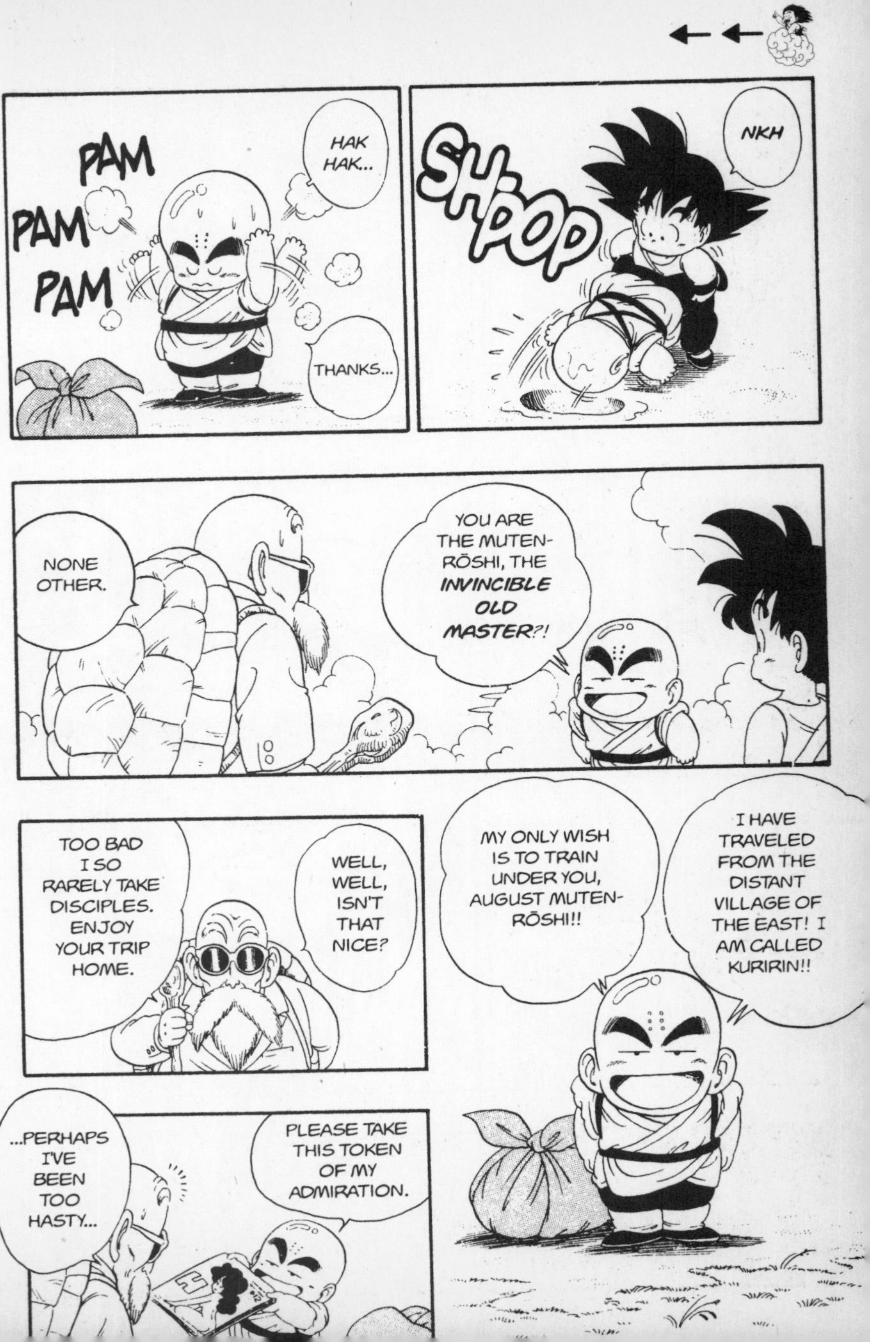
SHPOP
NKH
PAM PAM PAM
HAK HAK...
THANKS...
YOU ARE THE MUTEN-RŌSHI, THE *INVINCIBLE OLD MASTER*?!
NONE OTHER.
I HAVE TRAVELED FROM THE DISTANT VILLAGE OF THE EAST! I AM CALLED KURIRIN!!
MY ONLY WISH IS TO TRAIN UNDER YOU, AUGUST MUTEN-RŌSHI!!
WELL, WELL, ISN'T THAT NICE?
TOO BAD I SO RARELY TAKE DISCIPLES. ENJOY YOUR TRIP HOME.
PLEASE TAKE THIS TOKEN OF MY ADMIRATION.
...PERHAPS I'VE BEEN TOO HASTY...

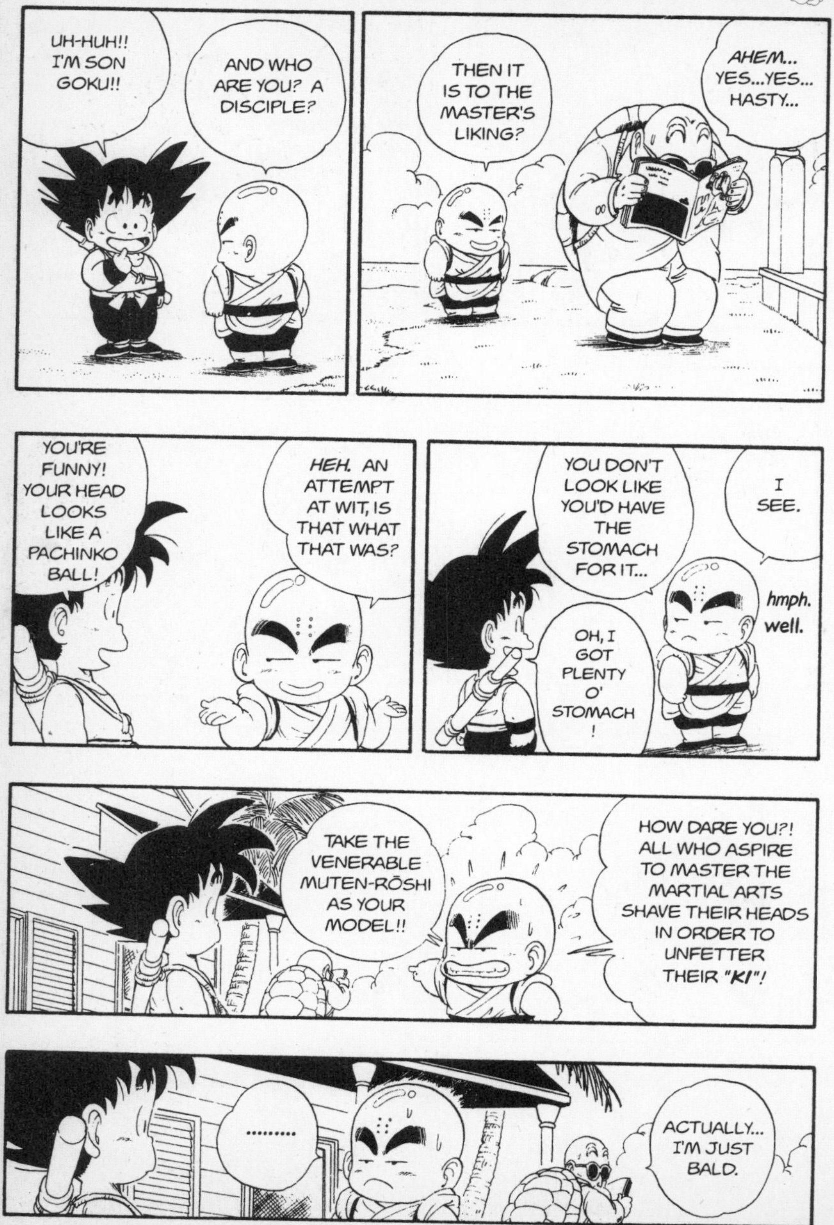
AHEM... YES...YES... HASTY...
THEN IT IS TO THE MASTER'S LIKING?
AND WHO ARE YOU? A DISCIPLE?
UH-HUH!! I'M SON GOKU!!
I SEE.
YOU DON'T LOOK LIKE YOU'D HAVE THE STOMACH FOR IT...
hmph. well.
OH, I GOT PLENTY O' STOMACH!
HEH. AN ATTEMPT AT WIT, IS THAT WHAT THAT WAS?
YOU'RE FUNNY! YOUR HEAD LOOKS LIKE A PACHINKO BALL!
HOW DARE YOU?! ALL WHO ASPIRE TO MASTER THE MARTIAL ARTS SHAVE THEIR HEADS IN ORDER TO UNFETTER THEIR "KI"!
TAKE THE VENERABLE MUTEN-RŌSHI AS YOUR MODEL!!
ACTUALLY... I'M JUST BALD.
....

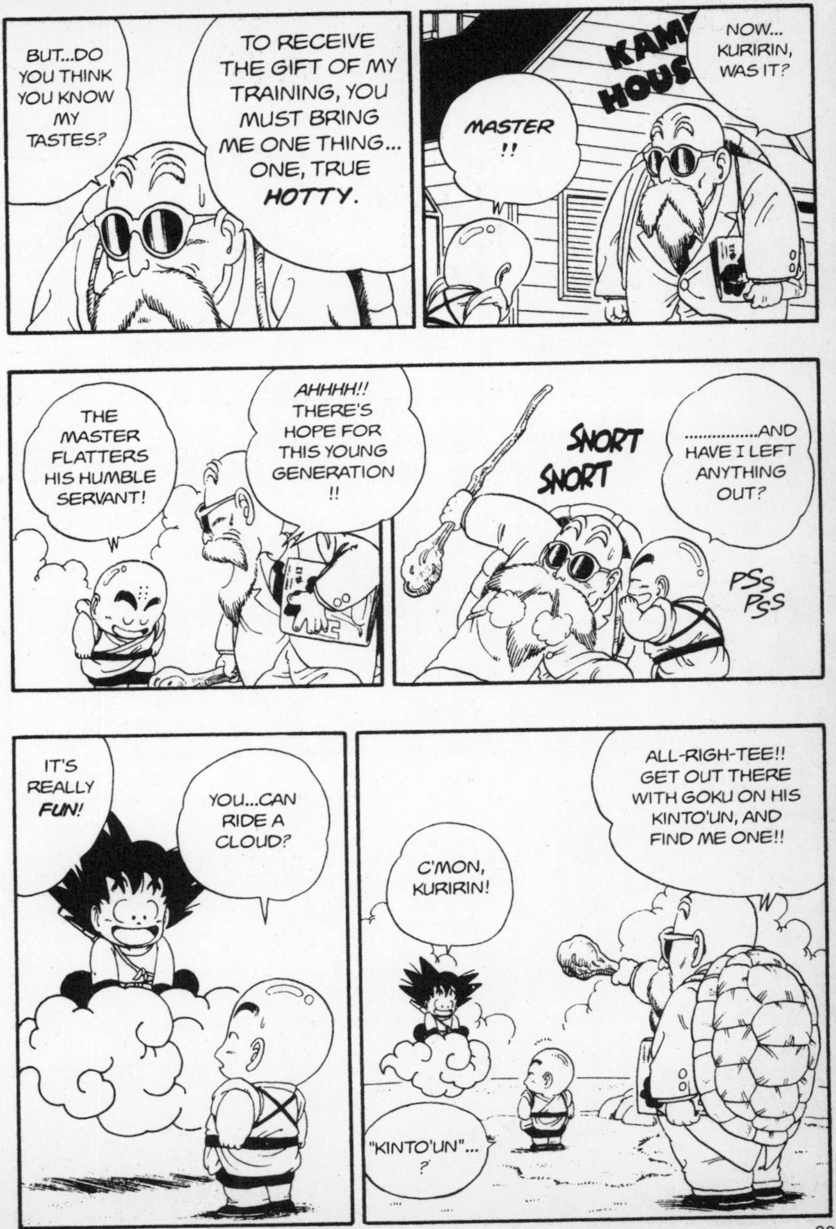
NOW... KURIRIN, WAS IT?
MASTER !!
TO RECEIVE THE GIFT OF MY TRAINING, YOU MUST BRING ME ONE THING... ONE, TRUE HOTTY.
BUT...DO YOU THINK YOU KNOW MY TASTES?
...............AND HAVE I LEFT ANYTHING OUT?
SNORT SNORT
PSS PSS
AHHHH!! THERE'S HOPE FOR THIS YOUNG GENERATION !!
THE MASTER FLATTERS HIS HUMBLE SERVANT!
ALL-RIGH-TEE!! GET OUT THERE WITH GOKU ON HIS KINTO'UN, AND FIND ME ONE!!
C'MON, KURIRIN!
"KINTO'UN"... ?
YOU...CAN RIDE A CLOUD?
IT'S REALLY FUN!

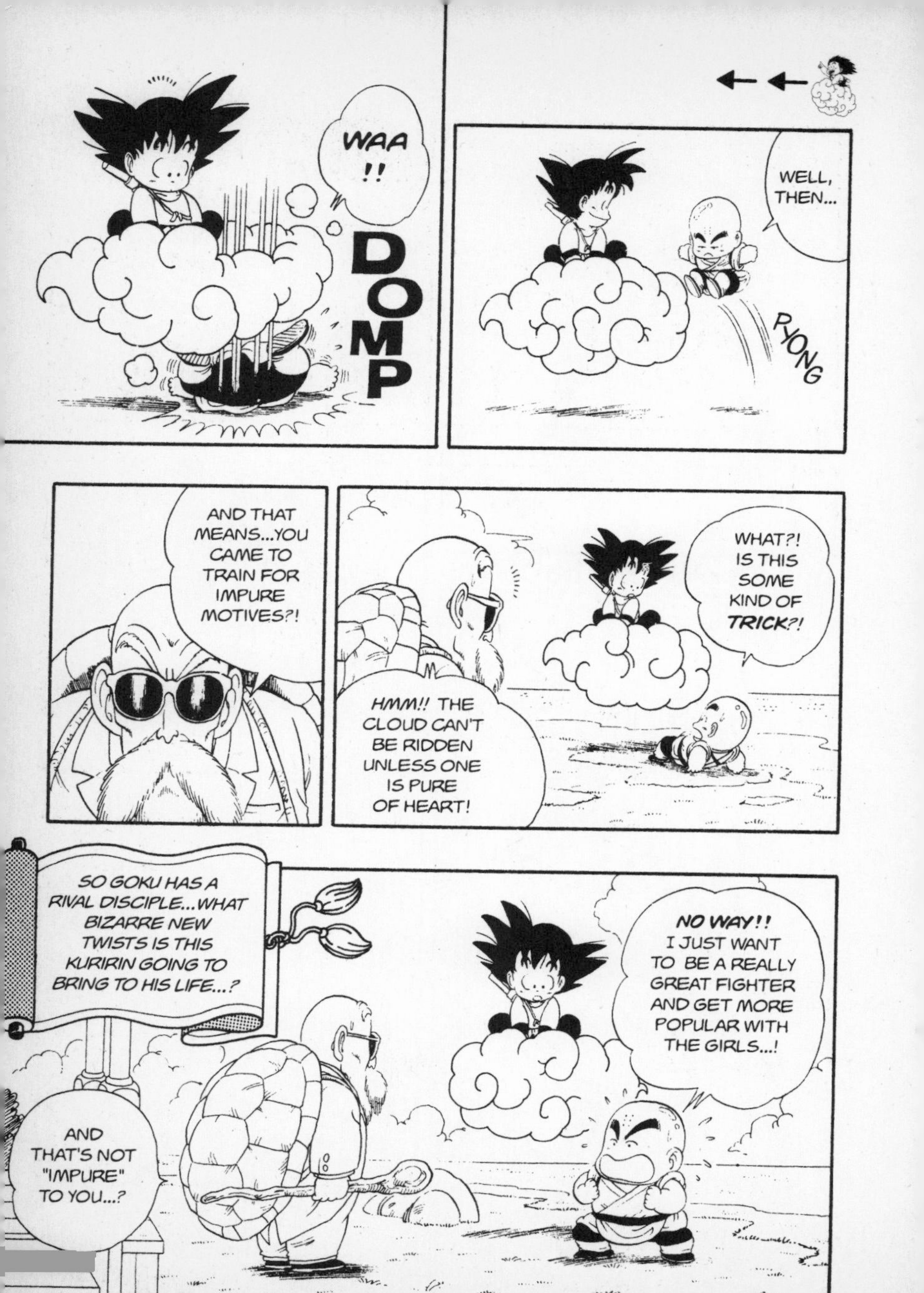
WELL, THEN...
PYONG
WAA!!
DOMP
WHAT?! IS THIS SOME KIND OF TRICK?!
HMM!! THE CLOUD CAN'T BE RIDDEN UNLESS ONE IS PURE OF HEART!
AND THAT MEANS...YOU CAME TO TRAIN FOR IMPURE MOTIVES?!
NO WAY!! I JUST WANT TO BE A REALLY GREAT FIGHTER AND GET MORE POPULAR WITH THE GIRLS...!
SO GOKU HAS A RIVAL DISCIPLE...WHAT BIZARRE NEW TWISTS IS THIS KURIRIN GOING TO BRING TO HIS LIFE...?
AND THAT'S NOT "IMPURE" TO YOU...?

NEXT: A Very... Interesting Girl

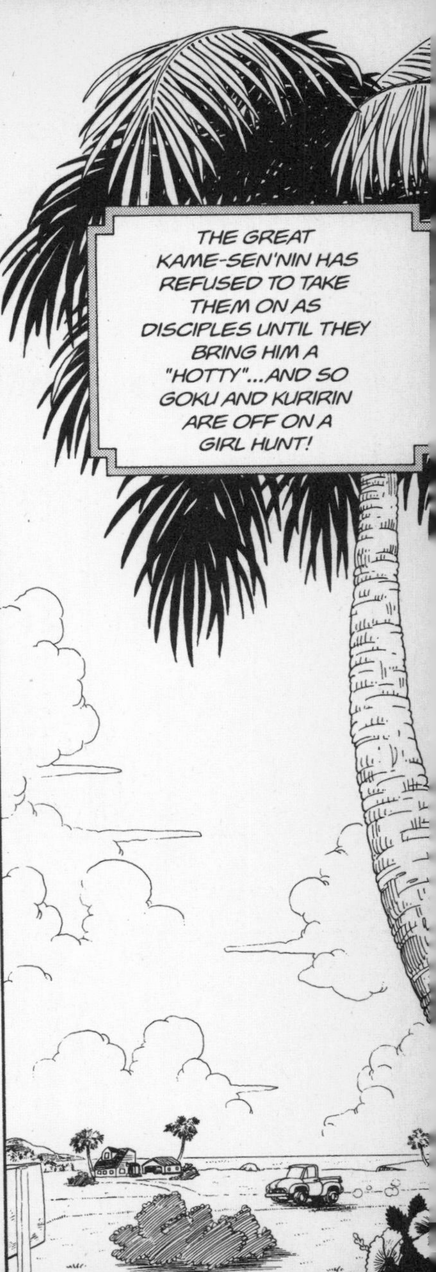
THE GREAT KAME-SEN'NIN HAS REFUSED TO TAKE THEM ON AS DISCIPLES UNTIL THEY BRING HIM A "HOTTY"...AND SO GOKU AND KURIRIN ARE OFF ON A GIRL HUNT!

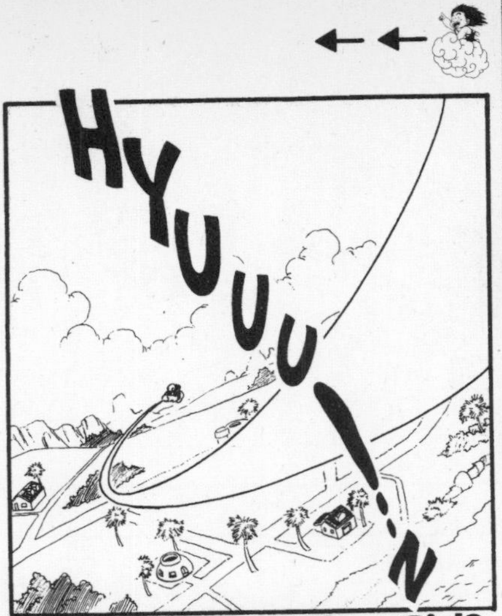
HYUUUU!!N

Tale 26 • Who's That Girl?

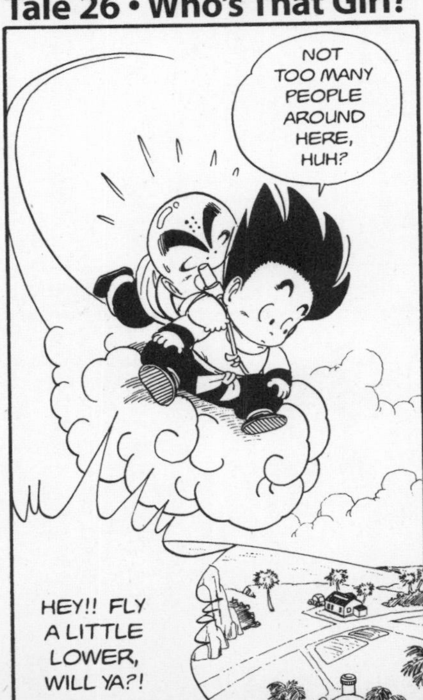
NOT TOO MANY PEOPLE AROUND HERE, HUH?
HEY!! FLY A LITTLE LOWER, WILL YA?!

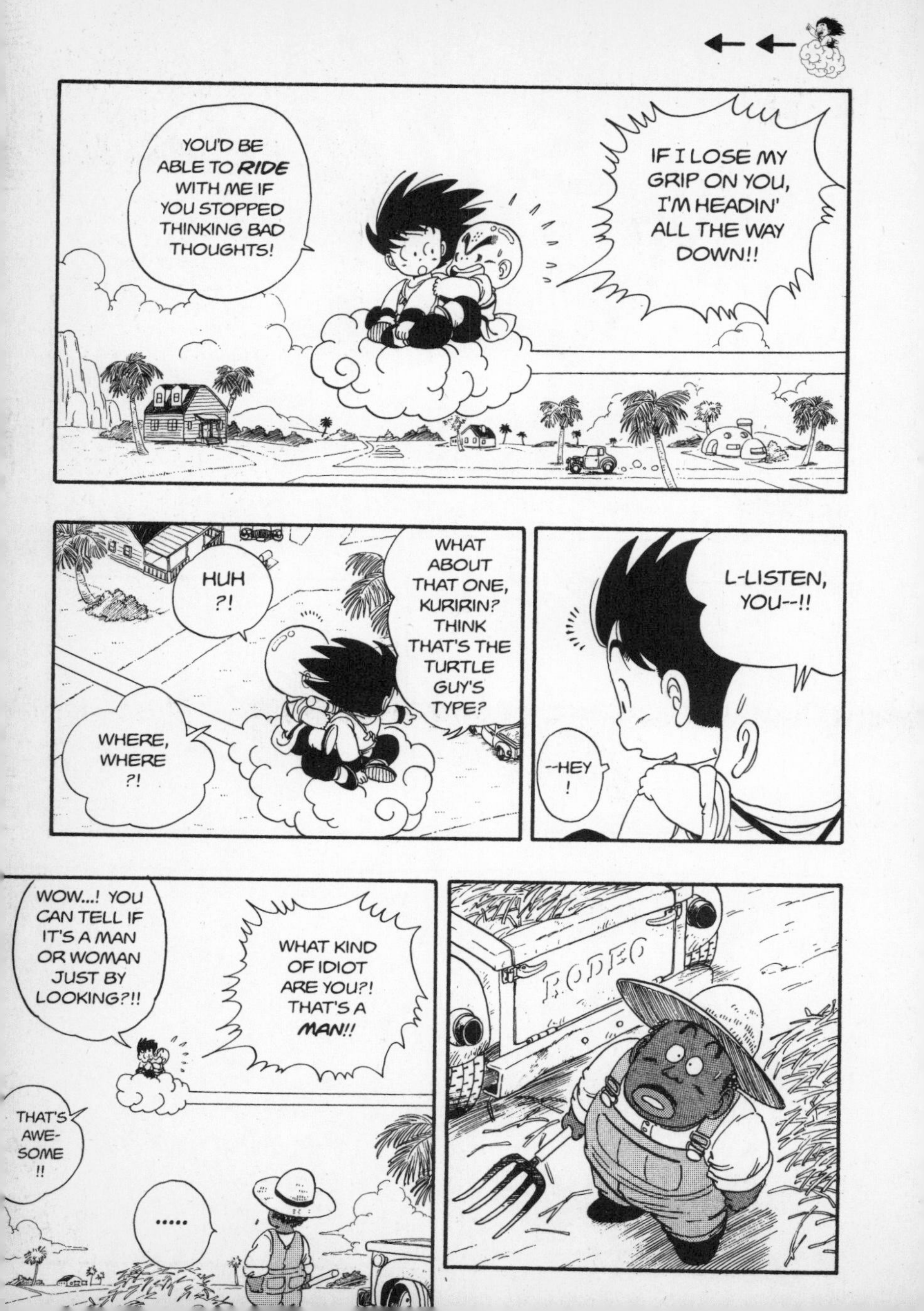
IF I LOSE MY GRIP ON YOU, I'M HEADIN' ALL THE WAY DOWN!!
YOU'D BE ABLE TO **RIDE** WITH ME IF YOU STOPPED THINKING BAD THOUGHTS!
L-LISTEN, YOU--!!
--HEY !
WHAT ABOUT THAT ONE, KURIRIN? THINK THAT'S THE TURTLE GUY'S TYPE?
HUH ?!
WHERE, WHERE ?!
RODEO
WHAT KIND OF IDIOT ARE YOU?! THAT'S A **MAN**!!
WOW...! YOU CAN TELL IF IT'S A MAN OR WOMAN JUST BY LOOKING?!!
THAT'S AWE-SOME !!
.....

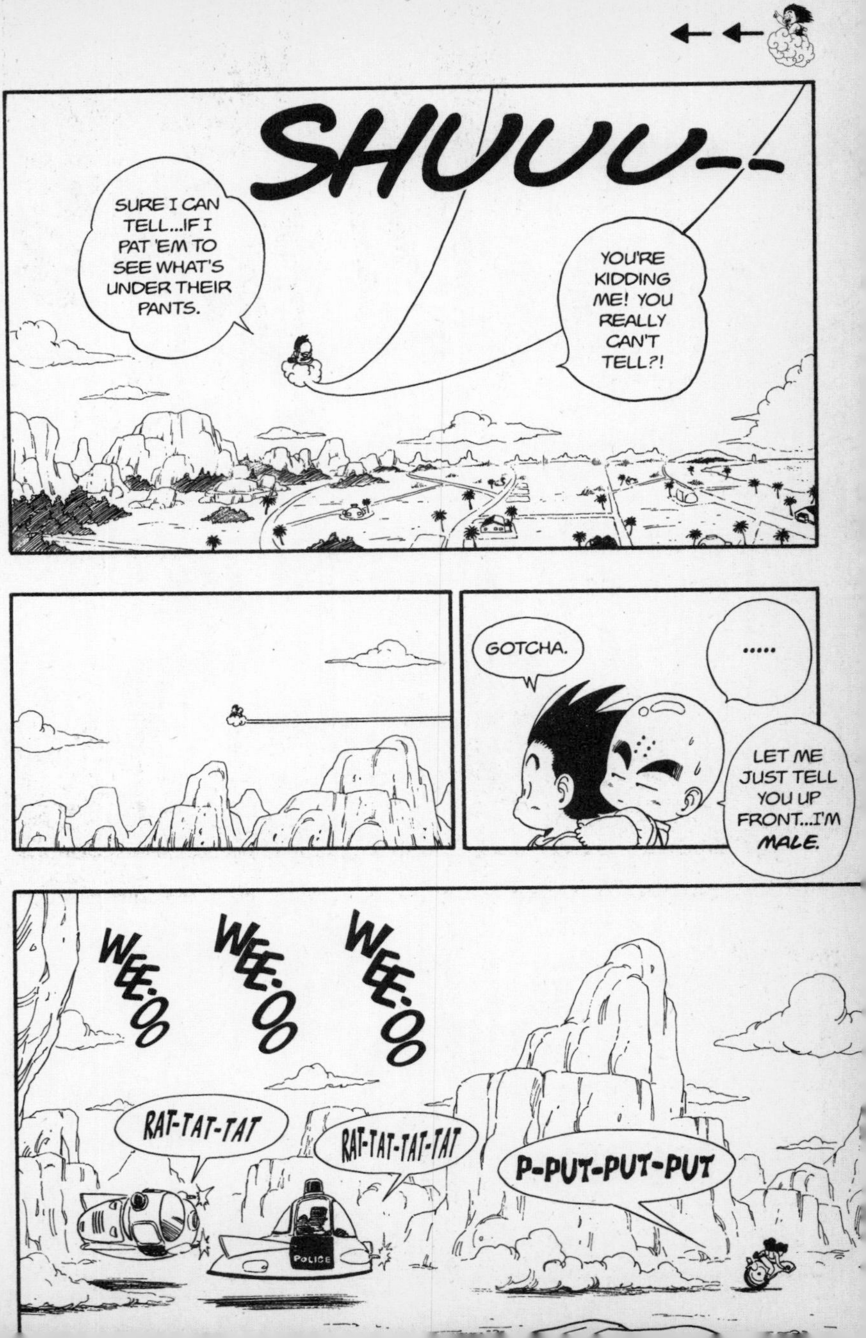
SHUUU--
YOU'RE KIDDING ME! YOU REALLY CAN'T TELL?!
SURE I CAN TELL...IF I PAT 'EM TO SEE WHAT'S UNDER THEIR PANTS.
.....
LET ME JUST TELL YOU UP FRONT...I'M MALE.
GOTCHA.
WEE-OO
WEE-OO
WEE-OO
P-PUT-PUT-PUT
RAT-TAT-TAT-TAT
RAT-TAT-TAT
POLICE

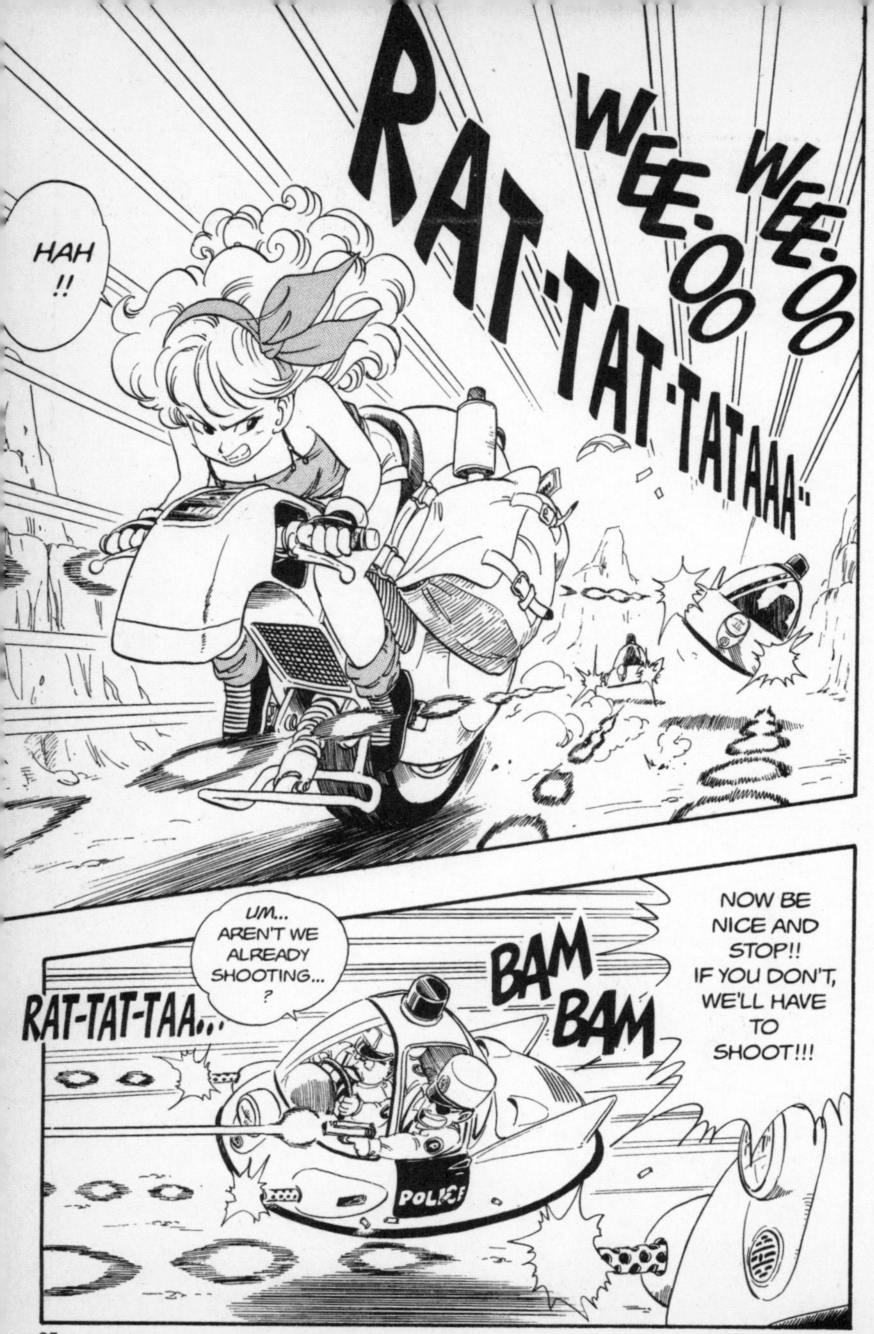
WEE-OO WEE-OO
RAT-TAT-TATAAA
HAH!!
NOW BE NICE AND STOP!! IF YOU DON'T, WE'LL HAVE TO SHOOT!!!
BAM BAM
UM... AREN'T WE ALREADY SHOOTING...?
RAT-TAT-TAA...

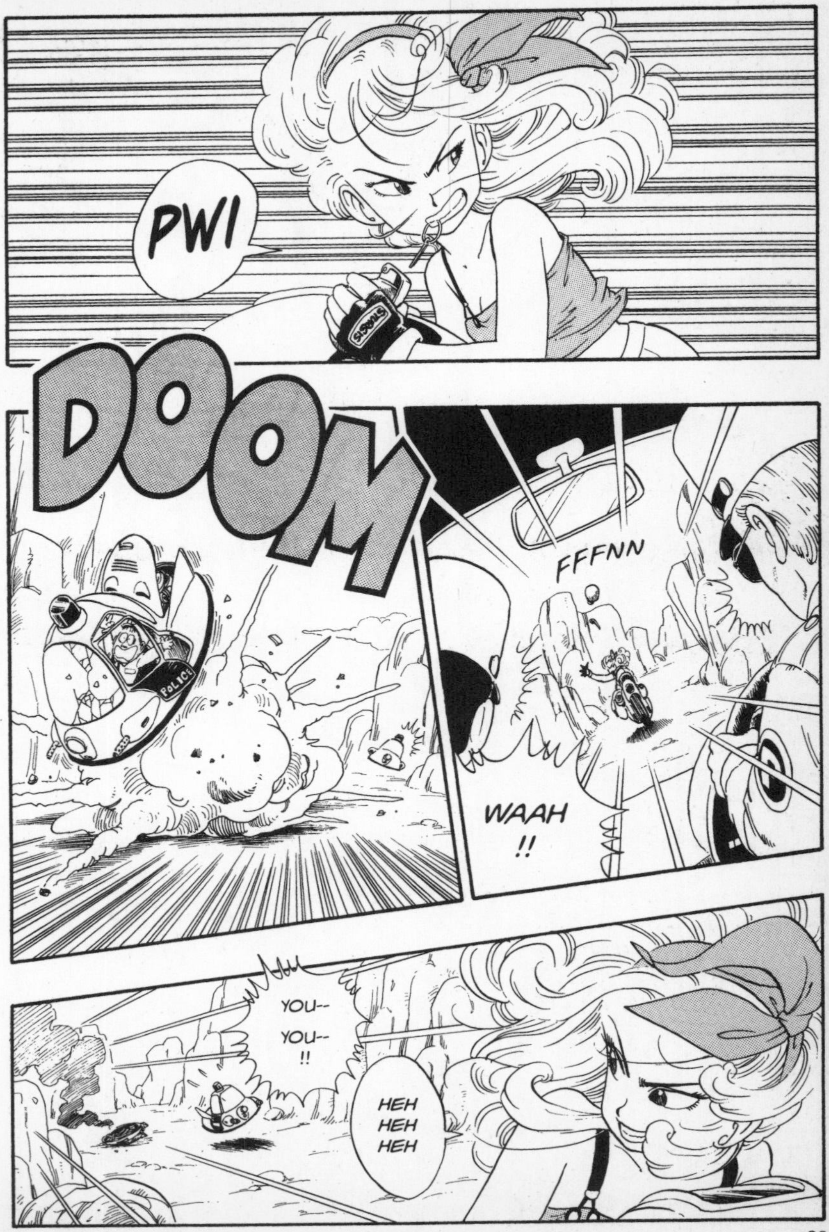
PWI
FFFNN
WAAH !!
DOOM
POLICE
YOU--
YOU-- !!
HEH HEH HEH

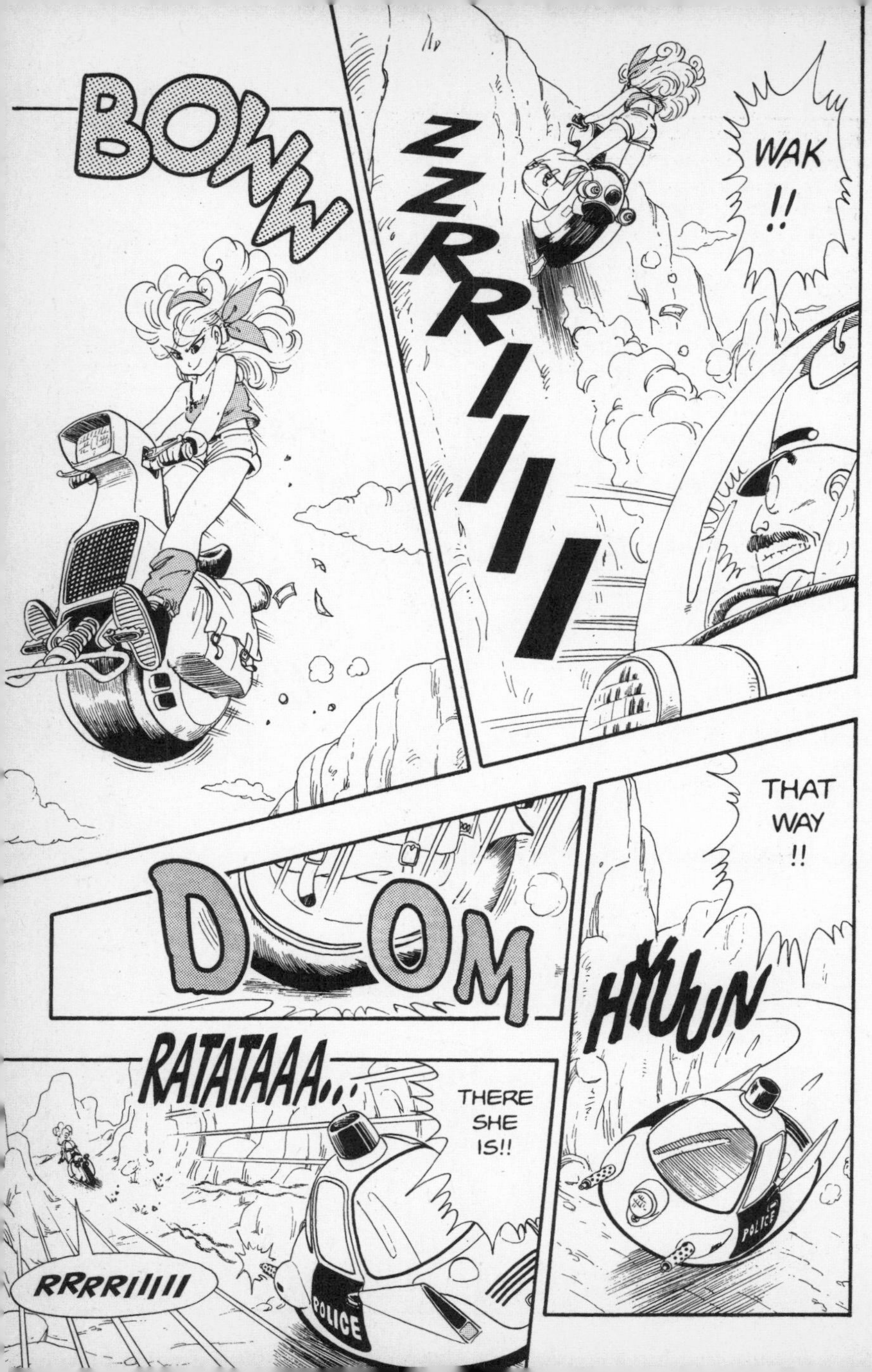
ZZRRIIIII
WAK !!
BOWWW
THAT WAY !!
HYUUN
POLICE
DOOM
RATATAAA...
THERE SHE IS!!
RRRRIIIII
POLICE

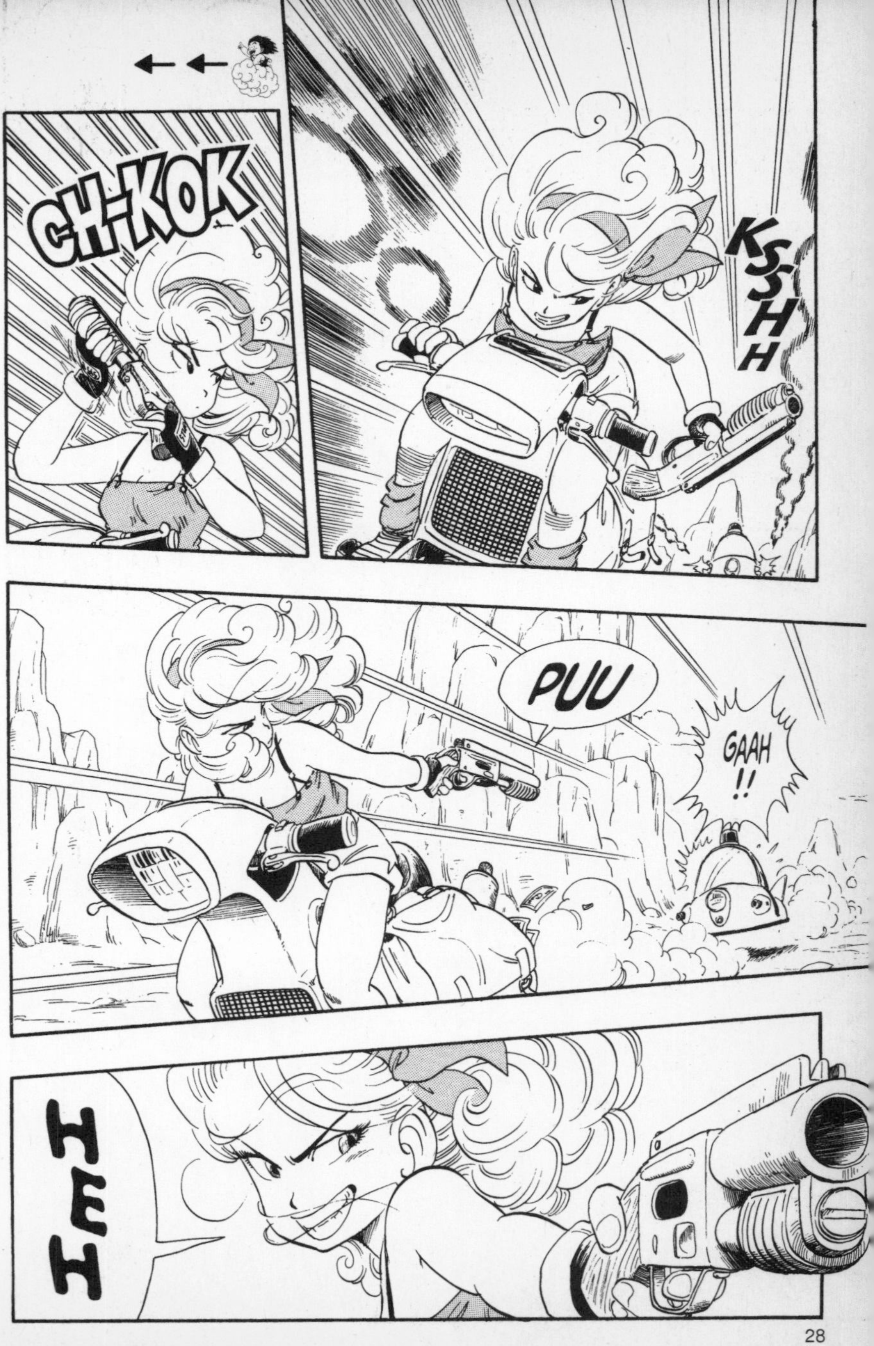
KSSHH
CH-KOK
PUU
GAAH!!
HEH

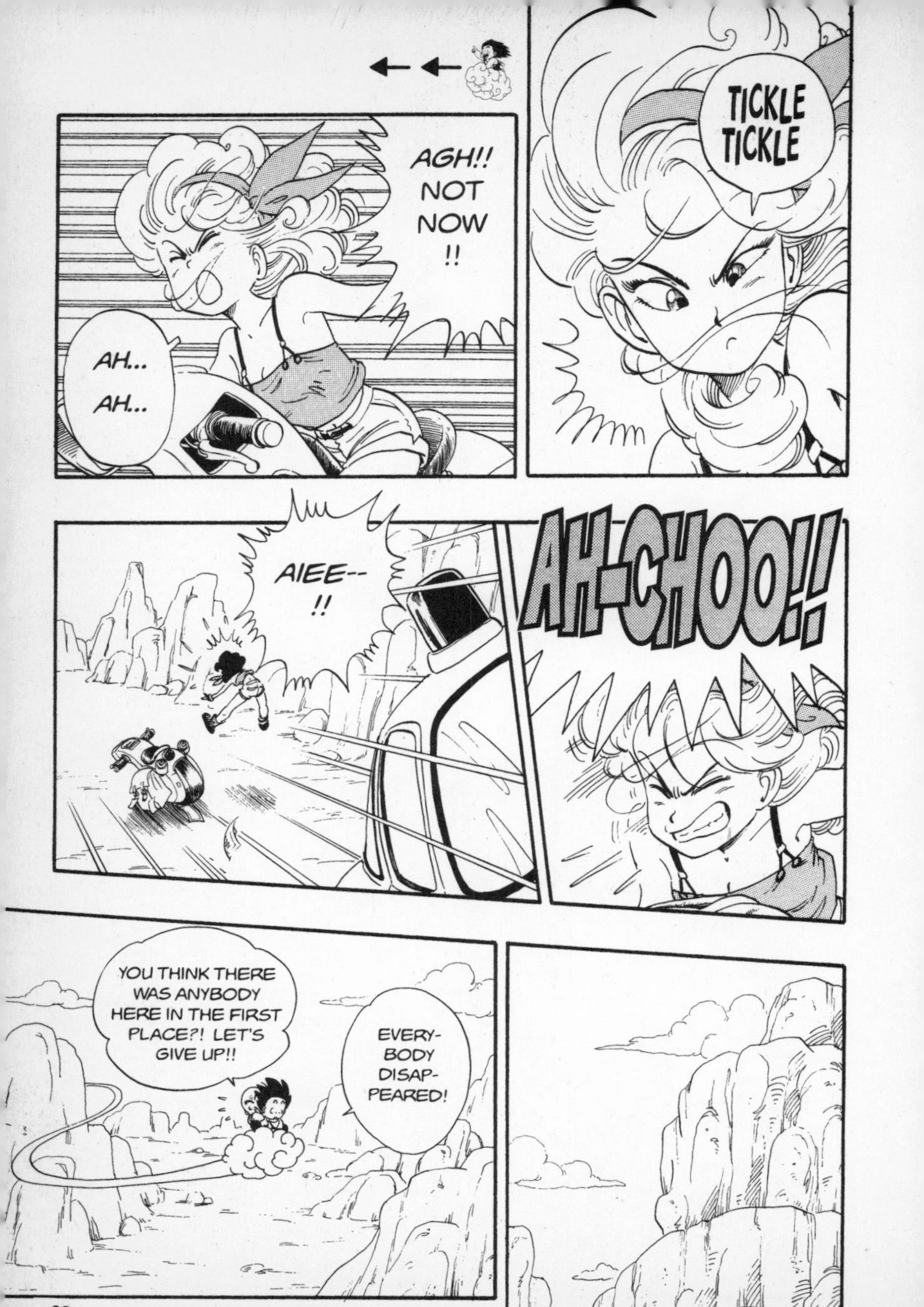

TICKLE TICKLE
AGH!! NOT NOW!!
AH... AH...
AH-CHOO!!
AIEE--!!
EVERY-BODY DISAP-PEARED!
YOU THINK THERE WAS ANYBODY HERE IN THE FIRST PLACE?! LET'S GIVE UP!!

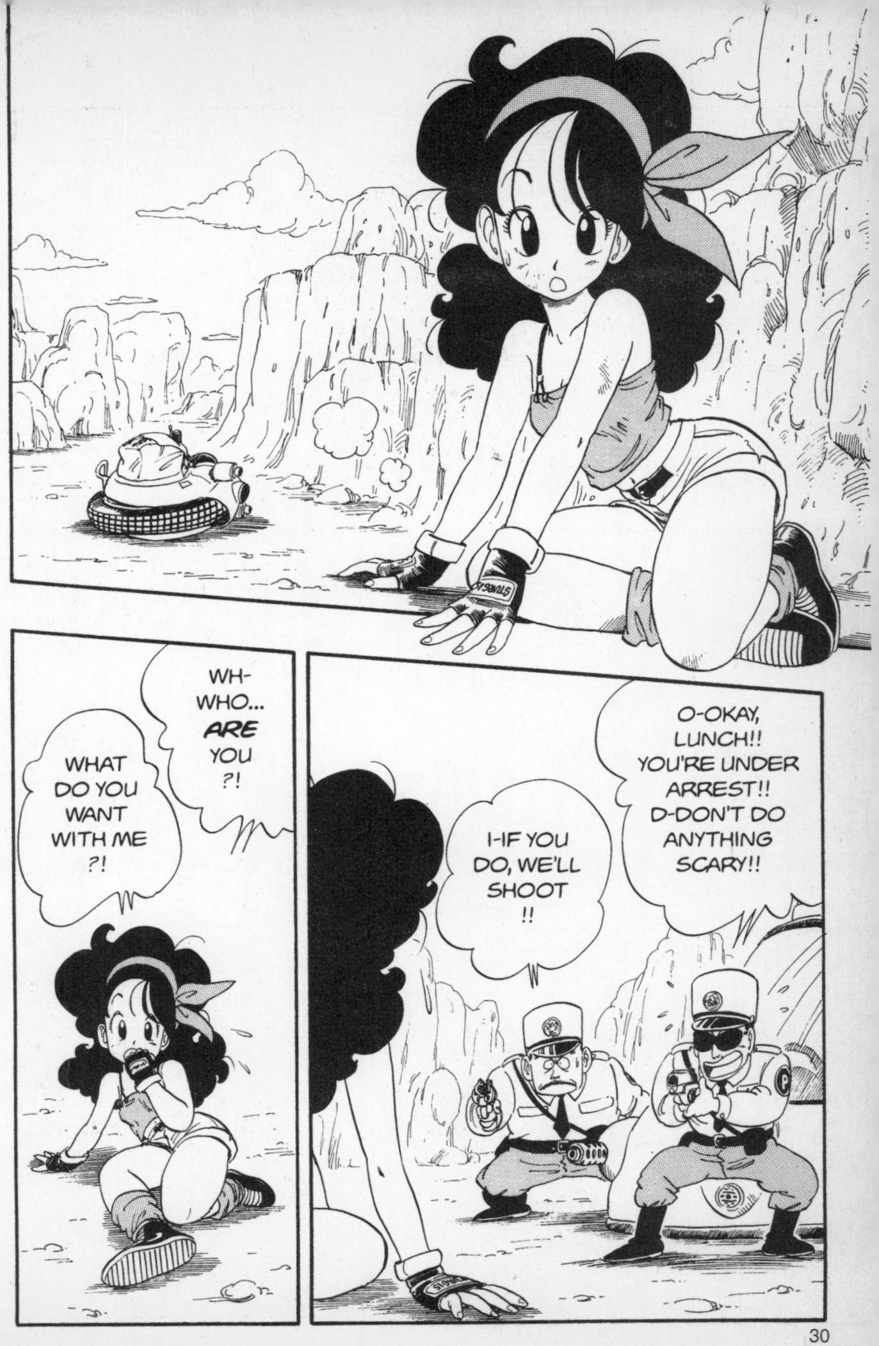
O-OKAY, LUNCH!! YOU'RE UNDER ARREST!! D-DON'T DO ANYTHING SCARY!!
I-IF YOU DO, WE'LL SHOOT !!
WH- WHO... ***ARE*** YOU ?!
WHAT DO YOU WANT WITH ME ?!

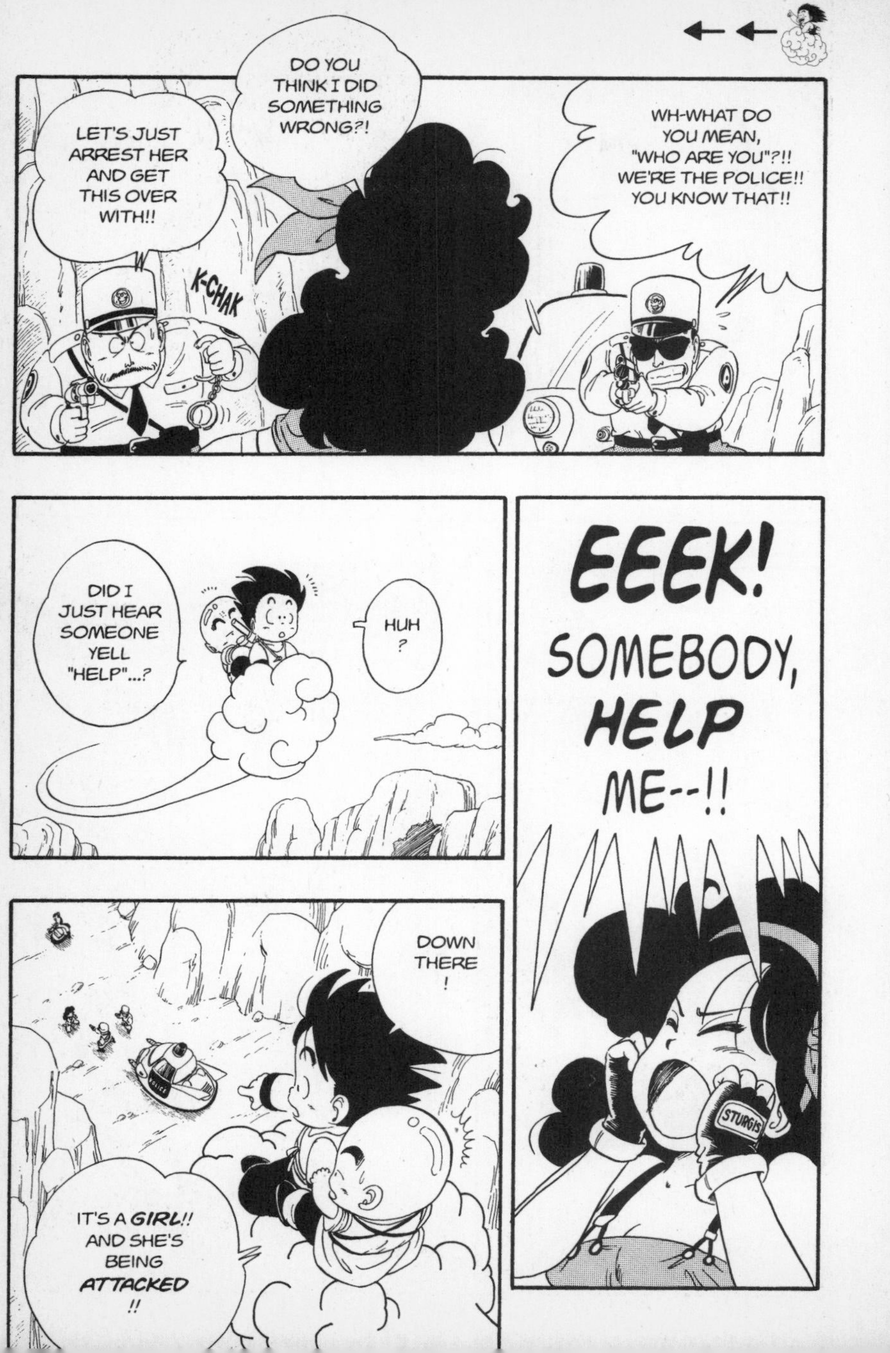
WH-WHAT DO YOU MEAN, "WHO ARE YOU"?!! WE'RE THE POLICE!! YOU KNOW THAT!!
DO YOU THINK I DID SOMETHING WRONG?!
LET'S JUST ARREST HER AND GET THIS OVER WITH!!
K-CHAK
EEEK! SOMEBODY, HELP ME--!!
STURGIS
HUH ?
DID I JUST HEAR SOMEONE YELL "HELP"...?
DOWN THERE !
IT'S A GIRL!! AND SHE'S BEING ATTACKED !!

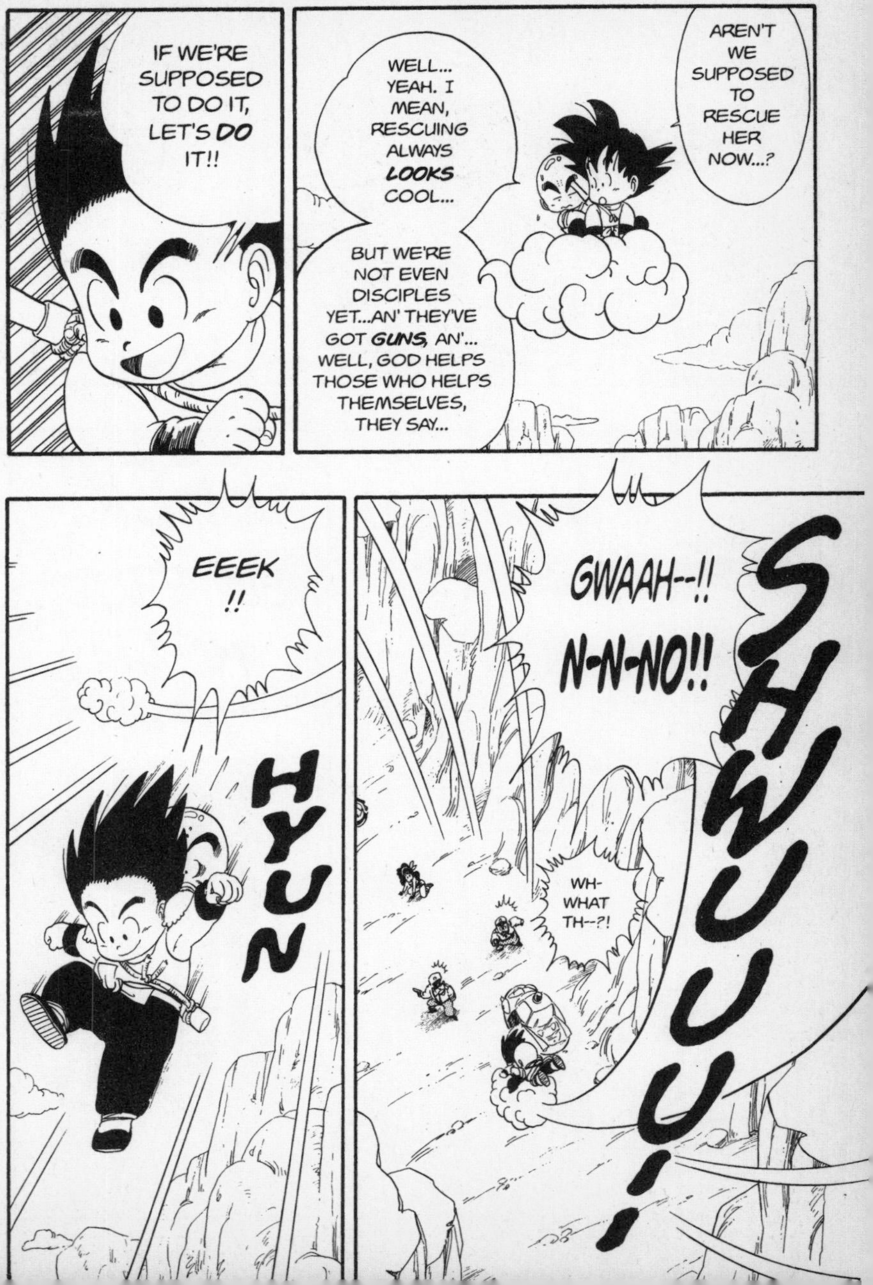
AREN'T WE SUPPOSED TO RESCUE HER NOW...?
WELL... YEAH. I MEAN, RESCUING ALWAYS *LOOKS* COOL...
BUT WE'RE NOT EVEN DISCIPLES YET...AN' THEY'VE GOT *GUNS*, AN'... WELL, GOD HELPS THOSE WHO HELPS THEMSELVES, THEY SAY...
IF WE'RE SUPPOSED TO DO IT, LET'S *DO* IT!!
SHWUUUU!!
GWAAH--!!
N-N-NO!!
WH- WHAT TH--?!
EEEK !!
HYUN

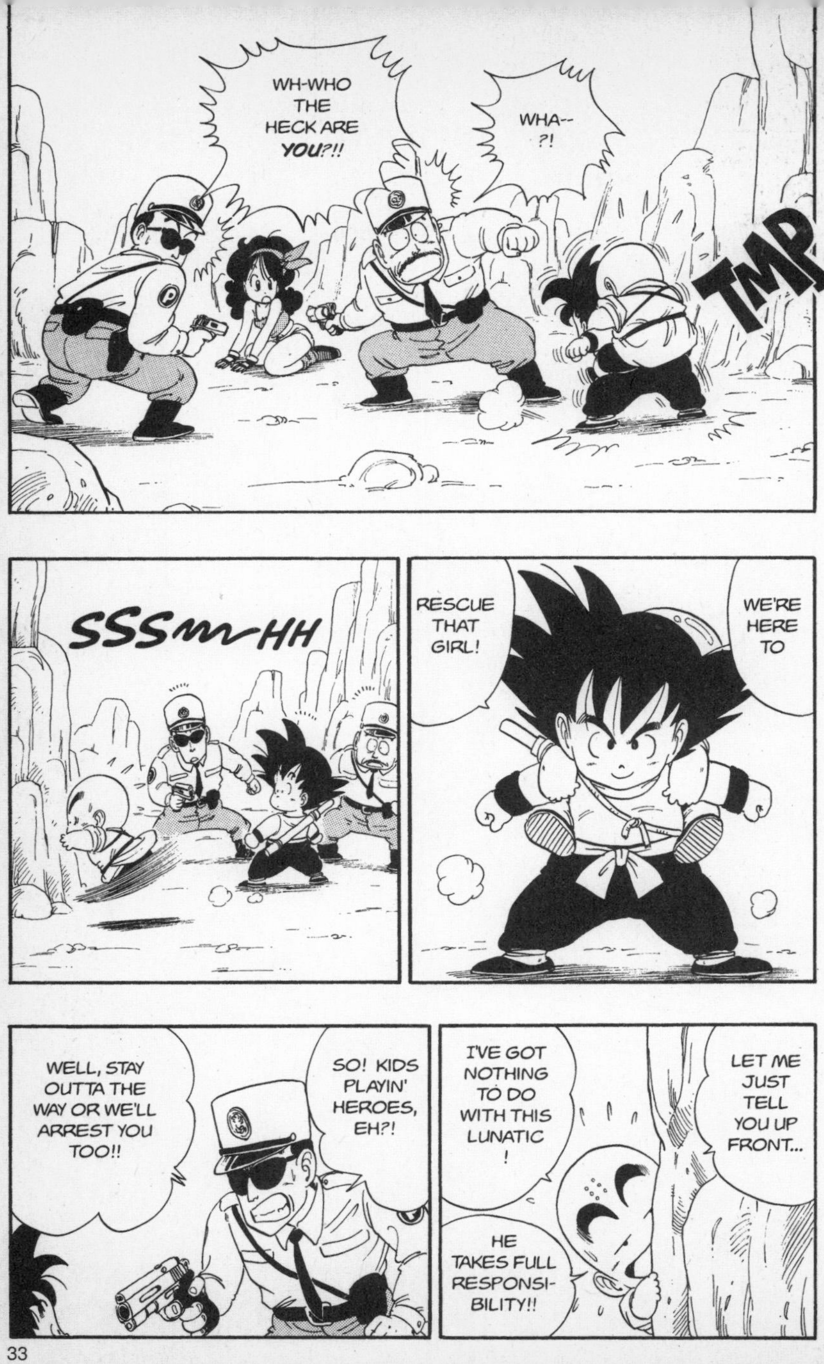
WHA-- ?!
WH-WHO THE HECK ARE YOU?!!
TMP
WE'RE HERE TO
RESCUE THAT GIRL!
SSS~HH
LET ME JUST TELL YOU UP FRONT...
I'VE GOT NOTHING TO DO WITH THIS LUNATIC!
HE TAKES FULL RESPONSIBILITY!!
SO! KIDS PLAYIN' HEROES, EH?!
WELL, STAY OUTTA THE WAY OR WE'LL ARREST YOU TOO!!

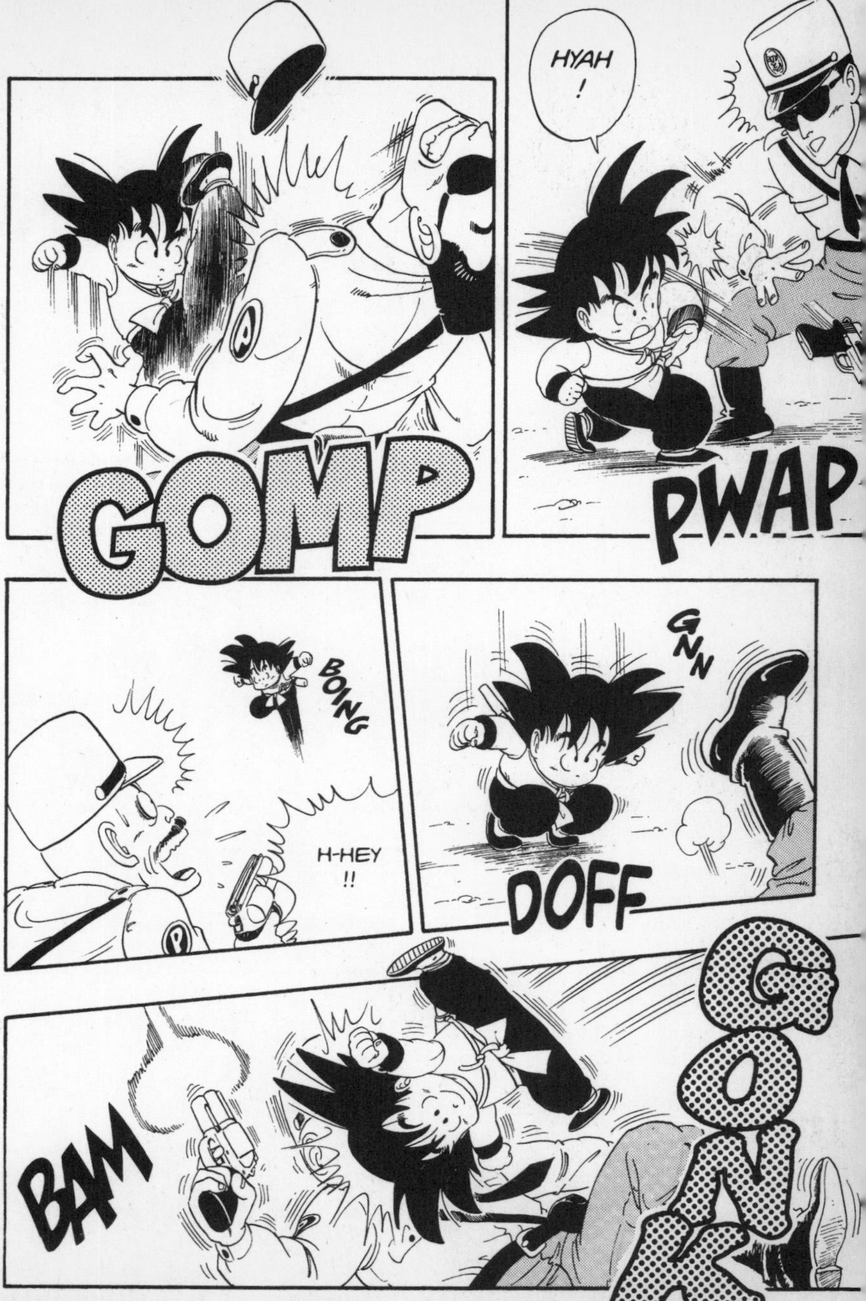
HYAH !
PWAP
GOMP
GNN
DOFF
BOING
H-HEY !!
GONK
BAM

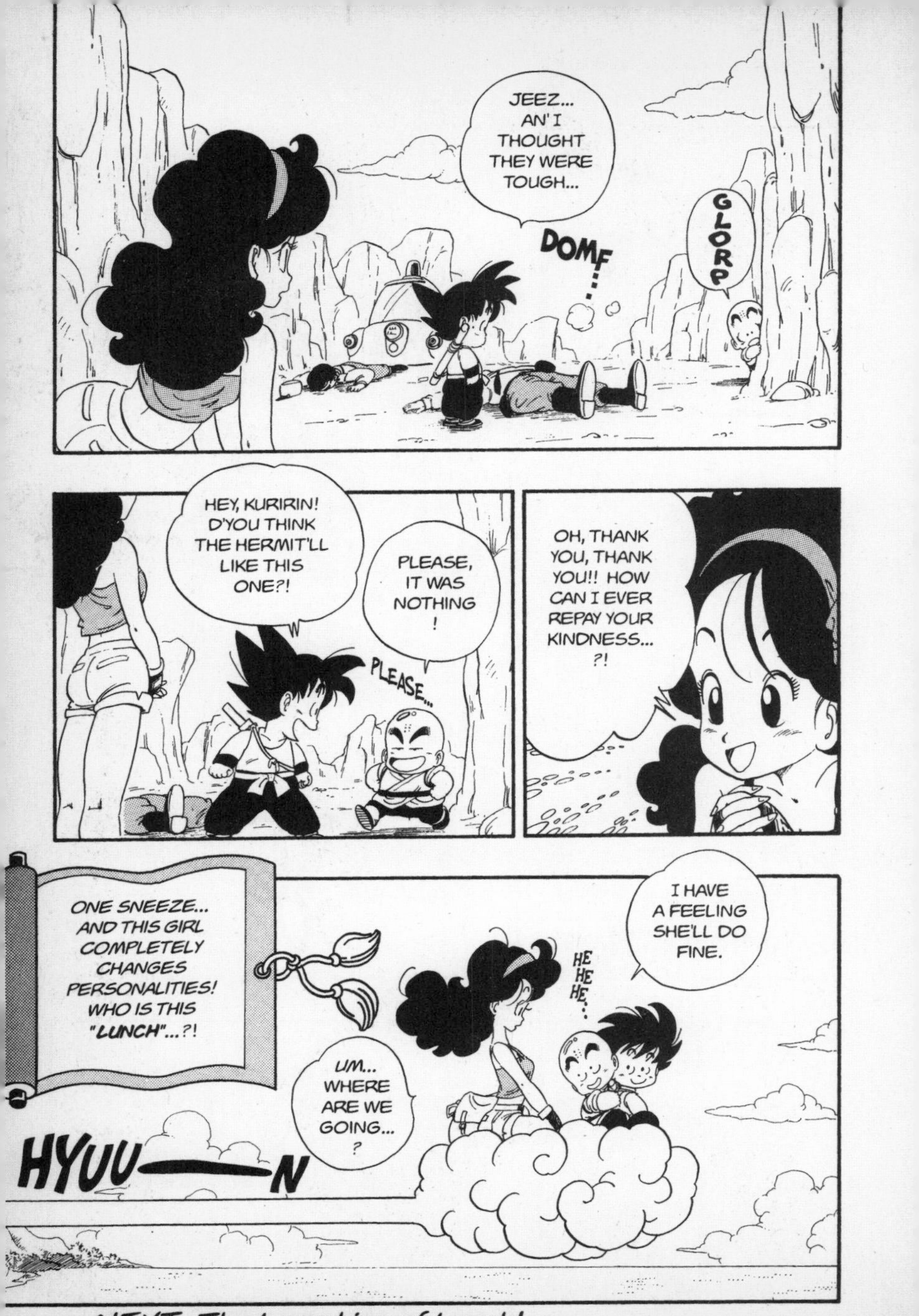
JEEZ... AN' I THOUGHT THEY WERE TOUGH...
GLORP
DOMF...
OH, THANK YOU, THANK YOU!! HOW CAN I EVER REPAY YOUR KINDNESS...?!
HEY, KURIRIN! D'YOU THINK THE HERMIT'LL LIKE THIS ONE?!
PLEASE, IT WAS NOTHING!
PLEASE...
I HAVE A FEELING SHE'LL DO FINE.
HE HE HE...
UM... WHERE ARE WE GOING...?
ONE SNEEZE... AND THIS GIRL COMPLETELY CHANGES PERSONALITIES! WHO IS THIS "LUNCH"...?!
HYUU——N

NEXT: The Launching of Lunch!

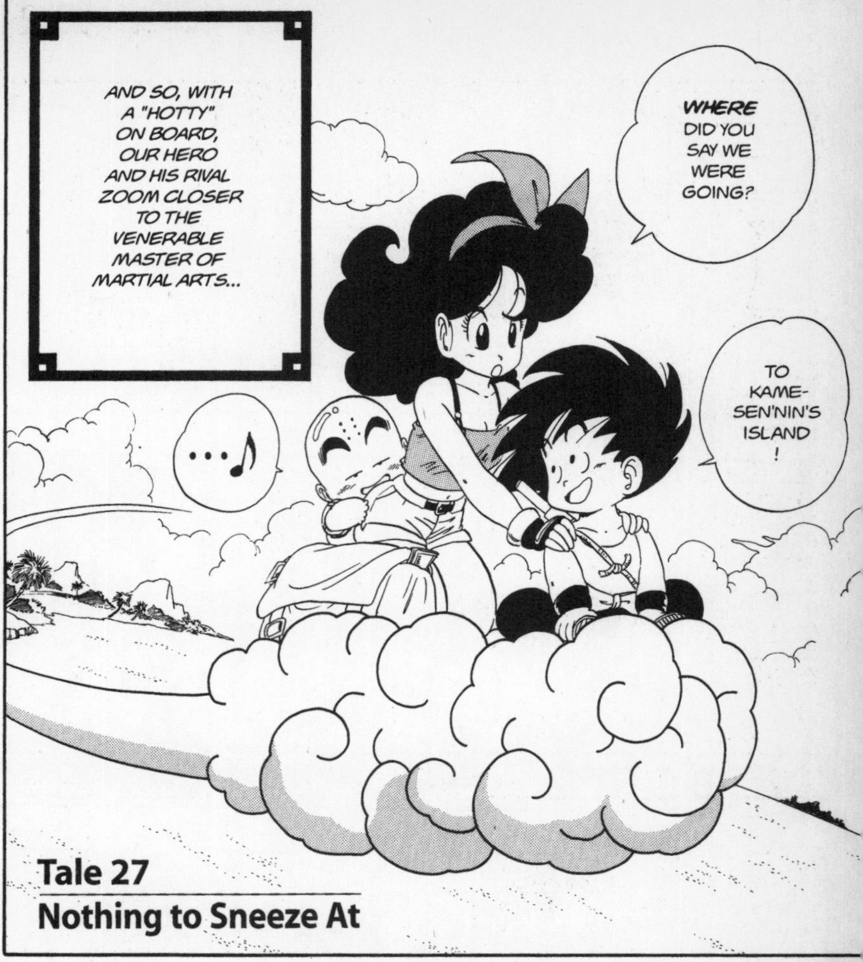
WHERE DID YOU SAY WE WERE GOING?
AND SO, WITH A "HOTTY" ON BOARD, OUR HERO AND HIS RIVAL ZOOM CLOSER TO THE VENERABLE MASTER OF MARTIAL ARTS...
TO KAME-SEN'NIN'S ISLAND!
...♪
Tale 27
Nothing to Sneeze At
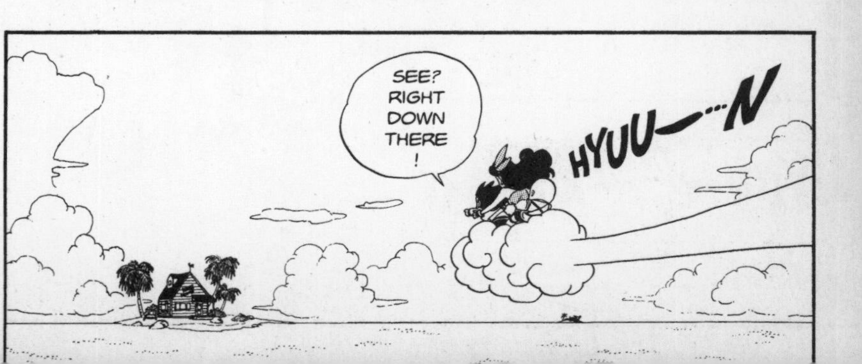
HYUU—...N
SEE? RIGHT DOWN THERE!

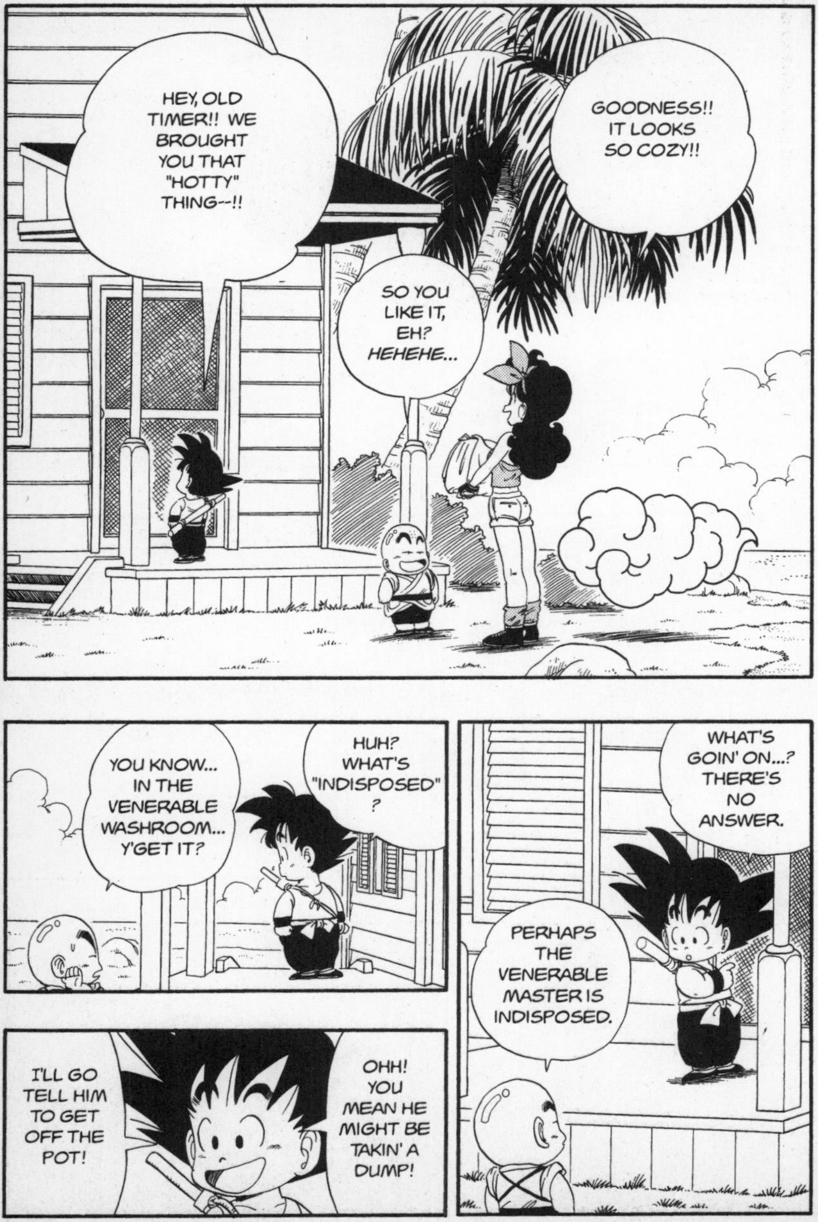
GOODNESS!! IT LOOKS SO COZY!!
HEY, OLD TIMER!! WE BROUGHT YOU THAT "HOTTY" THING--!!
SO YOU LIKE IT, EH? HEHEHE...
WHAT'S GOIN' ON...? THERE'S NO ANSWER.
PERHAPS THE VENERABLE MASTER IS INDISPOSED.
HUH? WHAT'S "INDISPOSED" ?
YOU KNOW... IN THE VENERABLE WASHROOM... Y'GET IT?
OHH! YOU MEAN HE MIGHT BE TAKIN' A DUMP!
I'LL GO TELL HIM TO GET OFF THE POT!

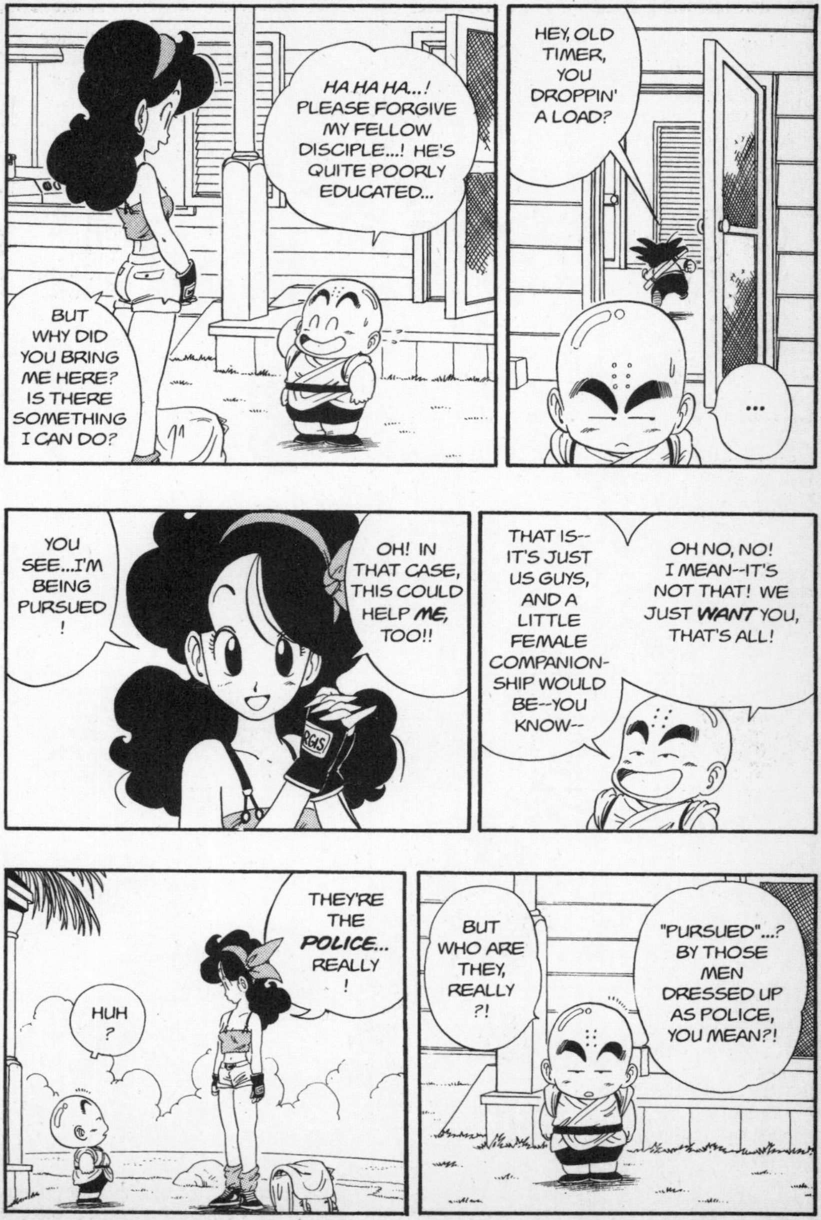
HEY, OLD TIMER, YOU DROPPIN' A LOAD?
...
HA HA HA...! PLEASE FORGIVE MY FELLOW DISCIPLE...! HE'S QUITE POORLY EDUCATED...
BUT WHY DID YOU BRING ME HERE? IS THERE SOMETHING I CAN DO?
OH NO, NO! I MEAN--IT'S NOT THAT! WE JUST WANT YOU, THAT'S ALL!
THAT IS-- IT'S JUST US GUYS, AND A LITTLE FEMALE COMPANIONSHIP WOULD BE--YOU KNOW--
OH! IN THAT CASE, THIS COULD HELP ME, TOO!!
YOU SEE...I'M BEING PURSUED!
"PURSUED"...? BY THOSE MEN DRESSED UP AS POLICE, YOU MEAN?!
BUT WHO ARE THEY, REALLY?!
THEY'RE THE POLICE... REALLY!
HUH?

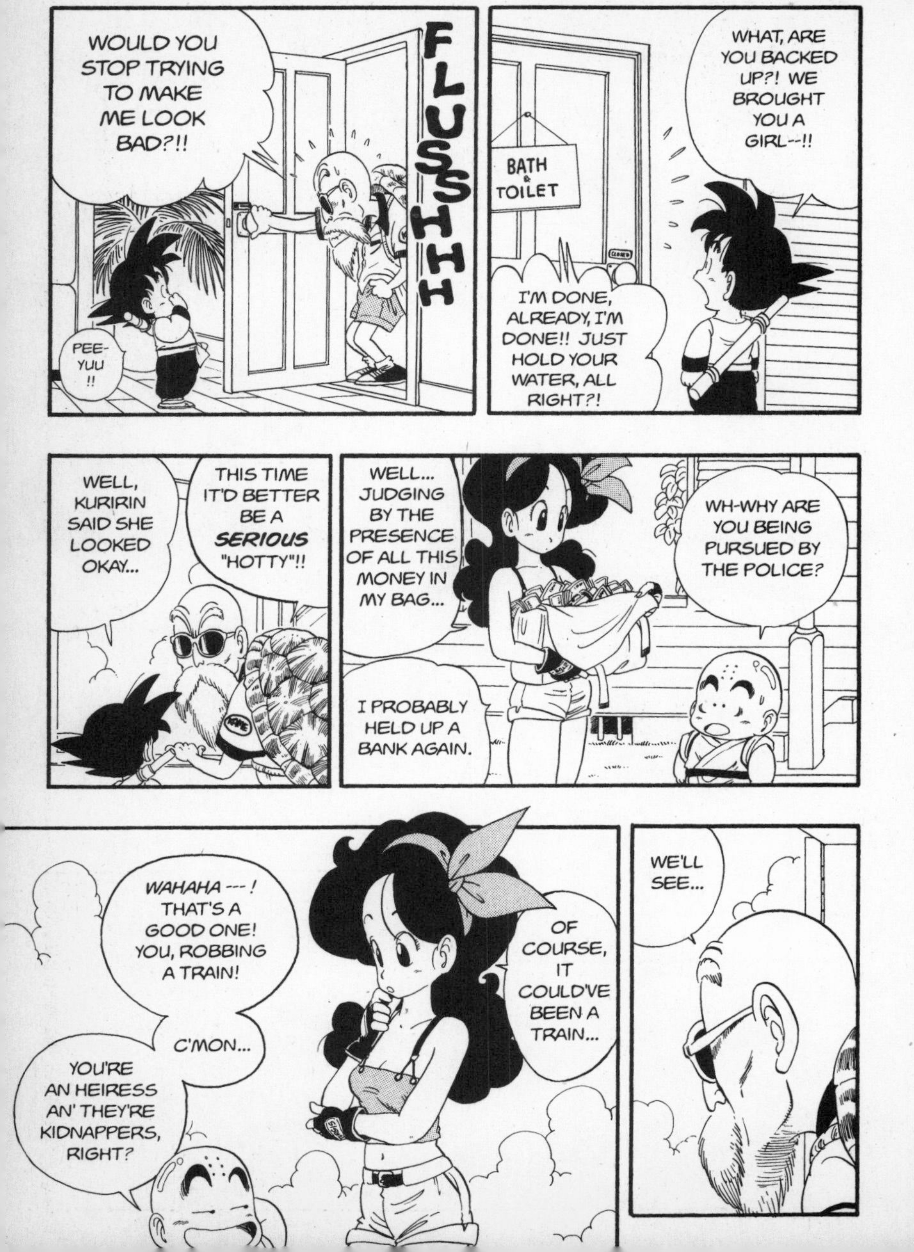
WHAT, ARE YOU BACKED UP?! WE BROUGHT YOU A GIRL--!!
BATH & TOILET
I'M DONE, ALREADY, I'M DONE!! JUST HOLD YOUR WATER, ALL RIGHT?!
FLUSSHHH
WOULD YOU STOP TRYING TO MAKE ME LOOK BAD?!!
PEE-YUU!!
WH-WHY ARE YOU BEING PURSUED BY THE POLICE?
WELL... JUDGING BY THE PRESENCE OF ALL THIS MONEY IN MY BAG...
I PROBABLY HELD UP A BANK AGAIN.
THIS TIME IT'D BETTER BE A *SERIOUS* "HOTTY"!!
WELL, KURIRIN SAID SHE LOOKED OKAY...
WE'LL SEE...
OF COURSE, IT COULD'VE BEEN A TRAIN...
WAHAHA ---! THAT'S A GOOD ONE! YOU, ROBBING A TRAIN!
C'MON...
YOU'RE AN HEIRESS AN' THEY'RE KIDNAPPERS, RIGHT?

SEE...

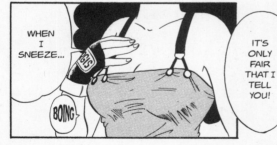

WHEN
I
SNEEZE...

BOING

IT'S
ONLY
FAIR
THAT I
TELL
YOU!

poing

...I
CHANGE
PERSON-
ALITIES.

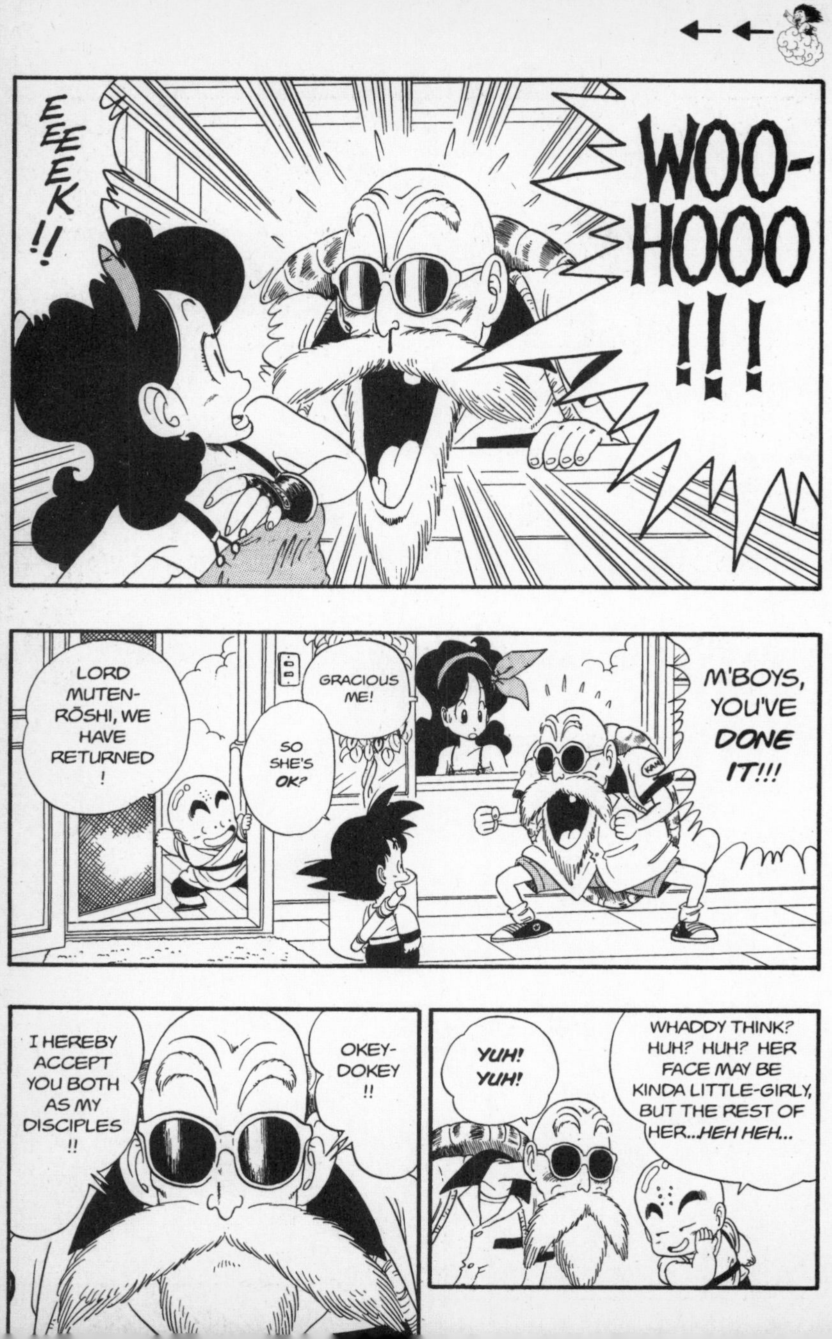
WOO-HOOO!!!
EEEEK!!
M'BOYS, YOU'VE DONE IT!!!
GRACIOUS ME!
SO SHE'S OK?
LORD MUTEN-RŌSHI, WE HAVE RETURNED!
WHADDY THINK? HUH? HUH? HER FACE MAY BE KINDA LITTLE-GIRLY, BUT THE REST OF HER...HEH HEH...
YUH! YUH!
OKEY-DOKEY!!
I HEREBY ACCEPT YOU BOTH AS MY DISCIPLES!!

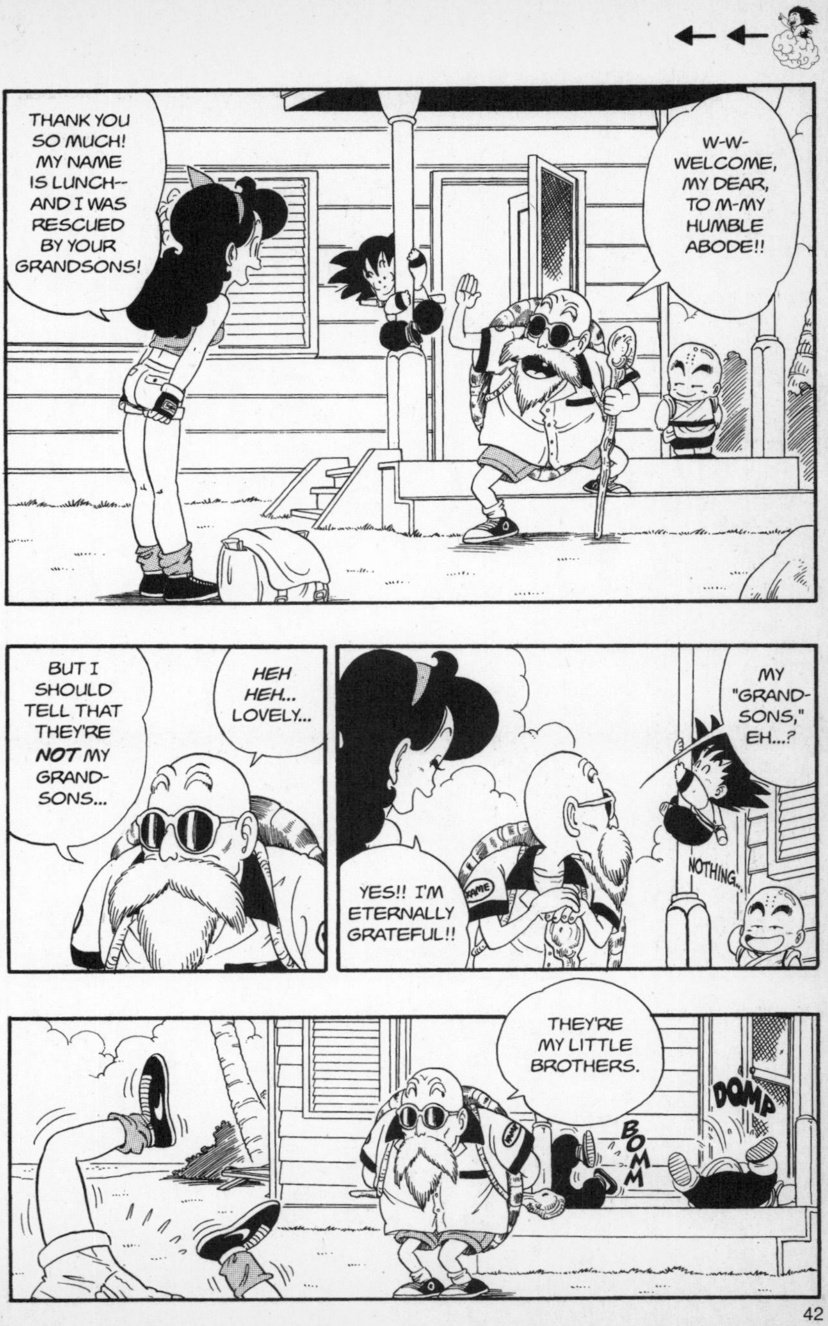
W-W-WELCOME, MY DEAR, TO M-MY HUMBLE ABODE!!
THANK YOU SO MUCH! MY NAME IS LUNCH--AND I WAS RESCUED BY YOUR GRANDSONS!
MY "GRAND-SONS," EH...?
NOTHING...
YES!! I'M ETERNALLY GRATEFUL!!
HEH HEH... LOVELY...
BUT I SHOULD TELL THAT THEY'RE NOT MY GRAND-SONS...
THEY'RE MY LITTLE BROTHERS.
DOMP
BOMM

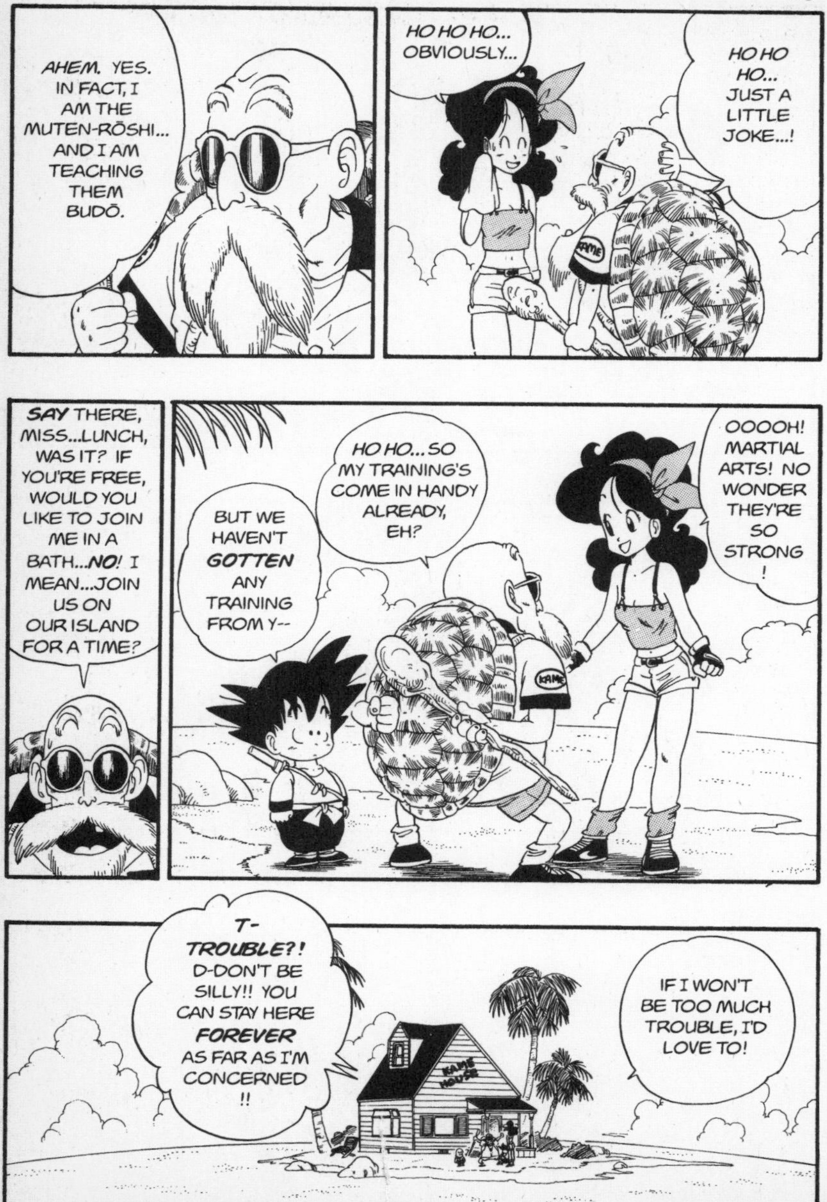
HO HO HO... JUST A LITTLE JOKE...!
HO HO HO... OBVIOUSLY...
AHEM. YES. IN FACT, I AM THE MUTEN-RŌSHI... AND I AM TEACHING THEM BUDŌ.
KAME
OOOOH! MARTIAL ARTS! NO WONDER THEY'RE SO STRONG!
HO HO... SO MY TRAINING'S COME IN HANDY ALREADY, EH?
BUT WE HAVEN'T GOTTEN ANY TRAINING FROM Y--
KAME
SAY THERE, MISS...LUNCH, WAS IT? IF YOU'RE FREE, WOULD YOU LIKE TO JOIN ME IN A BATH...NO! I MEAN...JOIN US ON OUR ISLAND FOR A TIME?
IF I WON'T BE TOO MUCH TROUBLE, I'D LOVE TO!
T-TROUBLE?! D-DON'T BE SILLY!! YOU CAN STAY HERE FOREVER AS FAR AS I'M CONCERNED!!
KAME HOUSE

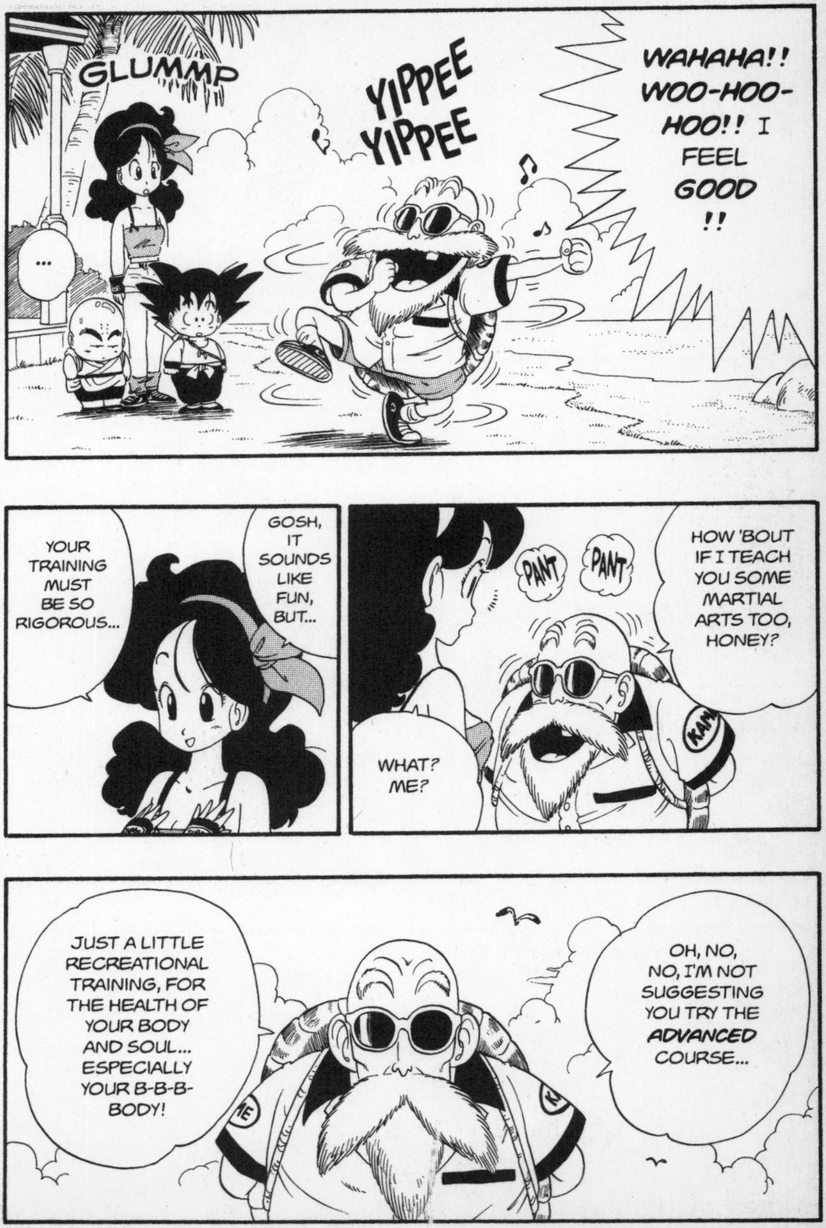
WAHAHA!! WOO-HOO-HOO!! I FEEL GOOD!!
YIPPEE YIPPEE
GLUMMP
...
HOW 'BOUT IF I TEACH YOU SOME MARTIAL ARTS TOO, HONEY?
PANT
PANT
WHAT? ME?
GOSH, IT SOUNDS LIKE FUN, BUT...
YOUR TRAINING MUST BE SO RIGOROUS...
OH, NO, NO, I'M NOT SUGGESTING YOU TRY THE ADVANCED COURSE...
JUST A LITTLE RECREATIONAL TRAINING, FOR THE HEALTH OF YOUR BODY AND SOUL... ESPECIALLY YOUR B-B-B-BODY!

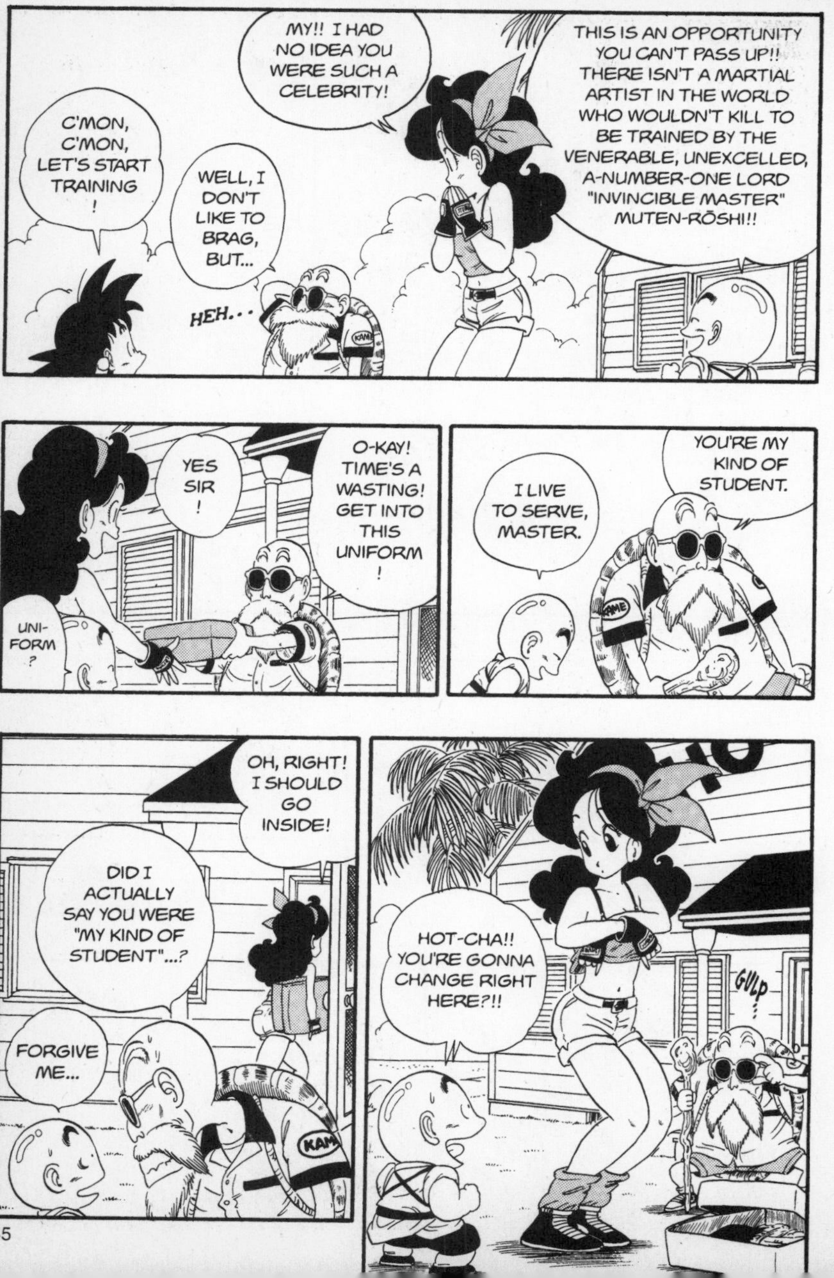
THIS IS AN OPPORTUNITY YOU CAN'T PASS UP!! THERE ISN'T A MARTIAL ARTIST IN THE WORLD WHO WOULDN'T KILL TO BE TRAINED BY THE VENERABLE, UNEXCELLED, A-NUMBER-ONE LORD "INVINCIBLE MASTER" MUTEN-RŌSHI!!
MY!! I HAD NO IDEA YOU WERE SUCH A CELEBRITY!
WELL, I DON'T LIKE TO BRAG, BUT...
HEH...
C'MON, C'MON, LET'S START TRAINING!
YOU'RE MY KIND OF STUDENT.
I LIVE TO SERVE, MASTER.
O-KAY! TIME'S A WASTING! GET INTO THIS UNIFORM!
YES SIR!
UNI-FORM?
HOT-CHA!! YOU'RE GONNA CHANGE RIGHT HERE?!!
GULP
OH, RIGHT! I SHOULD GO INSIDE!
DID I ACTUALLY SAY YOU WERE "MY KIND OF STUDENT"...?
FORGIVE ME...

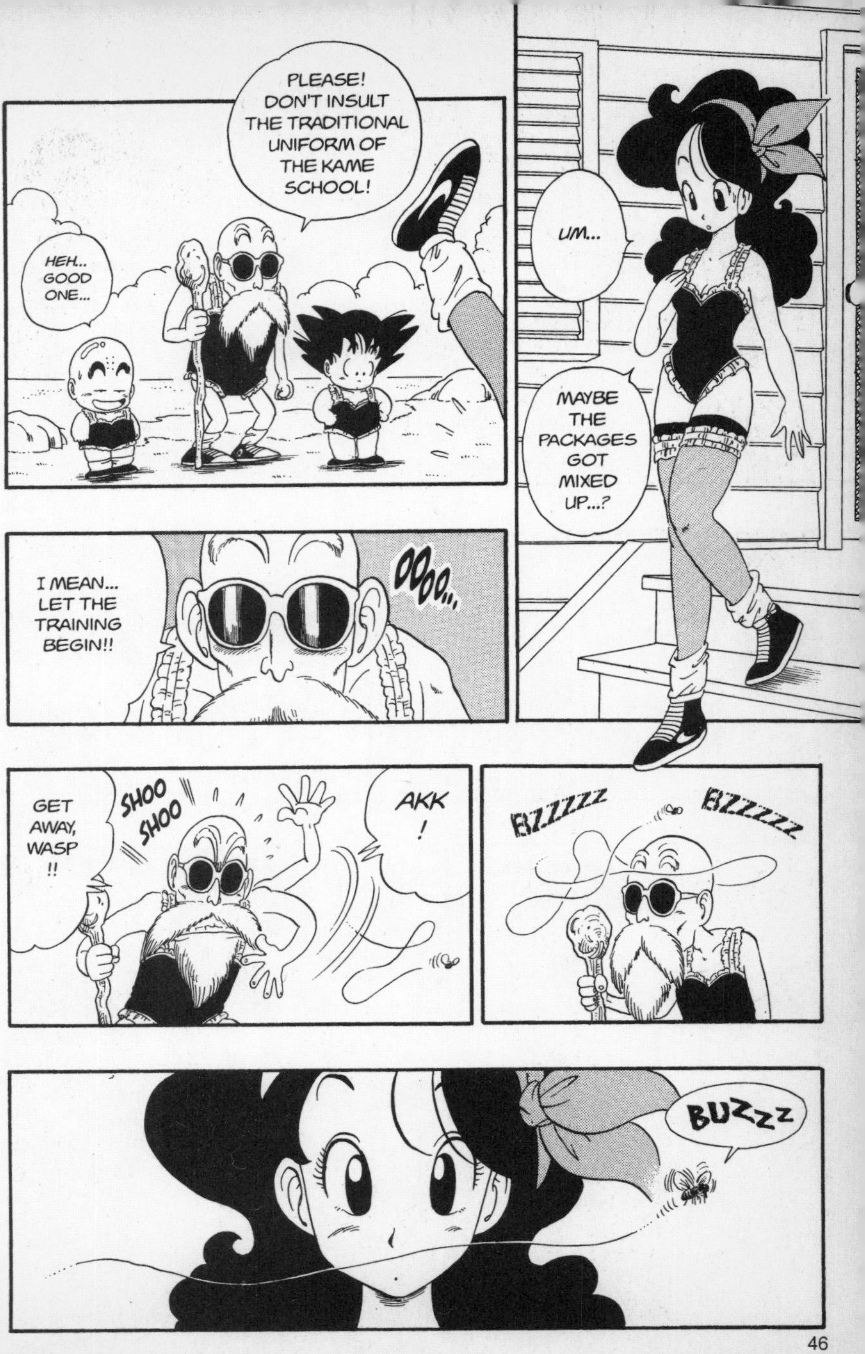
UM...
MAYBE THE PACKAGES GOT MIXED UP...?
PLEASE! DON'T INSULT THE TRADITIONAL UNIFORM OF THE KAME SCHOOL!
HEH.. GOOD ONE...
OOOO...
I MEAN... LET THE TRAINING BEGIN!!
BZZZZZ
BZZZZZZ
AKK !
SHOO SHOO
GET AWAY, WASP !!
BUZZZ

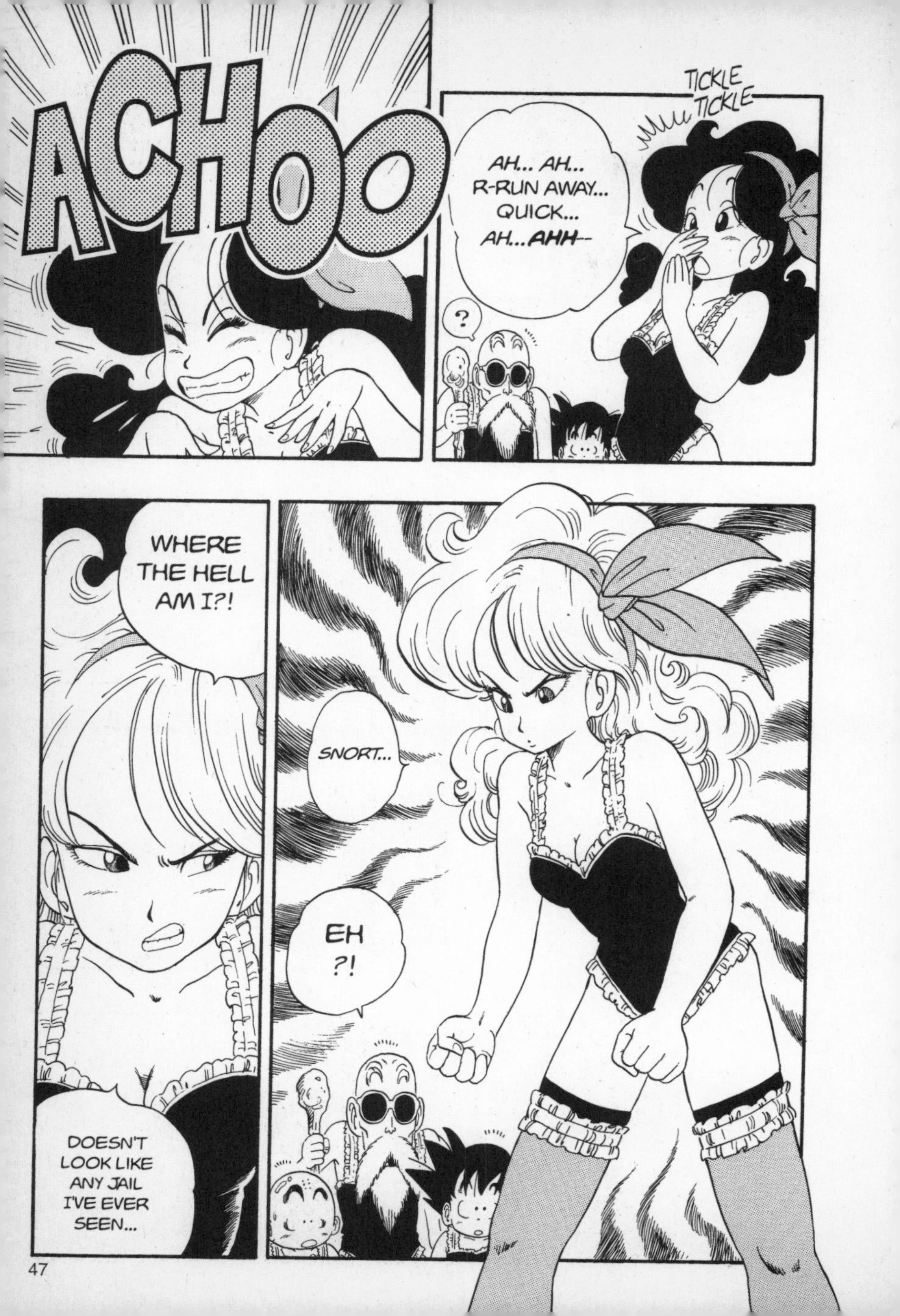
TICKLE TICKLE
AH... AH... R-RUN AWAY... QUICK... AH...AHH--
?
ACHOO
SNORT...
EH ?!
WHERE THE HELL AM I?!
DOESN'T LOOK LIKE ANY JAIL I'VE EVER SEEN...

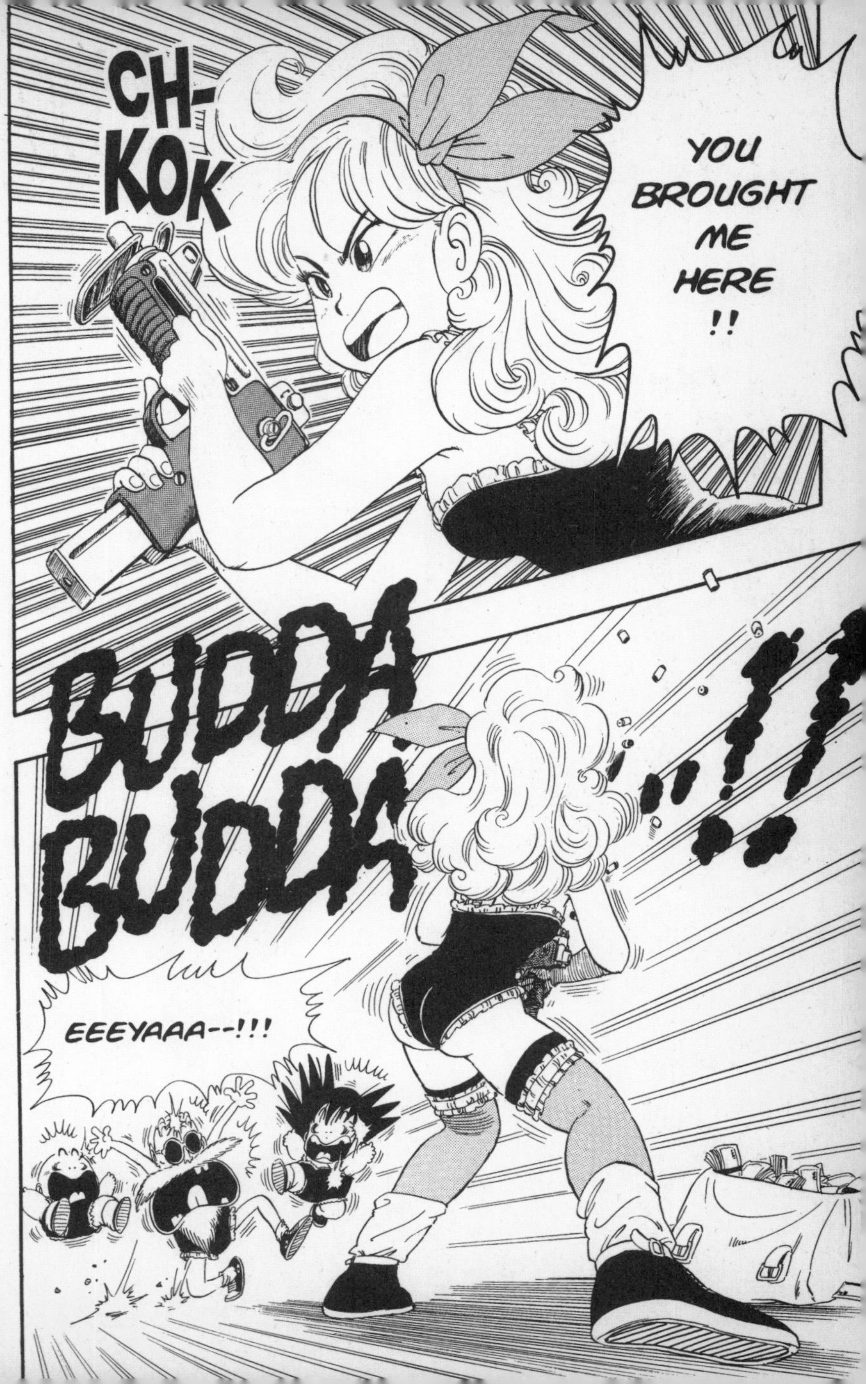
YOU BROUGHT ME HERE !!
CH-KOK
BUDDA BUDDA!!!
EEEYAAA--!!!

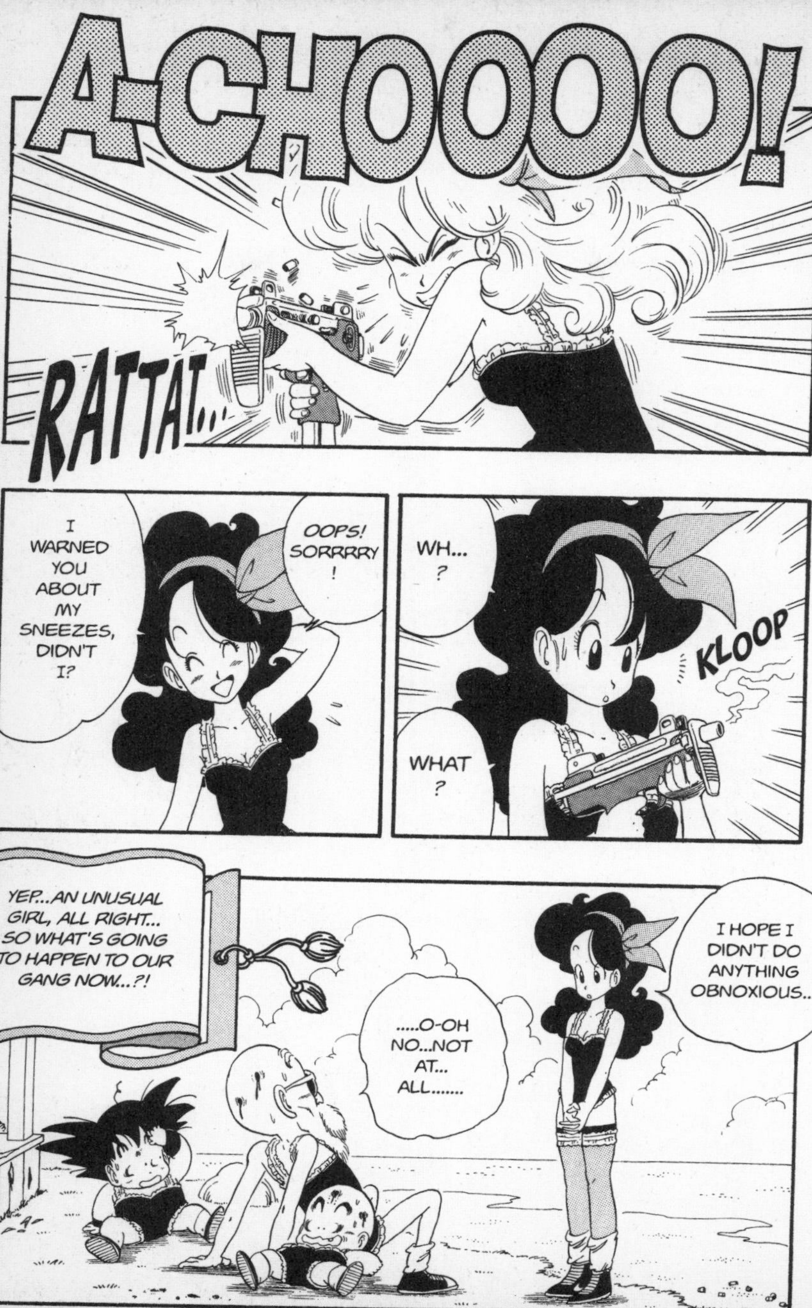
A-CHOOOO!
RATTAT...
WH...?
KLOOP
WHAT?
OOPS! SORRRRY!
I WARNED YOU ABOUT MY SNEEZES, DIDN'T I?
I HOPE I DIDN'T DO ANYTHING OBNOXIOUS...
.....O-OH NO...NOT AT... ALL.......
YEP...AN UNUSUAL GIRL, ALL RIGHT... SO WHAT'S GOING TO HAPPEN TO OUR GANG NOW...?!

NEXT: Let the Training Begin (Finally)!!

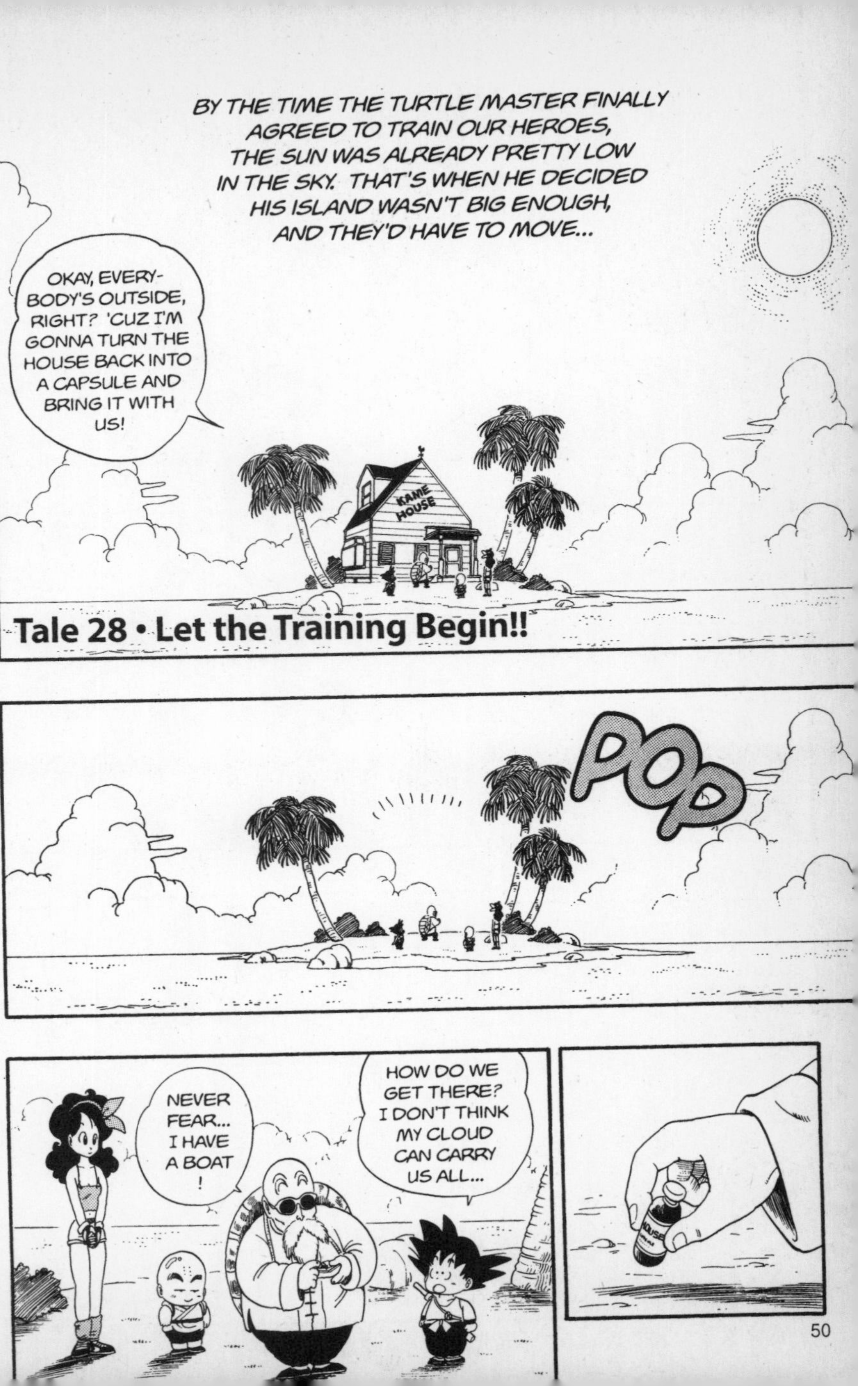
BY THE TIME THE TURTLE MASTER FINALLY AGREED TO TRAIN OUR HEROES, THE SUN WAS ALREADY PRETTY LOW IN THE SKY. THAT'S WHEN HE DECIDED HIS ISLAND WASN'T BIG ENOUGH, AND THEY'D HAVE TO MOVE...
OKAY, EVERYBODY'S OUTSIDE, RIGHT? 'CUZ I'M GONNA TURN THE HOUSE BACK INTO A CAPSULE AND BRING IT WITH US!
KAME HOUSE
Tale 28 • Let the Training Begin!!
POP
HOUSE
HOW DO WE GET THERE? I DON'T THINK MY CLOUD CAN CARRY US ALL...
NEVER FEAR... I HAVE A BOAT!

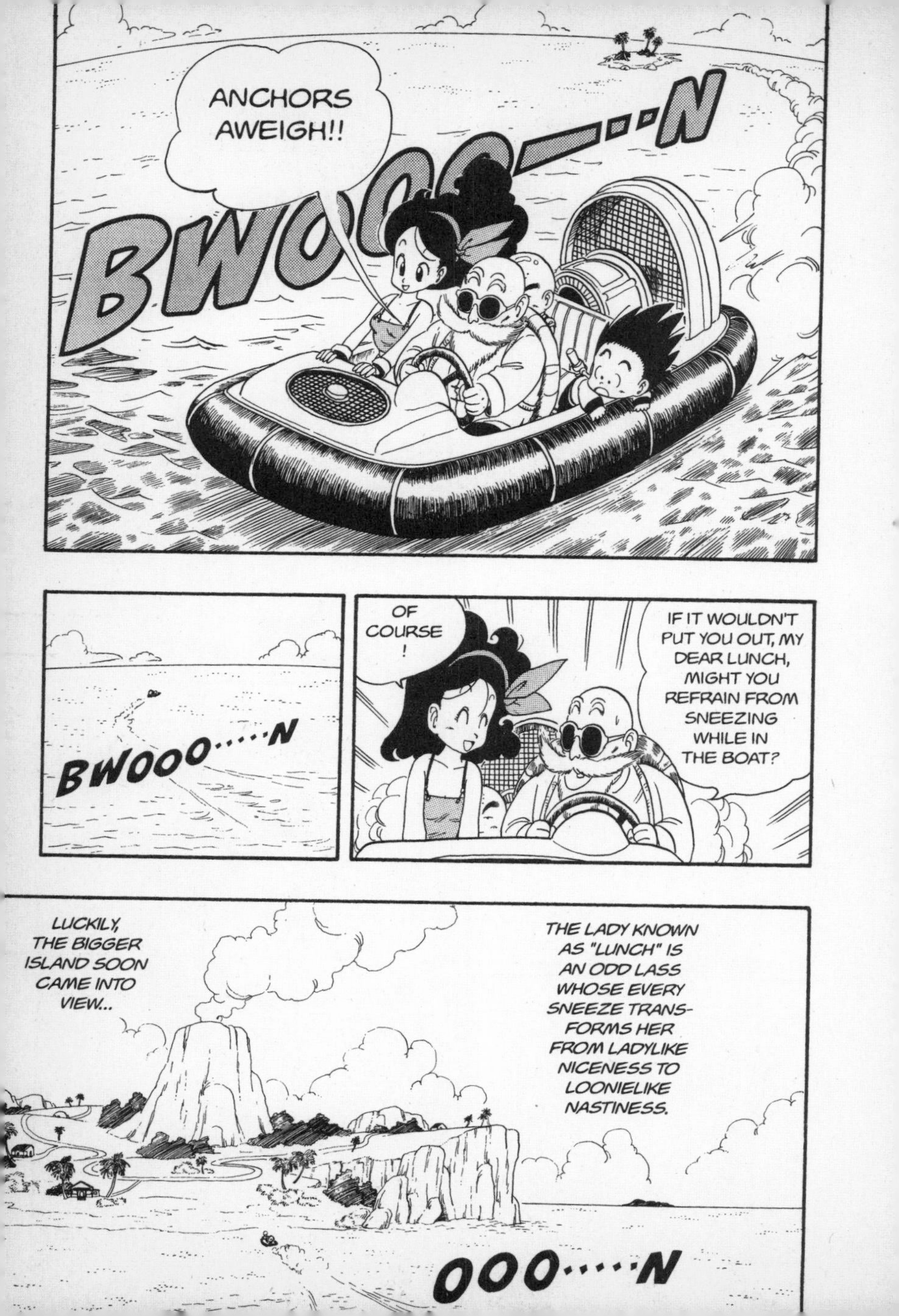
ANCHORS AWEIGH!!
BWOOO—··N
IF IT WOULDN'T PUT YOU OUT, MY DEAR LUNCH, MIGHT YOU REFRAIN FROM SNEEZING WHILE IN THE BOAT?
OF COURSE!
BWOOO·····N
THE LADY KNOWN AS "LUNCH" IS AN ODD LASS WHOSE EVERY SNEEZE TRANS-FORMS HER FROM LADYLIKE NICENESS TO LOONIELIKE NASTINESS.
LUCKILY, THE BIGGER ISLAND SOON CAME INTO VIEW...
OOO·····N

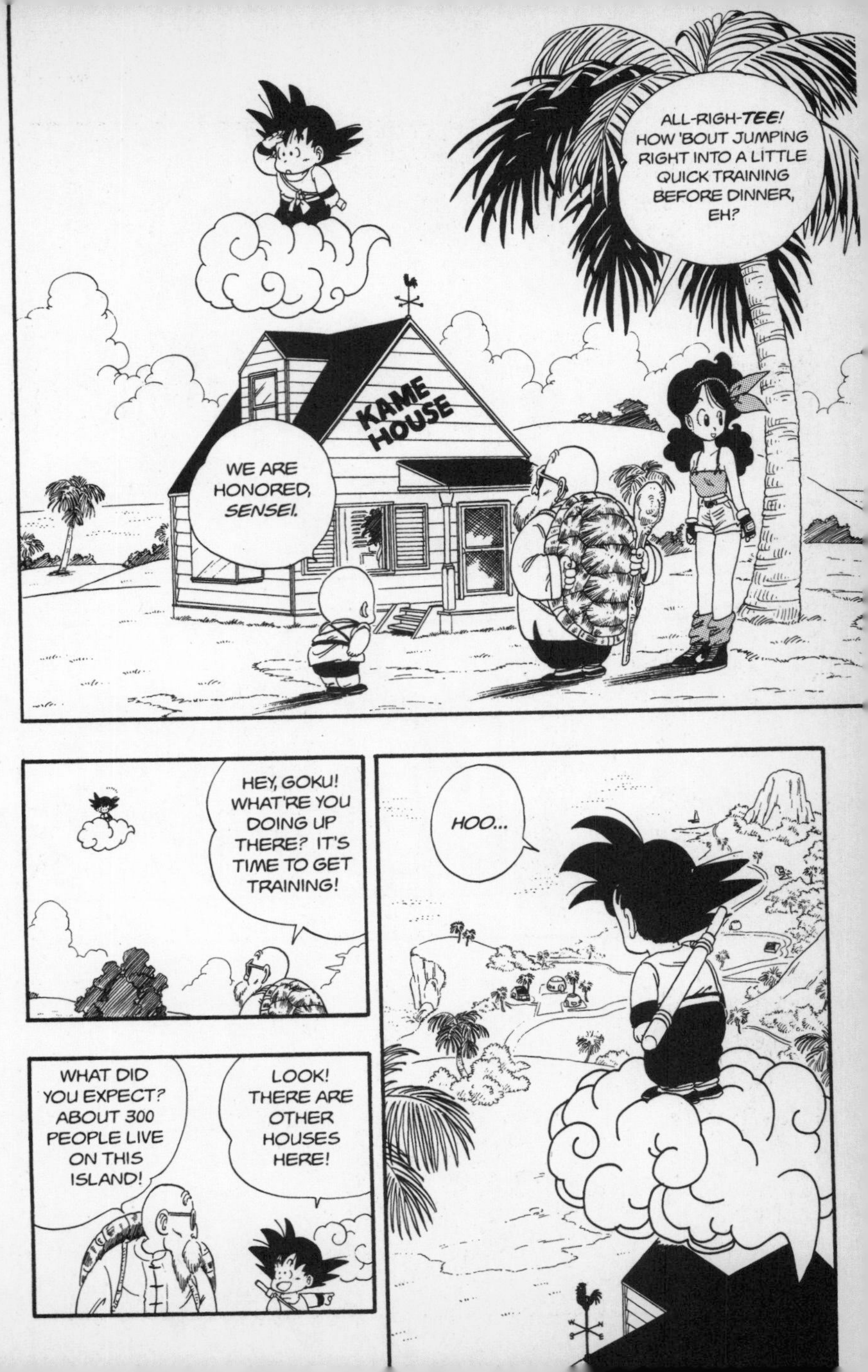
ALL-RIGH-TEE! HOW 'BOUT JUMPING RIGHT INTO A LITTLE QUICK TRAINING BEFORE DINNER, EH?
KAME HOUSE
WE ARE HONORED, SENSEI.
HOO...
HEY, GOKU! WHAT'RE YOU DOING UP THERE? IT'S TIME TO GET TRAINING!
LOOK! THERE ARE OTHER HOUSES HERE!
WHAT DID YOU EXPECT? ABOUT 300 PEOPLE LIVE ON THIS ISLAND!

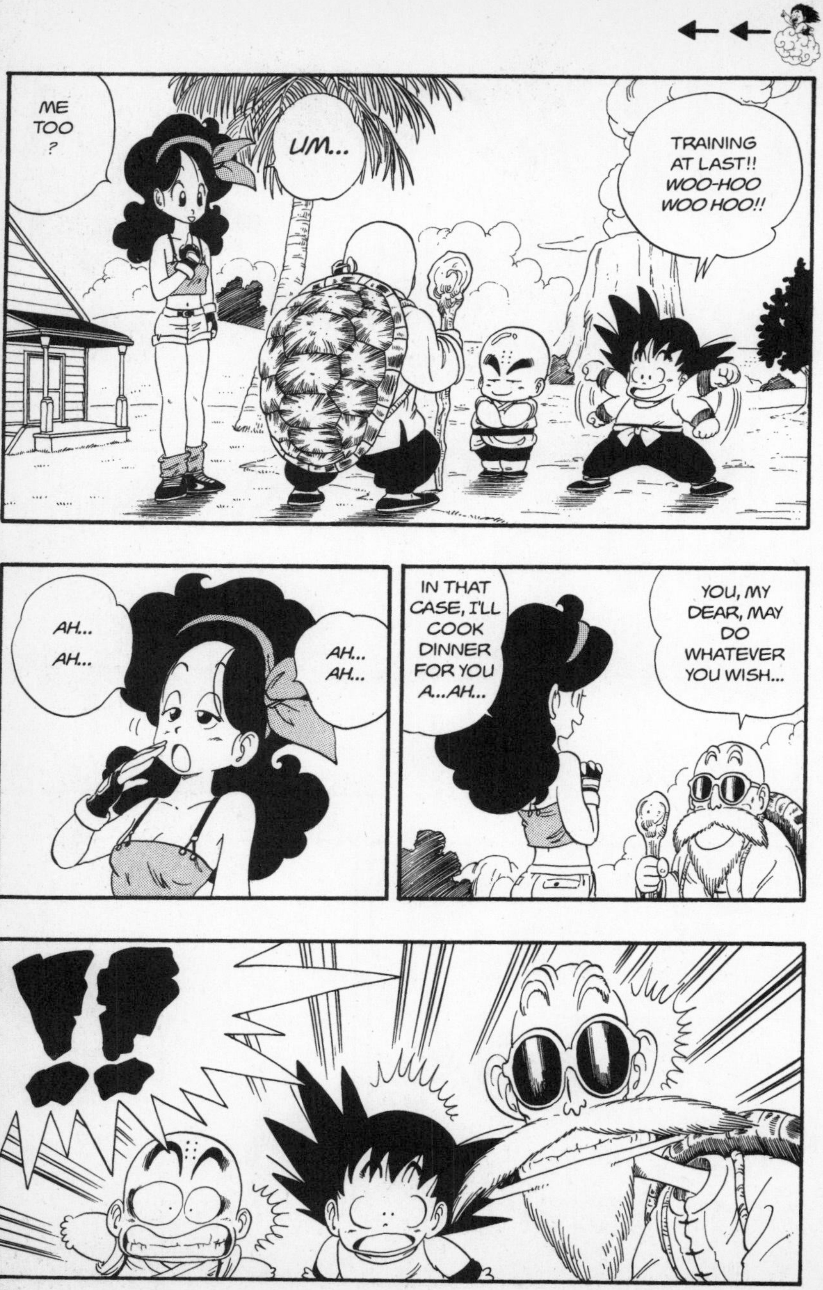
TRAINING AT LAST!! WOO-HOO WOO HOO!!
UM...
ME TOO ?
YOU, MY DEAR, MAY DO WHATEVER YOU WISH...
IN THAT CASE, I'LL COOK DINNER FOR YOU A...AH...
AH... AH...
AH... AH...

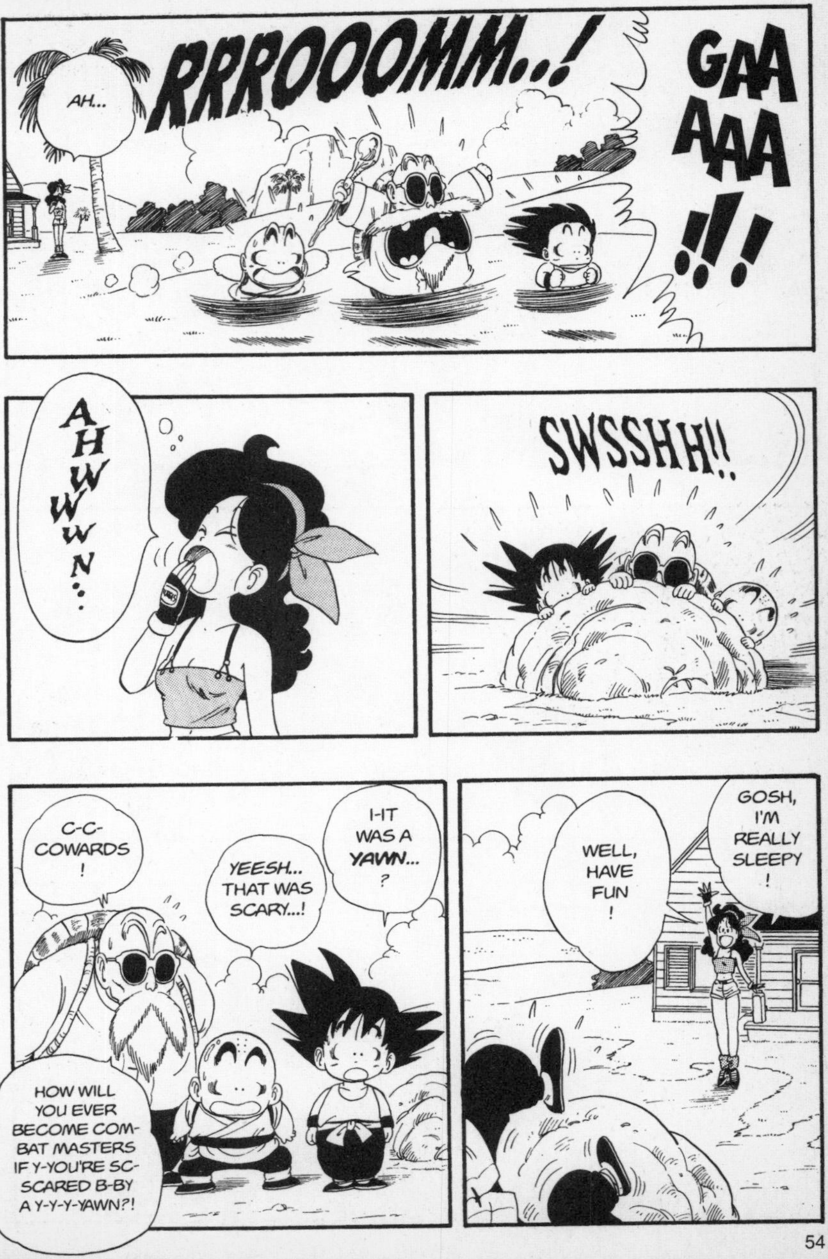
GAAAAA!!!
RRROOOMM..!
AH...
SWSSHH!!
AHWWWN...
GOSH, I'M REALLY SLEEPY!
WELL, HAVE FUN!
I-IT WAS A YAWN...?
YEESH... THAT WAS SCARY...!
C-C-COWARDS!
HOW WILL YOU EVER BECOME COMBAT MASTERS IF Y-YOU'RE SC-SCARED B-BY A Y-Y-Y-YAWN?!

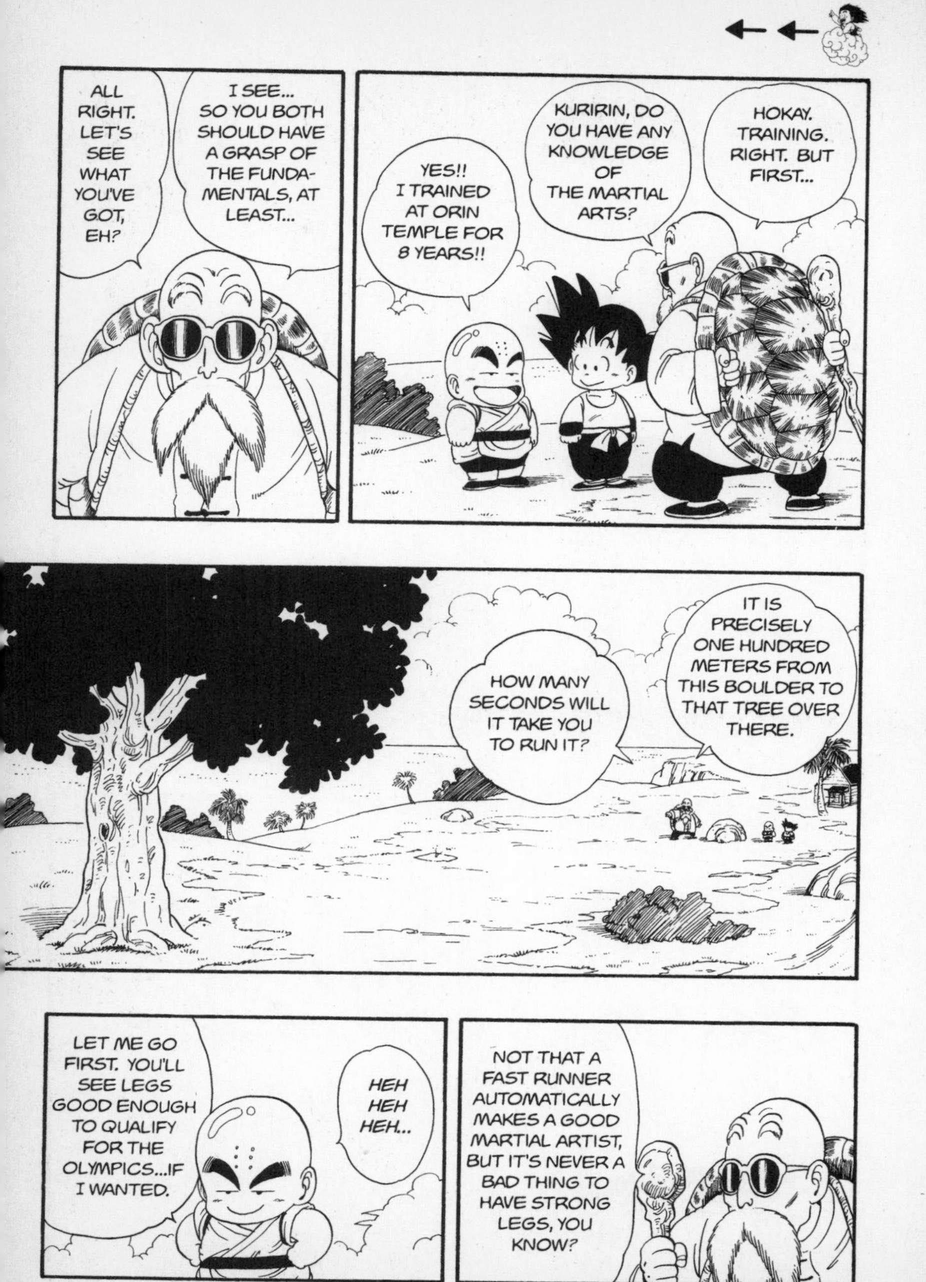
HOKAY. TRAINING. RIGHT. BUT FIRST...
KURIRIN, DO YOU HAVE ANY KNOWLEDGE OF THE MARTIAL ARTS?
YES!! I TRAINED AT ORIN TEMPLE FOR 8 YEARS!!
I SEE... SO YOU BOTH SHOULD HAVE A GRASP OF THE FUNDA-MENTALS, AT LEAST...
ALL RIGHT. LET'S SEE WHAT YOU'VE GOT, EH?
IT IS PRECISELY ONE HUNDRED METERS FROM THIS BOULDER TO THAT TREE OVER THERE.
HOW MANY SECONDS WILL IT TAKE YOU TO RUN IT?
NOT THAT A FAST RUNNER AUTOMATICALLY MAKES A GOOD MARTIAL ARTIST, BUT IT'S NEVER A BAD THING TO HAVE STRONG LEGS, YOU KNOW?
HEH HEH HEH...
LET ME GO FIRST. YOU'LL SEE LEGS GOOD ENOUGH TO QUALIFY FOR THE OLYMPICS...IF I WANTED.

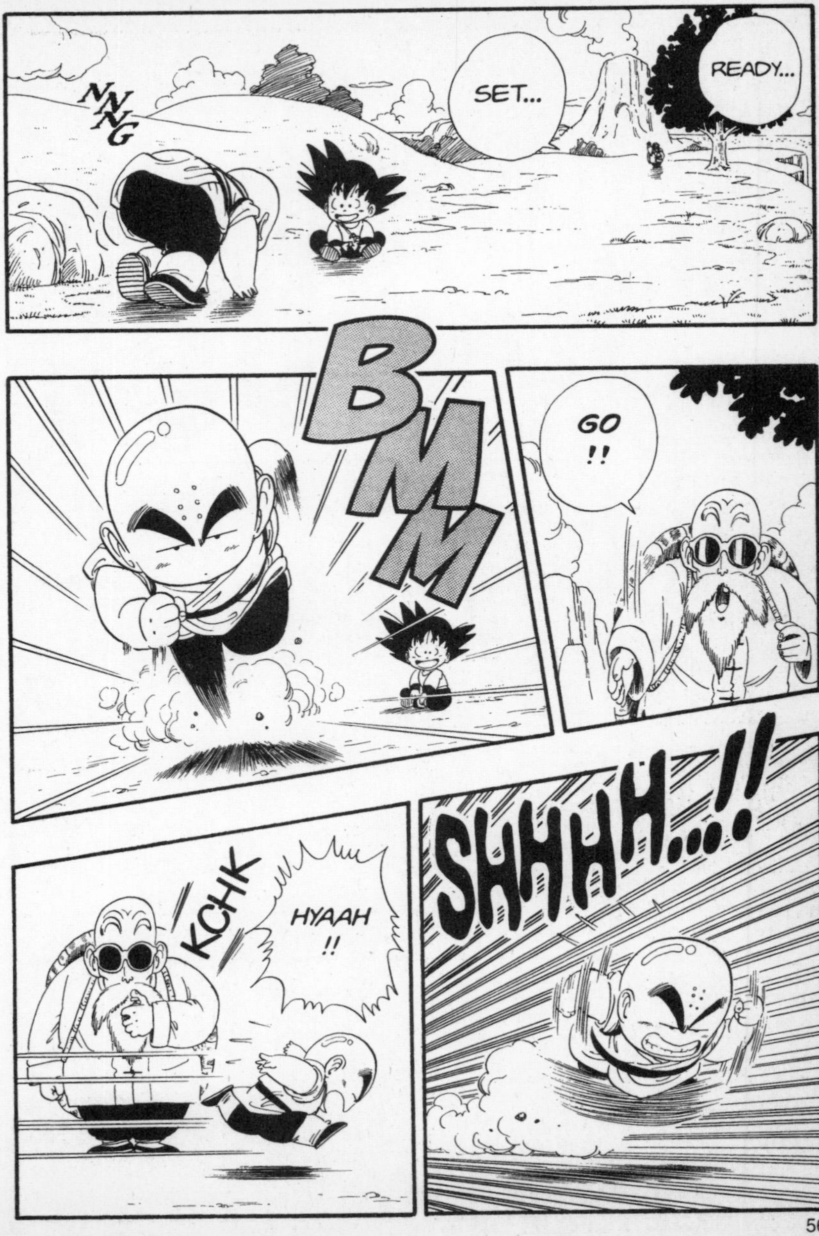
READY...
SET...
NNNG
GO !!
BMM
SHHHH...!!
KCHK
HYAAH !!

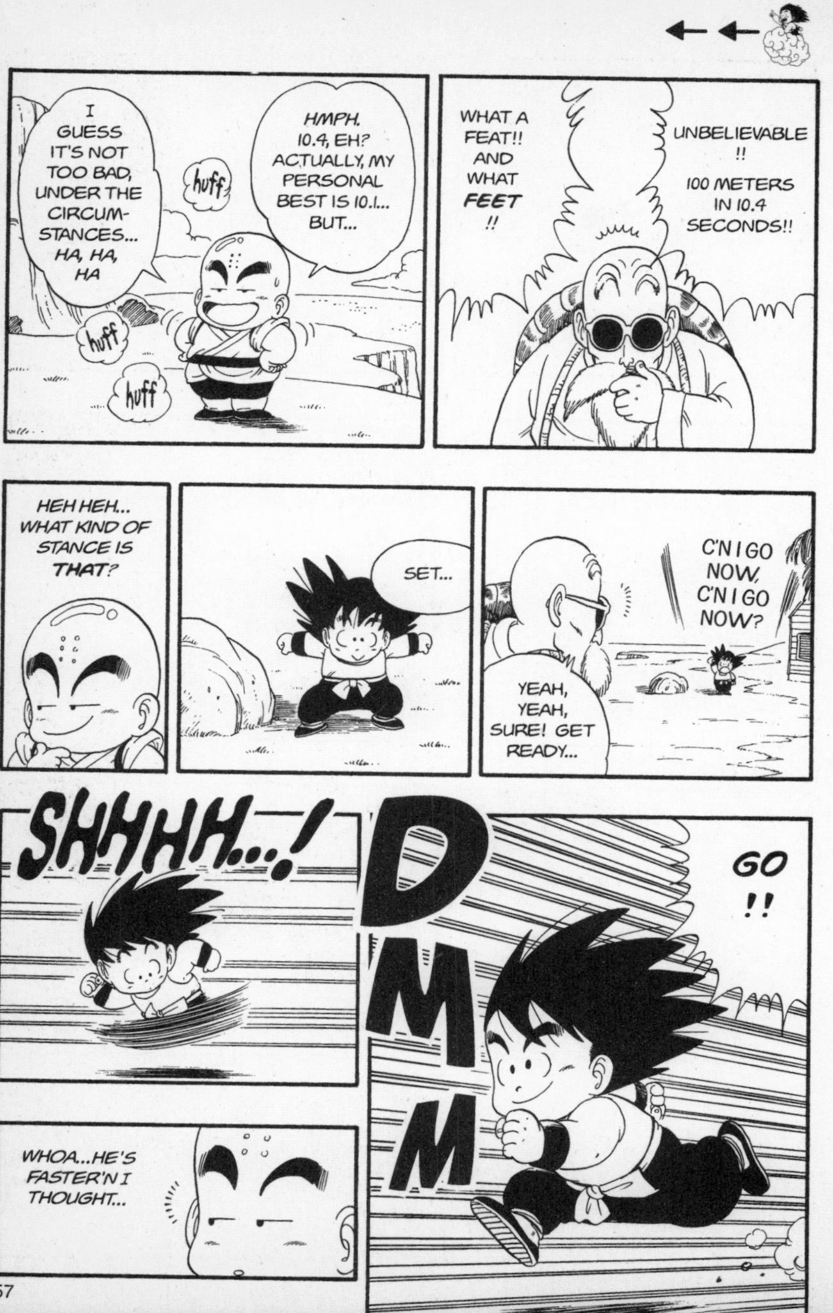
UNBELIEVABLE !! 100 METERS IN 10.4 SECONDS!!
WHAT A FEAT!! AND WHAT FEET !!
HMPH. 10.4, EH? ACTUALLY, MY PERSONAL BEST IS 10.1... BUT...
huff
I GUESS IT'S NOT TOO BAD, UNDER THE CIRCUM-STANCES... HA, HA, HA
huff
huff
C'N I GO NOW, C'N I GO NOW?
YEAH, YEAH, SURE! GET READY...
SET...
HEH HEH... WHAT KIND OF STANCE IS THAT?
GO !!
DMMM
SHHHH...!
WHOA...HE'S FASTER'N I THOUGHT...

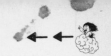

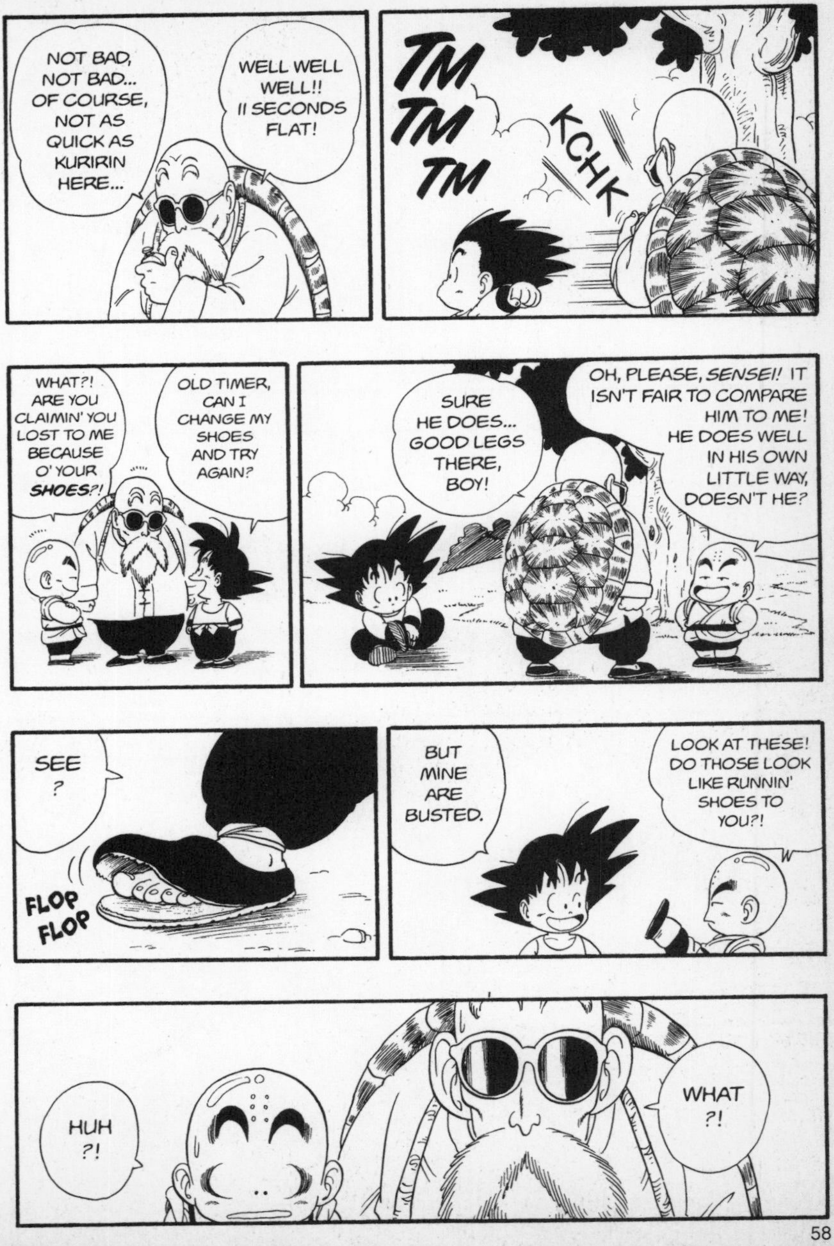
TM TM TM
KCHK
WELL WELL WELL!! 11 SECONDS FLAT!
NOT BAD, NOT BAD... OF COURSE, NOT AS QUICK AS KURIRIN HERE...
OH, PLEASE, SENSEI! IT ISN'T FAIR TO COMPARE HIM TO ME! HE DOES WELL IN HIS OWN LITTLE WAY, DOESN'T HE?
SURE HE DOES... GOOD LEGS THERE, BOY!
OLD TIMER, CAN I CHANGE MY SHOES AND TRY AGAIN?
WHAT?! ARE YOU CLAIMIN' YOU LOST TO ME BECAUSE O' YOUR SHOES?!
LOOK AT THESE! DO THOSE LOOK LIKE RUNNIN' SHOES TO YOU?!
BUT MINE ARE BUSTED.
SEE ?
FLOP FLOP
WHAT ?!
HUH ?!

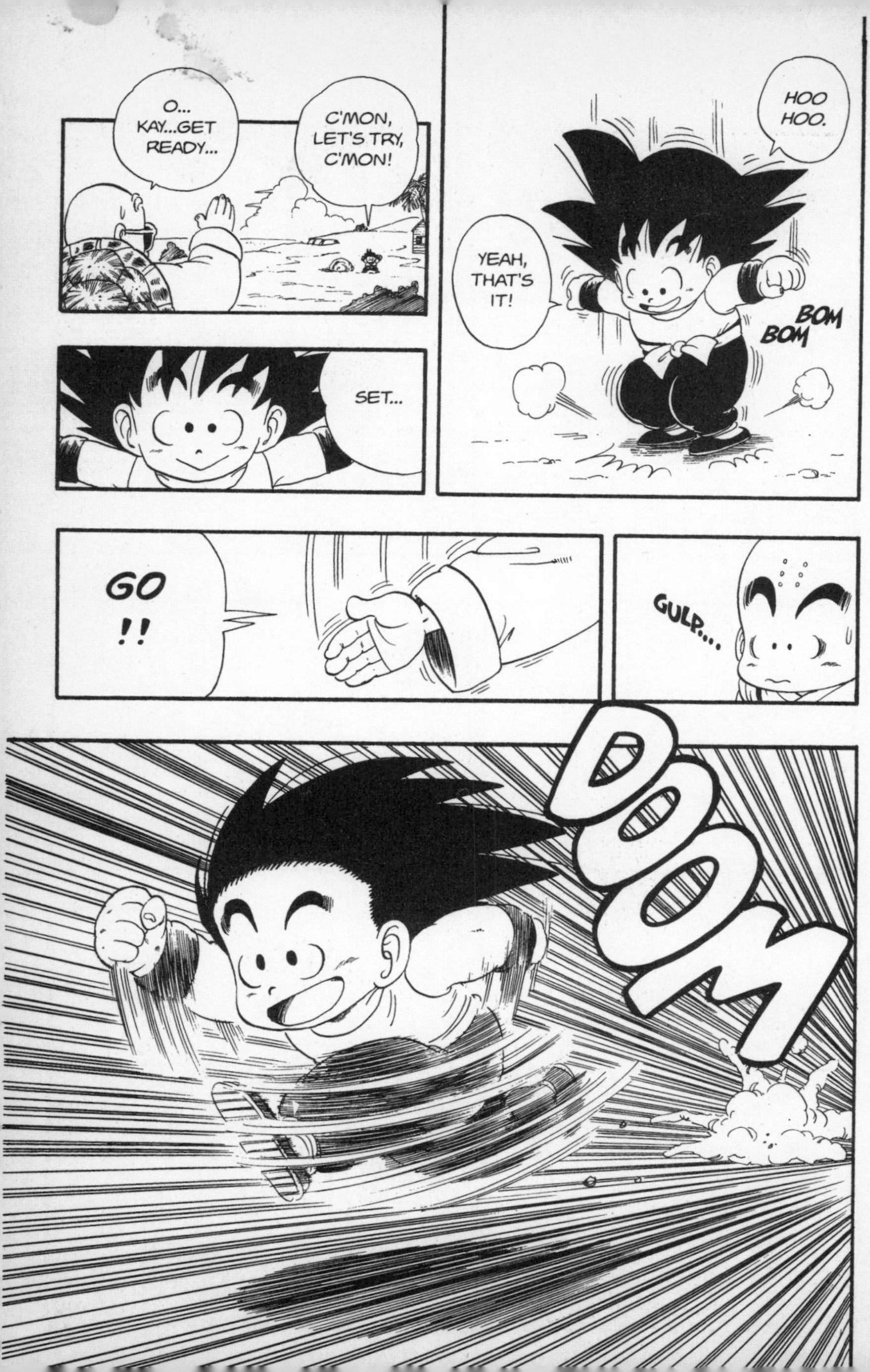
HOO HOO.
YEAH, THAT'S IT!
BOM BOM
C'MON, LET'S TRY, C'MON!
O... KAY...GET READY...
SET...
GULP....
GO !!
DOOOM

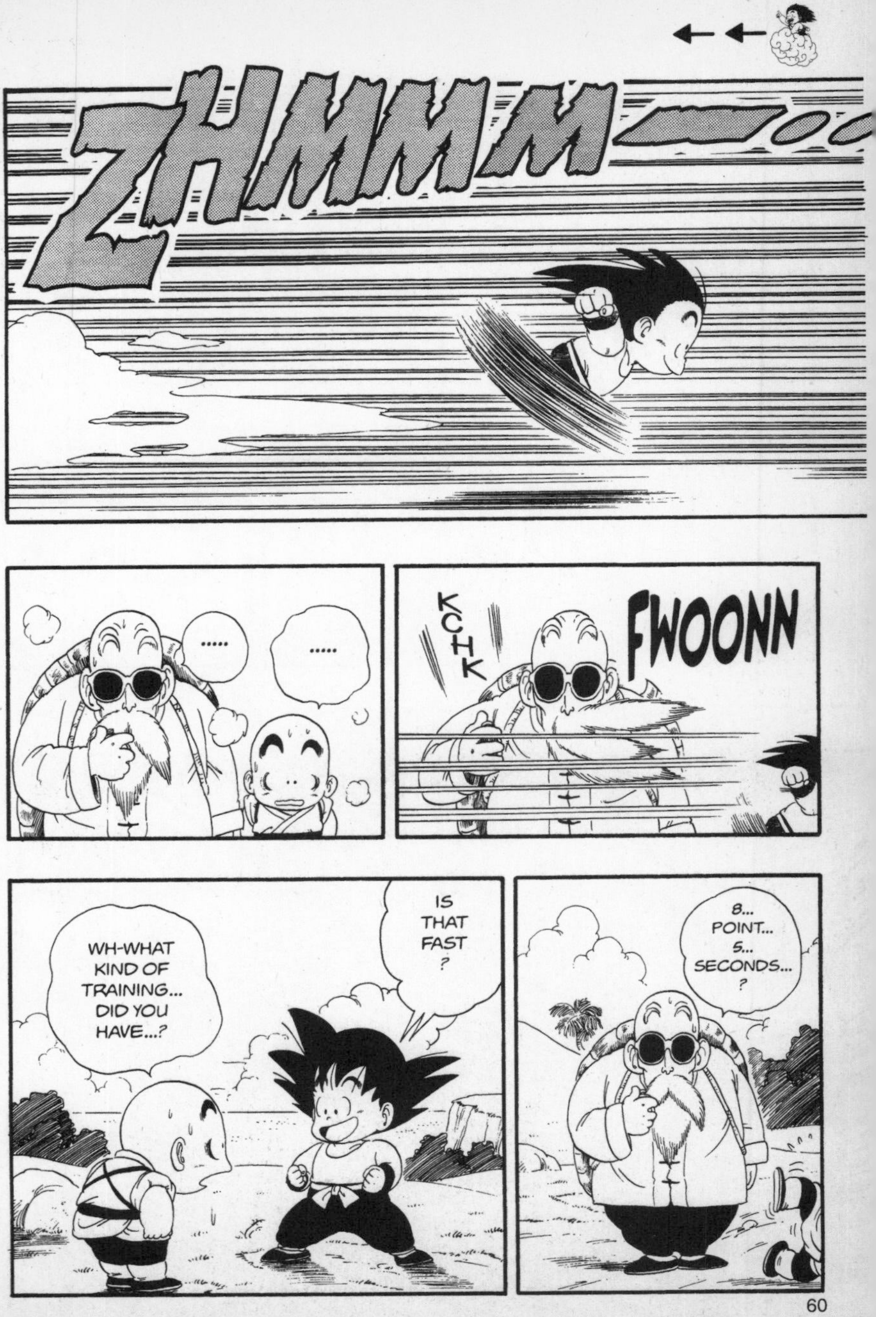

ZHMMM——...
FWOONN
KCHK
......
......
8... POINT... 5... SECONDS... ?
IS THAT FAST ?
WH-WHAT KIND OF TRAINING... DID YOU HAVE...?

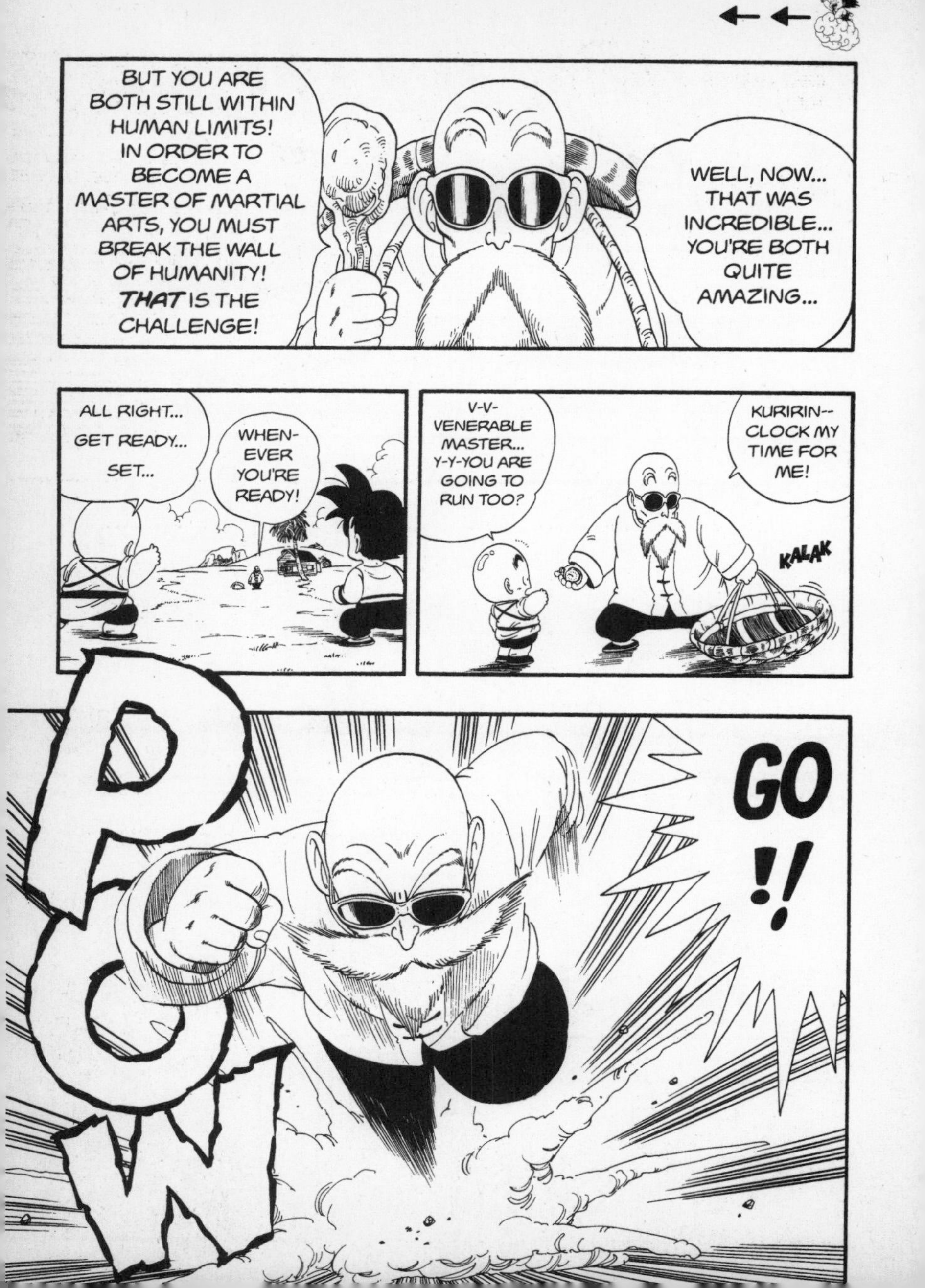
WELL, NOW... THAT WAS INCREDIBLE... YOU'RE BOTH QUITE AMAZING...
BUT YOU ARE BOTH STILL WITHIN HUMAN LIMITS! IN ORDER TO BECOME A MASTER OF MARTIAL ARTS, YOU MUST BREAK THE WALL OF HUMANITY! *THAT* IS THE CHALLENGE!
KURIRIN-- CLOCK MY TIME FOR ME!
V-V-VENERABLE MASTER... Y-Y-YOU ARE GOING TO RUN TOO?
KALAK
WHEN-EVER YOU'RE READY!
ALL RIGHT... GET READY... SET...
GO!!
POW

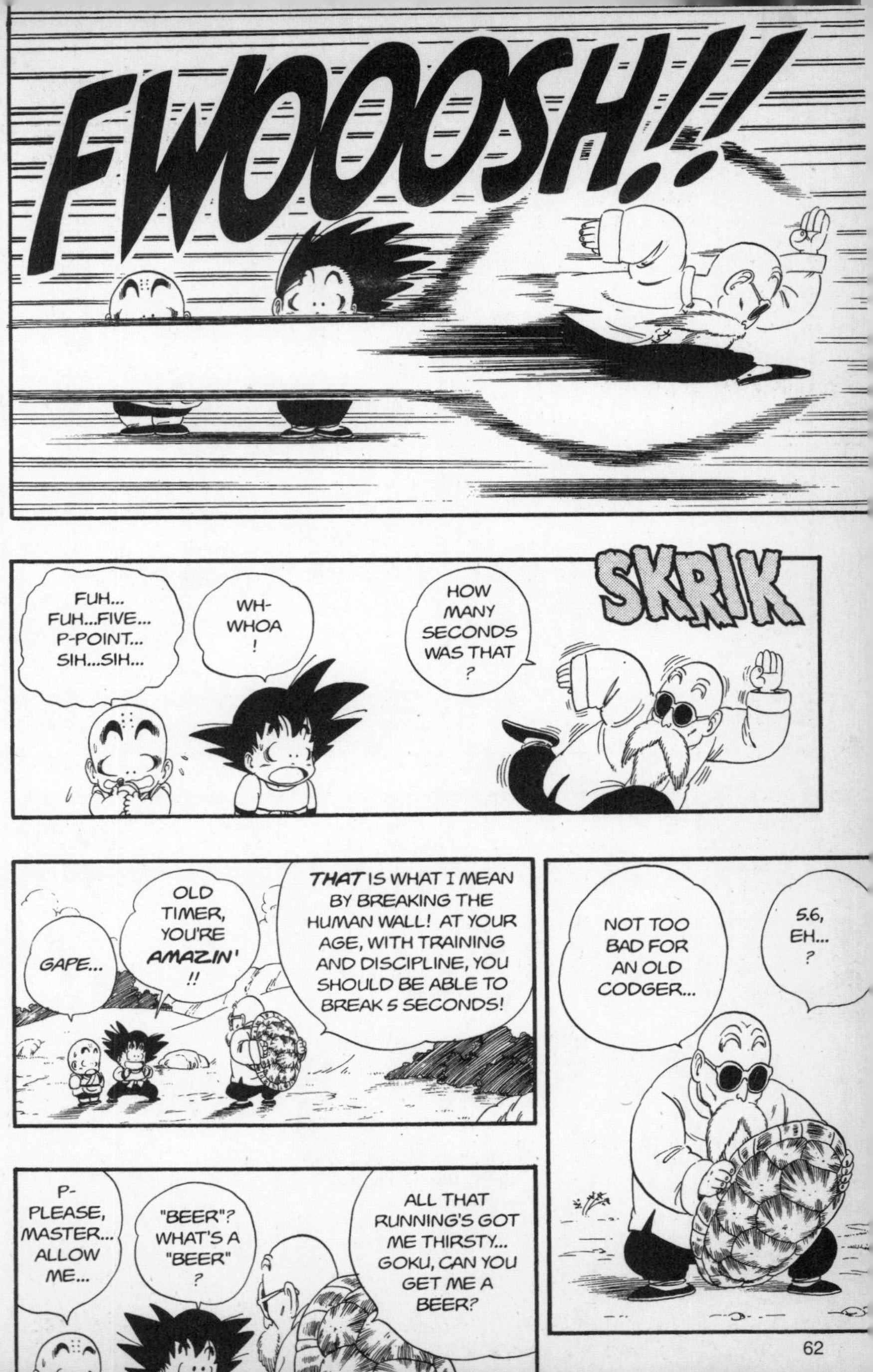
FWOOOSH!!
SKRIK
HOW MANY SECONDS WAS THAT ?
WH- WHOA !
FUH... FUH...FIVE... P-POINT... SIH...SIH...
5.6, EH... ?
NOT TOO BAD FOR AN OLD CODGER...
THAT IS WHAT I MEAN BY BREAKING THE HUMAN WALL! AT YOUR AGE, WITH TRAINING AND DISCIPLINE, YOU SHOULD BE ABLE TO BREAK 5 SECONDS!
OLD TIMER, YOU'RE AMAZIN' !!
GAPE...
ALL THAT RUNNING'S GOT ME THIRSTY... GOKU, CAN YOU GET ME A BEER?
"BEER"? WHAT'S A "BEER" ?
P- PLEASE, MASTER... ALLOW ME...

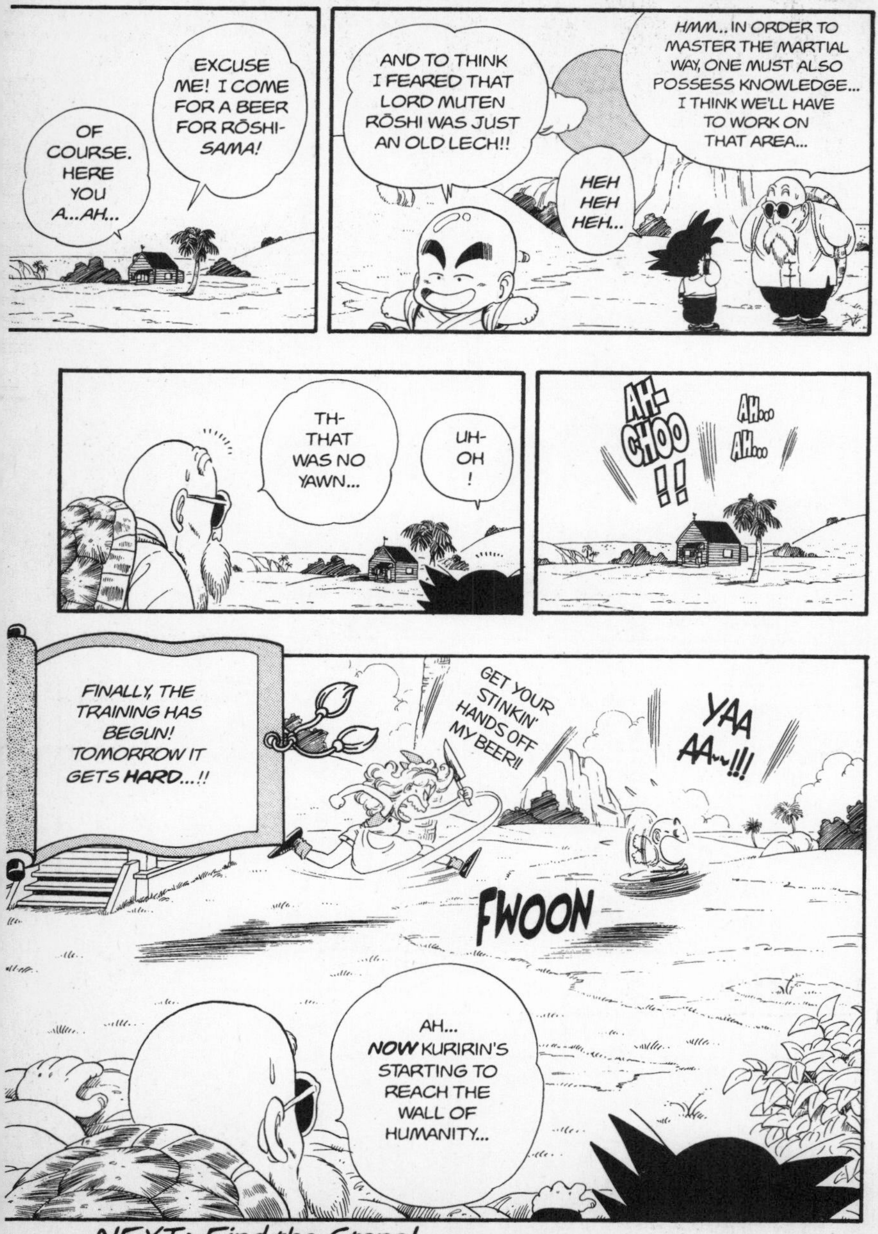
HMM... IN ORDER TO MASTER THE MARTIAL WAY, ONE MUST ALSO POSSESS KNOWLEDGE... I THINK WE'LL HAVE TO WORK ON THAT AREA...
AND TO THINK I FEARED THAT LORD MUTEN RŌSHI WAS JUST AN OLD LECH!!
HEH HEH HEH...
EXCUSE ME! I COME FOR A BEER FOR RŌSHI-SAMA!
OF COURSE. HERE YOU A...AH...
AH... AH...
AH-CHOO!!
UH-OH!
TH-THAT WAS NO YAWN...
YAAAA~!!!
GET YOUR STINKIN' HANDS OFF MY BEER!!
FWOON
FINALLY, THE TRAINING HAS BEGUN! TOMORROW IT GETS HARD...!!
AH... NOW KURIRIN'S STARTING TO REACH THE WALL OF HUMANITY...

NEXT: Find the Stone!

Tale 29
Bad Day at Turtle Rock

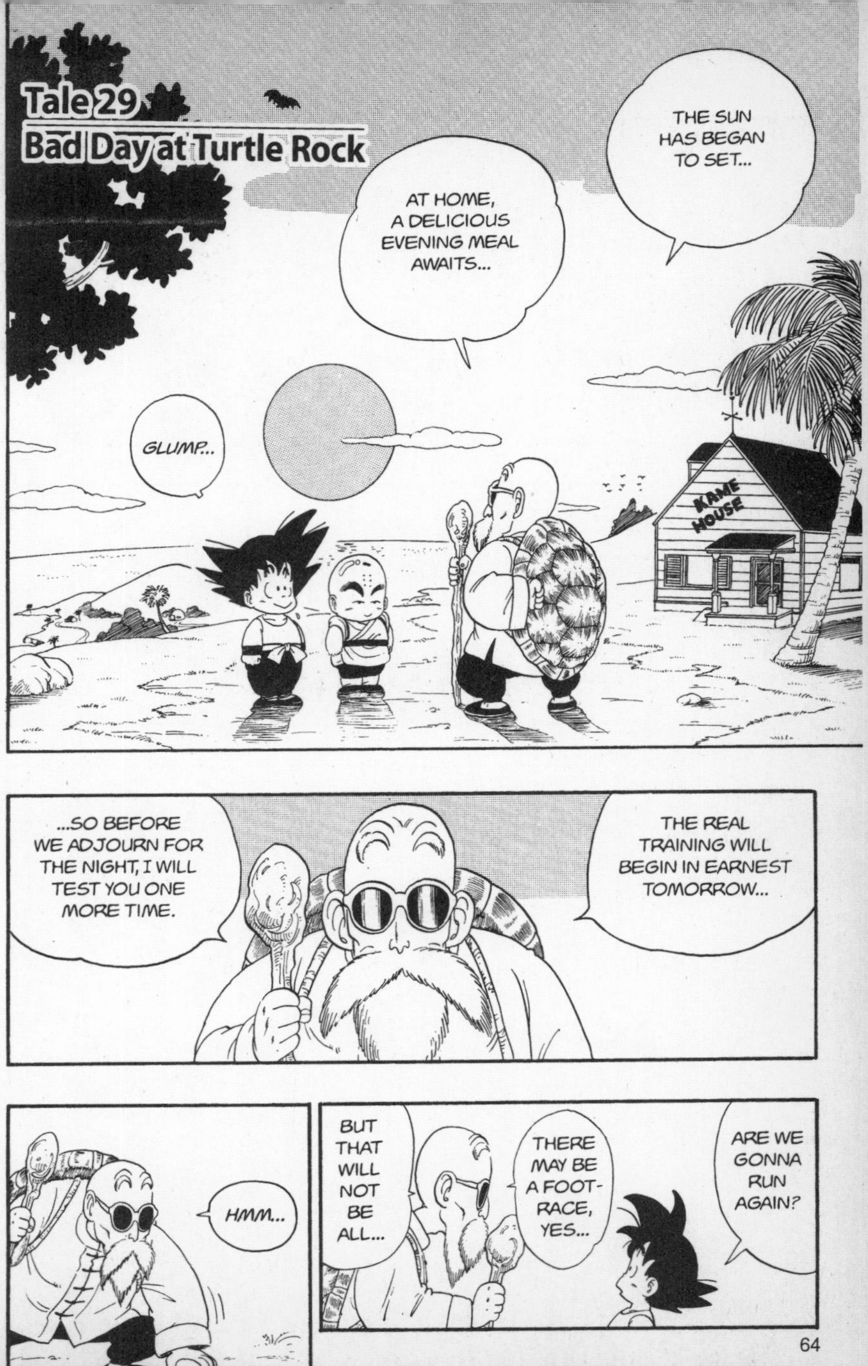
THE SUN HAS BEGAN TO SET...
AT HOME, A DELICIOUS EVENING MEAL AWAITS...
GLUMP...
KAME HOUSE
THE REAL TRAINING WILL BEGIN IN EARNEST TOMORROW...
...SO BEFORE WE ADJOURN FOR THE NIGHT, I WILL TEST YOU ONE MORE TIME.
ARE WE GONNA RUN AGAIN?
THERE MAY BE A FOOT-RACE, YES...
BUT THAT WILL NOT BE ALL...
HMM...

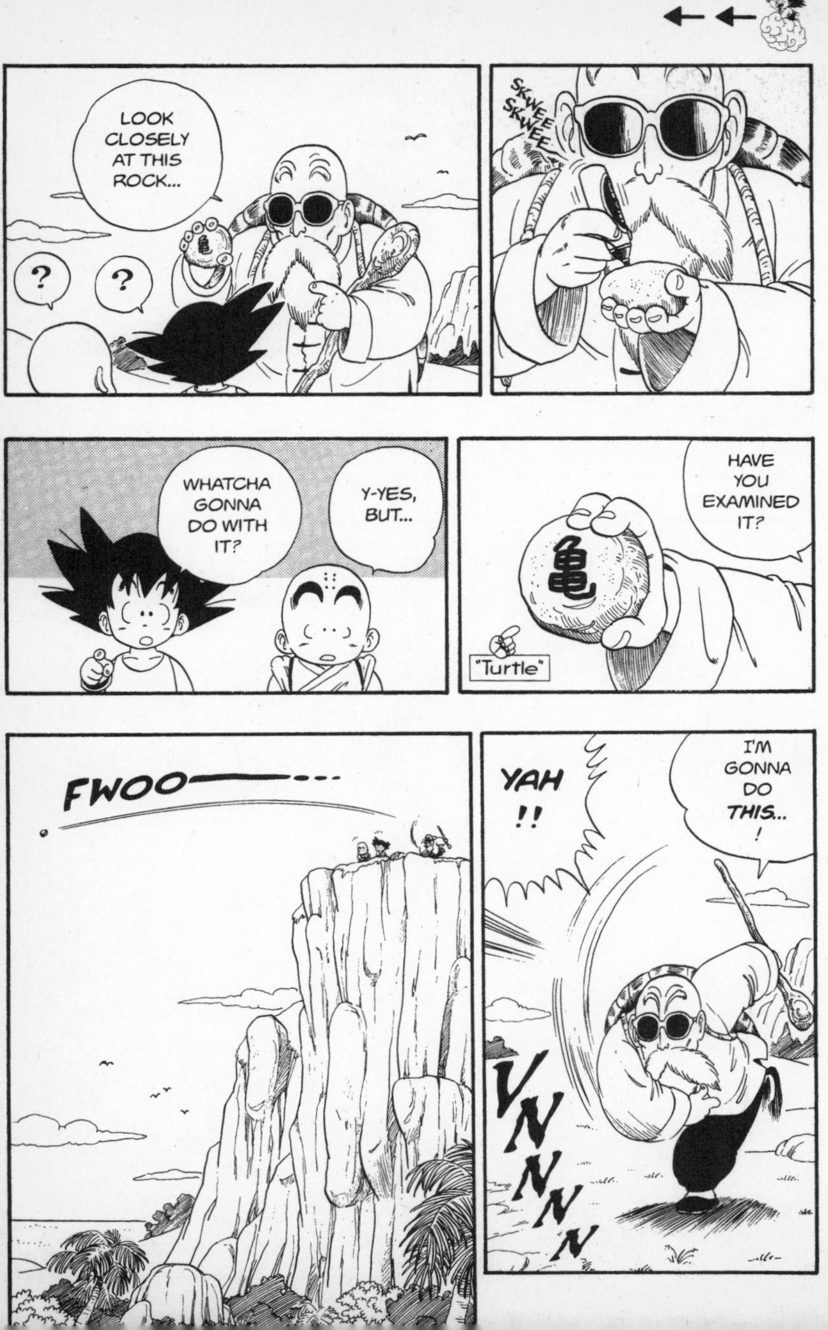
SKWEE
SKWEE
LOOK CLOSELY AT THIS ROCK...
?
?
HAVE YOU EXAMINED IT?
"Turtle"
Y-YES, BUT...
WHATCHA GONNA DO WITH IT?
I'M GONNA DO THIS...!
YAH!!
VNNNN
FWOO———...

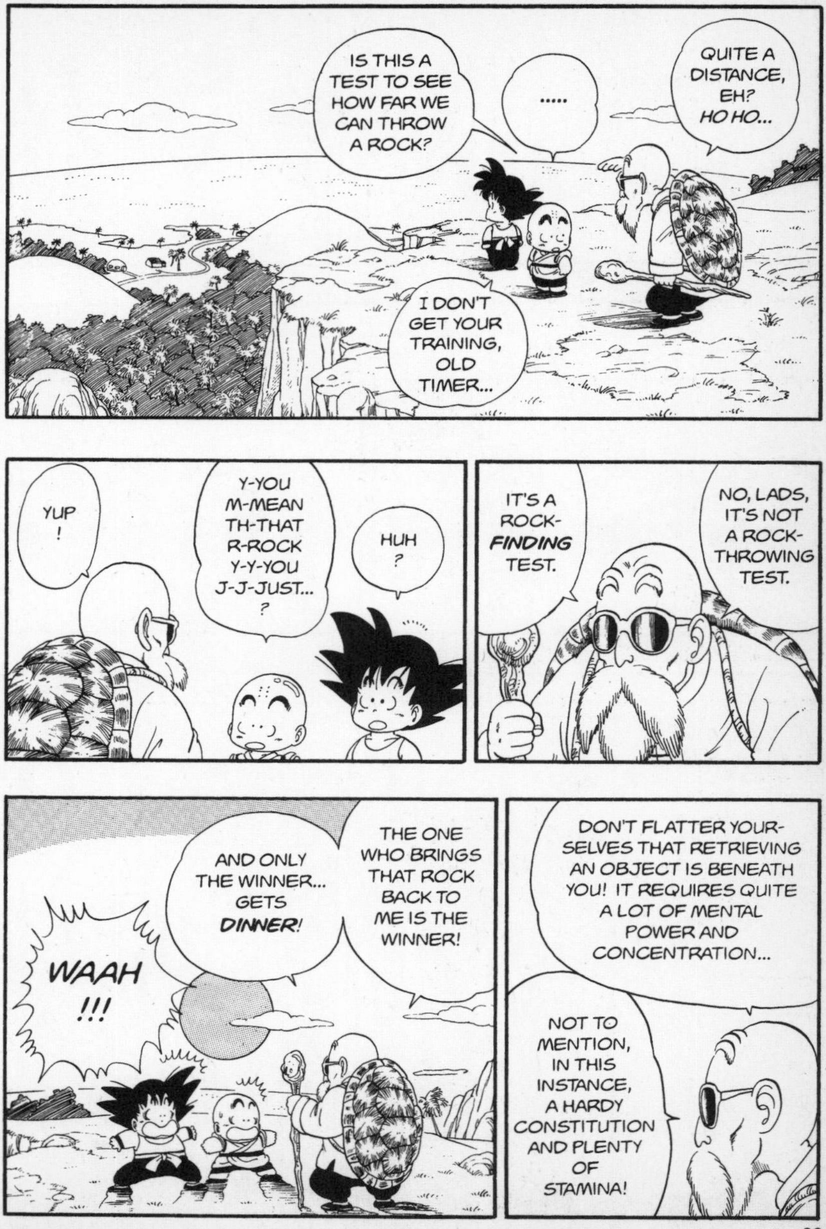
QUITE A DISTANCE, EH? HO HO...
.....
IS THIS A TEST TO SEE HOW FAR WE CAN THROW A ROCK?
I DON'T GET YOUR TRAINING, OLD TIMER...
NO, LADS, IT'S NOT A ROCK-THROWING TEST.
IT'S A ROCK-FINDING TEST.
HUH ?
Y-YOU M-MEAN TH-THAT R-ROCK Y-Y-YOU J-J-JUST... ?
YUP !
DON'T FLATTER YOURSELVES THAT RETRIEVING AN OBJECT IS BENEATH YOU! IT REQUIRES QUITE A LOT OF MENTAL POWER AND CONCENTRATION...
NOT TO MENTION, IN THIS INSTANCE, A HARDY CONSTITUTION AND PLENTY OF STAMINA!
THE ONE WHO BRINGS THAT ROCK BACK TO ME IS THE WINNER!
AND ONLY THE WINNER... GETS DINNER!
WAAH !!!

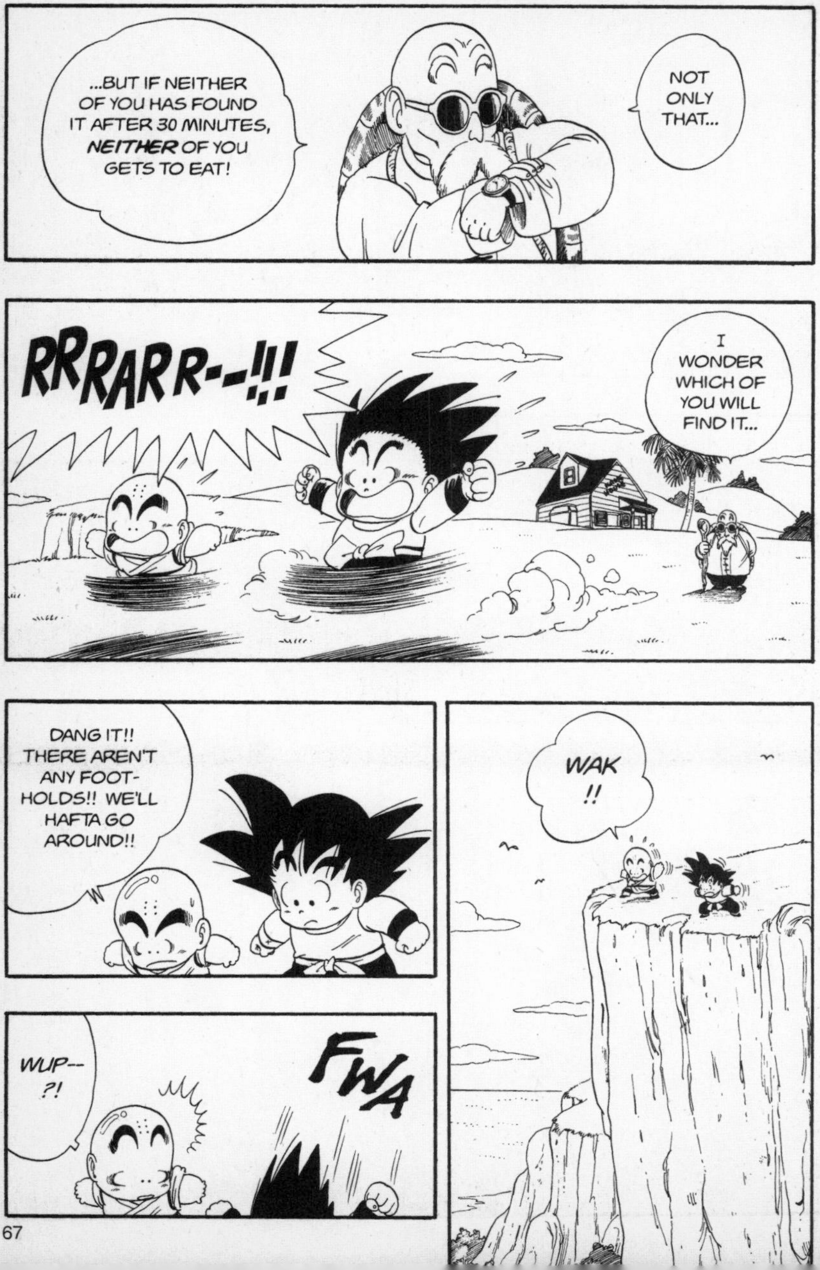
NOT ONLY THAT...
...BUT IF NEITHER OF YOU HAS FOUND IT AFTER 30 MINUTES, ***NEITHER*** OF YOU GETS TO EAT!
I WONDER WHICH OF YOU WILL FIND IT...
RRRARR--!!!
WAK !!
DANG IT!! THERE AREN'T ANY FOOT-HOLDS!! WE'LL HAFTA GO AROUND!!
FWA
WUP-- ?!

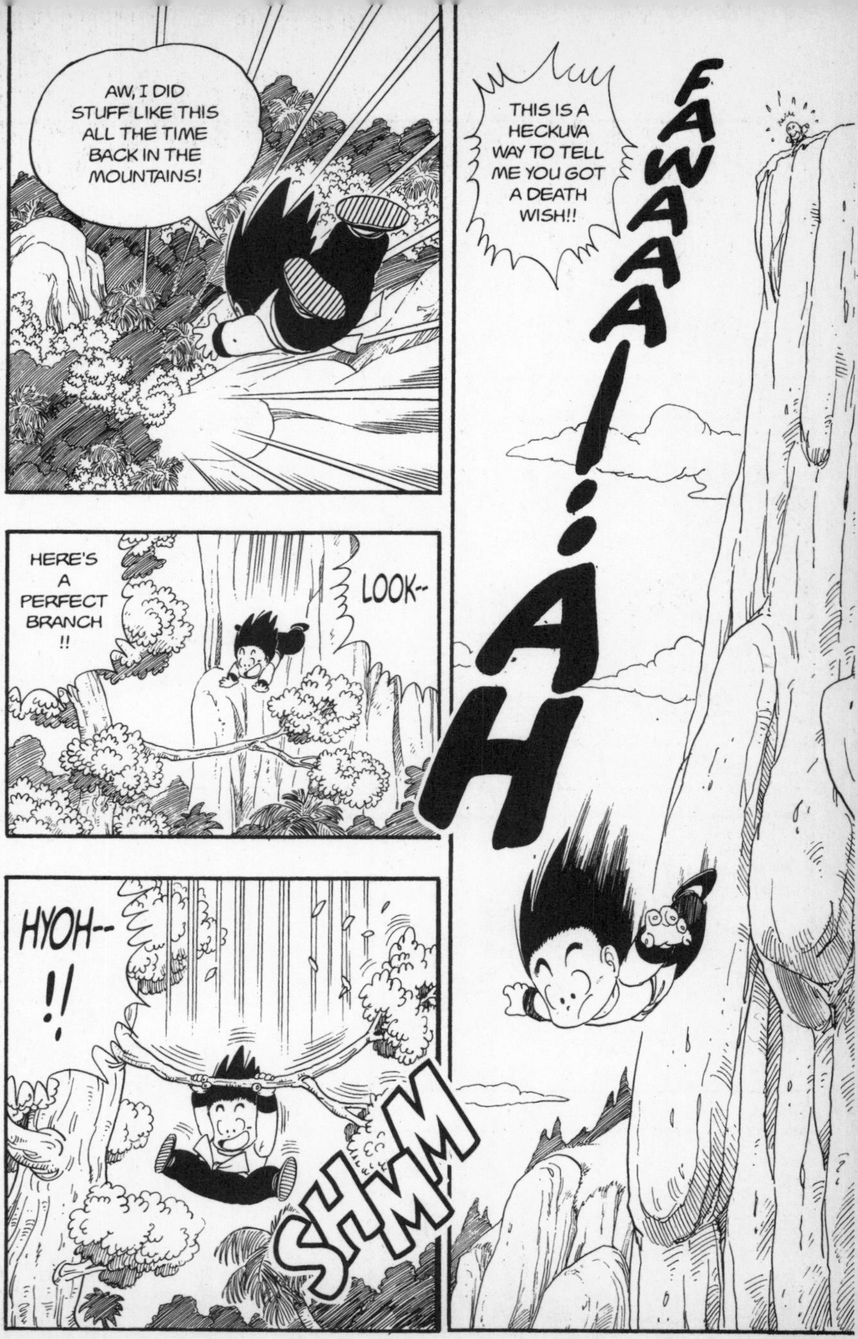
THIS IS A HECKUVA WAY TO TELL ME YOU GOT A DEATH WISH!!
FAWAAA!!AH
AW, I DID STUFF LIKE THIS ALL THE TIME BACK IN THE MOUNTAINS!
LOOK--
HERE'S A PERFECT BRANCH !!
HYOH-- !!
SHMM

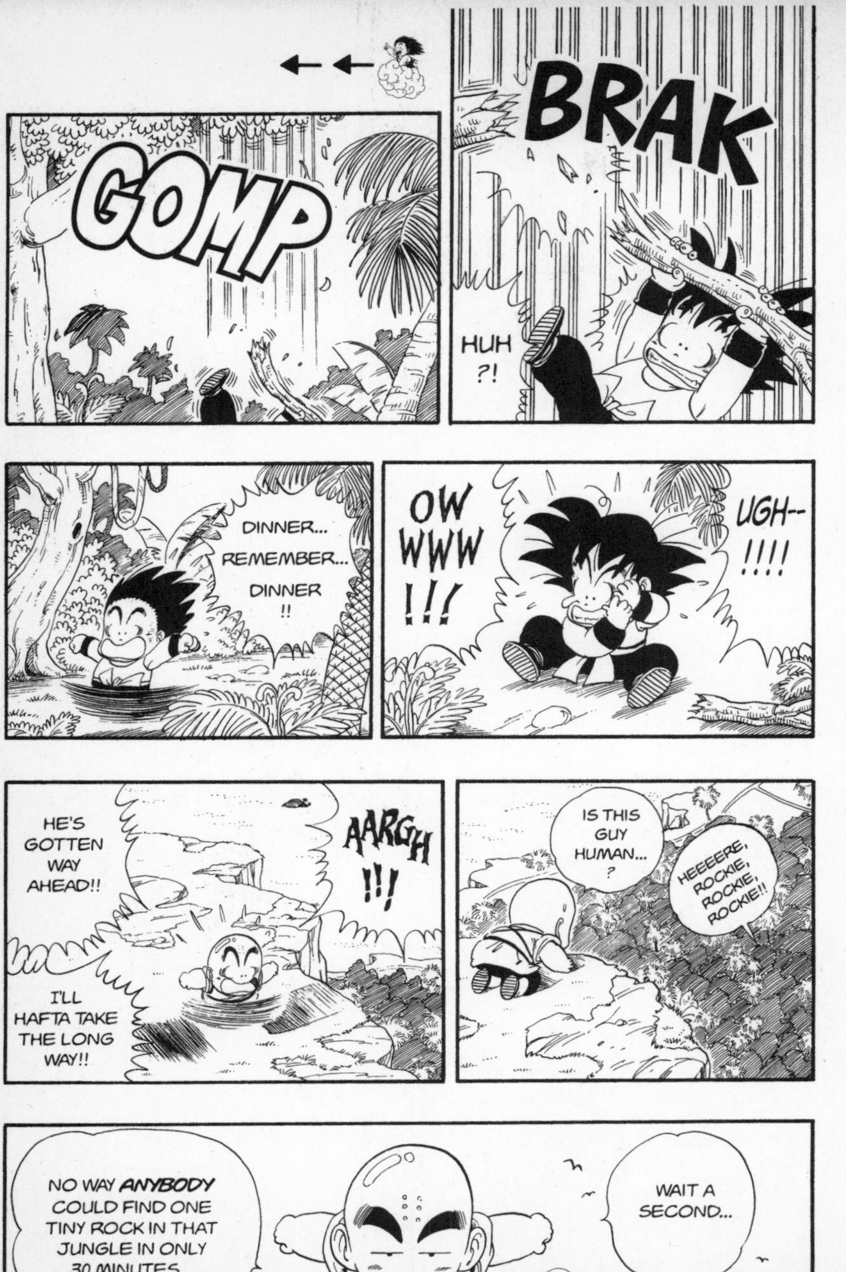
BRAK
HUH ?!
GOMP
UGH-- !!!!
OW WWW !!!
DINNER... REMEMBER... DINNER !!
HEEEERE, ROCKIE, ROCKIE, ROCKIE!!
IS THIS GUY HUMAN... ?
AARGH !!!
HE'S GOTTEN WAY AHEAD!!
I'LL HAFTA TAKE THE LONG WAY!!
WAIT A SECOND...
NO WAY **ANYBODY** COULD FIND ONE TINY ROCK IN THAT JUNGLE IN ONLY 30 MINUTES...

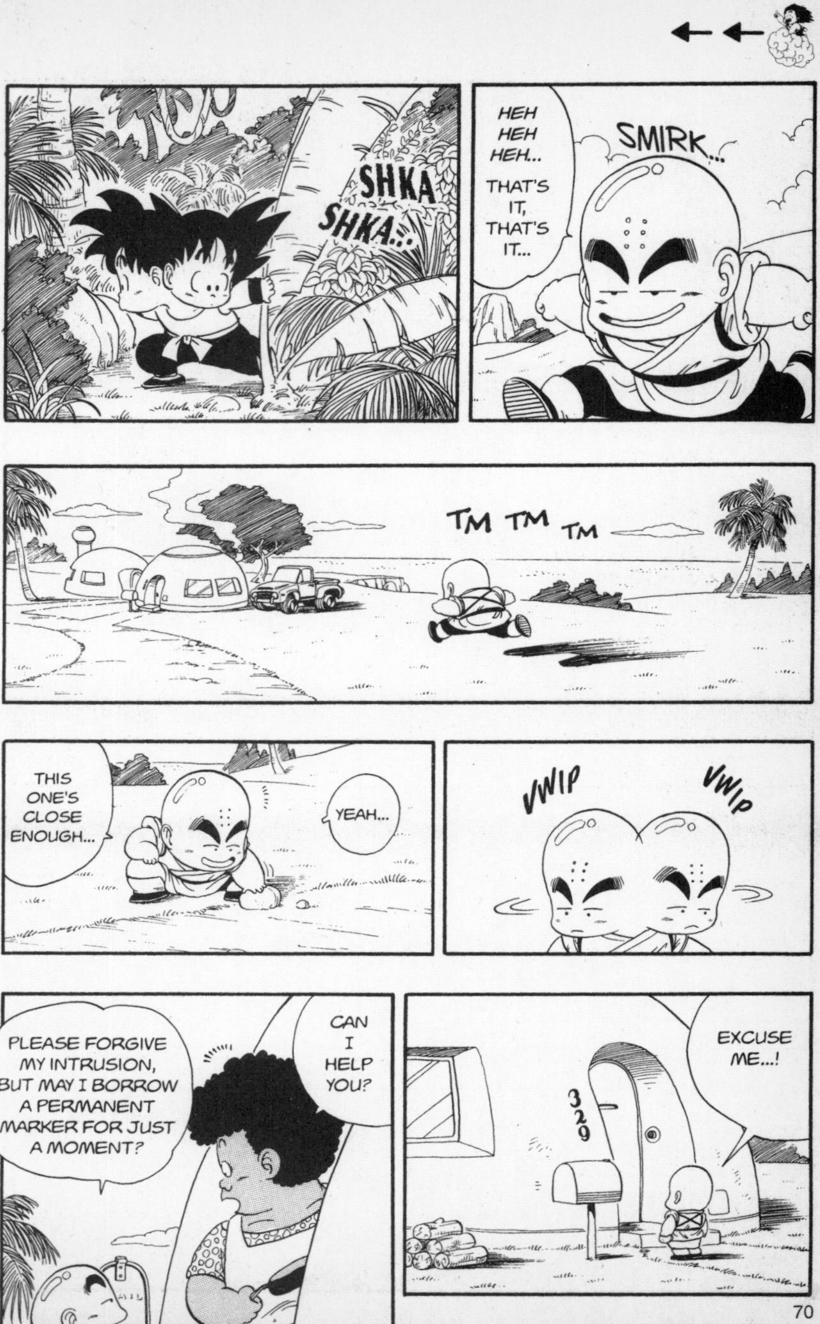
SMIRK...
HEH HEH HEH...
THAT'S IT, THAT'S IT...
SHKA SHKA...
TM TM TM
VWIP VWIP
THIS ONE'S CLOSE ENOUGH...
YEAH...
EXCUSE ME...!
329
CAN I HELP YOU?
PLEASE FORGIVE MY INTRUSION, BUT MAY I BORROW A PERMANENT MARKER FOR JUST A MOMENT?

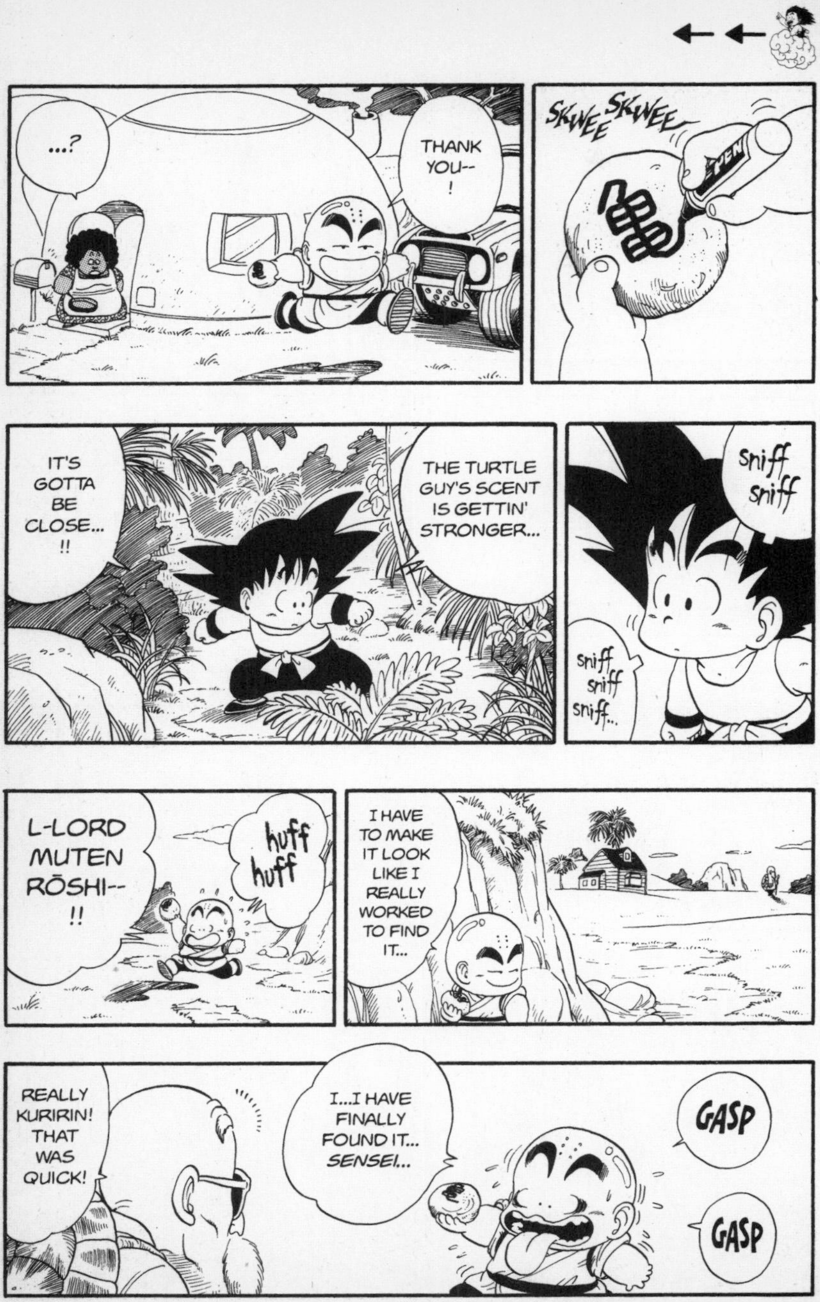
SKWEE SKWEE
PEN
THANK YOU--!
...?
sniff sniff
sniff sniff sniff...
THE TURTLE GUY'S SCENT IS GETTIN' STRONGER...
IT'S GOTTA BE CLOSE...!!
I HAVE TO MAKE IT LOOK LIKE I REALLY WORKED TO FIND IT...
huff huff
L-LORD MUTEN RŌSHI--!!
GASP
GASP
I...I HAVE FINALLY FOUND IT... SENSEI...
REALLY KURIRIN! THAT WAS QUICK!

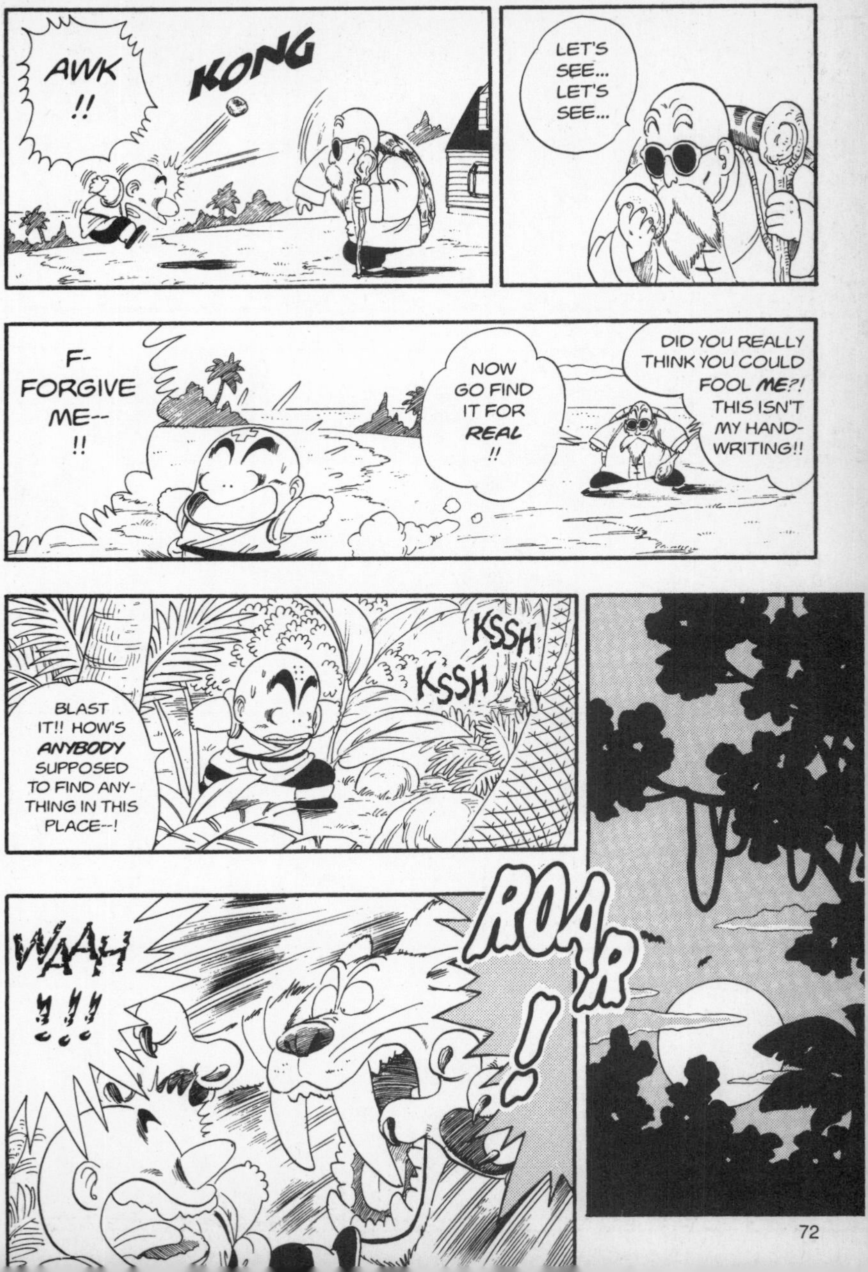
LET'S SEE... LET'S SEE...
KONG
AWK !!
DID YOU REALLY THINK YOU COULD FOOL ME?! THIS ISN'T MY HAND-WRITING!!
NOW GO FIND IT FOR REAL !!
F-FORGIVE ME-- !!
KSSH
KSSH
BLAST IT!! HOW'S ANYBODY SUPPOSED TO FIND ANY-THING IN THIS PLACE--!
ROAR !
WAAH !!!

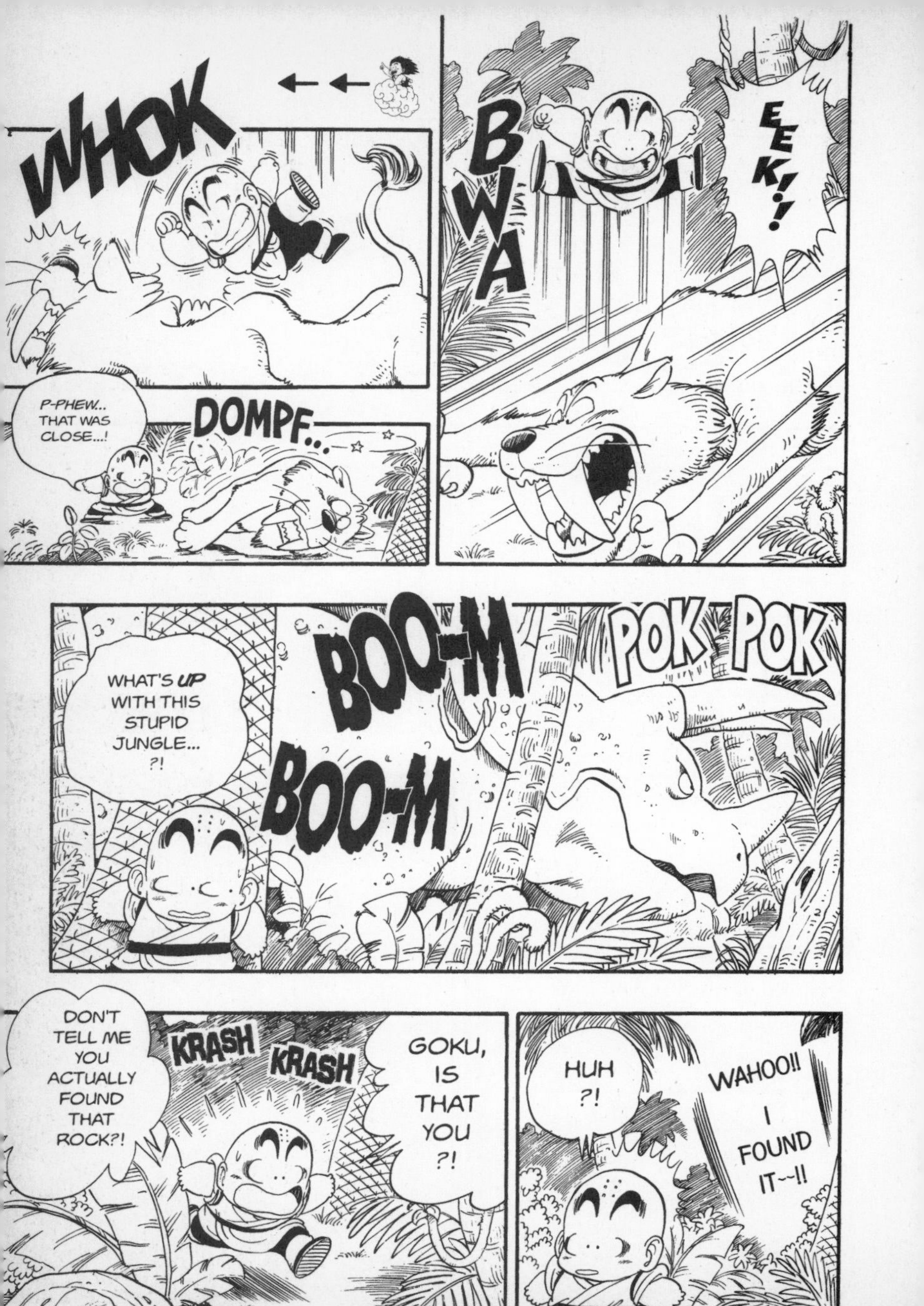
BWA
EEK!!
WHOK
P-PHEW... THAT WAS CLOSE...!
DOMPF...
POK POK
BOO-M
BOO-M
WHAT'S *UP* WITH THIS STUPID JUNGLE...?!
WAHOO!! I FOUND IT~~!!
HUH?!
GOKU, IS THAT YOU?!
KRASH
KRASH
DON'T TELL ME YOU ACTUALLY FOUND THAT ROCK?!

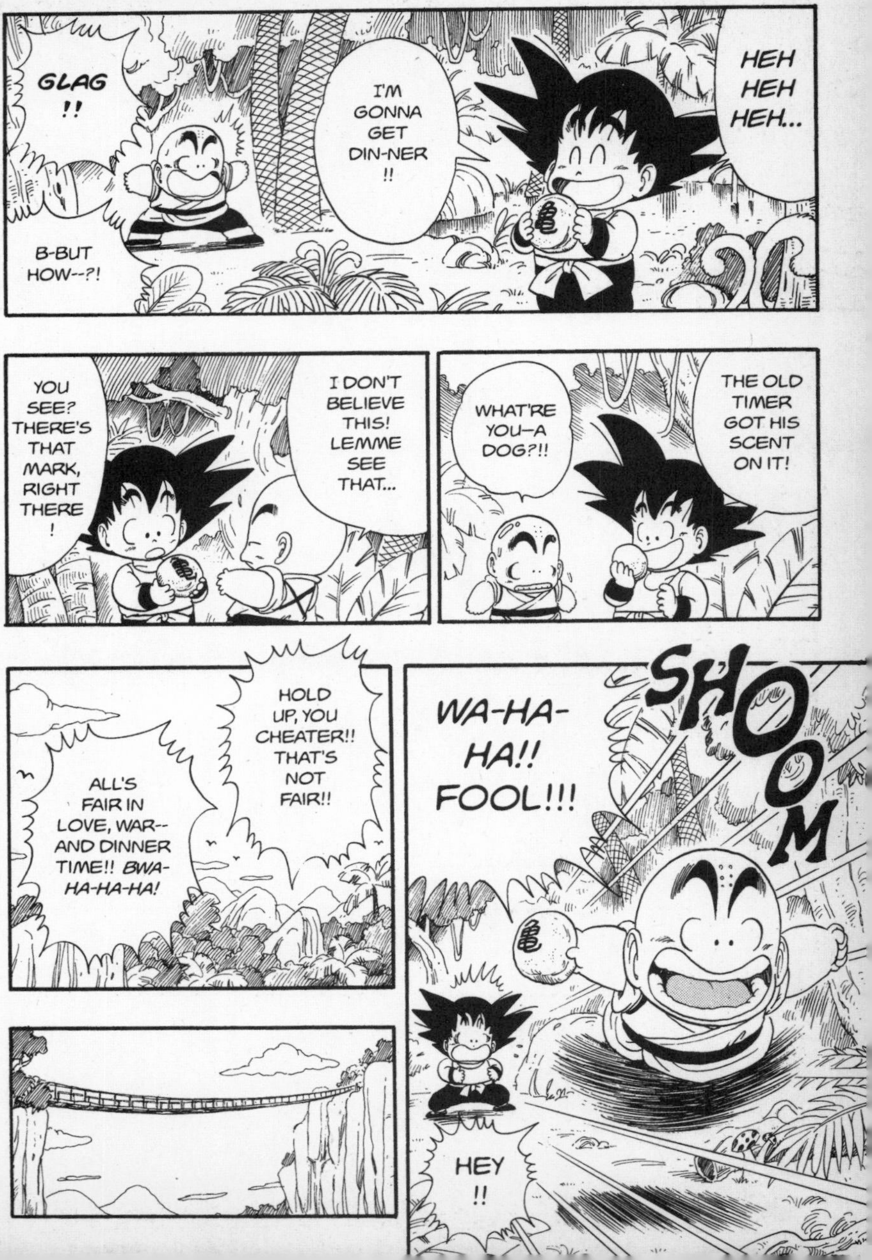
HEH HEH HEH...
I'M GONNA GET DIN-NER !!
GLAG !!
B-BUT HOW--?!
THE OLD TIMER GOT HIS SCENT ON IT!
WHAT'RE YOU—A DOG?!!
I DON'T BELIEVE THIS! LEMME SEE THAT...
YOU SEE? THERE'S THAT MARK, RIGHT THERE !
SHOOM
WA-HA-HA!! FOOL!!!
HEY !!
HOLD UP, YOU CHEATER!! THAT'S NOT FAIR!!
ALL'S FAIR IN LOVE, WAR-- AND DINNER TIME!! BWA-HA-HA-HA!

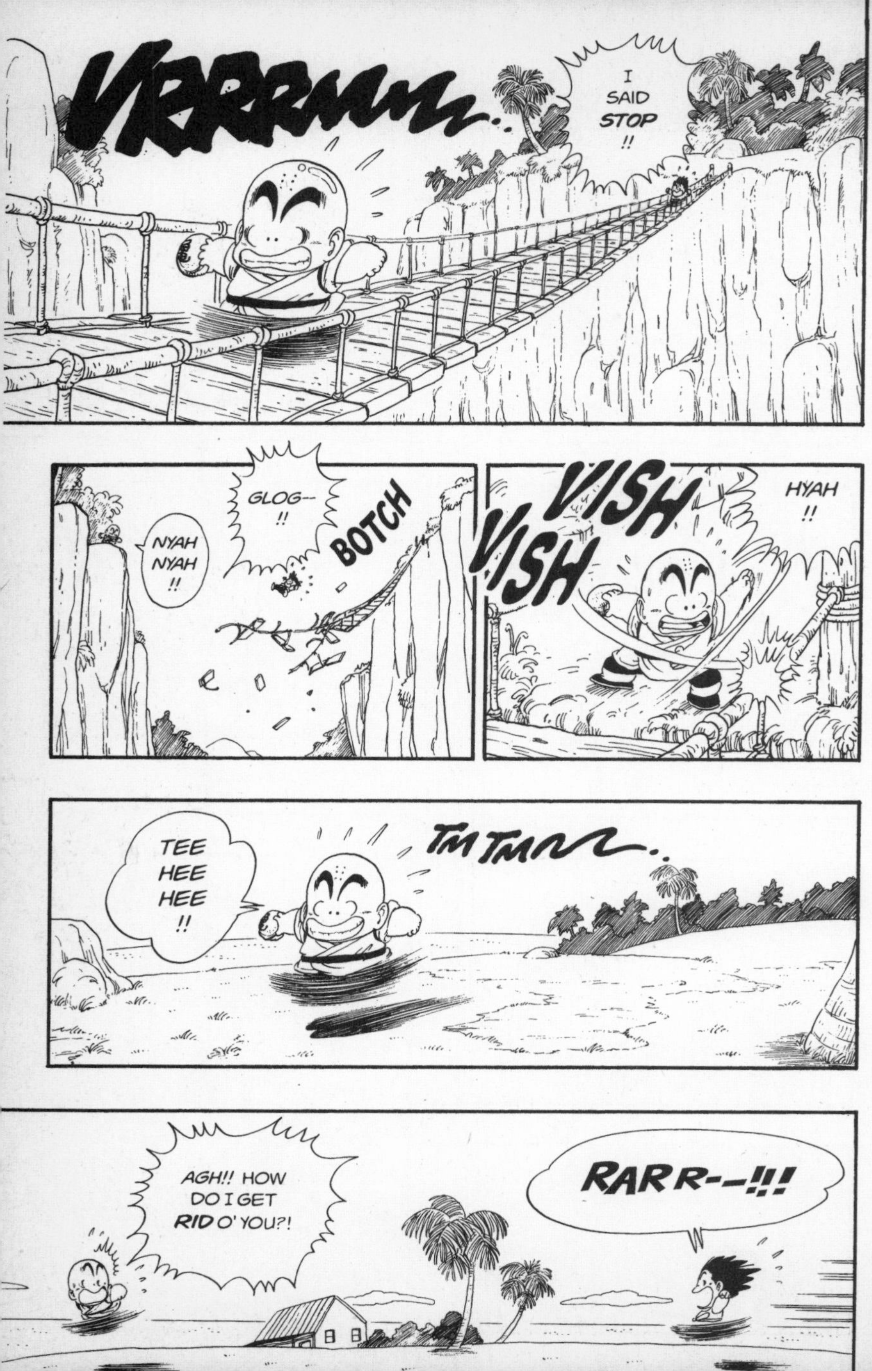
I SAID STOP !!
VRRRMMM..
HYAH !!
VISH
VISH
GLOG-- !!
BOTCH
NYAH NYAH !!
TM TMM..
TEE HEE HEE !!
RARR--!!!
AGH!! HOW DO I GET RID O' YOU?!

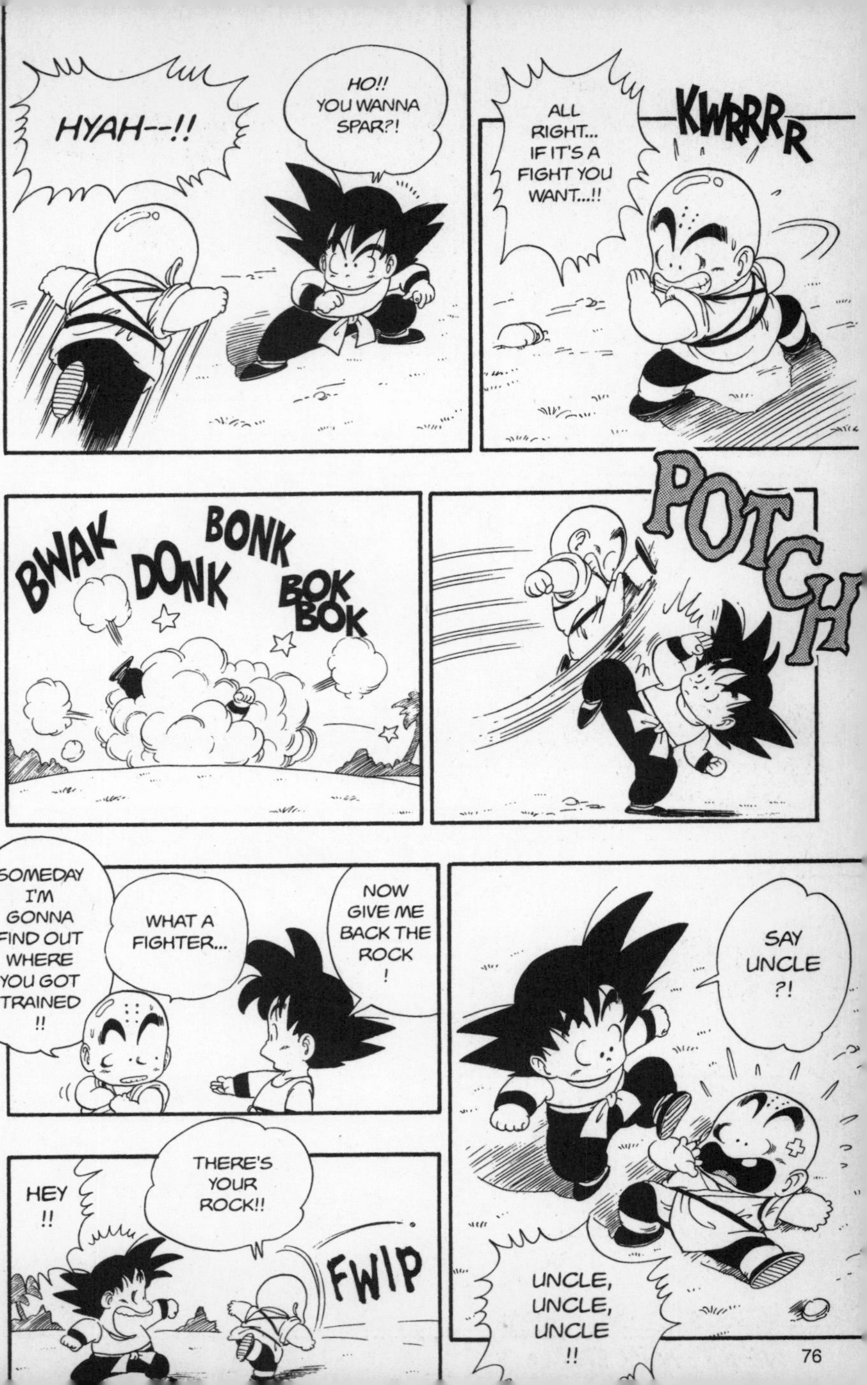
ALL RIGHT... IF IT'S A FIGHT YOU WANT...!!
KWRRRR
HYAH--!!
HO!! YOU WANNA SPAR?!
POTCH
BWAK
BONK
DONK
BOK BOK
SAY UNCLE ?!
UNCLE, UNCLE, UNCLE !!
NOW GIVE ME BACK THE ROCK !
WHAT A FIGHTER...
SOMEDAY I'M GONNA FIND OUT WHERE YOU GOT TRAINED !!
THERE'S YOUR ROCK!!
FWIP
HEY !!

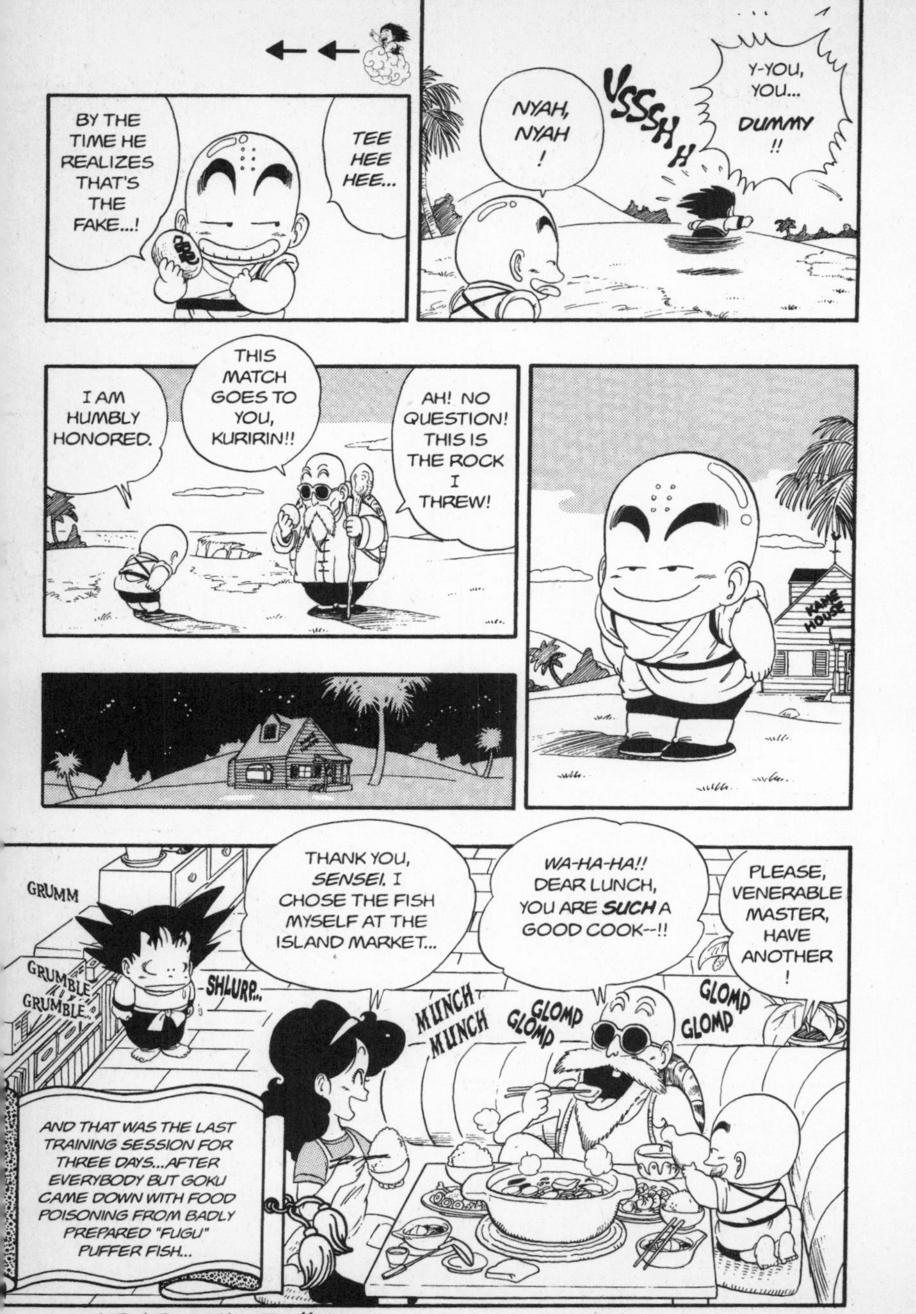
...
Y-YOU, YOU... DUMMY!!
VSSSHH
NYAH, NYAH!
TEE HEE HEE...
BY THE TIME HE REALIZES THAT'S THE FAKE...!
KAME HOUSE
AH! NO QUESTION! THIS IS THE ROCK I THREW!
THIS MATCH GOES TO YOU, KURIRIN!!
I AM HUMBLY HONORED.
PLEASE, VENERABLE MASTER, HAVE ANOTHER!
WA-HA-HA!! DEAR LUNCH, YOU ARE SUCH A GOOD COOK--!!
GLOMP GLOMP
GLOMP GLOMP
THANK YOU, SENSEI. I CHOSE THE FISH MYSELF AT THE ISLAND MARKET...
MUNCH MUNCH
SHLURP...
GRUMM
GRUMBLE GRUMBLE...
AND THAT WAS THE LAST TRAINING SESSION FOR THREE DAYS...AFTER EVERYBODY BUT GOKU CAME DOWN WITH FOOD POISONING FROM BADLY PREPARED "FUGU" PUFFER FISH...

NEXT: Milk Delivery

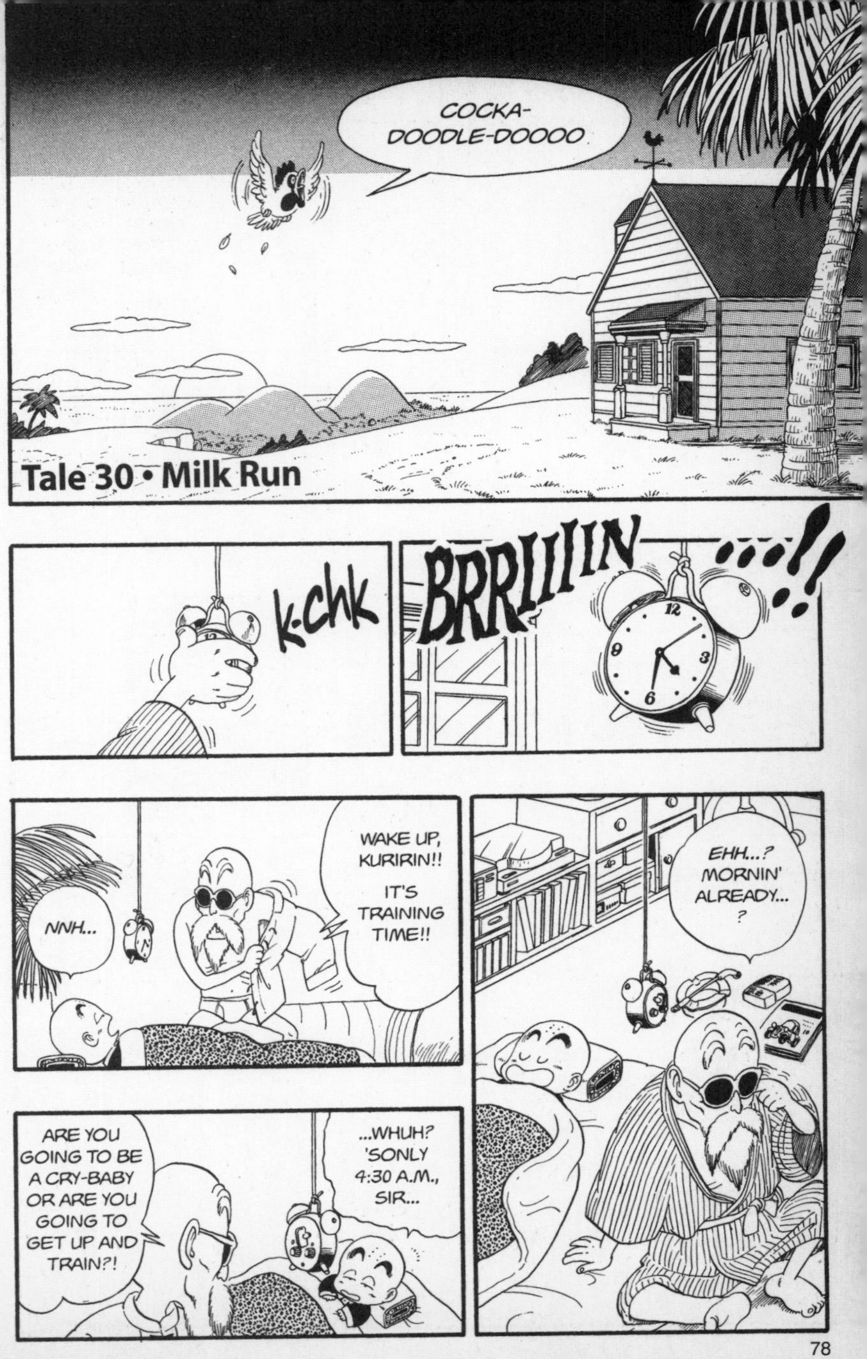
Tale 30 • Milk Run
COCKA-DOODLE-DOOOO
BRRIIIIN...!!
k-chk
EHH...? MORNIN' ALREADY...?
WAKE UP, KURIRIN!! IT'S TRAINING TIME!!
NNH...
...WHUH? 'SONLY 4:30 A.M., SIR...
ARE YOU GOING TO BE A CRY-BABY OR ARE YOU GOING TO GET UP AND TRAIN?!

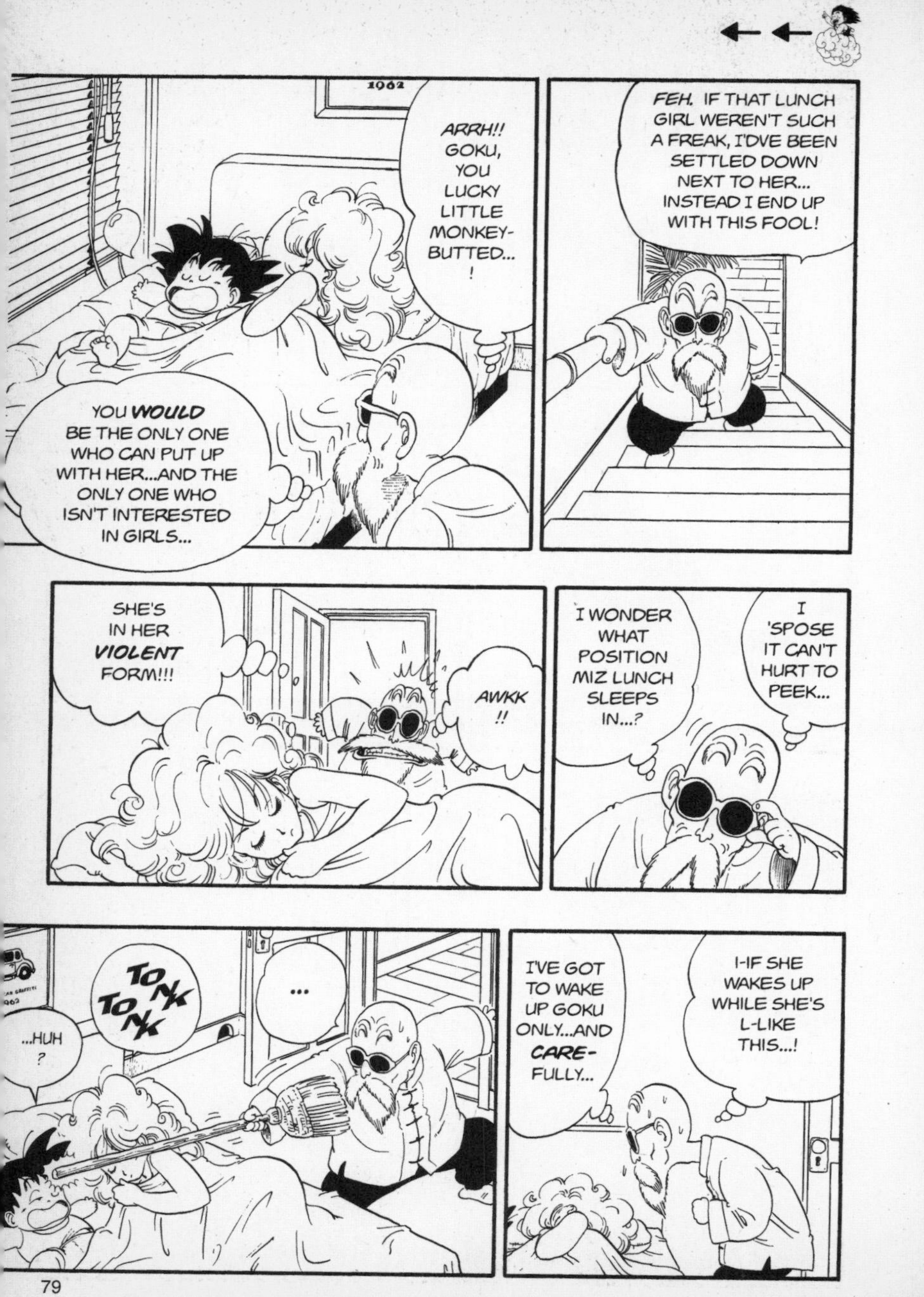
FEH. IF THAT LUNCH GIRL WEREN'T SUCH A FREAK, I'DVE BEEN SETTLED DOWN NEXT TO HER... INSTEAD I END UP WITH THIS FOOL!
1962
ARRH!! GOKU, YOU LUCKY LITTLE MONKEY-BUTTED... !
YOU ***WOULD*** BE THE ONLY ONE WHO CAN PUT UP WITH HER...AND THE ONLY ONE WHO ISN'T INTERESTED IN GIRLS...
I 'SPOSE IT CAN'T HURT TO PEEK...
I WONDER WHAT POSITION MIZ LUNCH SLEEPS IN...?
AWKK !!
SHE'S IN HER ***VIOLENT*** FORM!!!
I-IF SHE WAKES UP WHILE SHE'S L-LIKE THIS...!
I'VE GOT TO WAKE UP GOKU ONLY...AND ***CARE-*** FULLY...
...
TONK TONK
...HUH ?

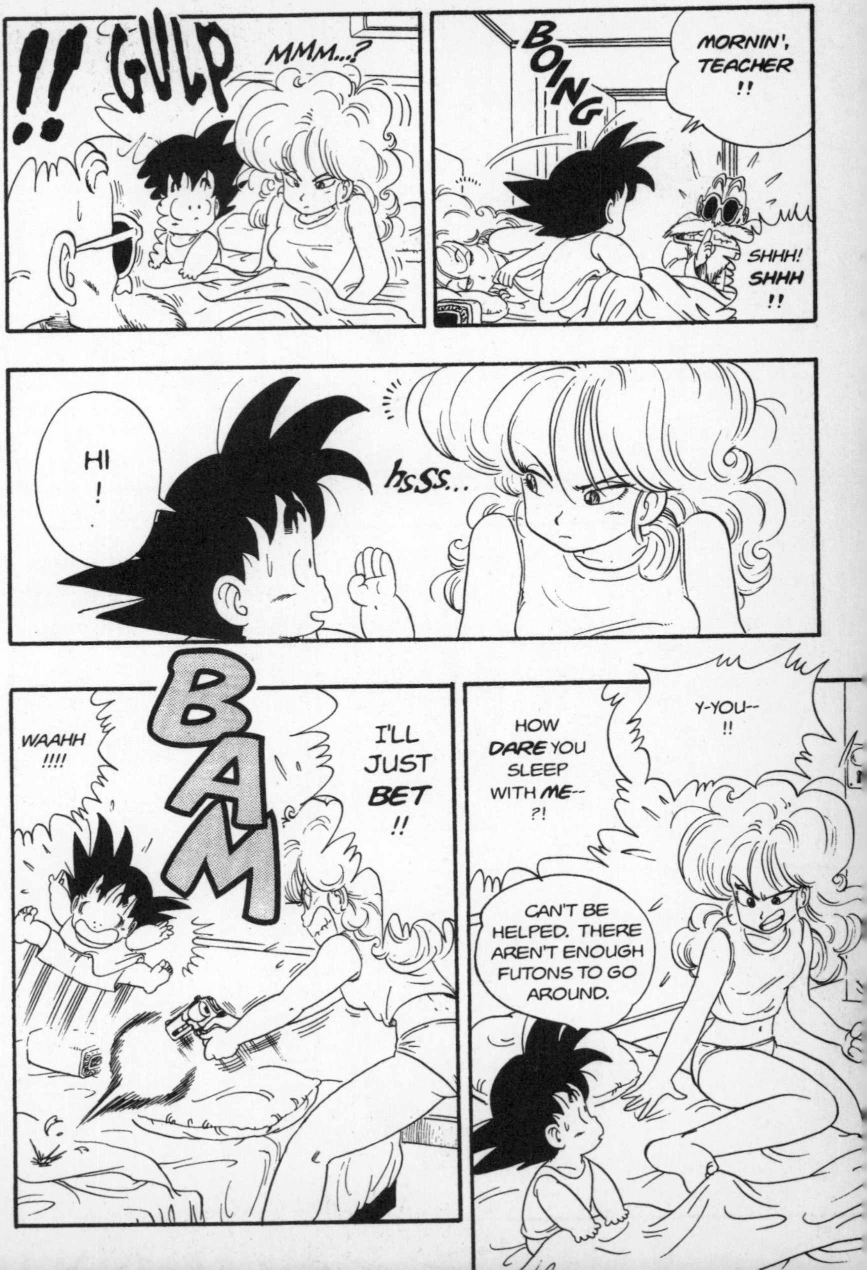
BOING
MORNIN', TEACHER !!
SHHH! SHHH !!
!! GULP
MMM...?
HI !
hsss...
Y-YOU-- !!
HOW DARE YOU SLEEP WITH ME-- ?!
CAN'T BE HELPED. THERE AREN'T ENOUGH FUTONS TO GO AROUND.
I'LL JUST BET !!
BAM
WAAHH !!!!

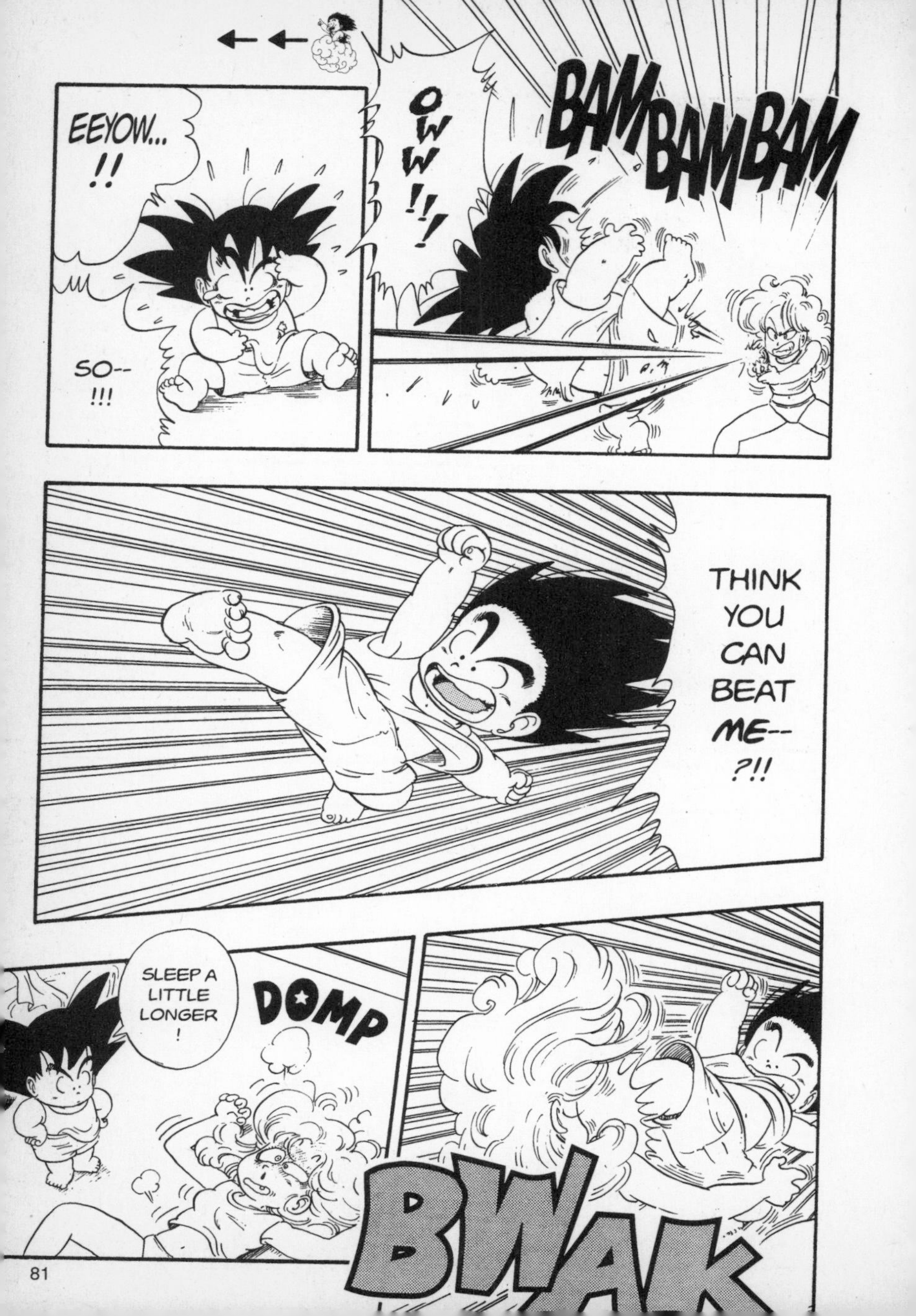
BAM BAM BAM
OWW!!!
EEYOW... !!
SO-- !!!
THINK YOU CAN BEAT ME-- ?!!
BWAK
SLEEP A LITTLE LONGER !
DOMP

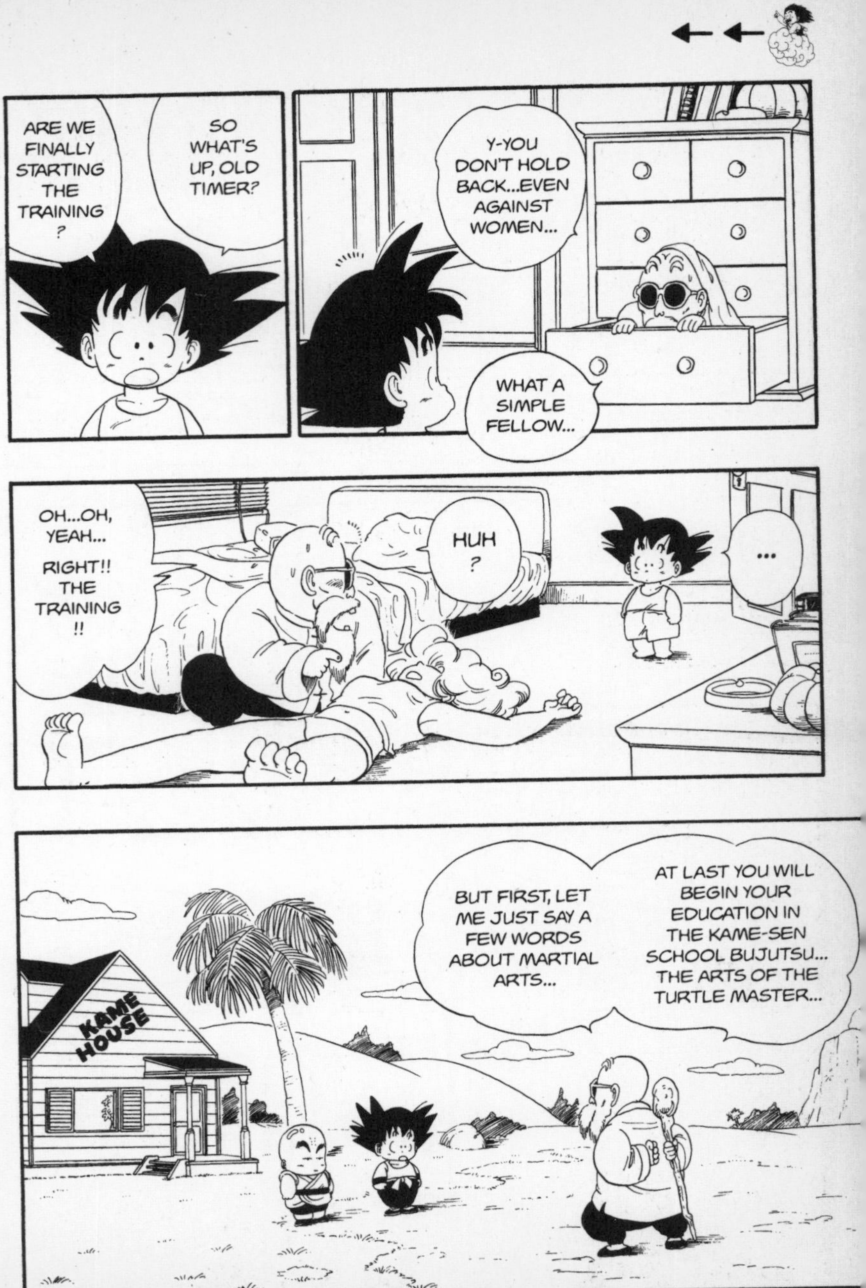
Y-YOU DON'T HOLD BACK...EVEN AGAINST WOMEN...
WHAT A SIMPLE FELLOW...
SO WHAT'S UP, OLD TIMER?
ARE WE FINALLY STARTING THE TRAINING ?
...
HUH ?
OH...OH, YEAH... RIGHT!! THE TRAINING !!
AT LAST YOU WILL BEGIN YOUR EDUCATION IN THE KAME-SEN SCHOOL BUJUTSU... THE ARTS OF THE TURTLE MASTER...
BUT FIRST, LET ME JUST SAY A FEW WORDS ABOUT MARTIAL ARTS...
KAME HOUSE

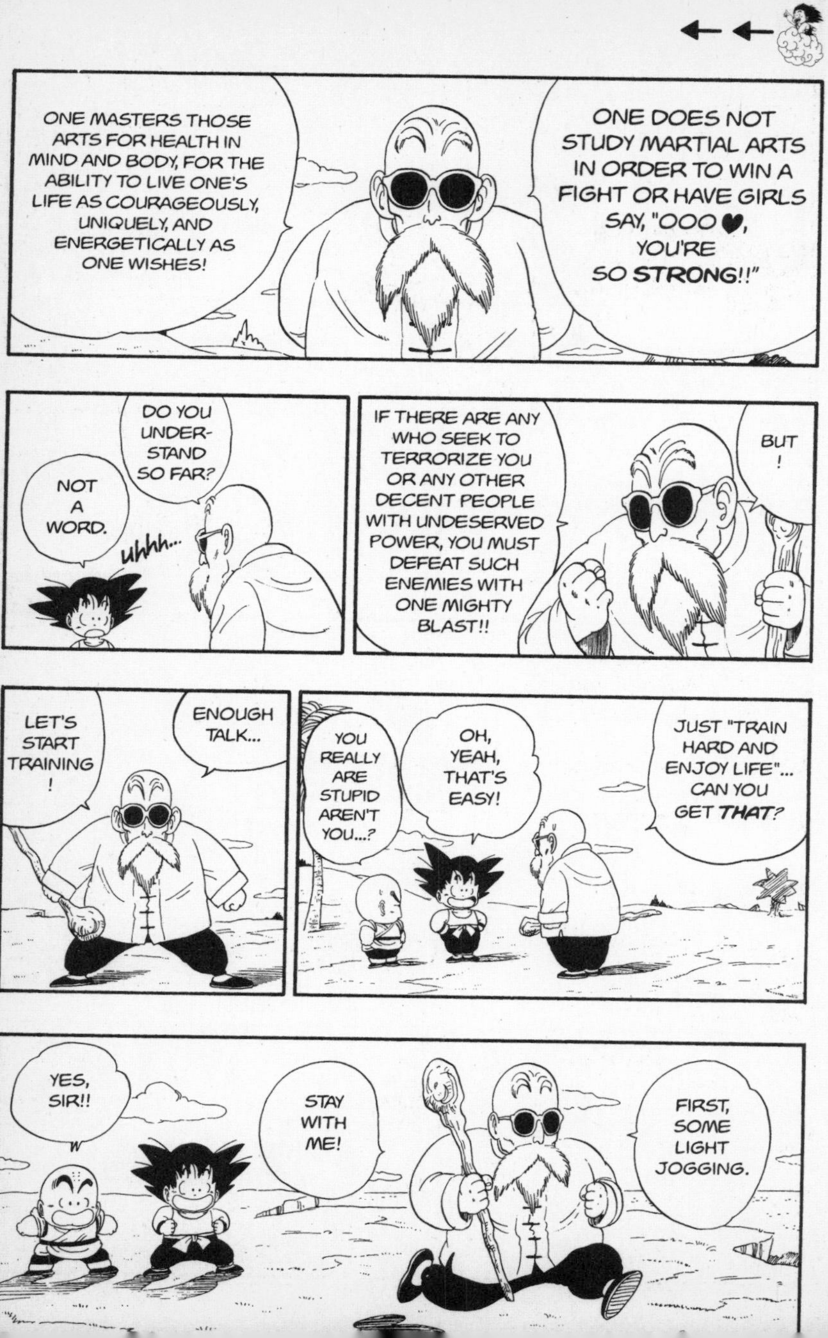
ONE DOES NOT STUDY MARTIAL ARTS IN ORDER TO WIN A FIGHT OR HAVE GIRLS SAY, "OOO ♥, YOU'RE SO STRONG!!"
ONE MASTERS THOSE ARTS FOR HEALTH IN MIND AND BODY, FOR THE ABILITY TO LIVE ONE'S LIFE AS COURAGEOUSLY, UNIQUELY, AND ENERGETICALLY AS ONE WISHES!
BUT!
IF THERE ARE ANY WHO SEEK TO TERRORIZE YOU OR ANY OTHER DECENT PEOPLE WITH UNDESERVED POWER, YOU MUST DEFEAT SUCH ENEMIES WITH ONE MIGHTY BLAST!!
DO YOU UNDER-STAND SO FAR?
NOT A WORD.
uhhh...
JUST "TRAIN HARD AND ENJOY LIFE"... CAN YOU GET THAT?
OH, YEAH, THAT'S EASY!
YOU REALLY ARE STUPID AREN'T YOU...?
ENOUGH TALK...
LET'S START TRAINING!
FIRST, SOME LIGHT JOGGING.
STAY WITH ME!
YES, SIR!!

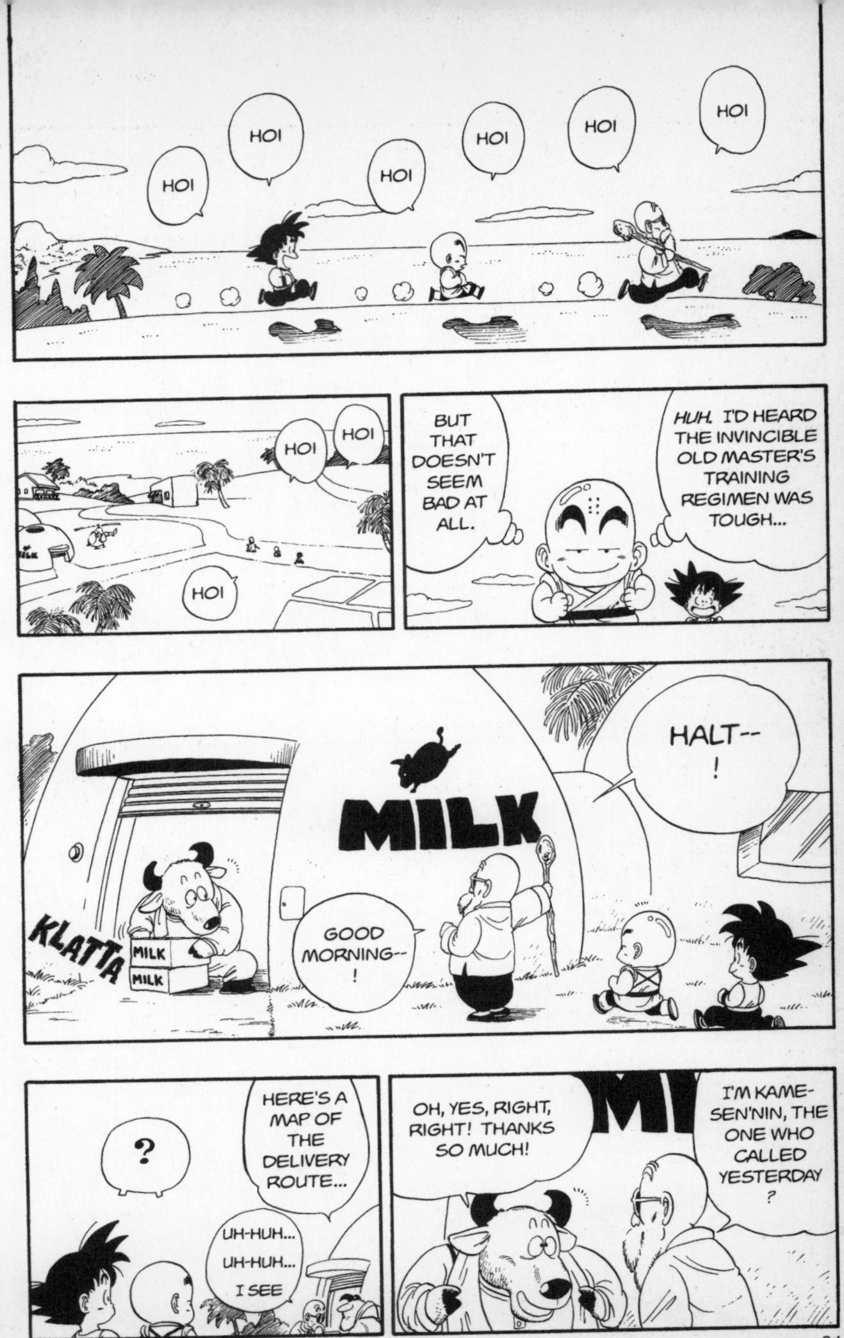
HOI
HOI
HOI
HOI
HOI
HOI
HOI
HUH. I'D HEARD THE INVINCIBLE OLD MASTER'S TRAINING REGIMEN WAS TOUGH...
BUT THAT DOESN'T SEEM BAD AT ALL.
HOI
HOI
HOI
HALT-- !
MILK
GOOD MORNING-- !
KLATTA
MILK
MILK
I'M KAME-SEN'NIN, THE ONE WHO CALLED YESTERDAY ?
OH, YES, RIGHT, RIGHT! THANKS SO MUCH!
HERE'S A MAP OF THE DELIVERY ROUTE...
?
UH-HUH... UH-HUH... I SEE

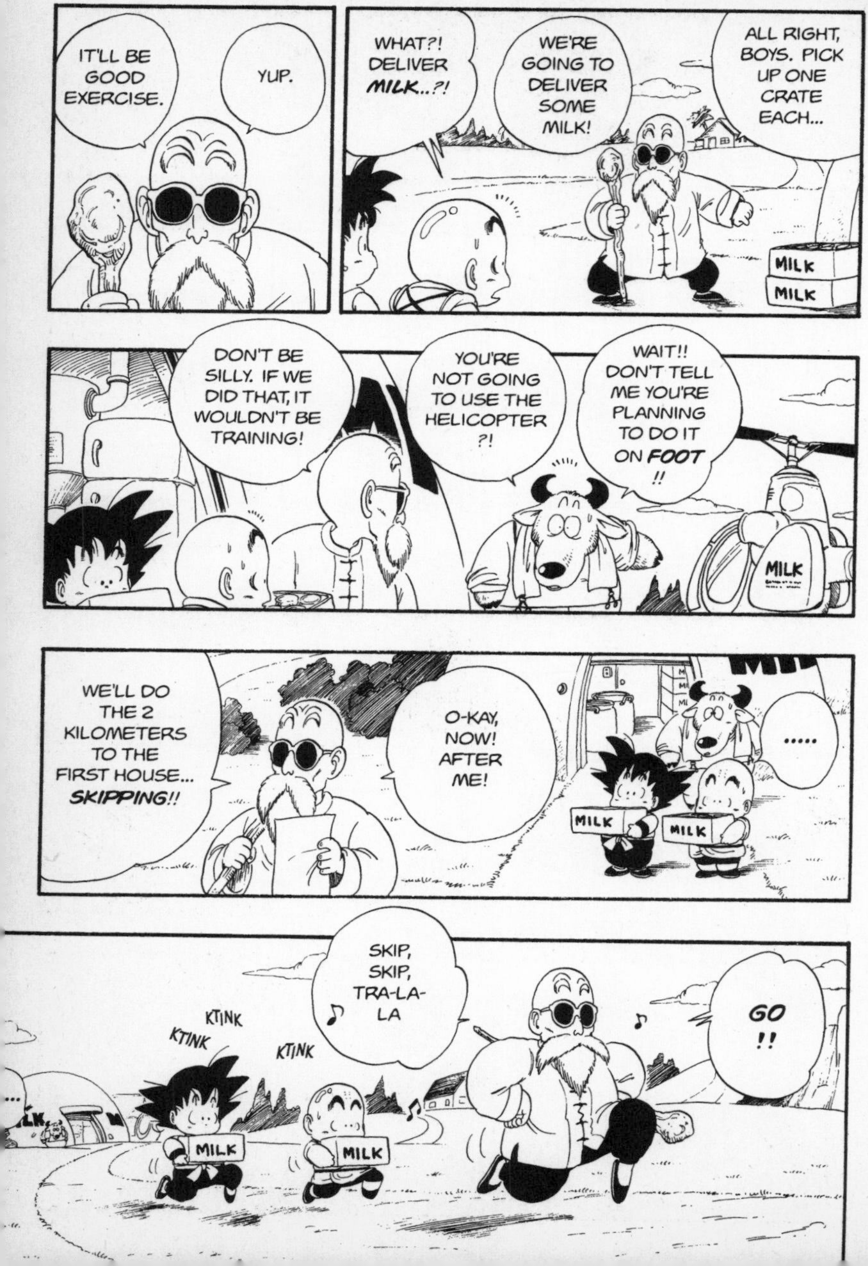
ALL RIGHT, BOYS. PICK UP ONE CRATE EACH...
WE'RE GOING TO DELIVER SOME MILK!
WHAT?! DELIVER MILK..?!
MILK
MILK
YUP.
IT'LL BE GOOD EXERCISE.
WAIT!! DON'T TELL ME YOU'RE PLANNING TO DO IT ON FOOT !!
YOU'RE NOT GOING TO USE THE HELICOPTER ?!
MILK
DON'T BE SILLY. IF WE DID THAT, IT WOULDN'T BE TRAINING!
.....
MILK
MILK
O-KAY, NOW! AFTER ME!
WE'LL DO THE 2 KILOMETERS TO THE FIRST HOUSE... SKIPPING!!
GO !!
SKIP, SKIP, TRA-LA-LA
KTINK
KTINK
KTINK
MILK
MILK

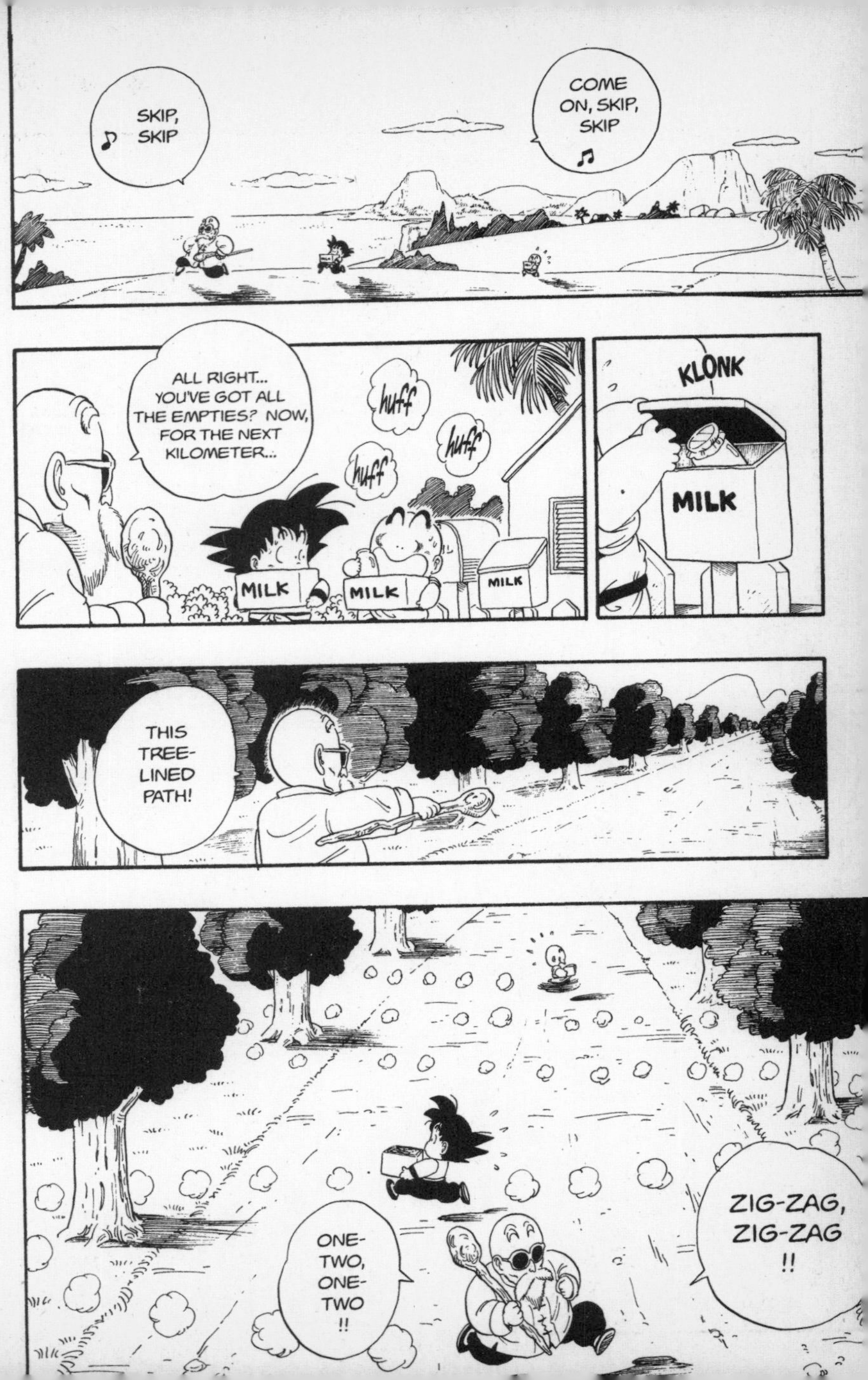
COME ON, SKIP, SKIP ♫
♪ SKIP, SKIP
KLONK
MILK
ALL RIGHT... YOU'VE GOT ALL THE EMPTIES? NOW, FOR THE NEXT KILOMETER...
huff
huff
huff
MILK
MILK
MILK
THIS TREE-LINED PATH!
ZIG-ZAG, ZIG-ZAG !!
ONE-TWO, ONE-TWO !!

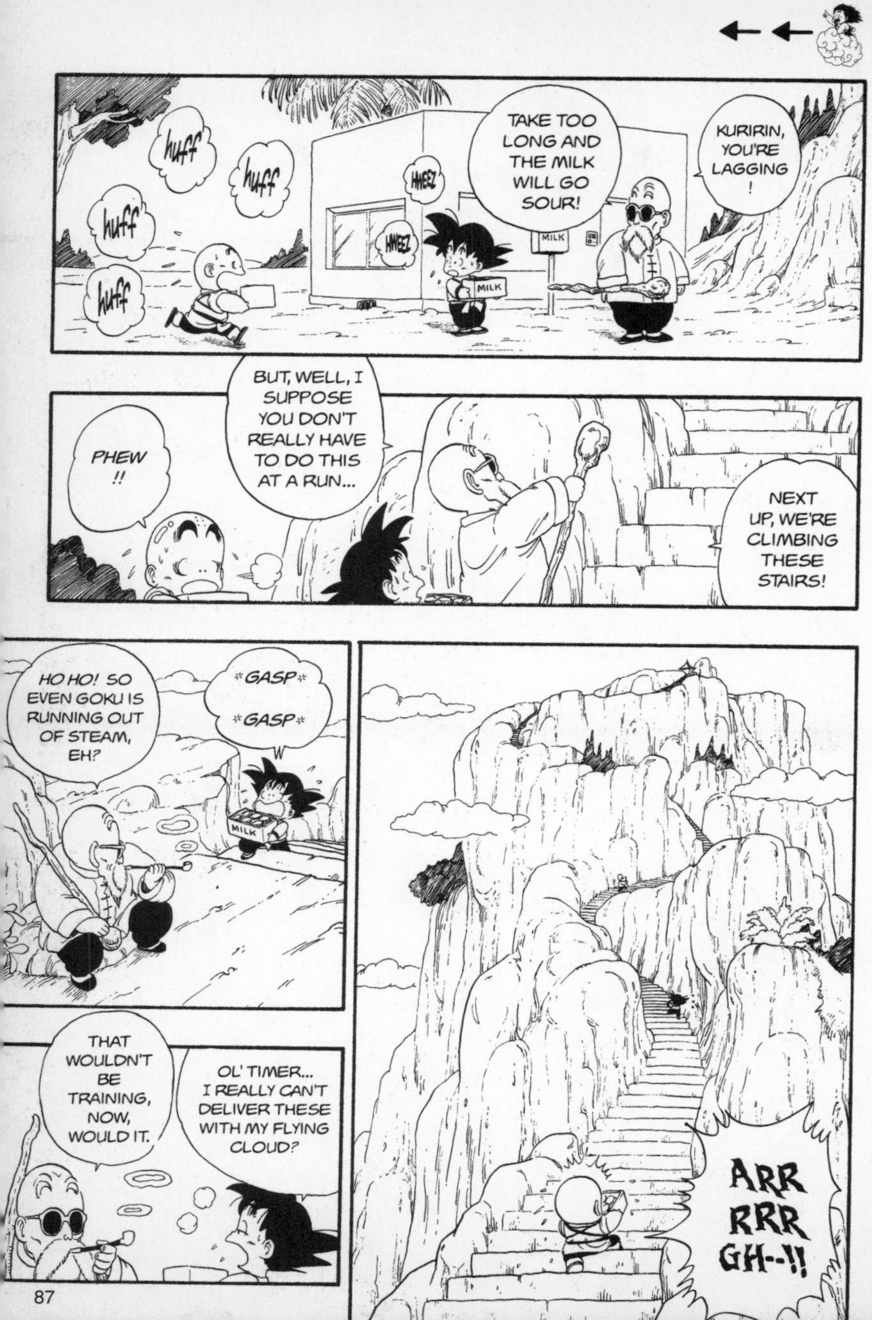
KURIRIN, YOU'RE LAGGING!
TAKE TOO LONG AND THE MILK WILL GO SOUR!
MILK
HWEEZ
HWEEZ
MILK
huff
huff
huff
huff
NEXT UP, WE'RE CLIMBING THESE STAIRS!
BUT, WELL, I SUPPOSE YOU DON'T REALLY HAVE TO DO THIS AT A RUN...
PHEW!!
ARR RRR GH--!!
GASP *GASP*
MILK
HO HO! SO EVEN GOKU IS RUNNING OUT OF STEAM, EH?
OL' TIMER... I REALLY CAN'T DELIVER THESE WITH MY FLYING CLOUD?
THAT WOULDN'T BE TRAINING, NOW, WOULD IT.

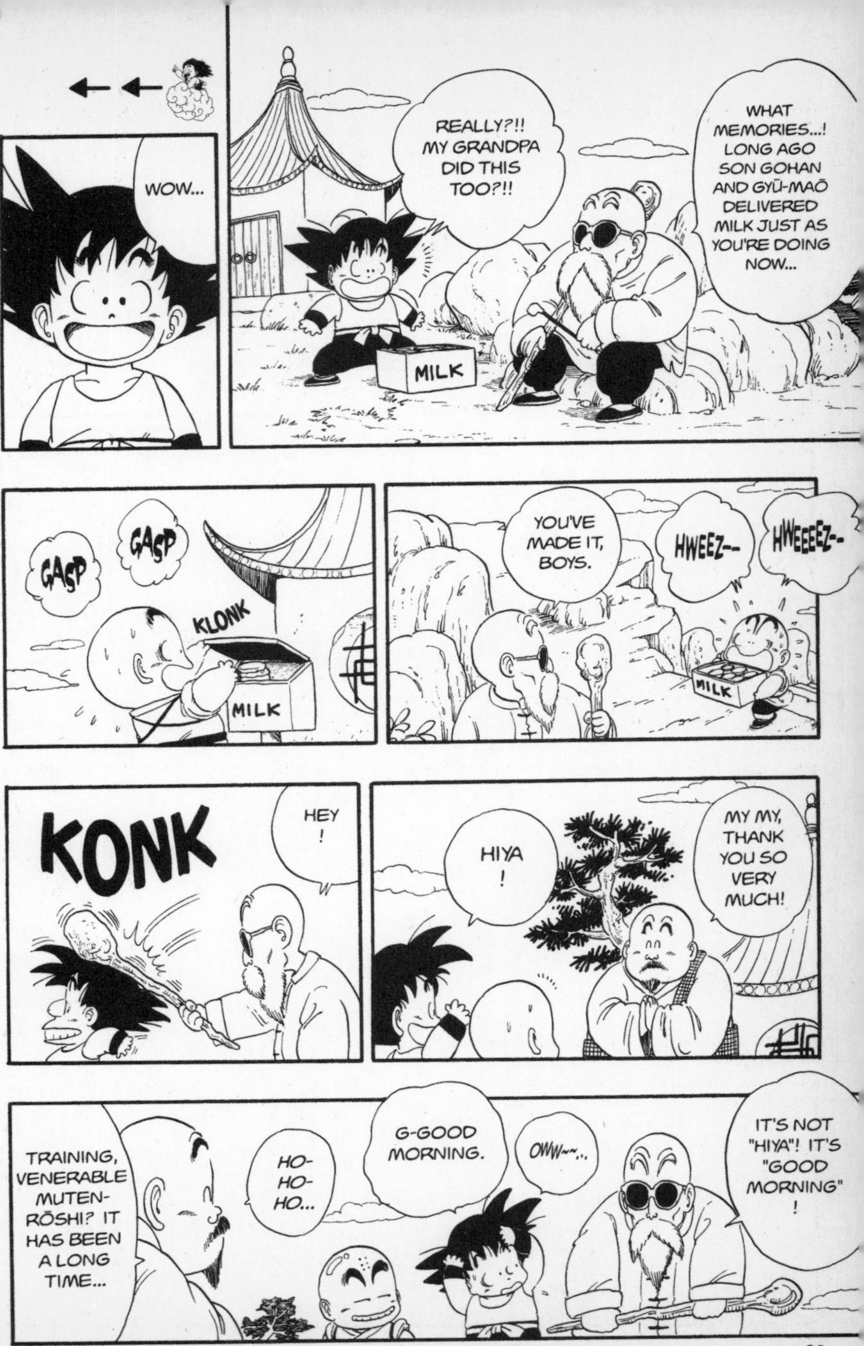
WHAT MEMORIES...! LONG AGO SON GOHAN AND GYŪ-MAŌ DELIVERED MILK JUST AS YOU'RE DOING NOW...
REALLY?!! MY GRANDPA DID THIS TOO?!!
MILK
WOW...
HWEEEEZ--
HWEEZ--
YOU'VE MADE IT, BOYS.
MILK
GASP
GASP
KLONK
MILK
MY MY, THANK YOU SO VERY MUCH!
HIYA !
HEY !
KONK
IT'S NOT "HIYA"! IT'S "GOOD MORNING" !
OWW~~..
G-GOOD MORNING.
HO-HO-HO...
TRAINING, VENERABLE MUTEN-RŌSHI? IT HAS BEEN A LONG TIME...

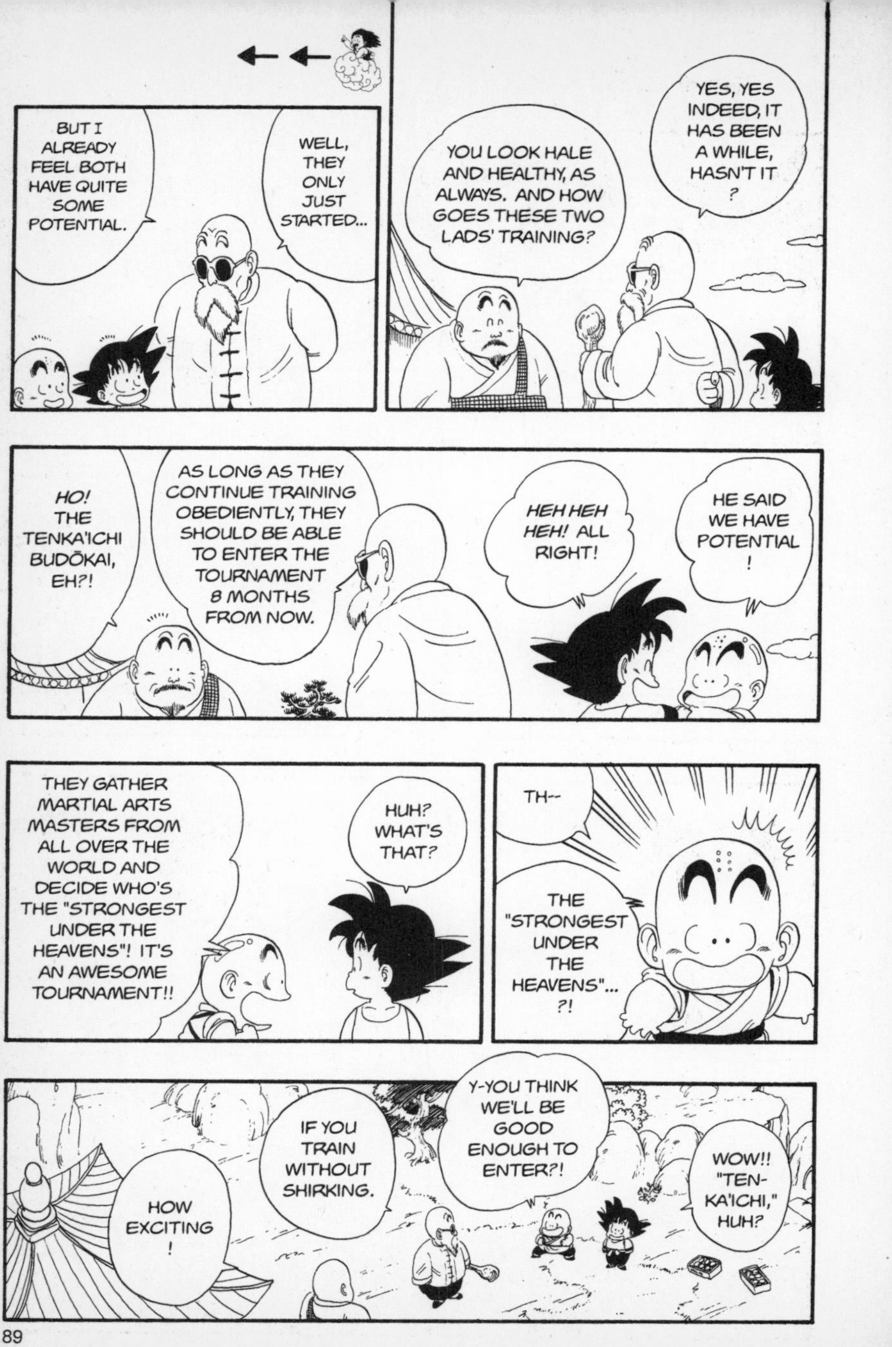

YES, YES INDEED, IT HAS BEEN A WHILE, HASN'T IT?
YOU LOOK HALE AND HEALTHY, AS ALWAYS. AND HOW GOES THESE TWO LADS' TRAINING?
WELL, THEY ONLY JUST STARTED...
BUT I ALREADY FEEL BOTH HAVE QUITE SOME POTENTIAL.
HE SAID WE HAVE POTENTIAL!
HEH HEH HEH! ALL RIGHT!
AS LONG AS THEY CONTINUE TRAINING OBEDIENTLY, THEY SHOULD BE ABLE TO ENTER THE TOURNAMENT 8 MONTHS FROM NOW.
HO! THE TENKA'ICHI BUDŌKAI, EH?!
TH--
THE "STRONGEST UNDER THE HEAVENS"...?!
HUH? WHAT'S THAT?
THEY GATHER MARTIAL ARTS MASTERS FROM ALL OVER THE WORLD AND DECIDE WHO'S THE "STRONGEST UNDER THE HEAVENS"! IT'S AN AWESOME TOURNAMENT!!
WOW!! "TEN-KA'ICHI," HUH?
Y-YOU THINK WE'LL BE GOOD ENOUGH TO ENTER?!
IF YOU TRAIN WITHOUT SHIRKING.
HOW EXCITING!

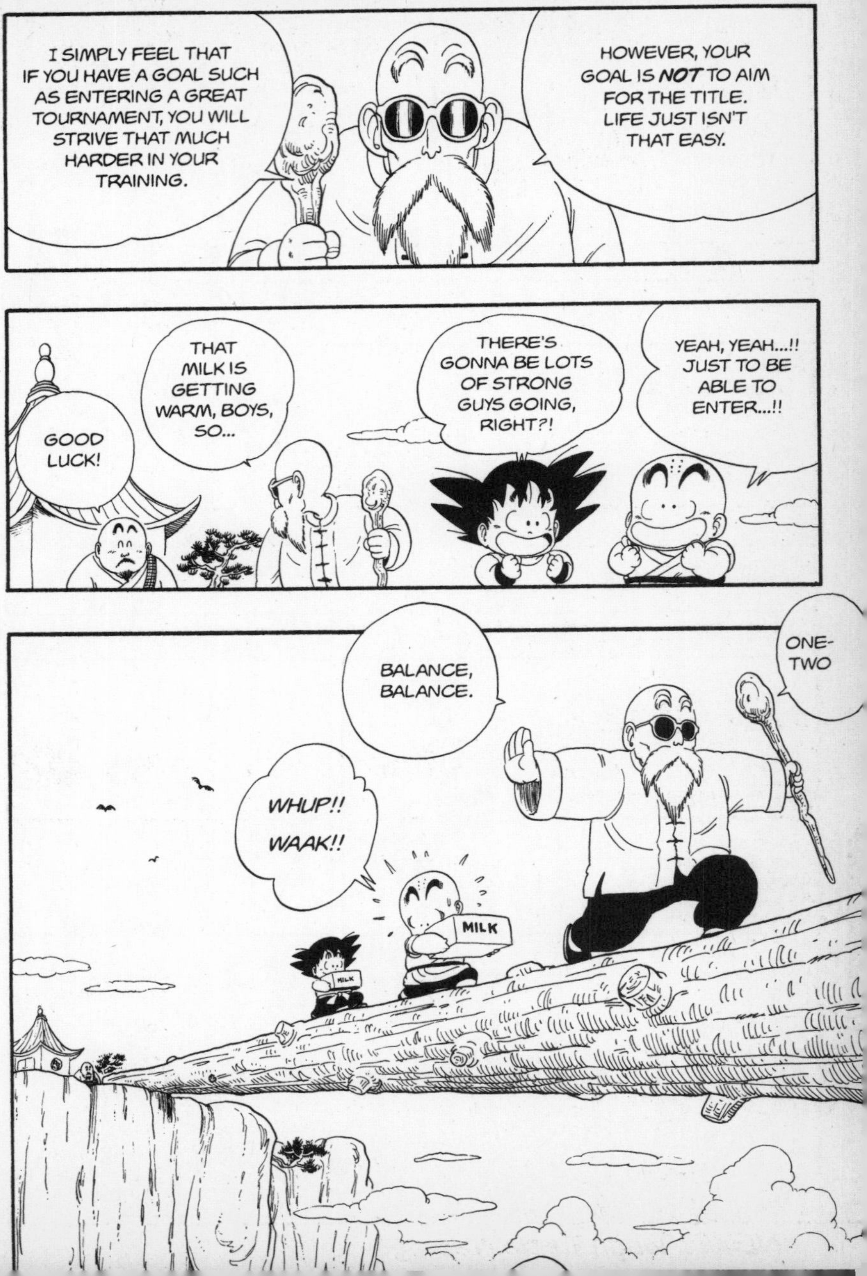
HOWEVER, YOUR GOAL IS **NOT** TO AIM FOR THE TITLE. LIFE JUST ISN'T THAT EASY.
I SIMPLY FEEL THAT IF YOU HAVE A GOAL SUCH AS ENTERING A GREAT TOURNAMENT, YOU WILL STRIVE THAT MUCH HARDER IN YOUR TRAINING.
YEAH, YEAH...!! JUST TO BE ABLE TO ENTER...!!
THERE'S GONNA BE LOTS OF STRONG GUYS GOING, RIGHT?!
THAT MILK IS GETTING WARM, BOYS, SO...
GOOD LUCK!
ONE-TWO
BALANCE, BALANCE.
WHUP!! WAAK!!
MILK
MILK

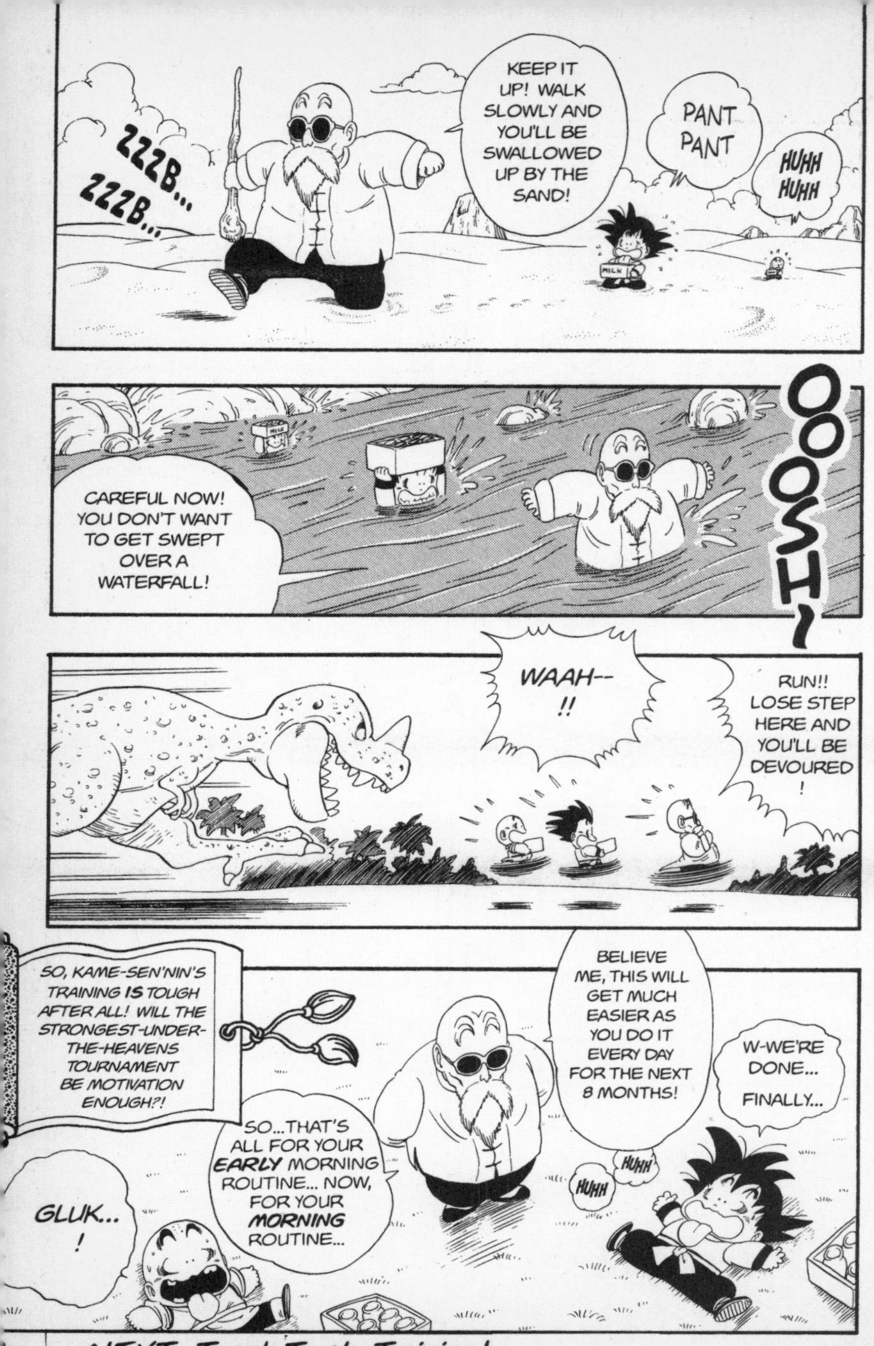
PANT PANT
HUHH HUHH
KEEP IT UP! WALK SLOWLY AND YOU'LL BE SWALLOWED UP BY THE SAND!
ZZZB... ZZZB...
OOOSH
CAREFUL NOW! YOU DON'T WANT TO GET SWEPT OVER A WATERFALL!
RUN!! LOSE STEP HERE AND YOU'LL BE DEVOURED!
WAAH-- !!
W-WE'RE DONE... FINALLY...
BELIEVE ME, THIS WILL GET MUCH EASIER AS YOU DO IT EVERY DAY FOR THE NEXT 8 MONTHS!
HUHH
HUHH
SO...THAT'S ALL FOR YOUR EARLY MORNING ROUTINE... NOW, FOR YOUR MORNING ROUTINE...
GLUK... !
SO, KAME-SEN'NIN'S TRAINING IS TOUGH AFTER ALL! WILL THE STRONGEST-UNDER-THE-HEAVENS TOURNAMENT BE MOTIVATION ENOUGH?!

NEXT: Tough Turtle Training!

Tale 31
It Only Gets Harder

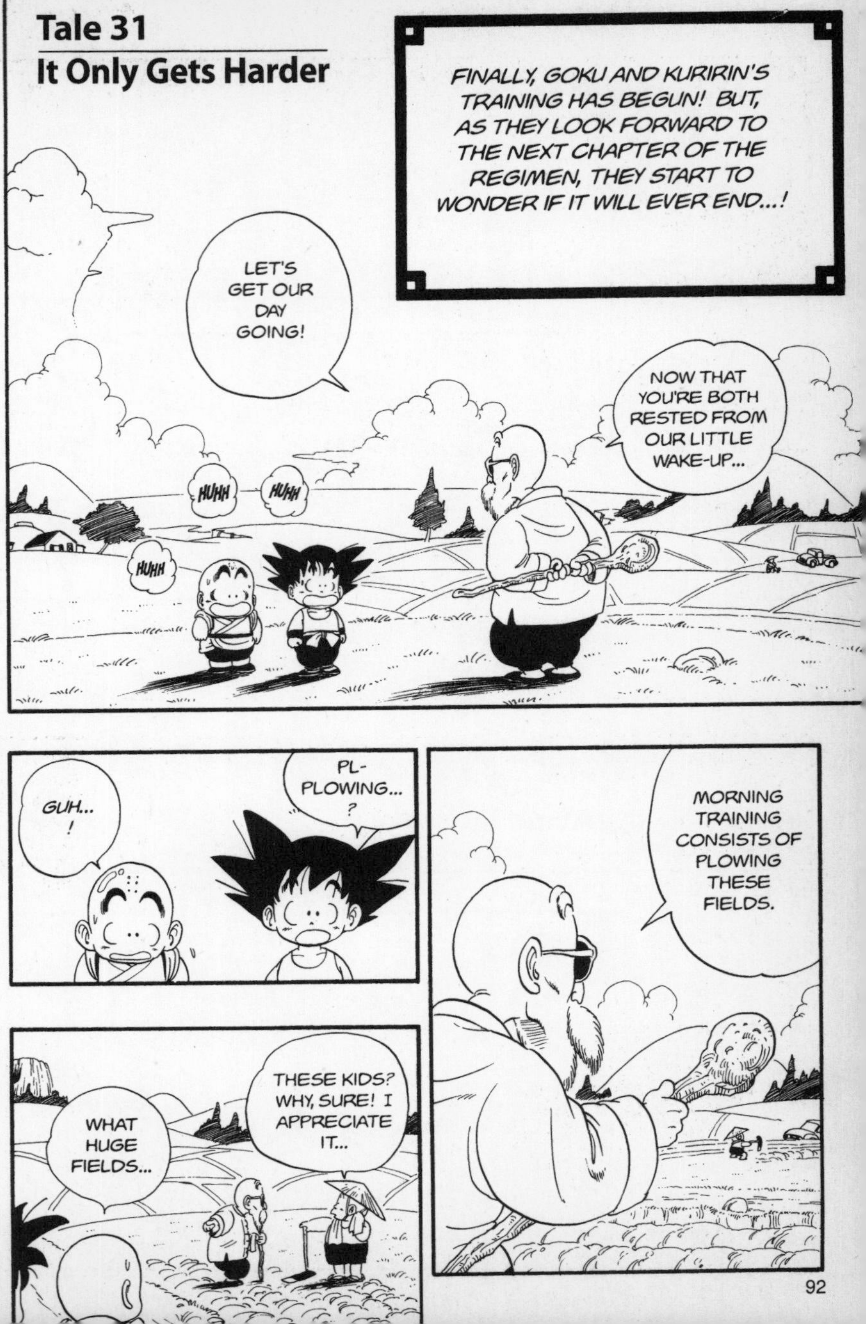
FINALLY, GOKU AND KURIRIN'S TRAINING HAS BEGUN! BUT, AS THEY LOOK FORWARD TO THE NEXT CHAPTER OF THE REGIMEN, THEY START TO WONDER IF IT WILL EVER END...!
NOW THAT YOU'RE BOTH RESTED FROM OUR LITTLE WAKE-UP...
LET'S GET OUR DAY GOING!
HUHH
HUHH
HUHH
MORNING TRAINING CONSISTS OF PLOWING THESE FIELDS.
PL- PLOWING... ?
GUH... !
THESE KIDS? WHY, SURE! I APPRECIATE IT...
WHAT HUGE FIELDS...

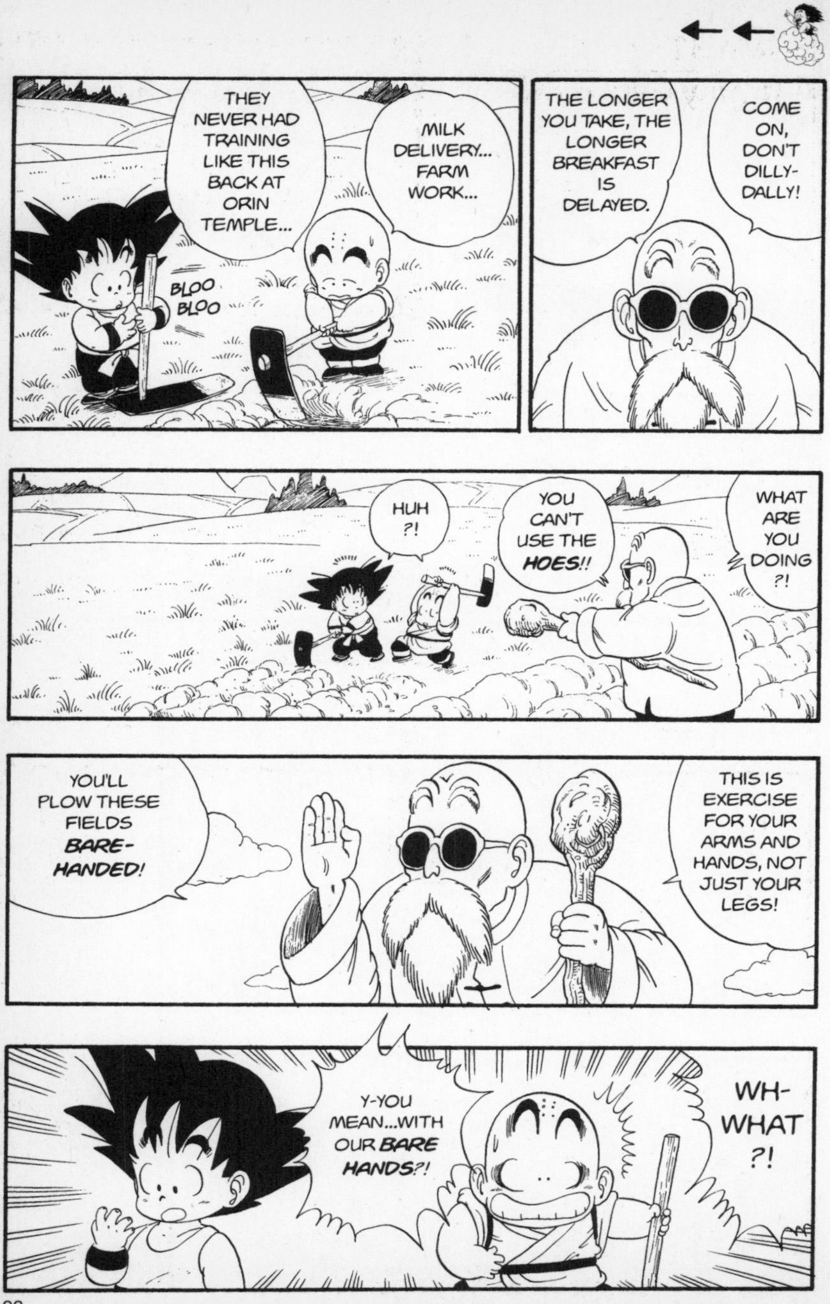
COME ON, DON'T DILLY-DALLY!
THE LONGER YOU TAKE, THE LONGER BREAKFAST IS DELAYED.
MILK DELIVERY... FARM WORK...
THEY NEVER HAD TRAINING LIKE THIS BACK AT ORIN TEMPLE...
BLOO BLOO
WHAT ARE YOU DOING ?!
YOU CAN'T USE THE HOES!!
HUH ?!
THIS IS EXERCISE FOR YOUR ARMS AND HANDS, NOT JUST YOUR LEGS!
YOU'LL PLOW THESE FIELDS BARE-HANDED!
WH-WHAT ?!
Y-YOU MEAN...WITH OUR BARE HANDS?!

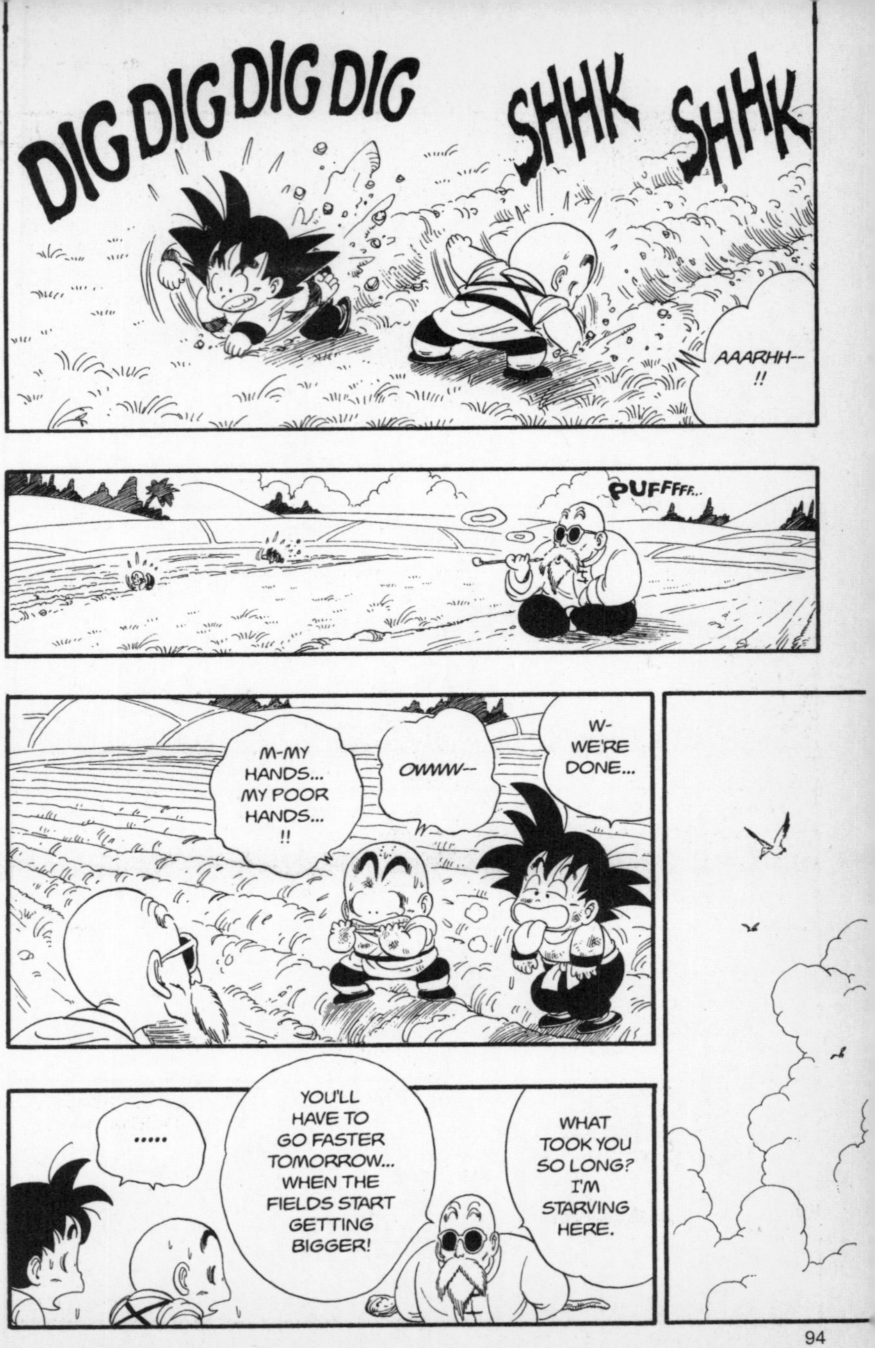
SHHK SHHK
DIG DIG DIG DIG
AAARHH--!!
PUFFFFF...
W- WE'RE DONE...
OWWW--
M-MY HANDS... MY POOR HANDS... !!
WHAT TOOK YOU SO LONG? I'M STARVING HERE.
YOU'LL HAVE TO GO FASTER TOMORROW... WHEN THE FIELDS START GETTING BIGGER!
......

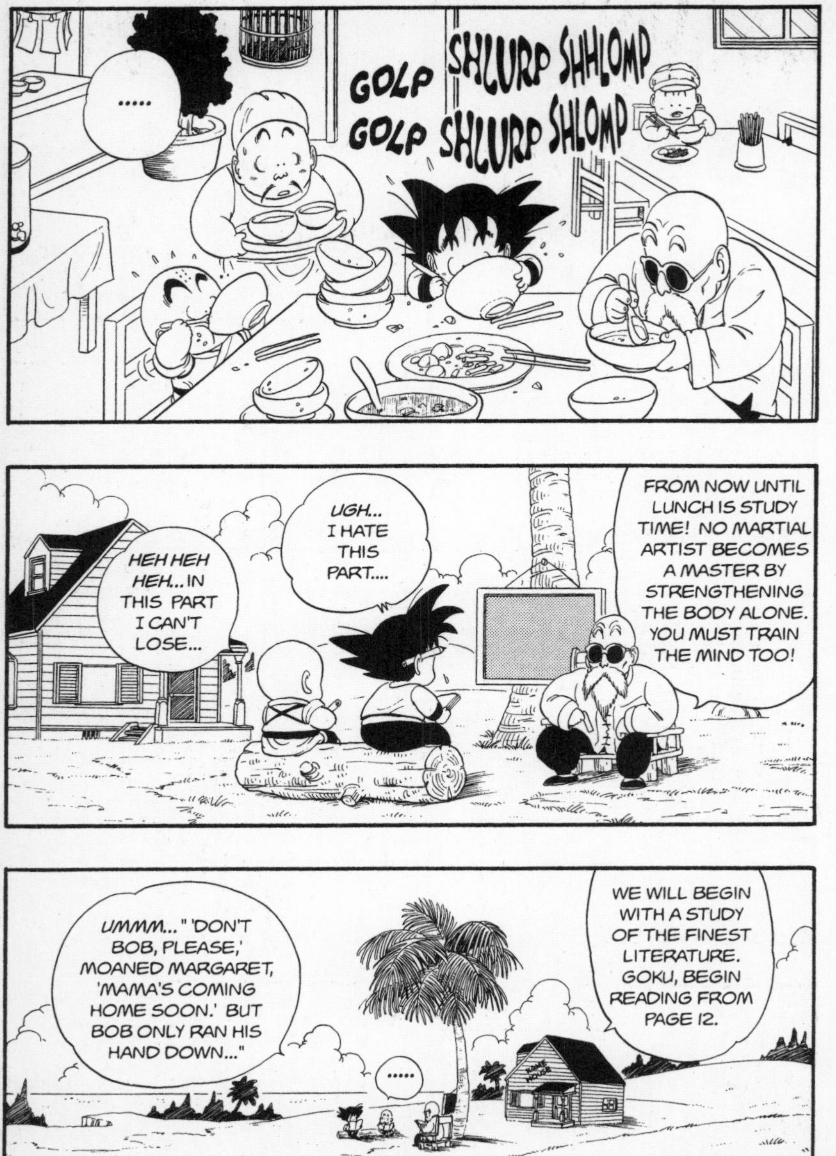
GOLP SHLURP SHHLOMP
GOLP SHLURP SHLOMP
.....
FROM NOW UNTIL LUNCH IS STUDY TIME! NO MARTIAL ARTIST BECOMES A MASTER BY STRENGTHENING THE BODY ALONE. YOU MUST TRAIN THE MIND TOO!
UGH... I HATE THIS PART....
HEH HEH HEH... IN THIS PART I CAN'T LOSE...
WE WILL BEGIN WITH A STUDY OF THE FINEST LITERATURE. GOKU, BEGIN READING FROM PAGE 12.
UMMM..." 'DON'T BOB, PLEASE,' MOANED MARGARET, 'MAMA'S COMING HOME SOON.' BUT BOB ONLY RAN HIS HAND DOWN..."
.....

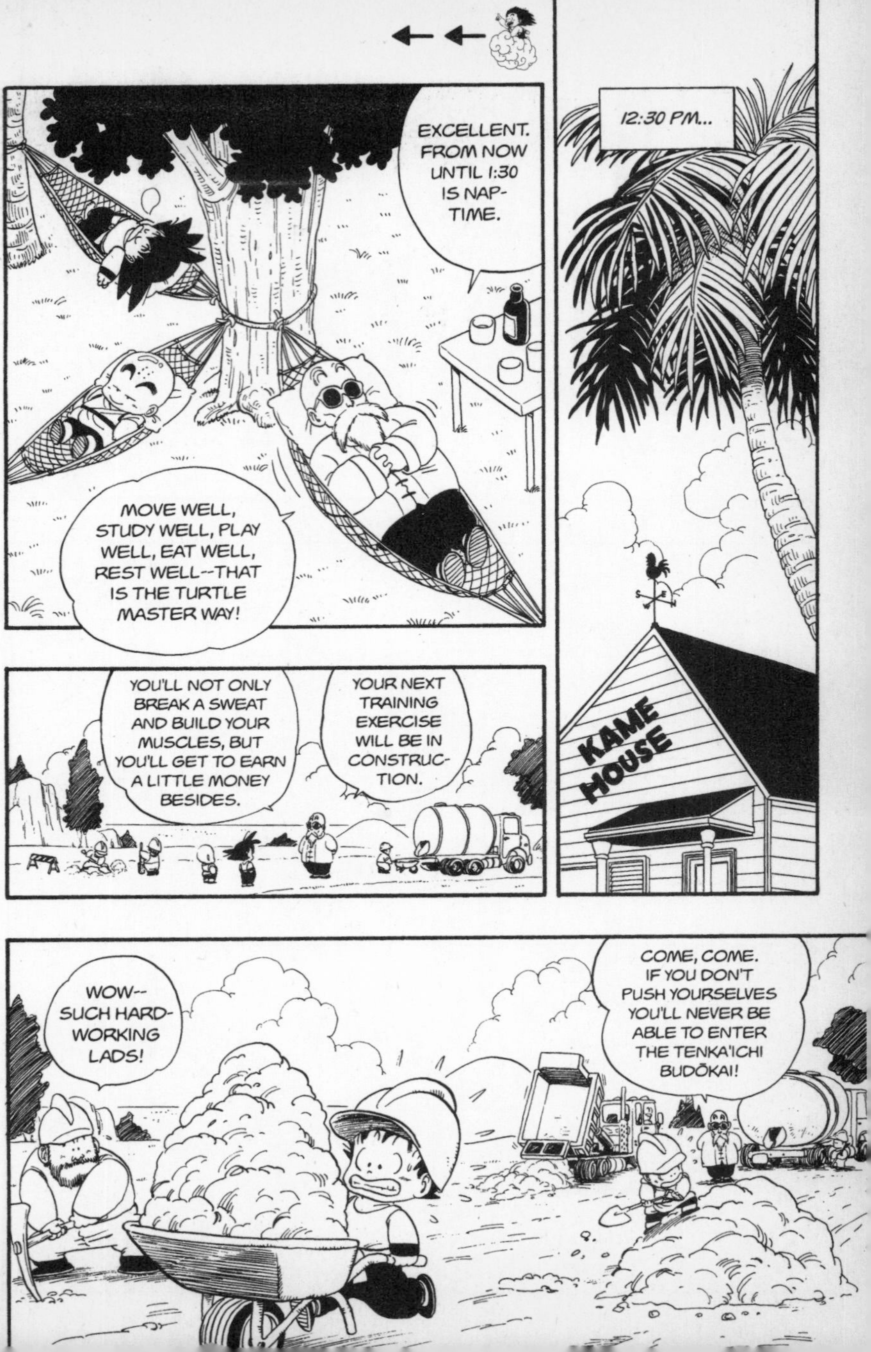
12:30 PM...
KAME HOUSE
EXCELLENT. FROM NOW UNTIL 1:30 IS NAP-TIME.
MOVE WELL, STUDY WELL, PLAY WELL, EAT WELL, REST WELL--THAT IS THE TURTLE MASTER WAY!
YOUR NEXT TRAINING EXERCISE WILL BE IN CONSTRUC-TION.
YOU'LL NOT ONLY BREAK A SWEAT AND BUILD YOUR MUSCLES, BUT YOU'LL GET TO EARN A LITTLE MONEY BESIDES.
COME, COME. IF YOU DON'T PUSH YOURSELVES YOU'LL NEVER BE ABLE TO ENTER THE TENKA'ICHI BUDŌKAI!
WOW-- SUCH HARD-WORKING LADS!

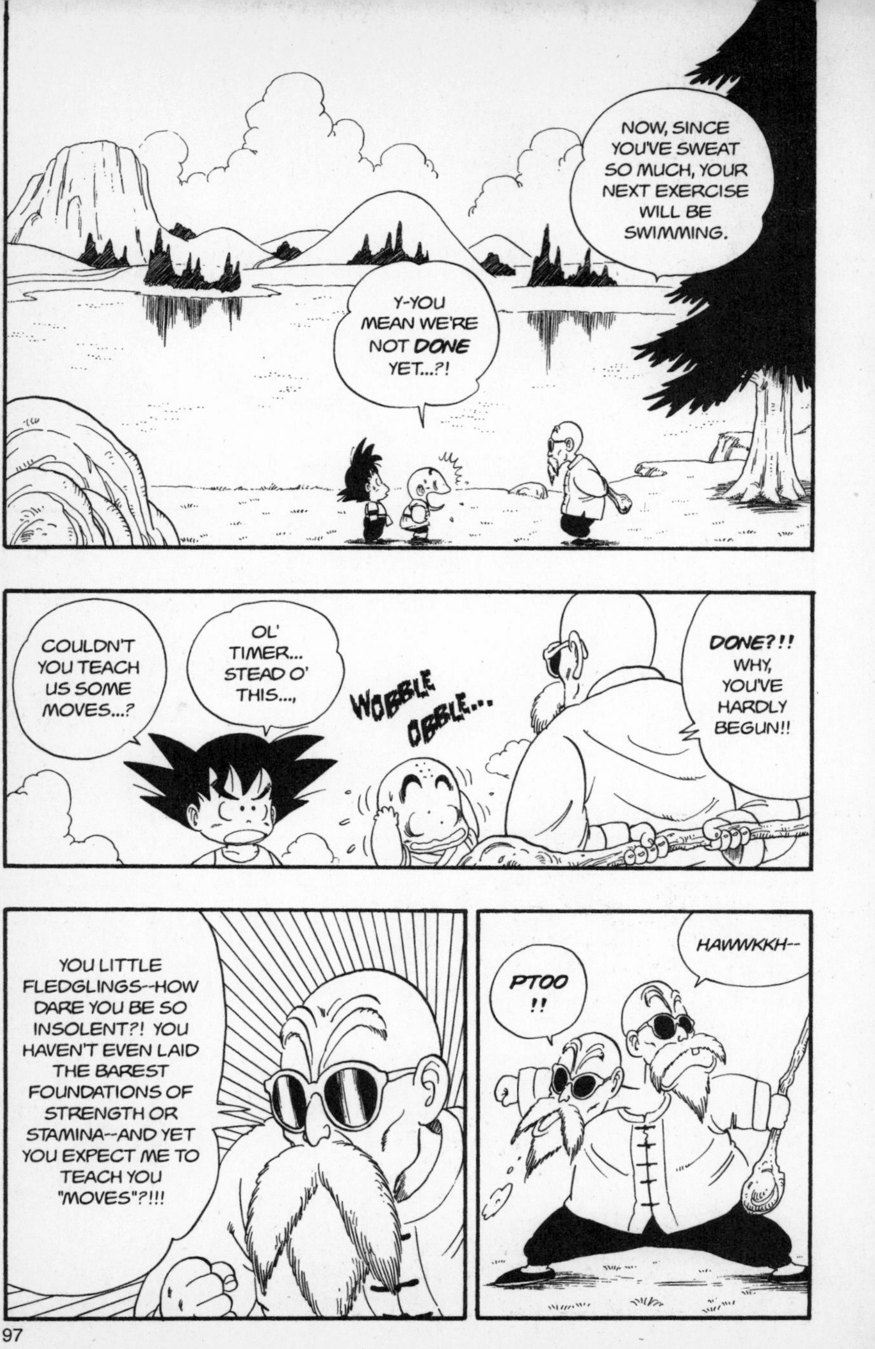
NOW, SINCE YOU'VE SWEAT SO MUCH, YOUR NEXT EXERCISE WILL BE SWIMMING.
Y-YOU MEAN WE'RE NOT DONE YET...?!
DONE?!! WHY, YOU'VE HARDLY BEGUN!!
WOBBLE OBBLE...
OL' TIMER... STEAD O' THIS...,
COULDN'T YOU TEACH US SOME MOVES...?
HAWWKKH--
PTOO !!
YOU LITTLE FLEDGLINGS--HOW DARE YOU BE SO INSOLENT?! YOU HAVEN'T EVEN LAID THE BAREST FOUNDATIONS OF STRENGTH OR STAMINA--AND YET YOU EXPECT ME TO TEACH YOU "MOVES"?!!!

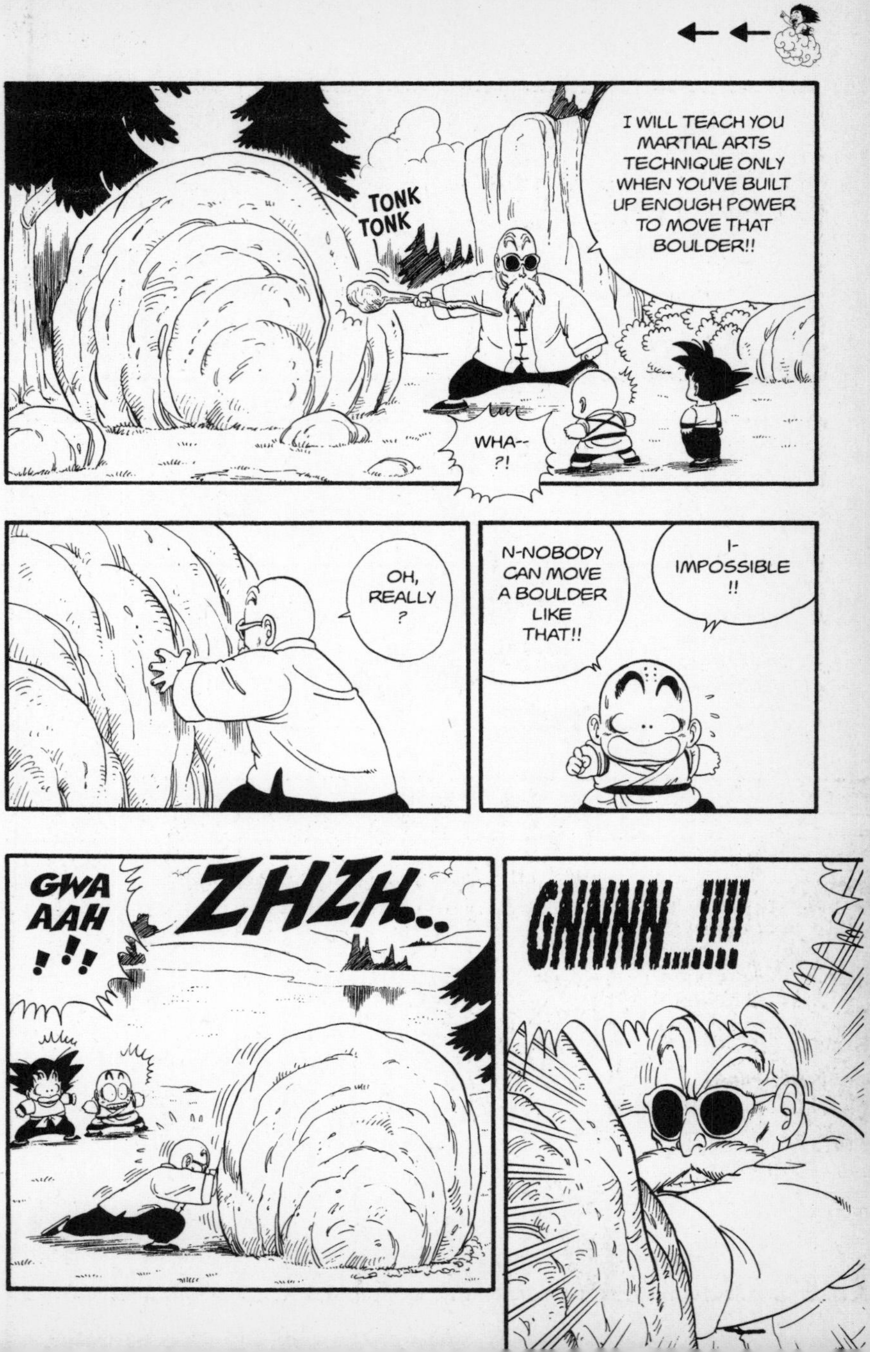
I WILL TEACH YOU MARTIAL ARTS TECHNIQUE ONLY WHEN YOU'VE BUILT UP ENOUGH POWER TO MOVE THAT BOULDER!!
TONK TONK
WHA--?!
I- IMPOSSIBLE!!
N-NOBODY CAN MOVE A BOULDER LIKE THAT!!
OH, REALLY?
GNNNN...!!!!
ZHZH...
GWAAAH!!!

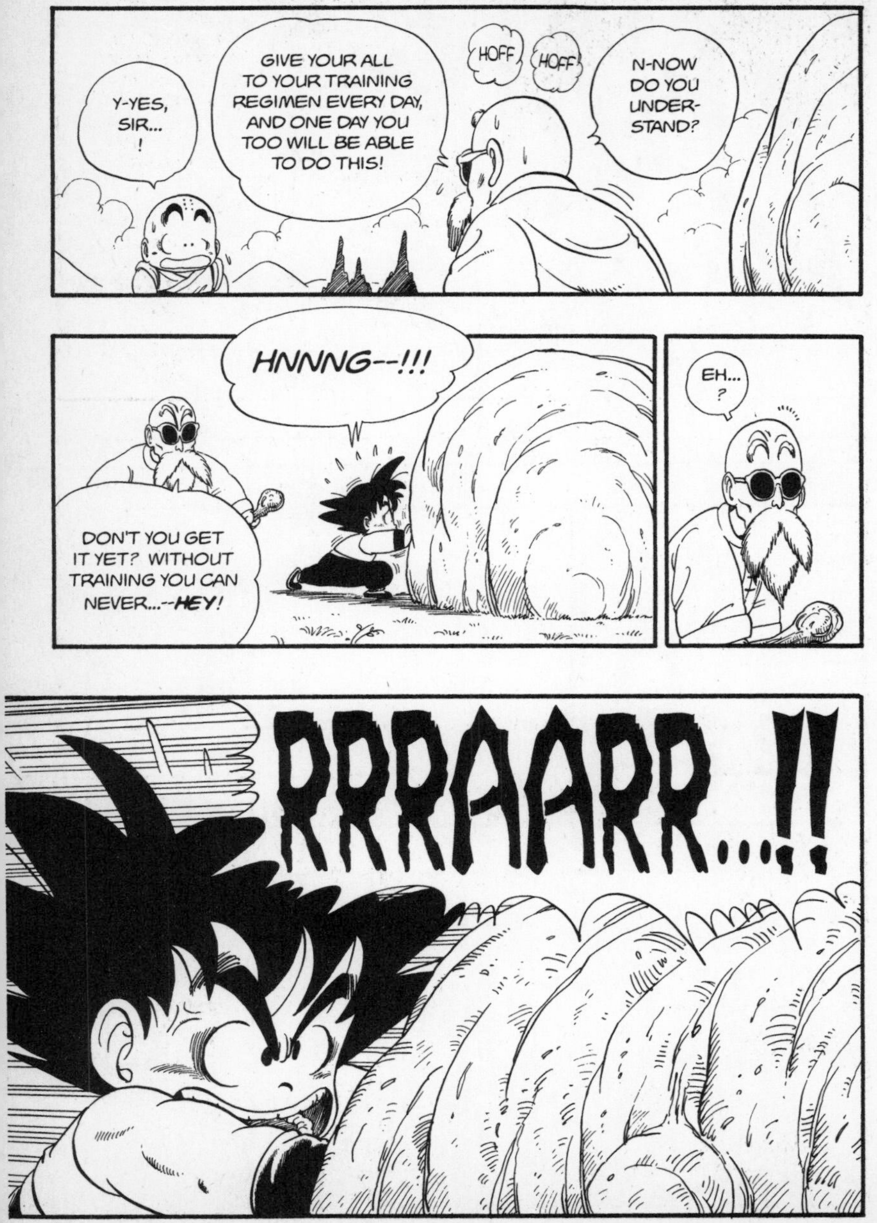
N-NOW DO YOU UNDER-STAND?
HOFF
HOFF
GIVE YOUR ALL TO YOUR TRAINING REGIMEN EVERY DAY, AND ONE DAY YOU TOO WILL BE ABLE TO DO THIS!
Y-YES, SIR... !
EH... ?
HNNNG--!!!
DON'T YOU GET IT YET? WITHOUT TRAINING YOU CAN NEVER...--HEY!
RRRAARR...!!

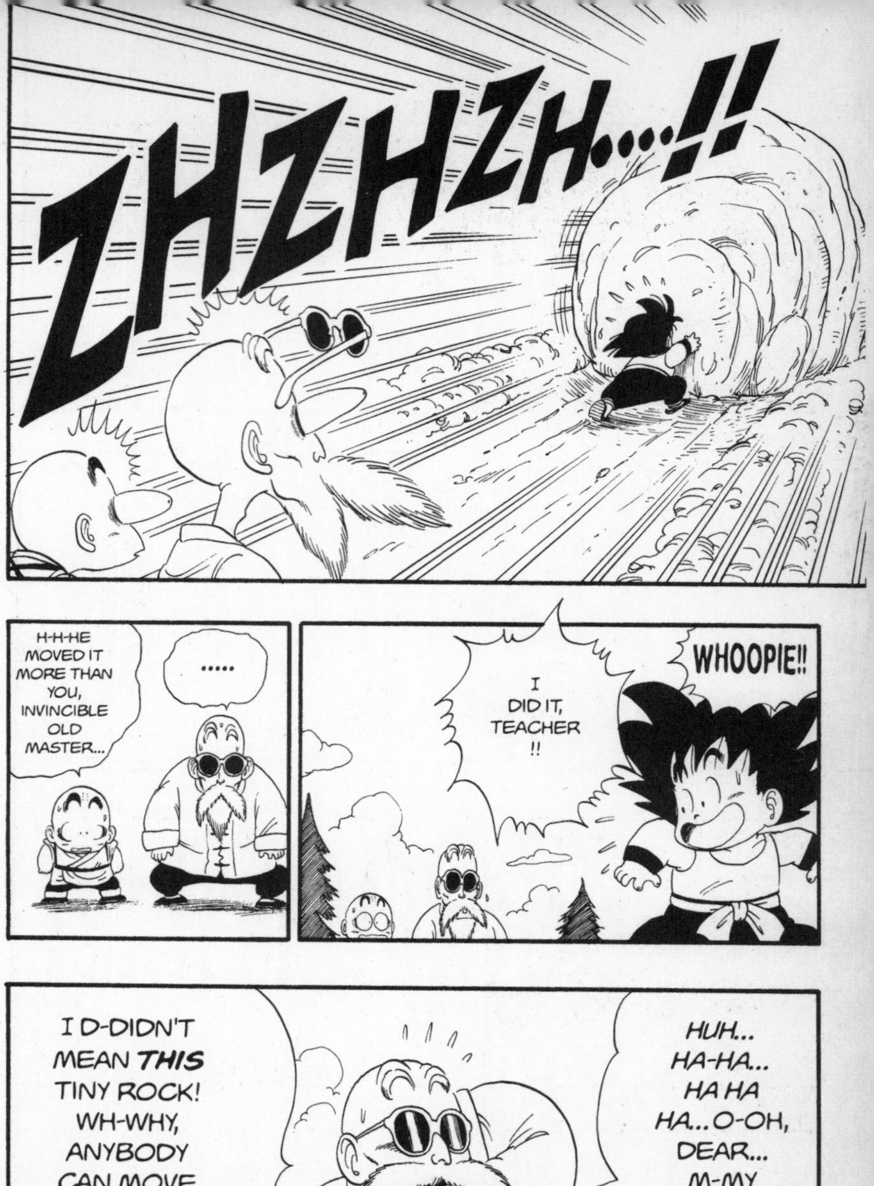
ZHZHZH...!!
WHOOPIE!!
I DID IT, TEACHER !!
H-H-HE MOVED IT MORE THAN YOU, INVINCIBLE OLD MASTER...
.....
HUH... HA-HA... HA HA HA...O-OH, DEAR... M-MY MISTAKE!
I D-DIDN'T MEAN THIS TINY ROCK! WH-WHY, ANYBODY CAN MOVE THIS!

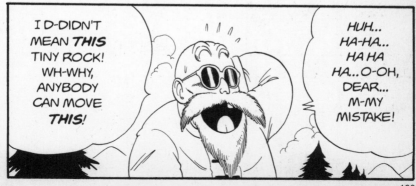

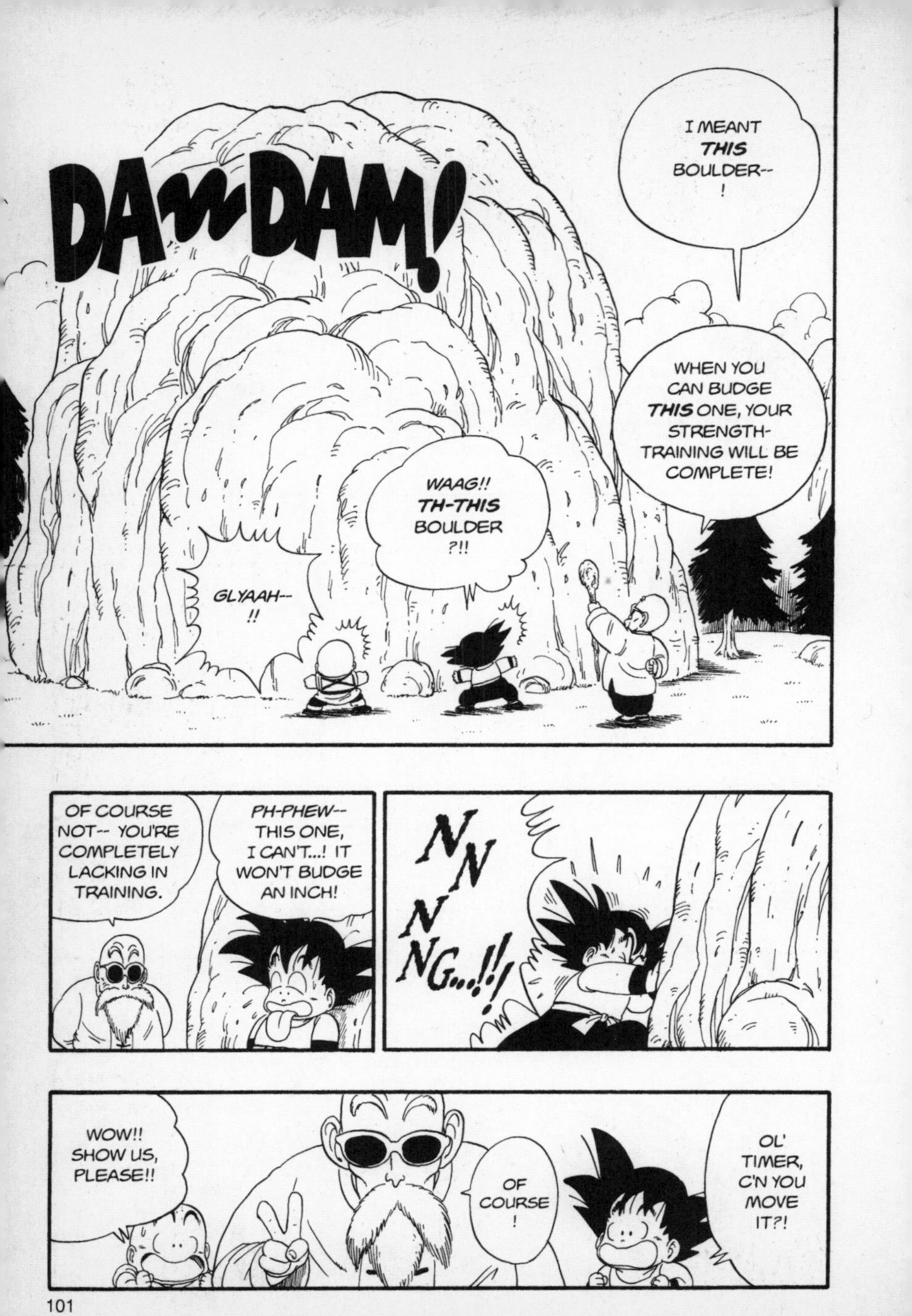

I MEANT THIS BOULDER--!
DAM DAM!
WHEN YOU CAN BUDGE THIS ONE, YOUR STRENGTH-TRAINING WILL BE COMPLETE!
WAAG!! TH-THIS BOULDER?!!
GLYAAH--!!
NNNNG...!!
PH-PHEW-- THIS ONE, I CAN'T...! IT WON'T BUDGE AN INCH!
OF COURSE NOT-- YOU'RE COMPLETELY LACKING IN TRAINING.
OL' TIMER, C'N YOU MOVE IT?!
OF COURSE!
WOW!! SHOW US, PLEASE!!

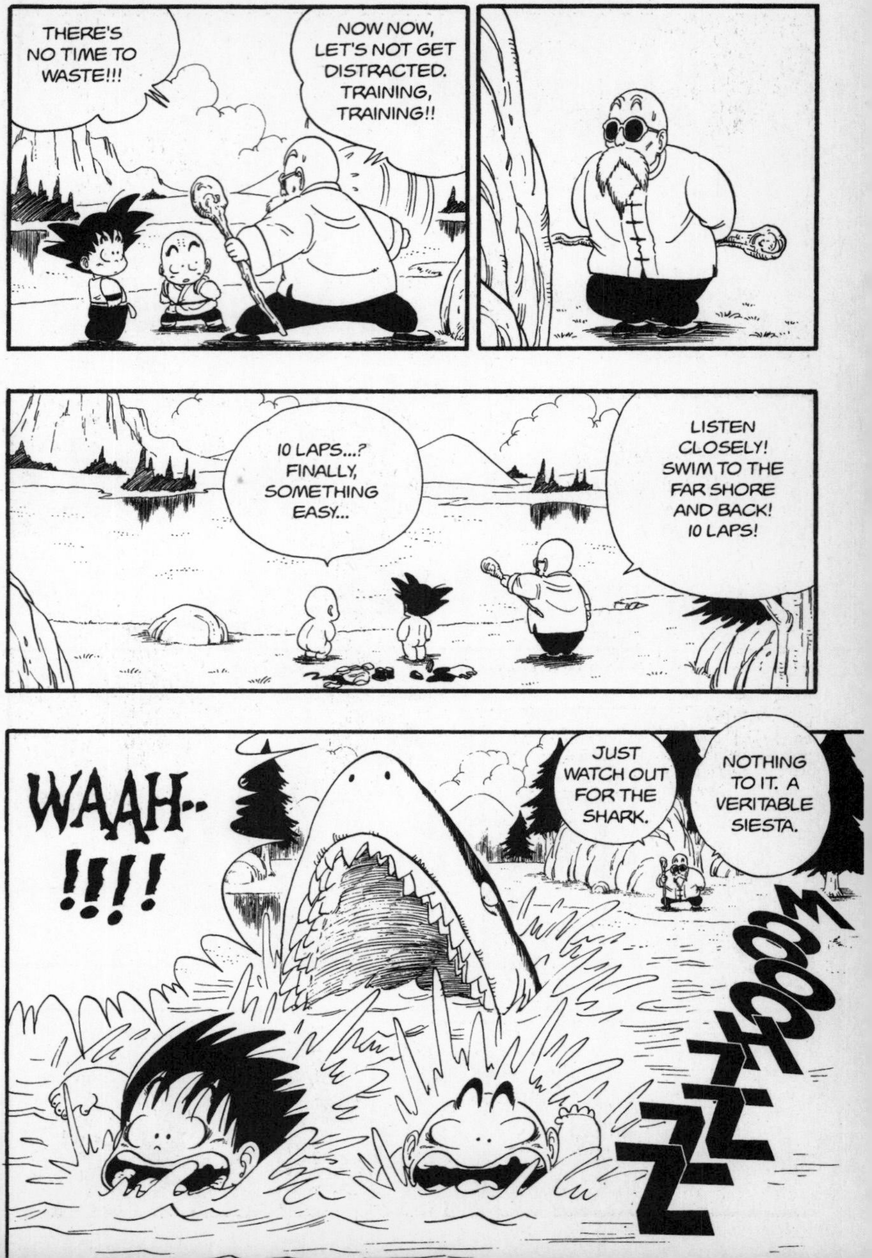
NOW NOW, LET'S NOT GET DISTRACTED. TRAINING, TRAINING!!
THERE'S NO TIME TO WASTE!!!
LISTEN CLOSELY! SWIM TO THE FAR SHORE AND BACK! 10 LAPS!
10 LAPS...? FINALLY, SOMETHING EASY...
NOTHING TO IT. A VERITABLE SIESTA.
JUST WATCH OUT FOR THE SHARK.
WOOOHZZZ
WAAH-- !!!!

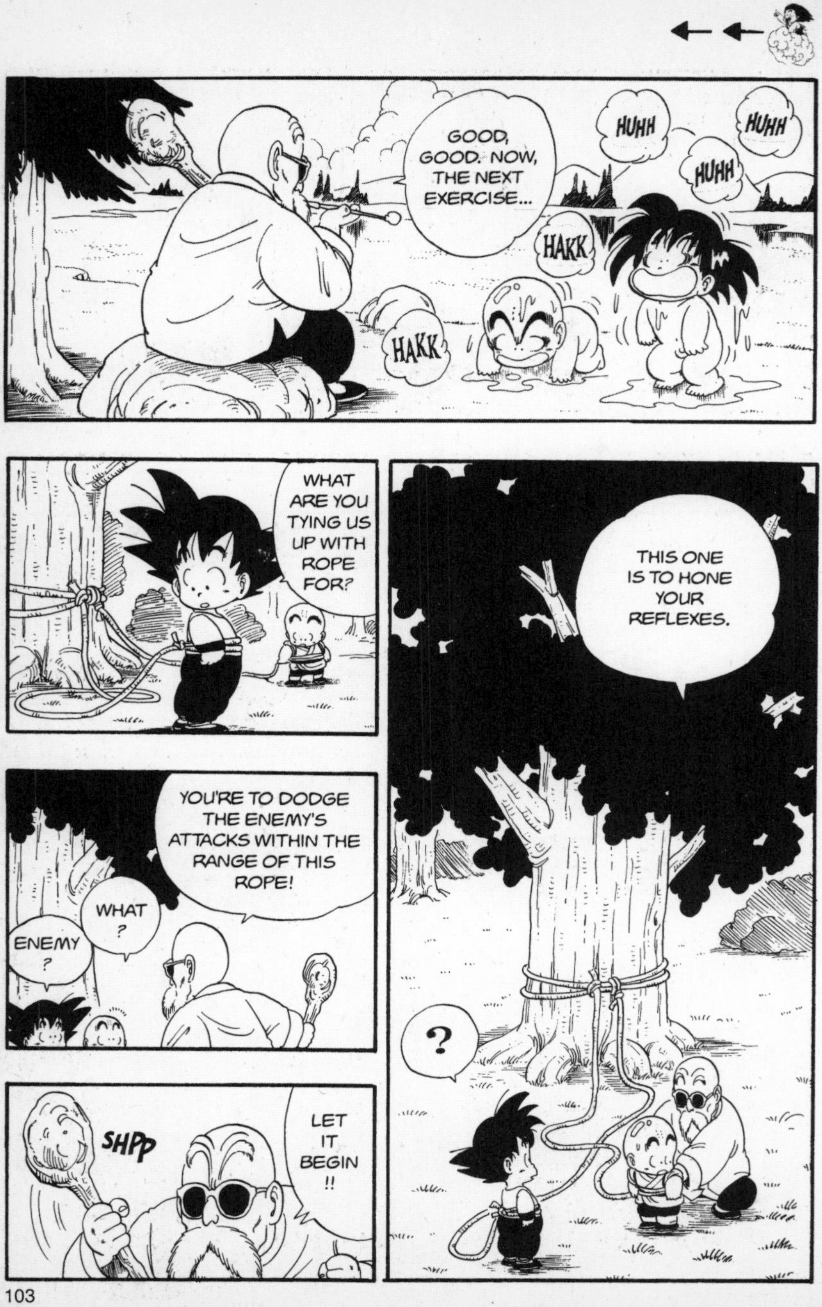
HUHH
HUHH
HUHH
GOOD, GOOD. NOW, THE NEXT EXERCISE...
HAKK
HAKK
THIS ONE IS TO HONE YOUR REFLEXES.
?
WHAT ARE YOU TYING US UP WITH ROPE FOR?
YOU'RE TO DODGE THE ENEMY'S ATTACKS WITHIN THE RANGE OF THIS ROPE!
WHAT ?
ENEMY ?
LET IT BEGIN !!
SHPP

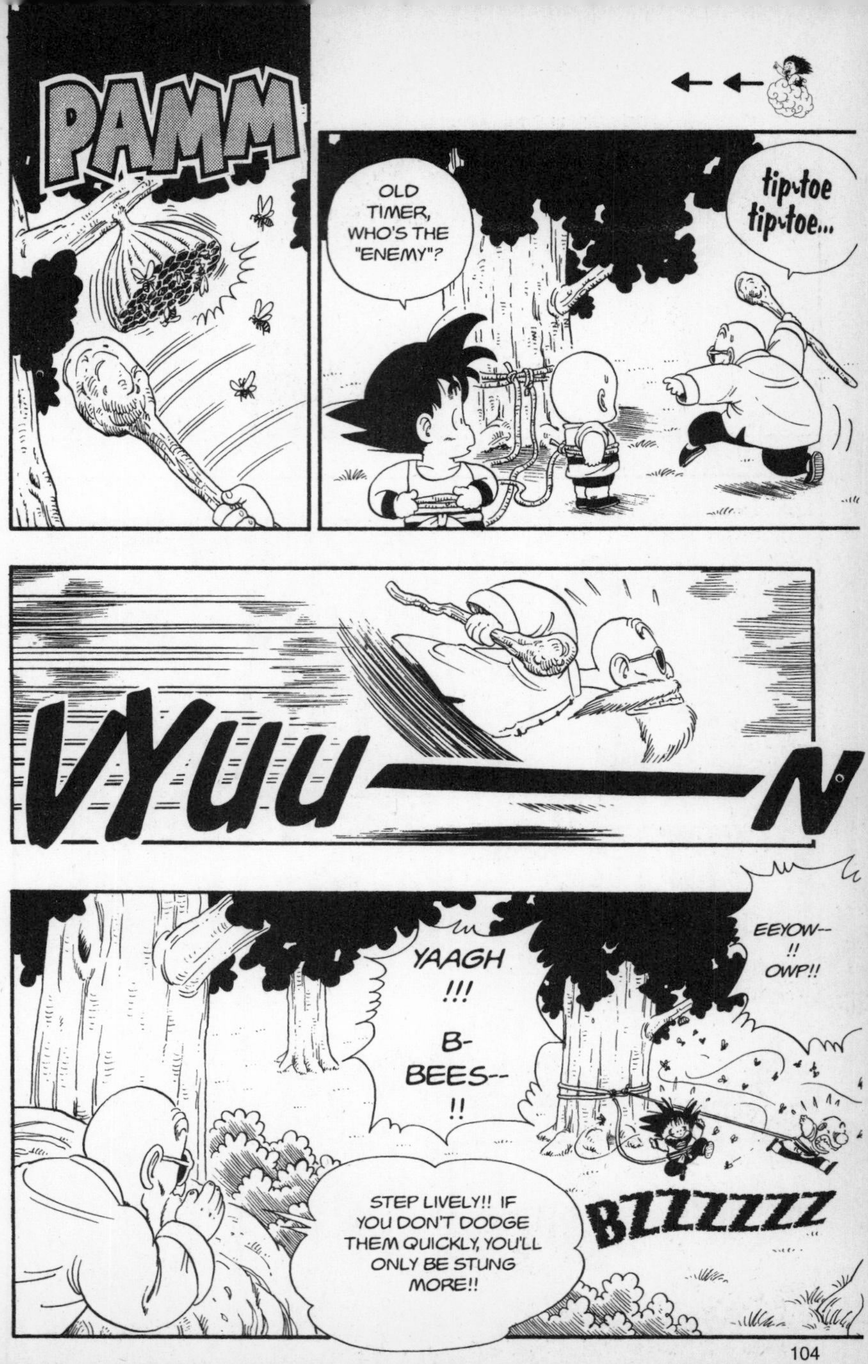
tip-toe tip-toe...
OLD TIMER, WHO'S THE "ENEMY"?
PAMM
VYUU——N
EEYOW-- !! OWP!!
YAAGH !!!
B- BEES-- !!
BZZZZZZZ
STEP LIVELY!! IF YOU DON'T DODGE THEM QUICKLY, YOU'LL ONLY BE STUNG MORE!!

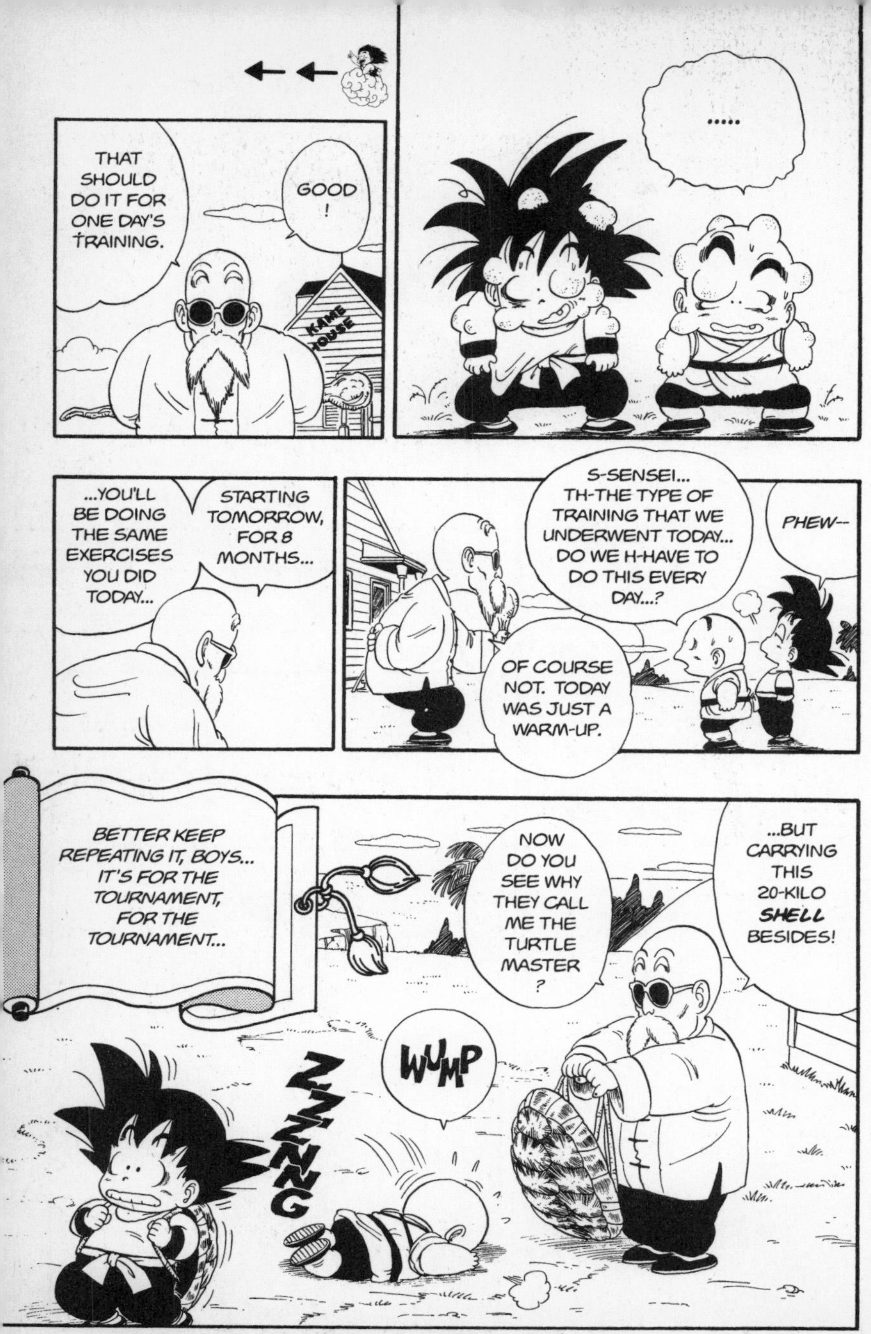
.....
THAT SHOULD DO IT FOR ONE DAY'S TRAINING.
GOOD !
KAME HOUSE
PHEW--
S-SENSEI... TH-THE TYPE OF TRAINING THAT WE UNDERWENT TODAY... DO WE H-HAVE TO DO THIS EVERY DAY...?
OF COURSE NOT. TODAY WAS JUST A WARM-UP.
STARTING TOMORROW, FOR 8 MONTHS...
...YOU'LL BE DOING THE SAME EXERCISES YOU DID TODAY...
...BUT CARRYING THIS 20-KILO SHELL BESIDES!
NOW DO YOU SEE WHY THEY CALL ME THE TURTLE MASTER ?
WUMP
ZZZNNG
BETTER KEEP REPEATING IT, BOYS... IT'S FOR THE TOURNAMENT, FOR THE TOURNAMENT...

NEXT: Let the Tournament Begin!

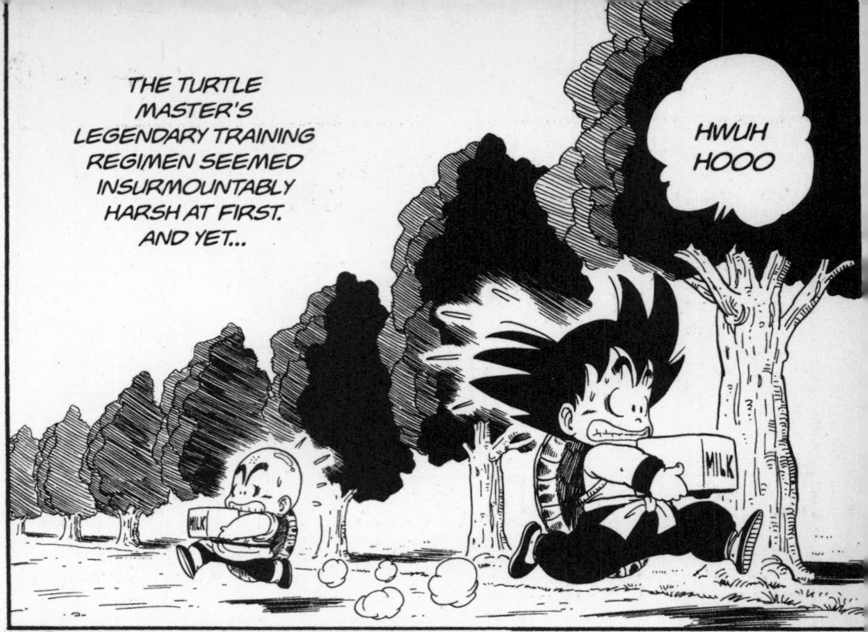
HWUH HOOO
THE TURTLE MASTER'S LEGENDARY TRAINING REGIMEN SEEMED INSURMOUNTABLY HARSH AT FIRST. AND YET...
MILK
MILK

Tale 32 • Let the Contest Begin!

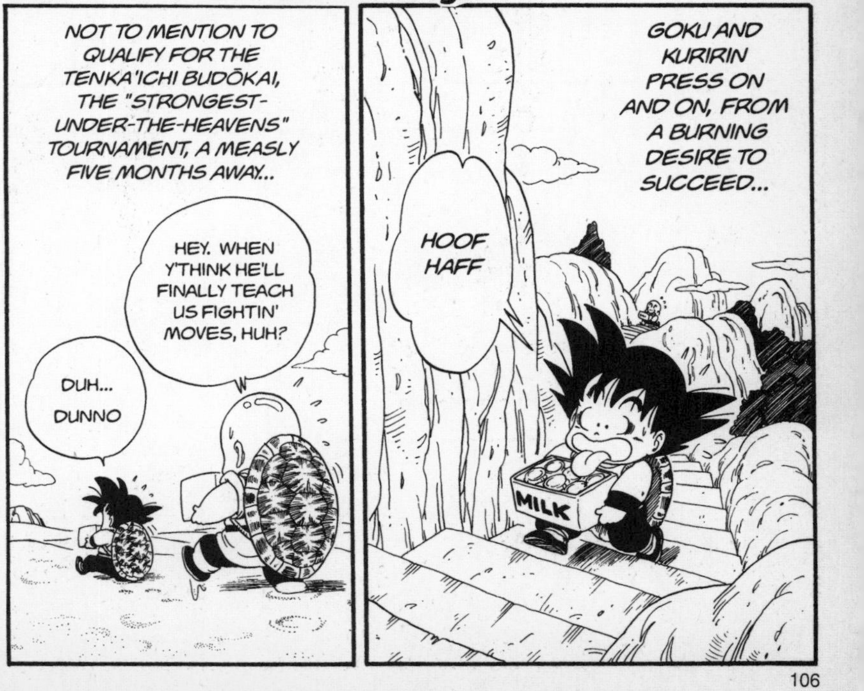
GOKU AND KURIRIN PRESS ON AND ON, FROM A BURNING DESIRE TO SUCCEED...
HOOF HAFF
MILK
NOT TO MENTION TO QUALIFY FOR THE TENKA'ICHI BUDŌKAI, THE "STRONGEST-UNDER-THE-HEAVENS" TOURNAMENT, A MEASLY FIVE MONTHS AWAY...
HEY. WHEN Y'THINK HE'LL FINALLY TEACH US FIGHTIN' MOVES, HUH?
DUH... DUNNO

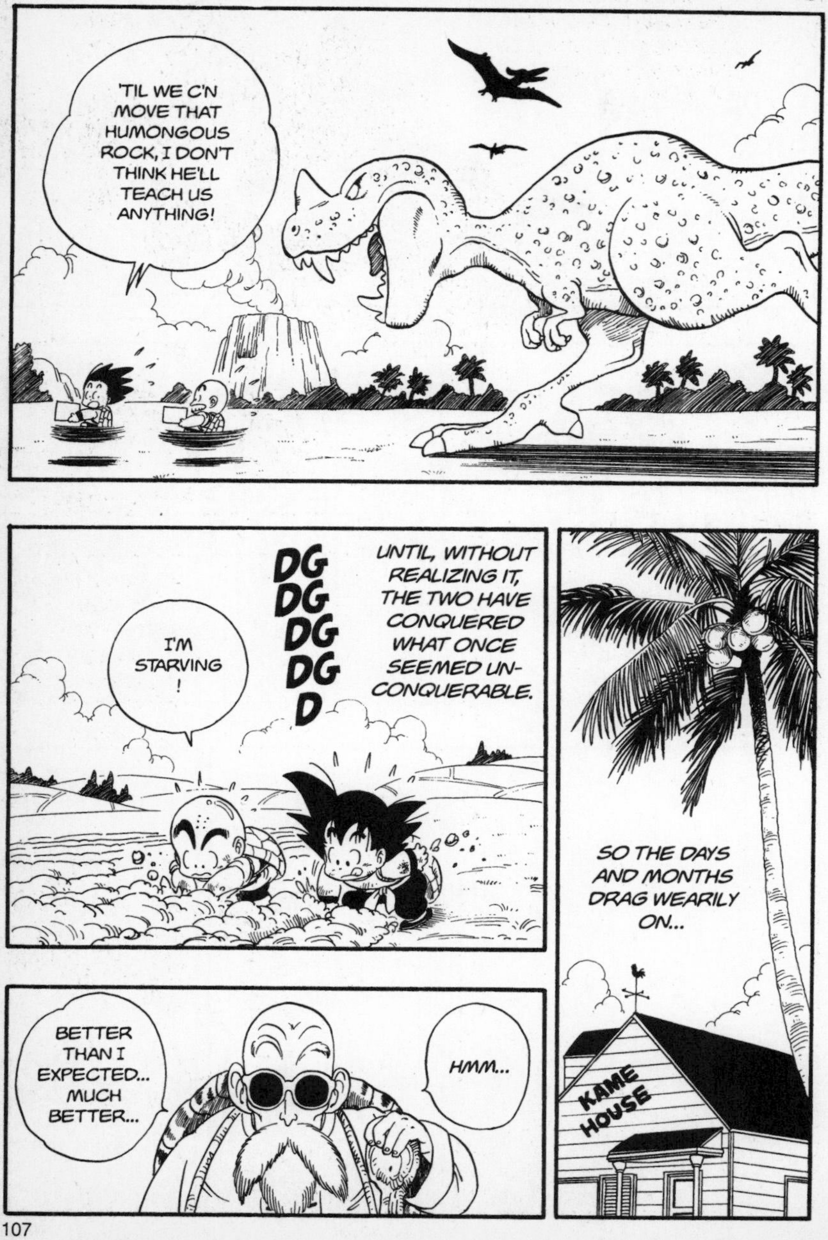
'TIL WE C'N MOVE THAT HUMONGOUS ROCK, I DON'T THINK HE'LL TEACH US ANYTHING!
SO THE DAYS AND MONTHS DRAG WEARILY ON...
KAME HOUSE
UNTIL, WITHOUT REALIZING IT, THE TWO HAVE CONQUERED WHAT ONCE SEEMED UN-CONQUERABLE.
DG DG DG DG D
I'M STARVING!
HMM...
BETTER THAN I EXPECTED... MUCH BETTER...

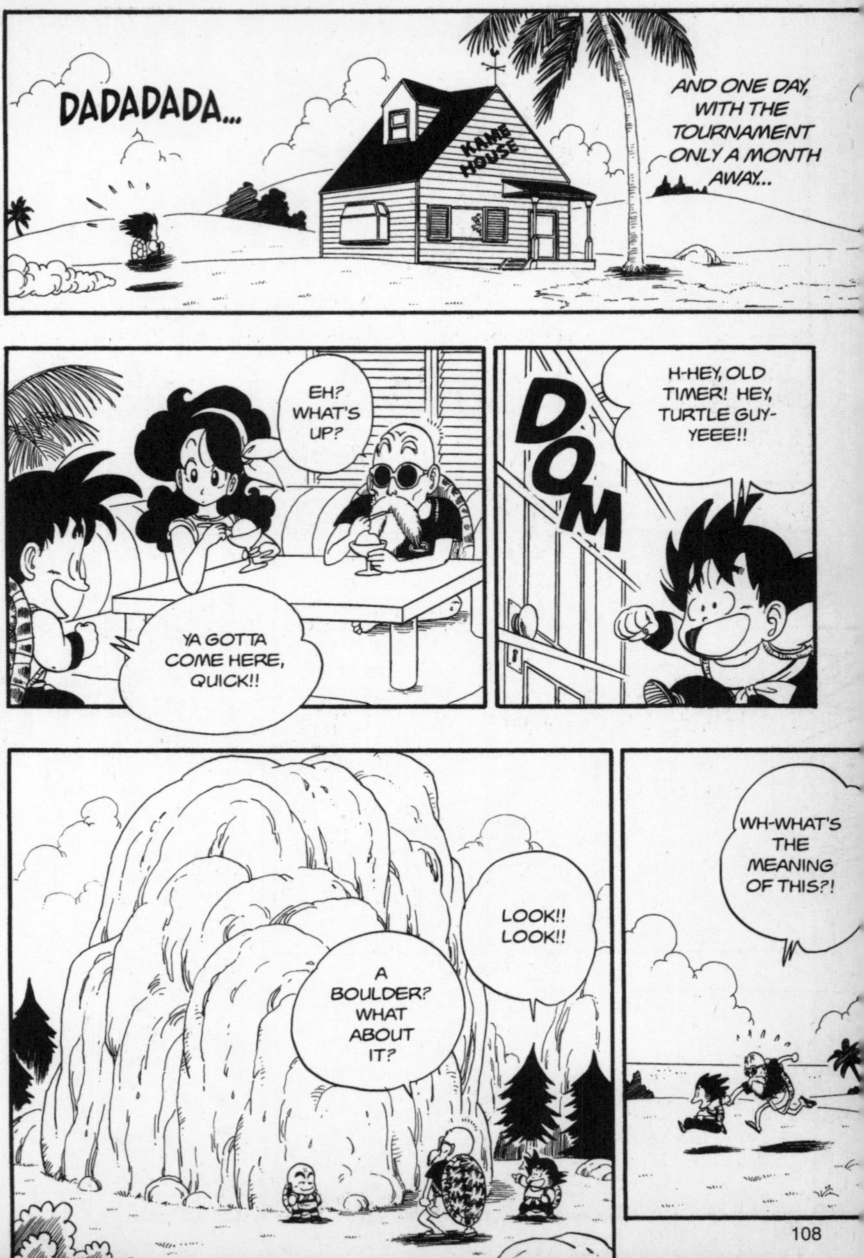
AND ONE DAY, WITH THE TOURNAMENT ONLY A MONTH AWAY...
DADADADA...
KAME HOUSE
H-HEY, OLD TIMER! HEY, TURTLE GUY-YEEE!!
DOM
EH? WHAT'S UP?
YA GOTTA COME HERE, QUICK!!
WH-WHAT'S THE MEANING OF THIS?!
LOOK!! LOOK!!
A BOULDER? WHAT ABOUT IT?

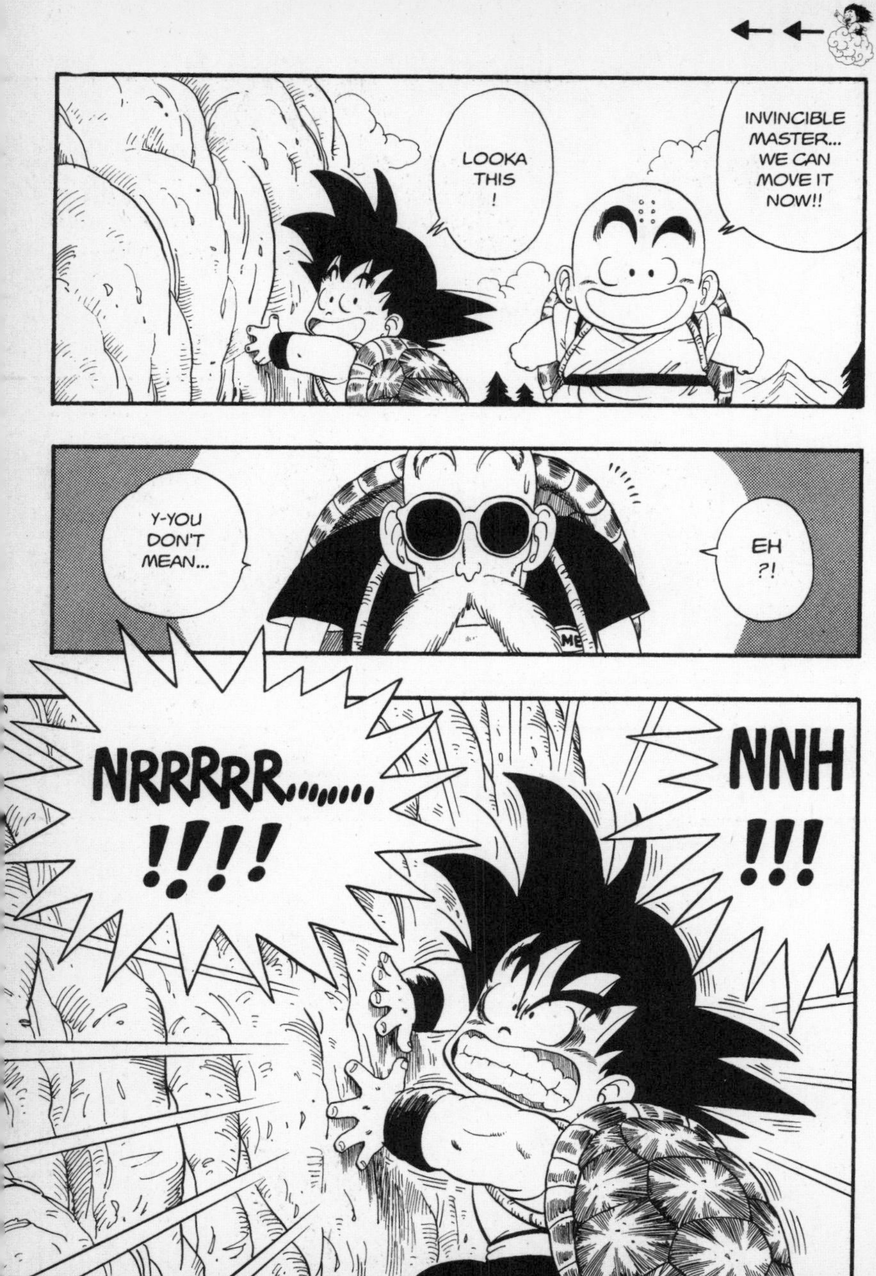
INVINCIBLE MASTER... WE CAN MOVE IT NOW!!
LOOKA THIS !
EH ?!
Y-YOU DON'T MEAN...
NNH !!!
NRRRRR........ !!!!

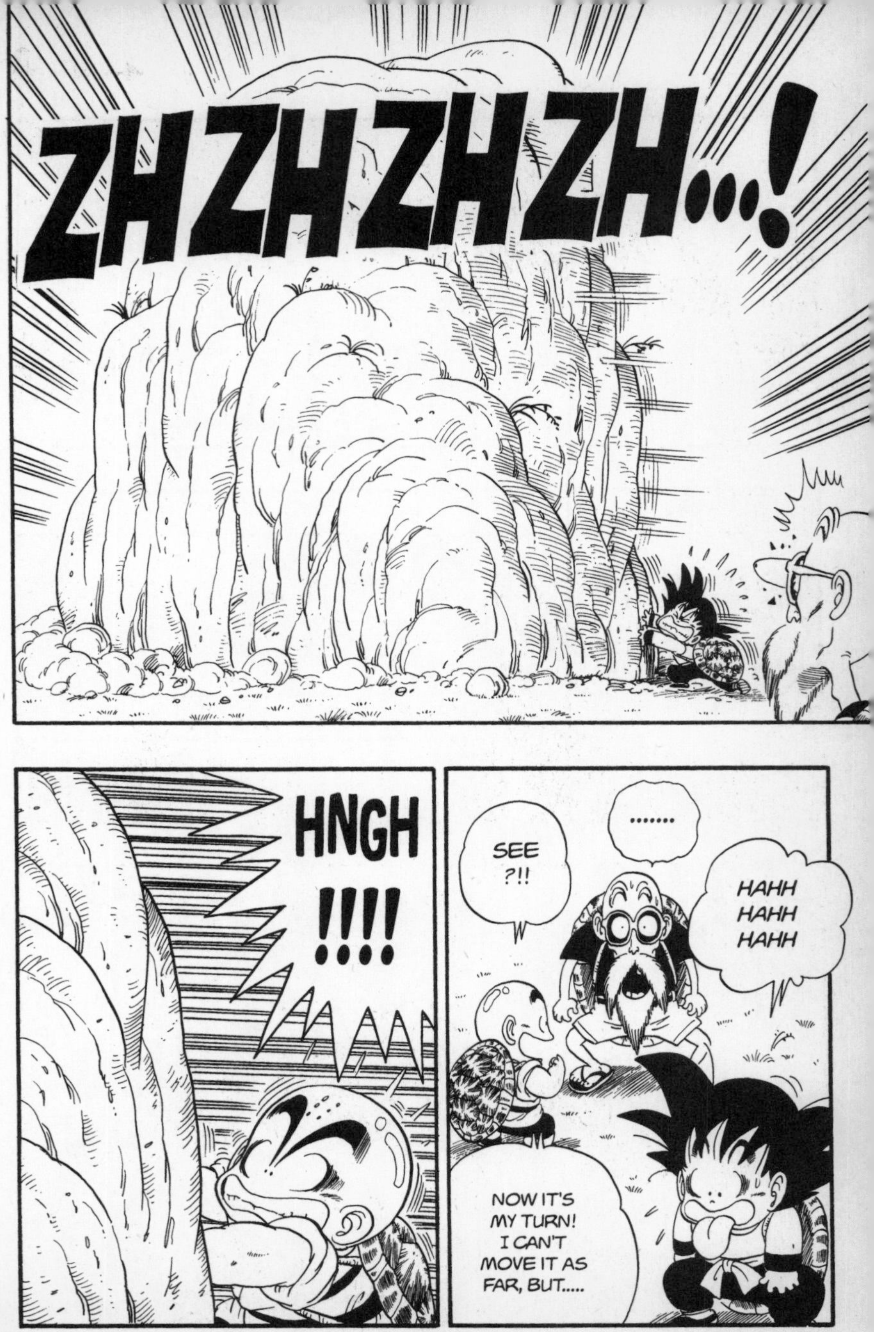
ZHZHZHZH...!
....
HAHH HAHH HAHH
SEE ?!!
NOW IT'S MY TURN! I CAN'T MOVE IT AS FAR, BUT.....
HNGH !!!!

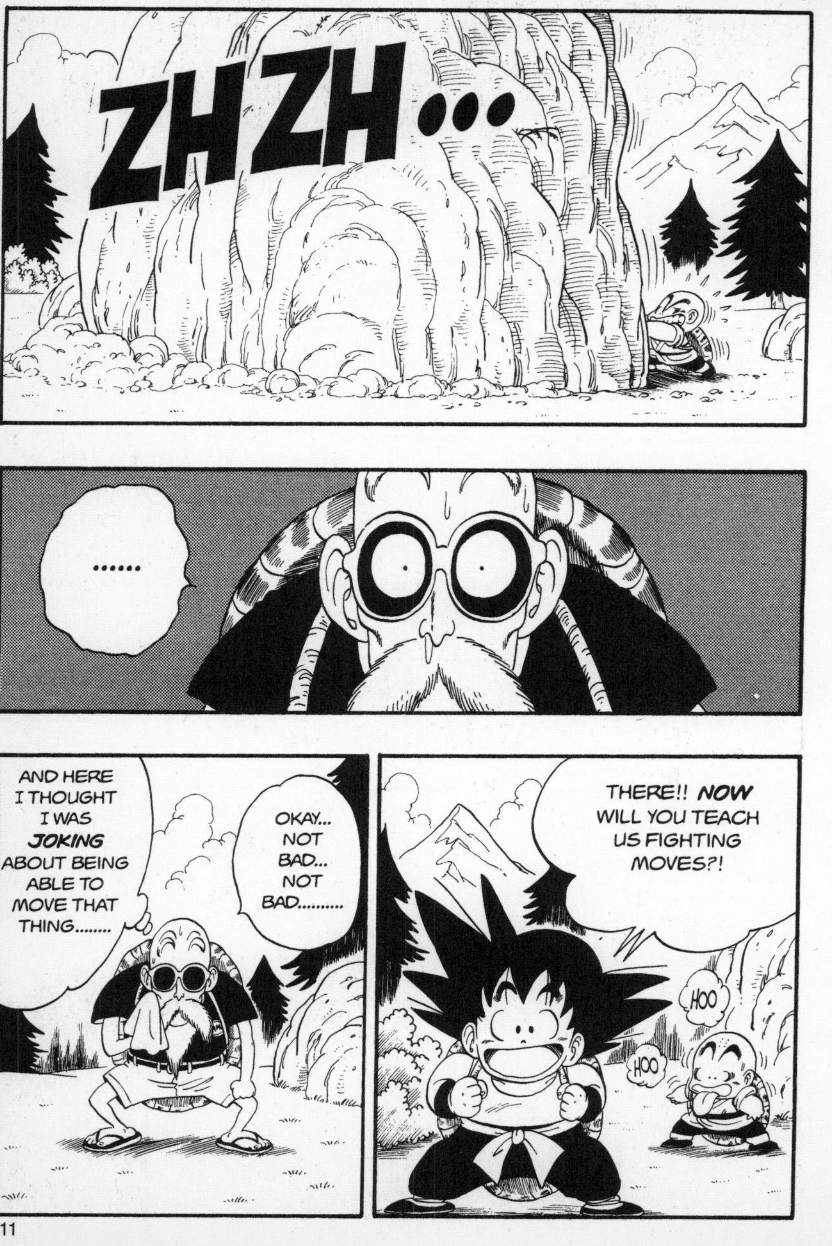
ZHZH...
......
THERE!! NOW WILL YOU TEACH US FIGHTING MOVES?!
HOO
HOO
OKAY... NOT BAD... NOT BAD.........
AND HERE I THOUGHT I WAS JOKING ABOUT BEING ABLE TO MOVE THAT THING........

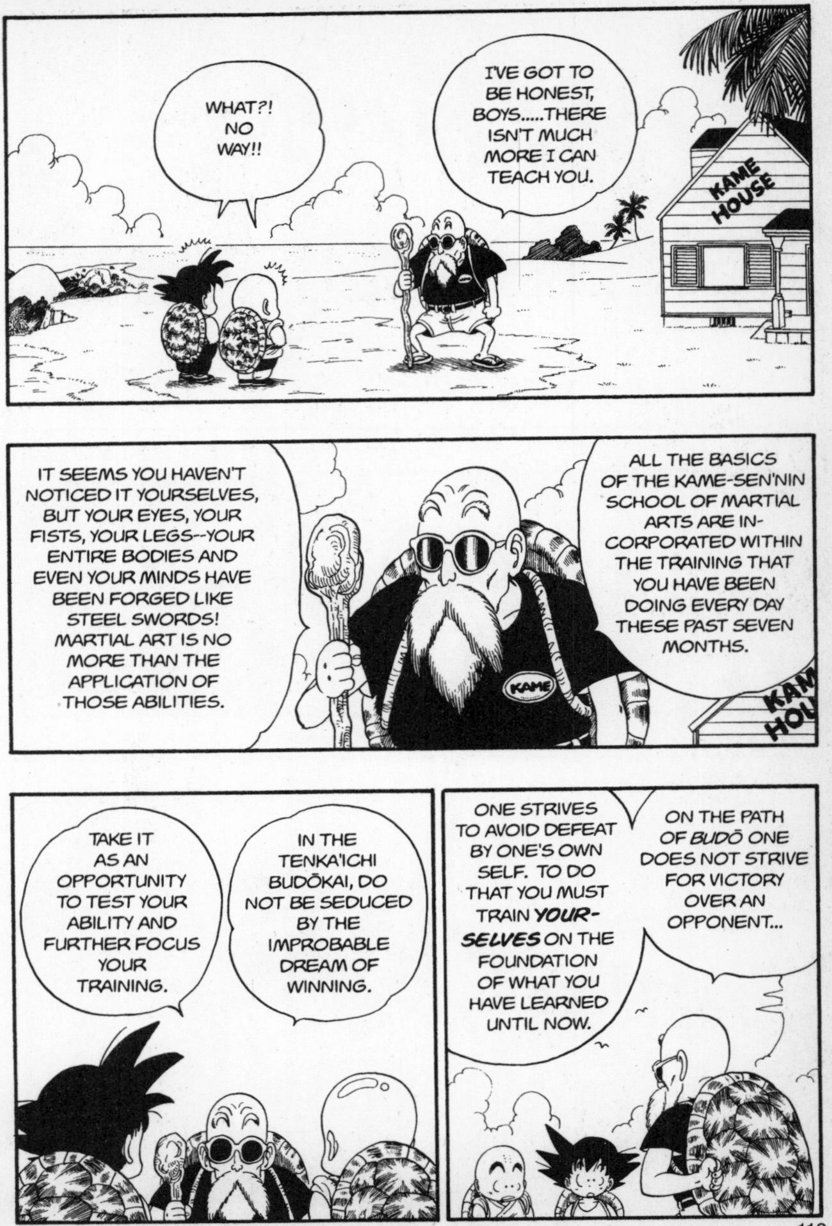
I'VE GOT TO BE HONEST, BOYS.....THERE ISN'T MUCH MORE I CAN TEACH YOU.
KAME HOUSE
WHAT?! NO WAY!!
ALL THE BASICS OF THE KAME-SEN'NIN SCHOOL OF MARTIAL ARTS ARE INCORPORATED WITHIN THE TRAINING THAT YOU HAVE BEEN DOING EVERY DAY THESE PAST SEVEN MONTHS.
IT SEEMS YOU HAVEN'T NOTICED IT YOURSELVES, BUT YOUR EYES, YOUR FISTS, YOUR LEGS--YOUR ENTIRE BODIES AND EVEN YOUR MINDS HAVE BEEN FORGED LIKE STEEL SWORDS! MARTIAL ART IS NO MORE THAN THE APPLICATION OF THOSE ABILITIES.
KAME
ON THE PATH OF *BUDŌ* ONE DOES NOT STRIVE FOR VICTORY OVER AN OPPONENT...
ONE STRIVES TO AVOID DEFEAT BY ONE'S OWN SELF. TO DO THAT YOU MUST TRAIN ***YOURSELVES*** ON THE FOUNDATION OF WHAT YOU HAVE LEARNED UNTIL NOW.
IN THE TENKA'ICHI BUDŌKAI, DO NOT BE SEDUCED BY THE IMPROBABLE DREAM OF WINNING.
TAKE IT AS AN OPPORTUNITY TO TEST YOUR ABILITY AND FURTHER FOCUS YOUR TRAINING.

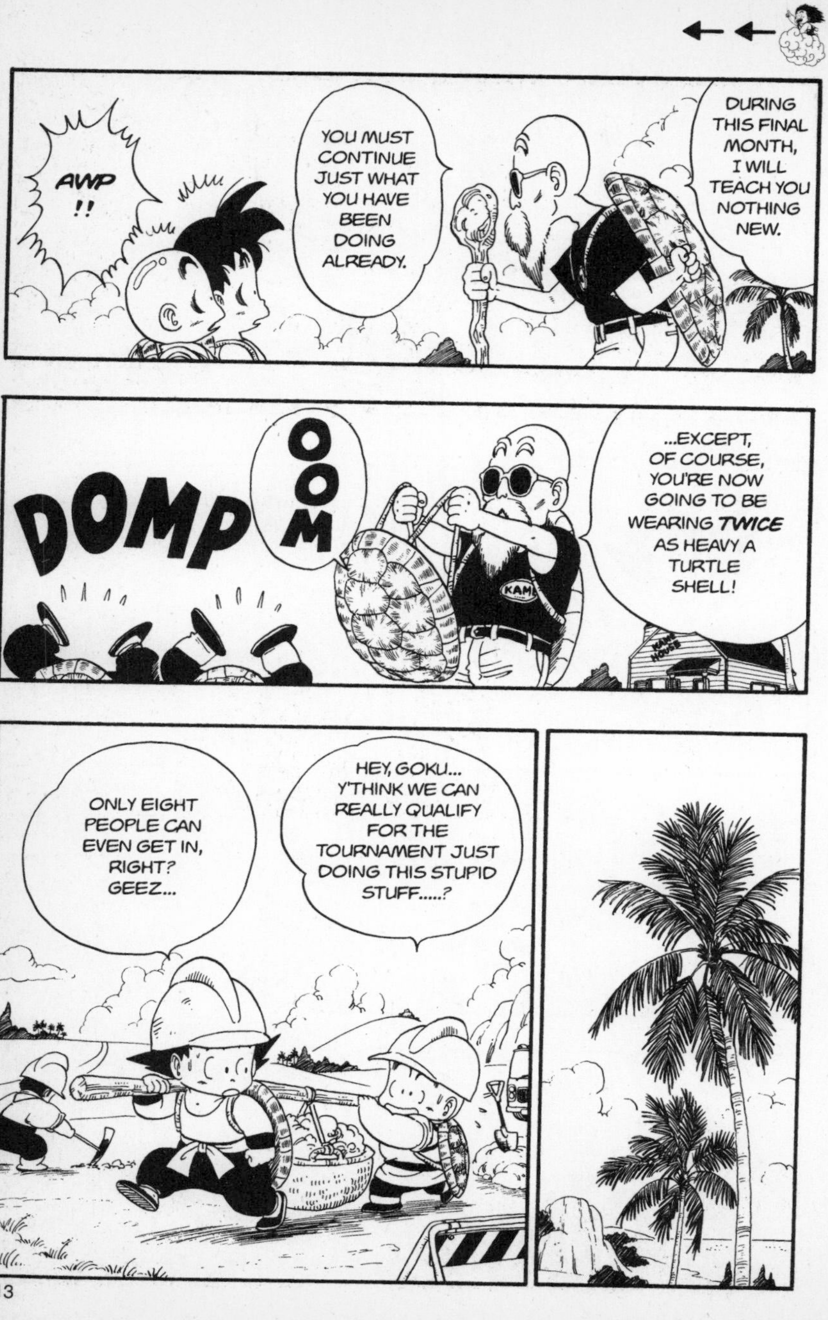
DURING THIS FINAL MONTH, I WILL TEACH YOU NOTHING NEW.
YOU MUST CONTINUE JUST WHAT YOU HAVE BEEN DOING ALREADY.
AWP !!
...EXCEPT, OF COURSE, YOU'RE NOW GOING TO BE WEARING **TWICE** AS HEAVY A TURTLE SHELL!
OOM
DOMP
HEY, GOKU... Y'THINK WE CAN REALLY QUALIFY FOR THE TOURNAMENT JUST DOING THIS STUPID STUFF.....?
ONLY EIGHT PEOPLE CAN EVEN GET IN, RIGHT? GEEZ...

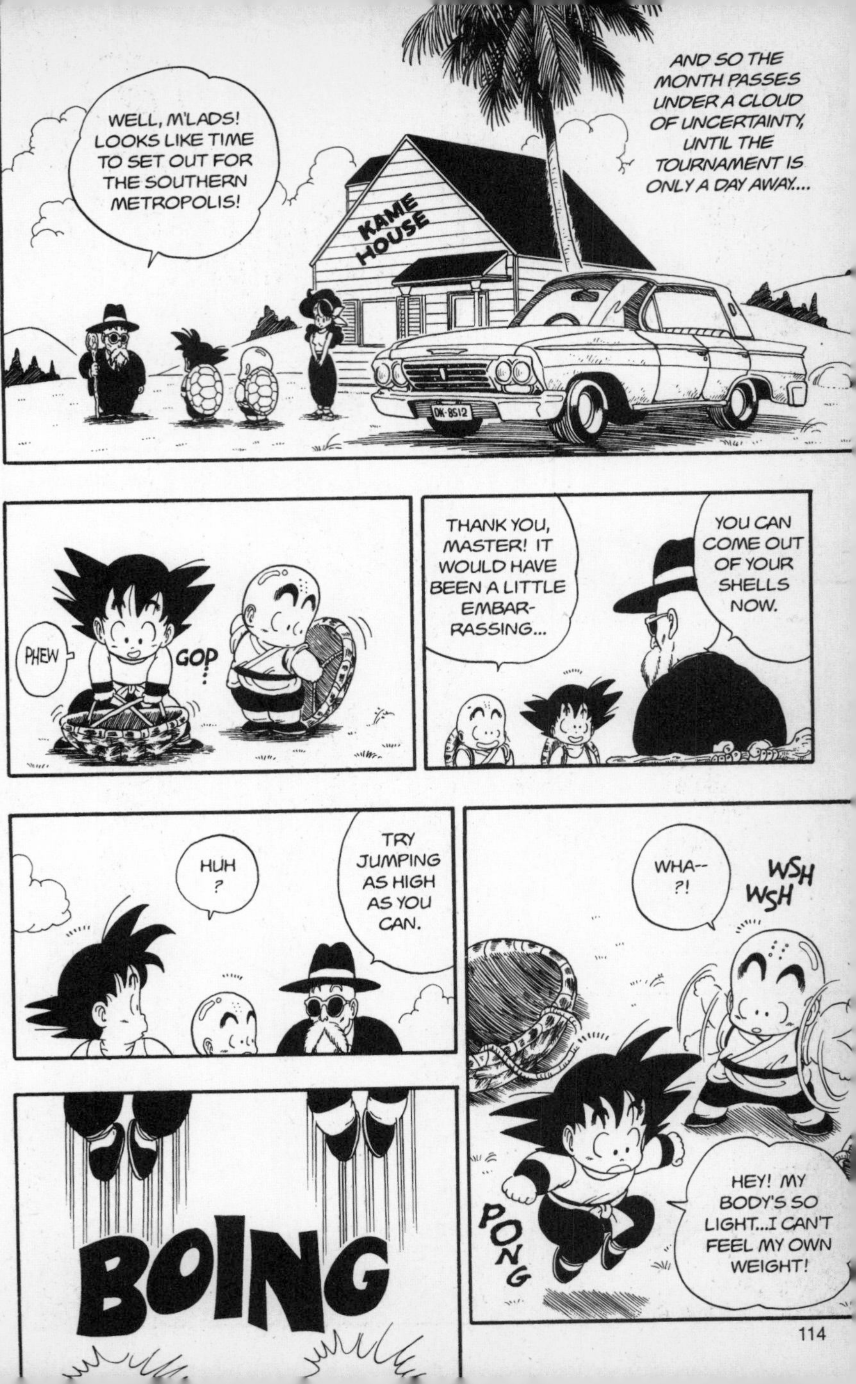
AND SO THE MONTH PASSES UNDER A CLOUD OF UNCERTAINTY, UNTIL THE TOURNAMENT IS ONLY A DAY AWAY....
KAME HOUSE
WELL, M'LADS! LOOKS LIKE TIME TO SET OUT FOR THE SOUTHERN METROPOLIS!
YOU CAN COME OUT OF YOUR SHELLS NOW.
THANK YOU, MASTER! IT WOULD HAVE BEEN A LITTLE EMBAR-RASSING...
GOP
PHEW
WSH WSH
WHA-- ?!
HEY! MY BODY'S SO LIGHT...I CAN'T FEEL MY OWN WEIGHT!
PONG
TRY JUMPING AS HIGH AS YOU CAN.
HUH ?
BOING

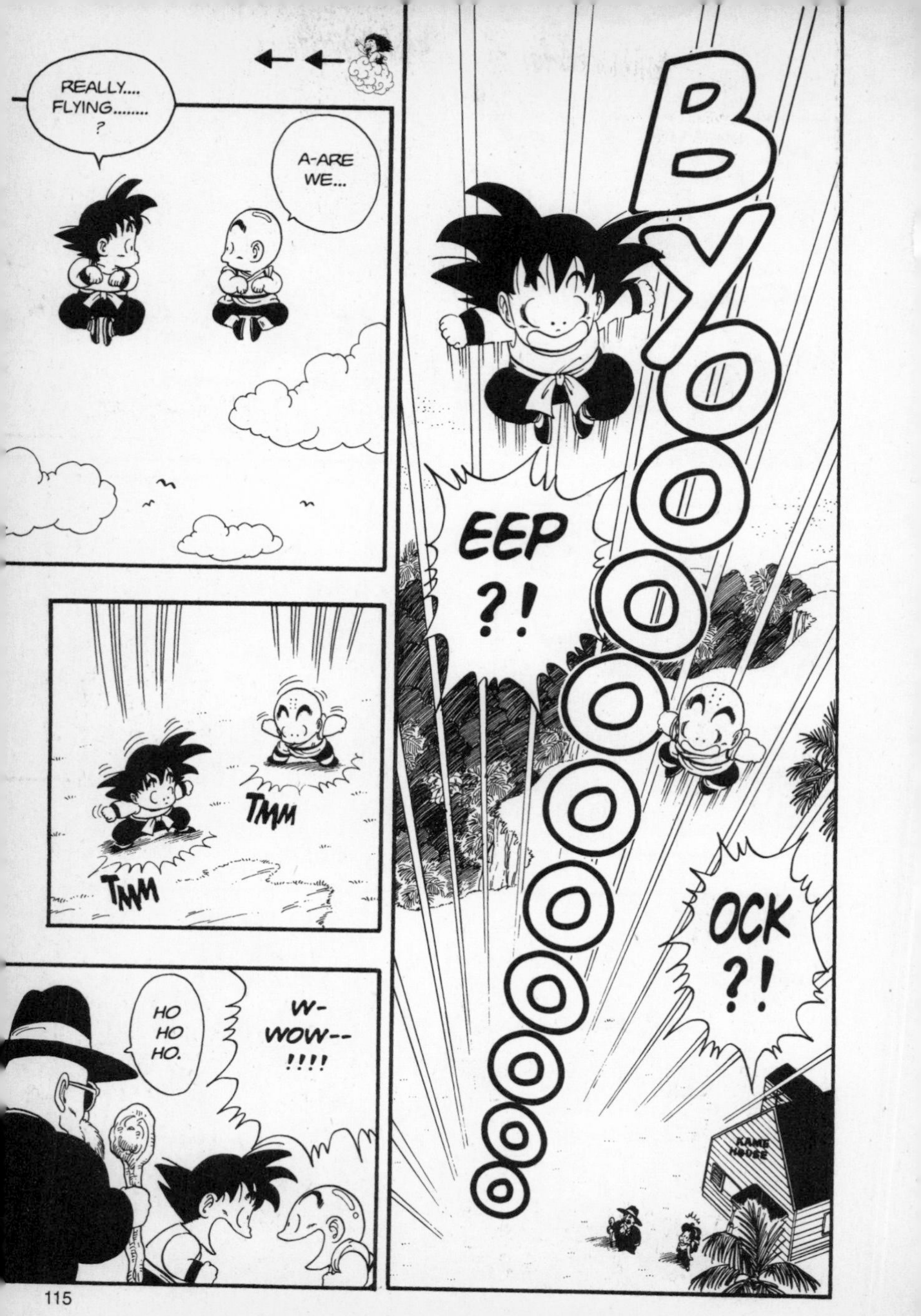

BYOOOOOOOOOOOOO
EEP ?!
OCK ?!
KAME HOUSE
A-ARE WE...
REALLY.... FLYING........ ?
TMM
TMM
W-WOW-- !!!!
HO HO HO.

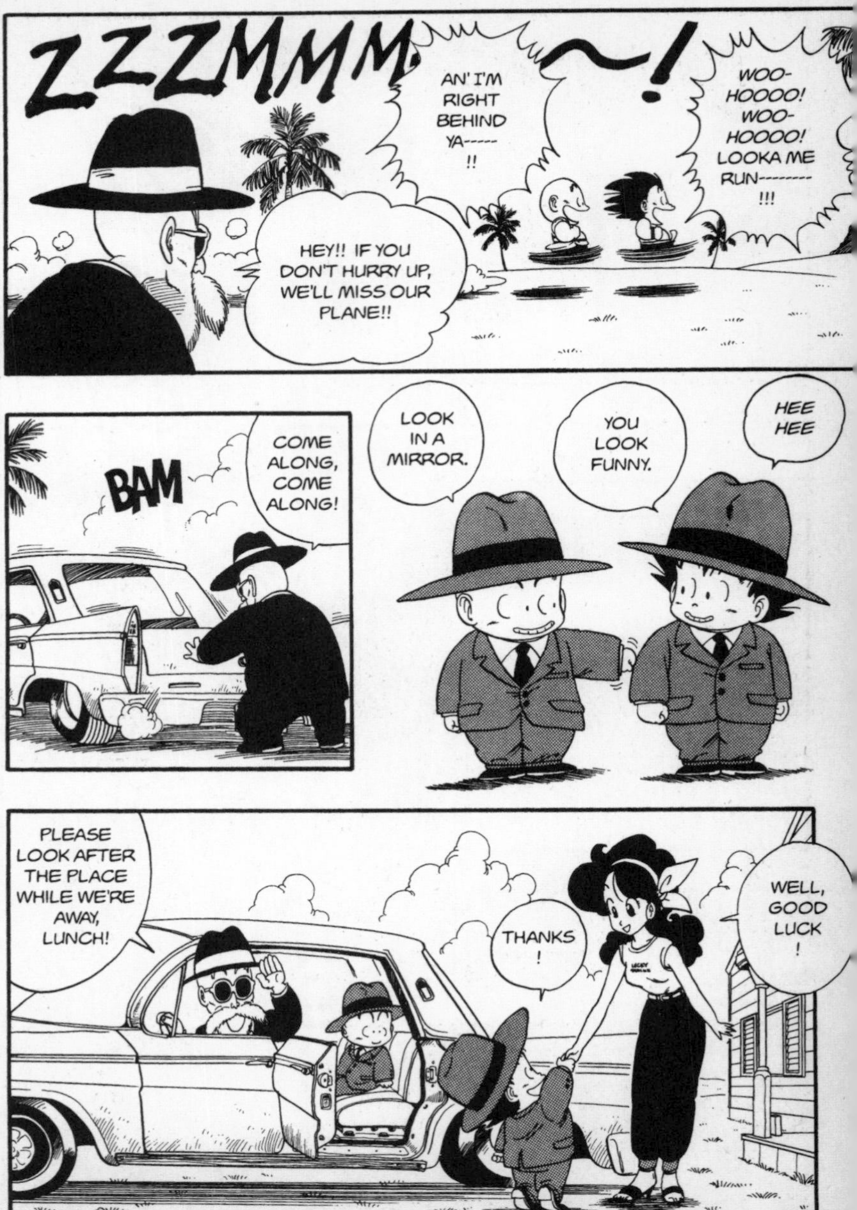
WOO-HOOOO! WOO-HOOOO! LOOKA ME RUN--------!!!
ZZZMMM~!
AN' I'M RIGHT BEHIND YA-----!!
HEY!! IF YOU DON'T HURRY UP, WE'LL MISS OUR PLANE!!
HEE HEE
YOU LOOK FUNNY.
LOOK IN A MIRROR.
COME ALONG, COME ALONG!
BAM
WELL, GOOD LUCK!
THANKS!
PLEASE LOOK AFTER THE PLACE WHILE WE'RE AWAY, LUNCH!

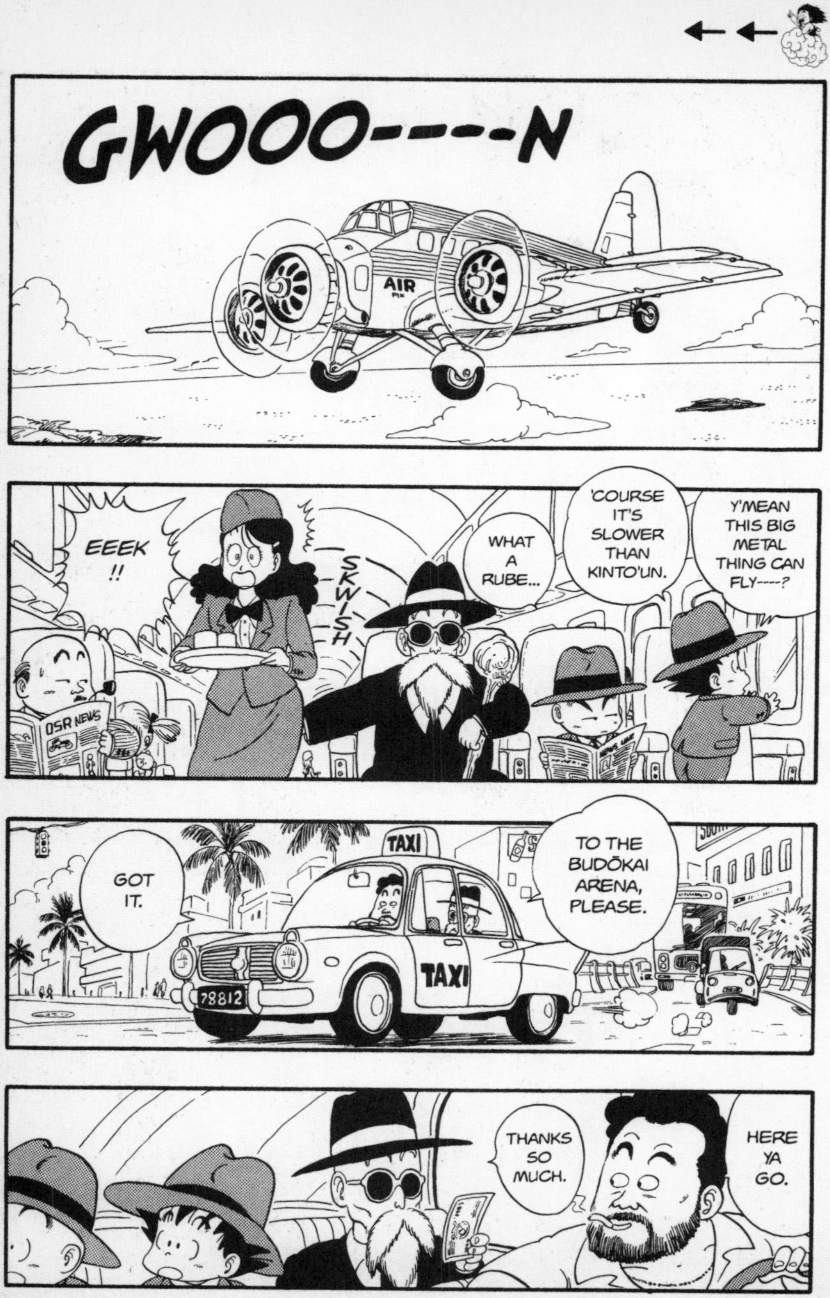
GWOOO---N
AIR
Y'MEAN THIS BIG METAL THING CAN FLY----?
'COURSE IT'S SLOWER THAN KINTO'UN.
WHAT A RUBE...
SKWISH
EEEK !!
OSR NEWS
TO THE BUDŌKAI ARENA, PLEASE.
TAXI
TAXI
78812
GOT IT.
HERE YA GO.
THANKS SO MUCH.

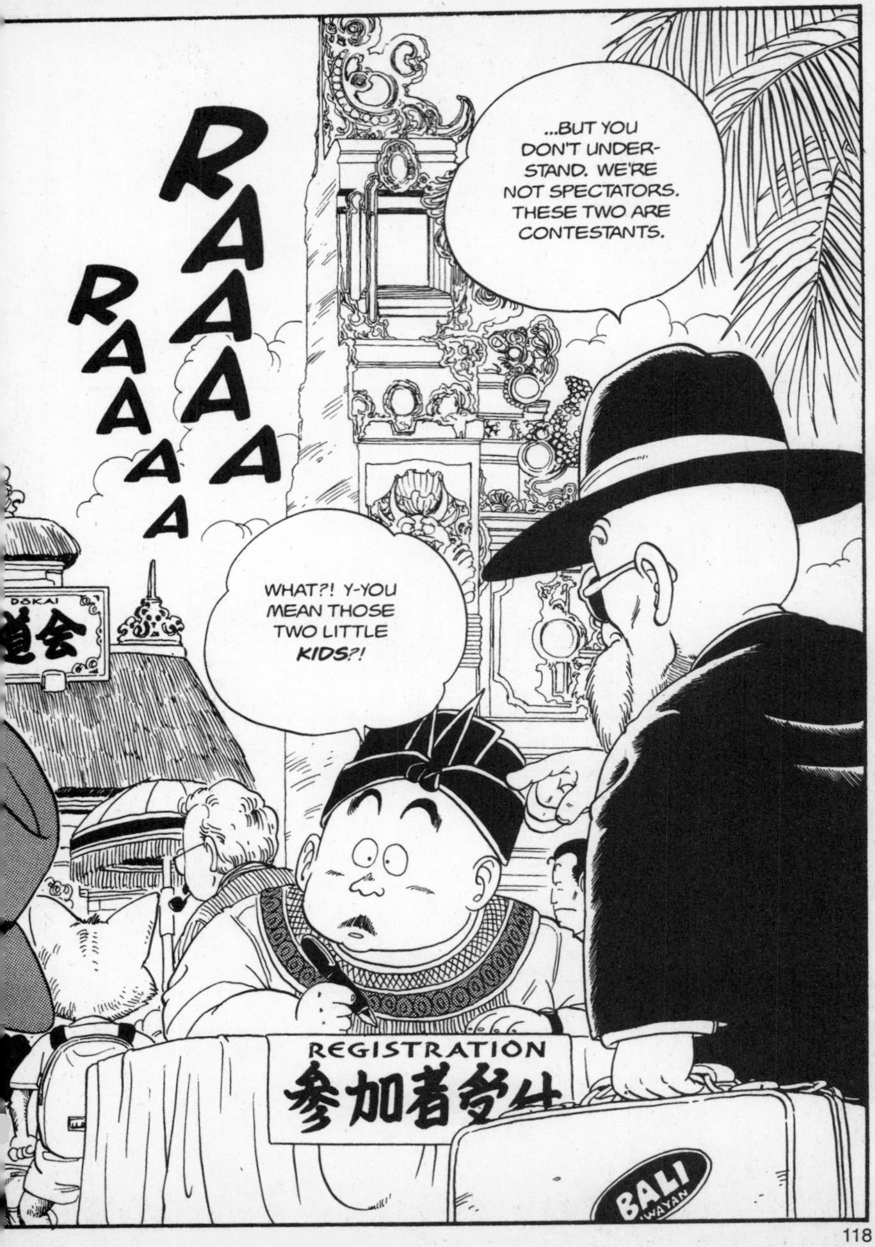
RAAAAA
RAAAA
...BUT YOU DON'T UNDER-STAND. WE'RE NOT SPECTATORS. THESE TWO ARE CONTESTANTS.
WHAT?! Y-YOU MEAN THOSE TWO LITTLE KIDS?!
DOKAI
道会
REGISTRATION
参加者受付
BALI
WAYAN

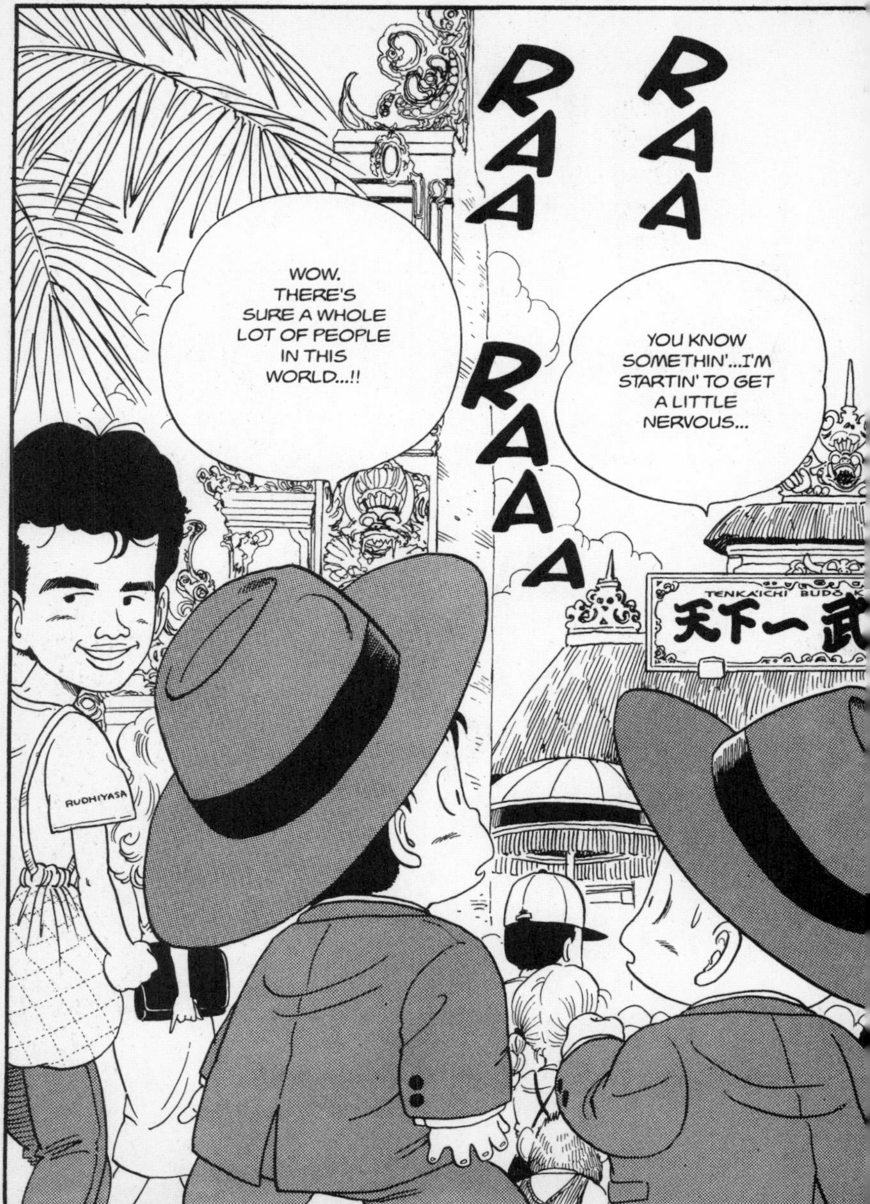
RAA
RAA
RAAAA
YOU KNOW SOMETHIN'...I'M STARTIN' TO GET A LITTLE NERVOUS...
WOW. THERE'S SURE A WHOLE LOT OF PEOPLE IN THIS WORLD...!!
TENKA'ICHI BUDŌ
天下一武
RUDHIYASA

NEXT: How Far Can They Go?!

Tale 33
Hard Work Pays!!

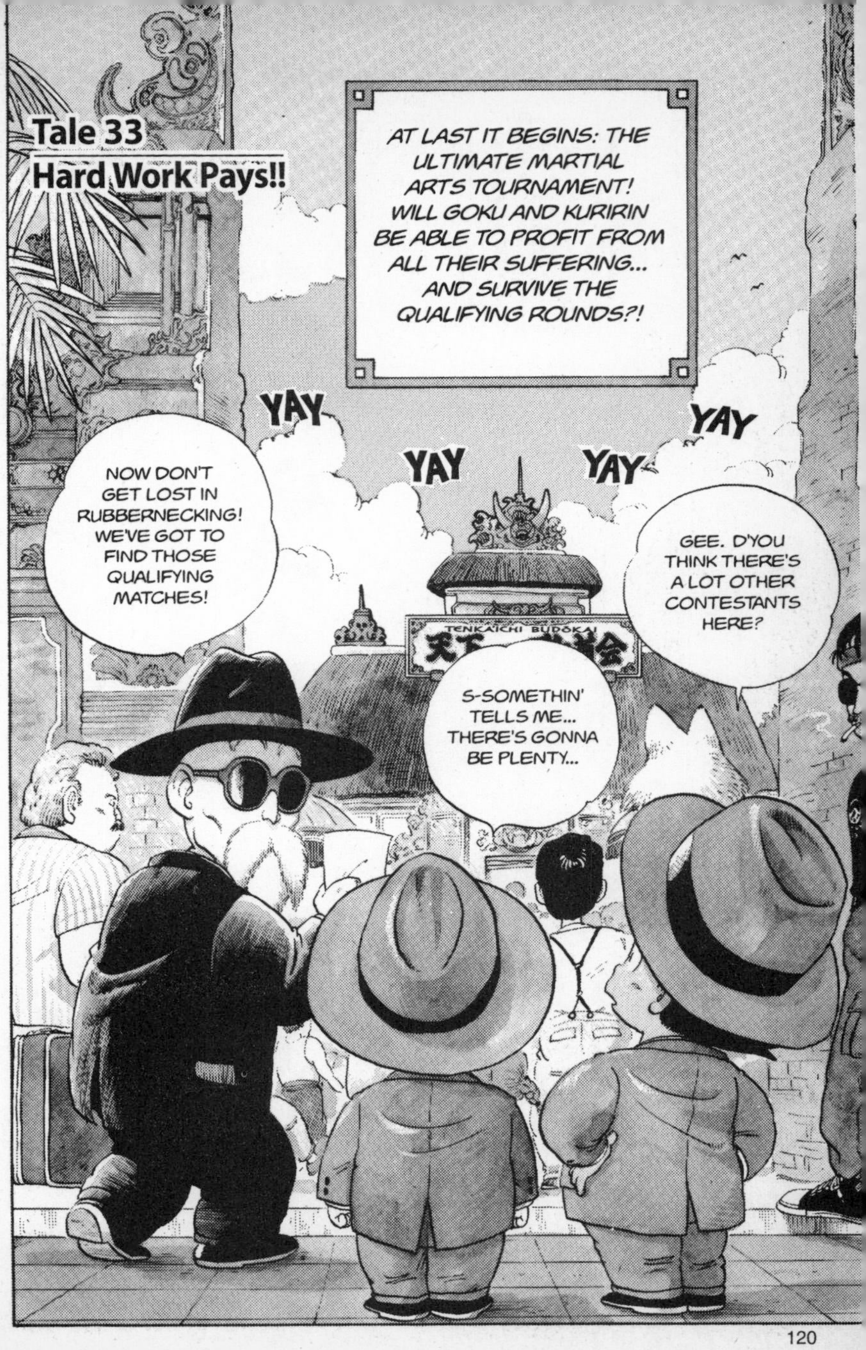
AT LAST IT BEGINS: THE ULTIMATE MARTIAL ARTS TOURNAMENT! WILL GOKU AND KURIRIN BE ABLE TO PROFIT FROM ALL THEIR SUFFERING... AND SURVIVE THE QUALIFYING ROUNDS?!
YAY
YAY
YAY
YAY
GEE. D'YOU THINK THERE'S A LOT OTHER CONTESTANTS HERE?
NOW DON'T GET LOST IN RUBBERNECKING! WE'VE GOT TO FIND THOSE QUALIFYING MATCHES!
TENKAICHI BUDOKAI
S-SOMETHIN' TELLS ME... THERE'S GONNA BE PLENTY...

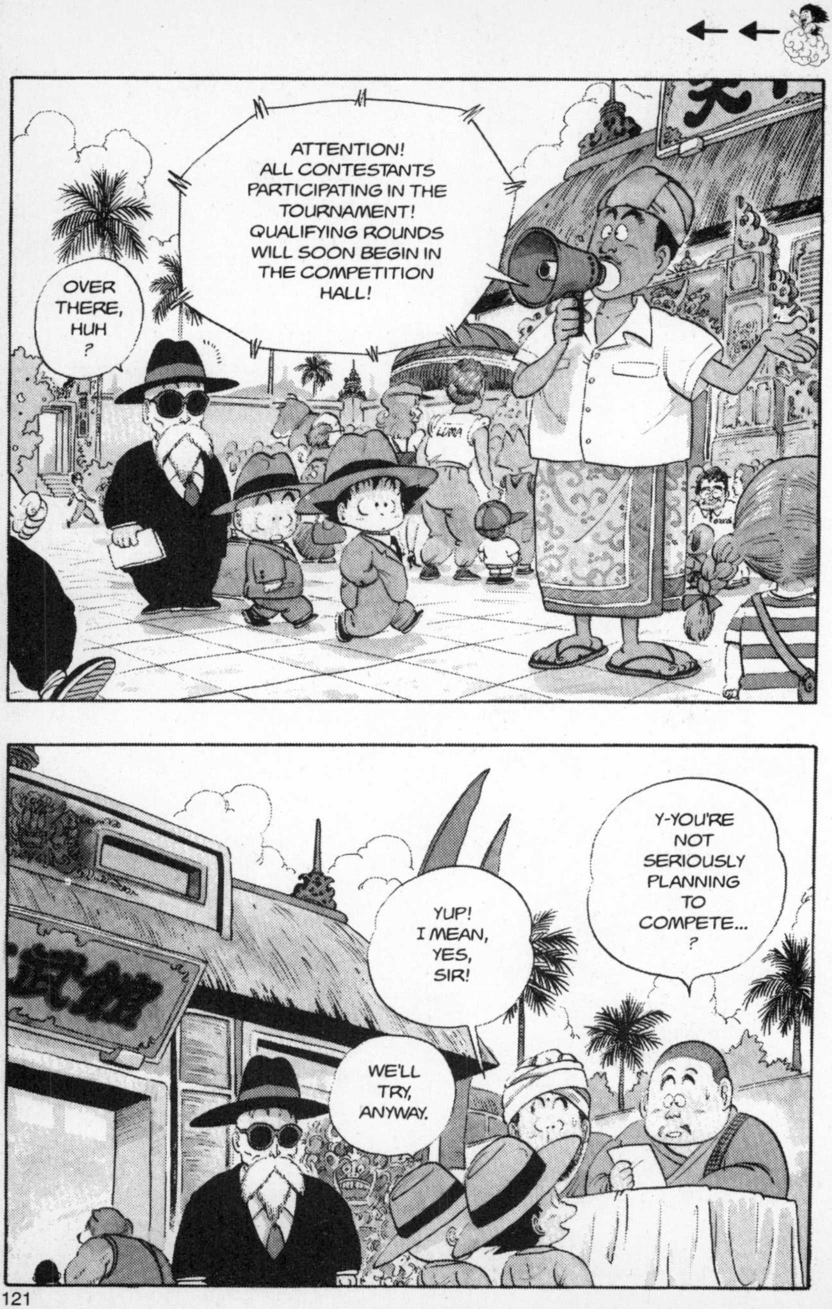
ATTENTION! ALL CONTESTANTS PARTICIPATING IN THE TOURNAMENT! QUALIFYING ROUNDS WILL SOON BEGIN IN THE COMPETITION HALL!
OVER THERE, HUH ?
Y-YOU'RE NOT SERIOUSLY PLANNING TO COMPETE... ?
YUP! I MEAN, YES, SIR!
WE'LL TRY, ANYWAY.

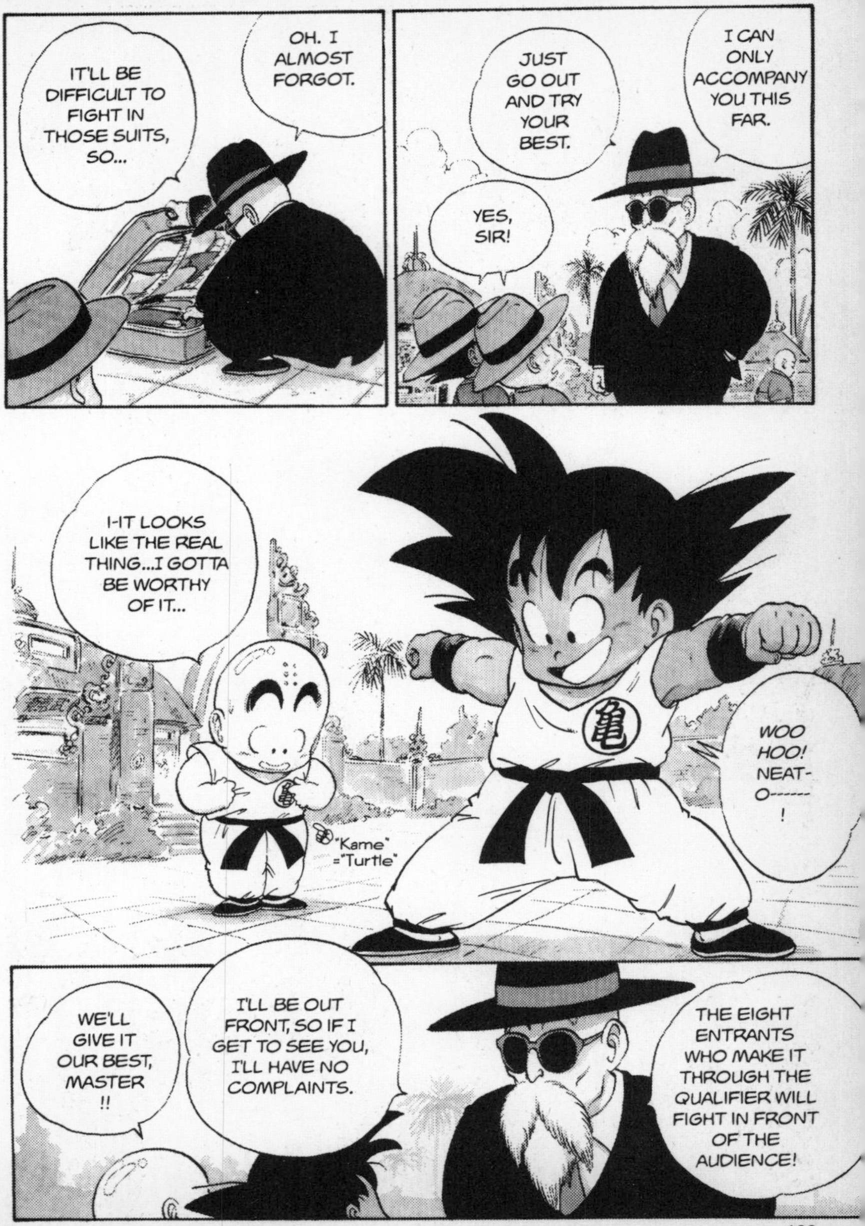
I CAN ONLY ACCOMPANY YOU THIS FAR.
JUST GO OUT AND TRY YOUR BEST.
YES, SIR!
OH. I ALMOST FORGOT.
IT'LL BE DIFFICULT TO FIGHT IN THOSE SUITS, SO...
WOO HOO! NEAT-O------!
I-IT LOOKS LIKE THE REAL THING...I GOTTA BE WORTHY OF IT...
"Kame" ="Turtle"
THE EIGHT ENTRANTS WHO MAKE IT THROUGH THE QUALIFIER WILL FIGHT IN FRONT OF THE AUDIENCE!
I'LL BE OUT FRONT, SO IF I GET TO SEE YOU, I'LL HAVE NO COMPLAINTS.
WE'LL GIVE IT OUR BEST, MASTER !!

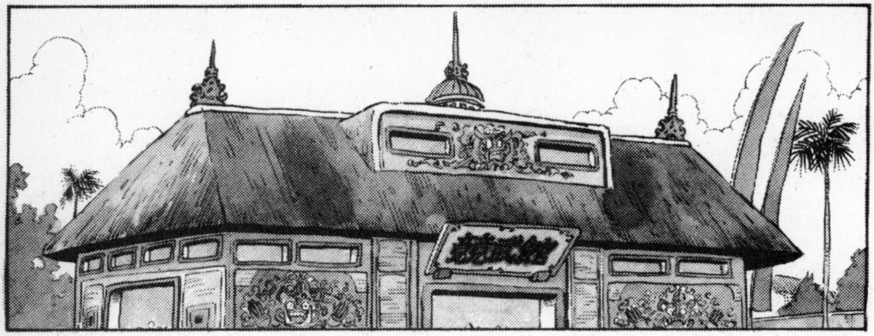

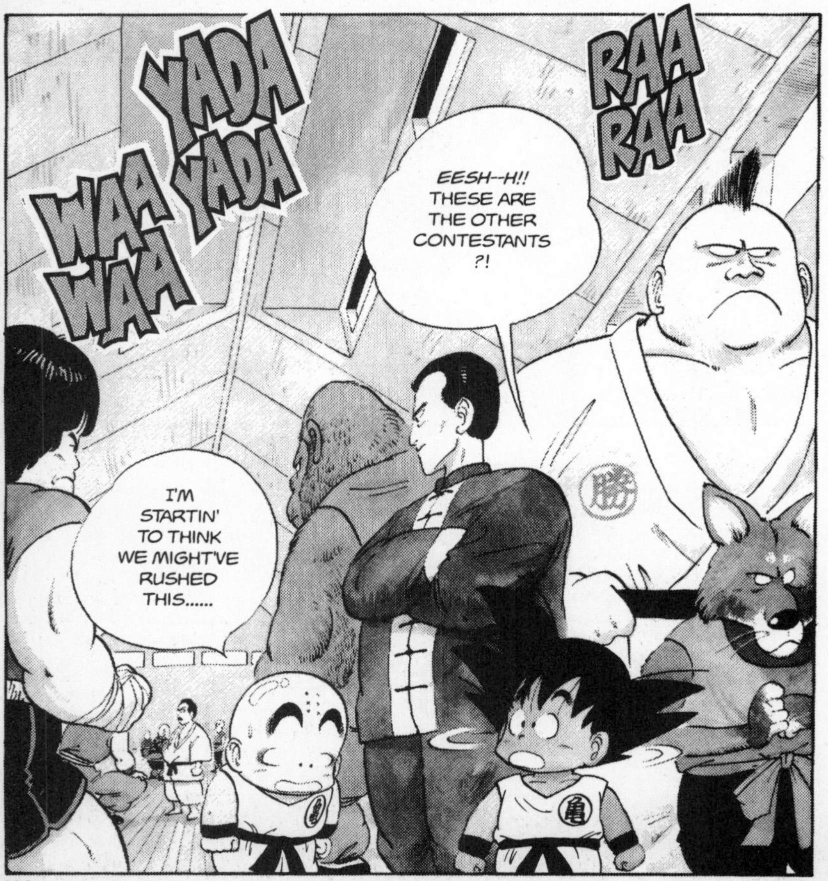

RAA RAA
EESH--H!! THESE ARE THE OTHER CONTESTANTS ?!
YADA YADA
WAA WAA
I'M STARTIN' TO THINK WE MIGHT'VE RUSHED THIS......

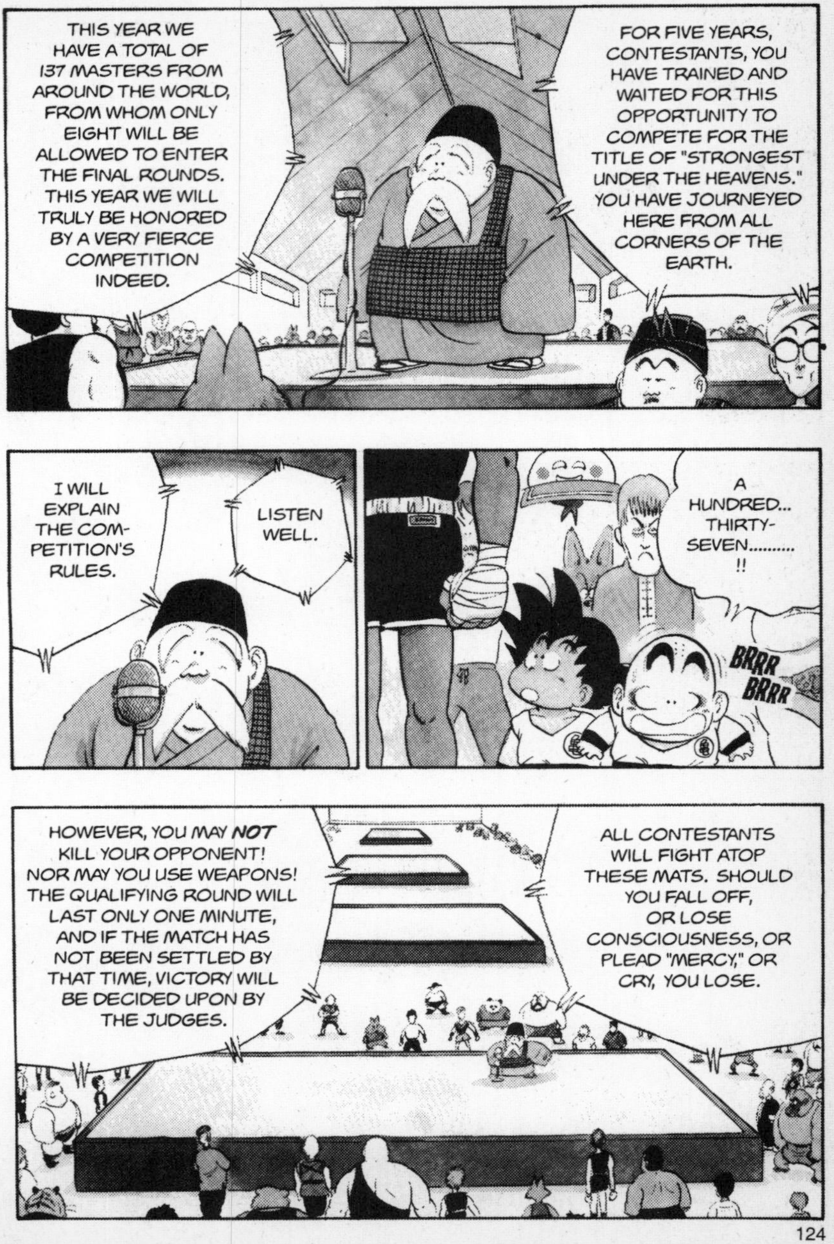
FOR FIVE YEARS, CONTESTANTS, YOU HAVE TRAINED AND WAITED FOR THIS OPPORTUNITY TO COMPETE FOR THE TITLE OF "STRONGEST UNDER THE HEAVENS." YOU HAVE JOURNEYED HERE FROM ALL CORNERS OF THE EARTH.
THIS YEAR WE HAVE A TOTAL OF 137 MASTERS FROM AROUND THE WORLD, FROM WHOM ONLY EIGHT WILL BE ALLOWED TO ENTER THE FINAL ROUNDS. THIS YEAR WE WILL TRULY BE HONORED BY A VERY FIERCE COMPETITION INDEED.
A HUNDRED... THIRTY-SEVEN.........!!
BRRR BRRR
LISTEN WELL.
I WILL EXPLAIN THE COMPETITION'S RULES.
ALL CONTESTANTS WILL FIGHT ATOP THESE MATS. SHOULD YOU FALL OFF, OR LOSE CONSCIOUSNESS, OR PLEAD "MERCY," OR CRY, YOU LOSE.
HOWEVER, YOU MAY ***NOT*** KILL YOUR OPPONENT! NOR MAY YOU USE WEAPONS! THE QUALIFYING ROUND WILL LAST ONLY ONE MINUTE, AND IF THE MATCH HAS NOT BEEN SETTLED BY THAT TIME, VICTORY WILL BE DECIDED UPON BY THE JUDGES.

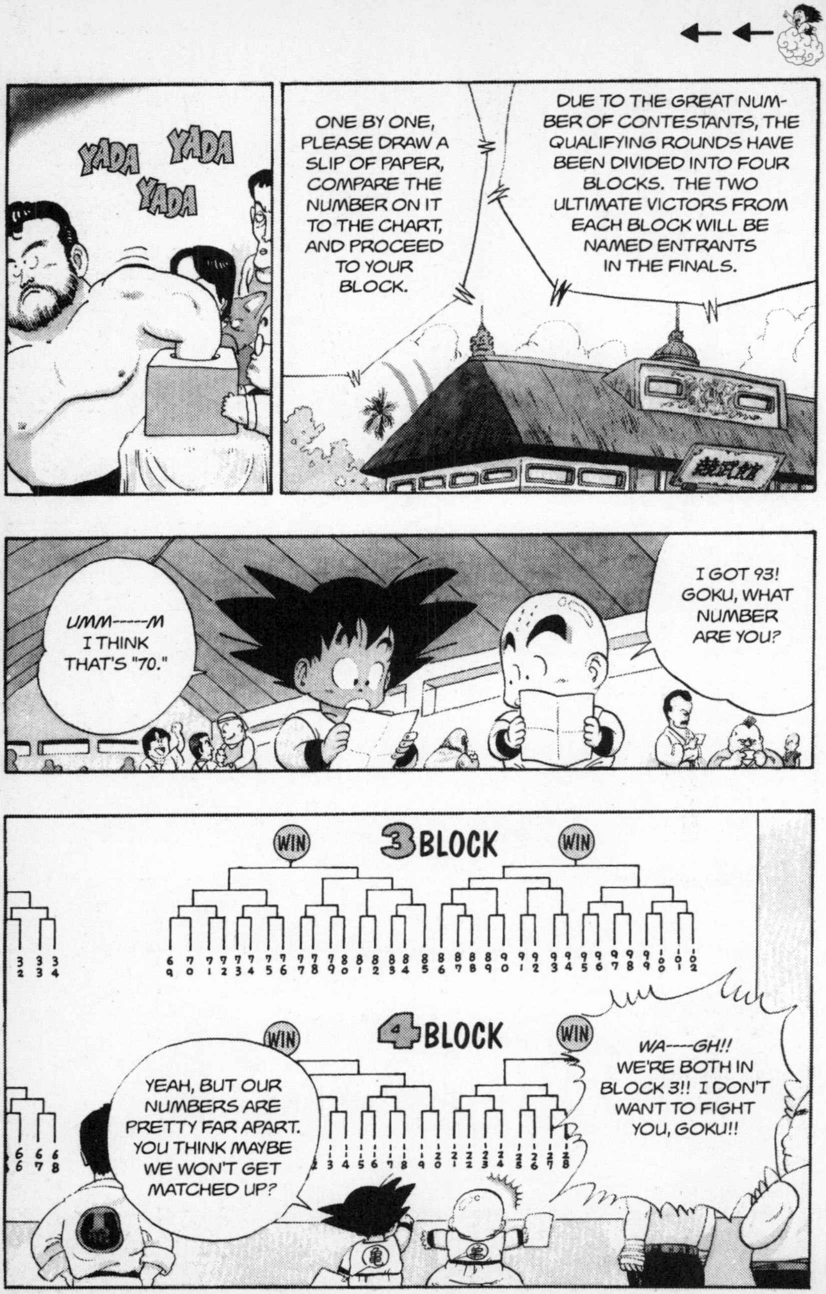
DUE TO THE GREAT NUMBER OF CONTESTANTS, THE QUALIFYING ROUNDS HAVE BEEN DIVIDED INTO FOUR BLOCKS. THE TWO ULTIMATE VICTORS FROM EACH BLOCK WILL BE NAMED ENTRANTS IN THE FINALS.
ONE BY ONE, PLEASE DRAW A SLIP OF PAPER, COMPARE THE NUMBER ON IT TO THE CHART, AND PROCEED TO YOUR BLOCK.
YADA YADA
YADA
I GOT 93! GOKU, WHAT NUMBER ARE YOU?
UMM-----M I THINK THAT'S "70."
WIN
3 BLOCK
WIN
WIN
4 BLOCK
WIN
WA----GH!! WE'RE BOTH IN BLOCK 3!! I DON'T WANT TO FIGHT YOU, GOKU!!
YEAH, BUT OUR NUMBERS ARE PRETTY FAR APART. YOU THINK MAYBE WE WON'T GET MATCHED UP?

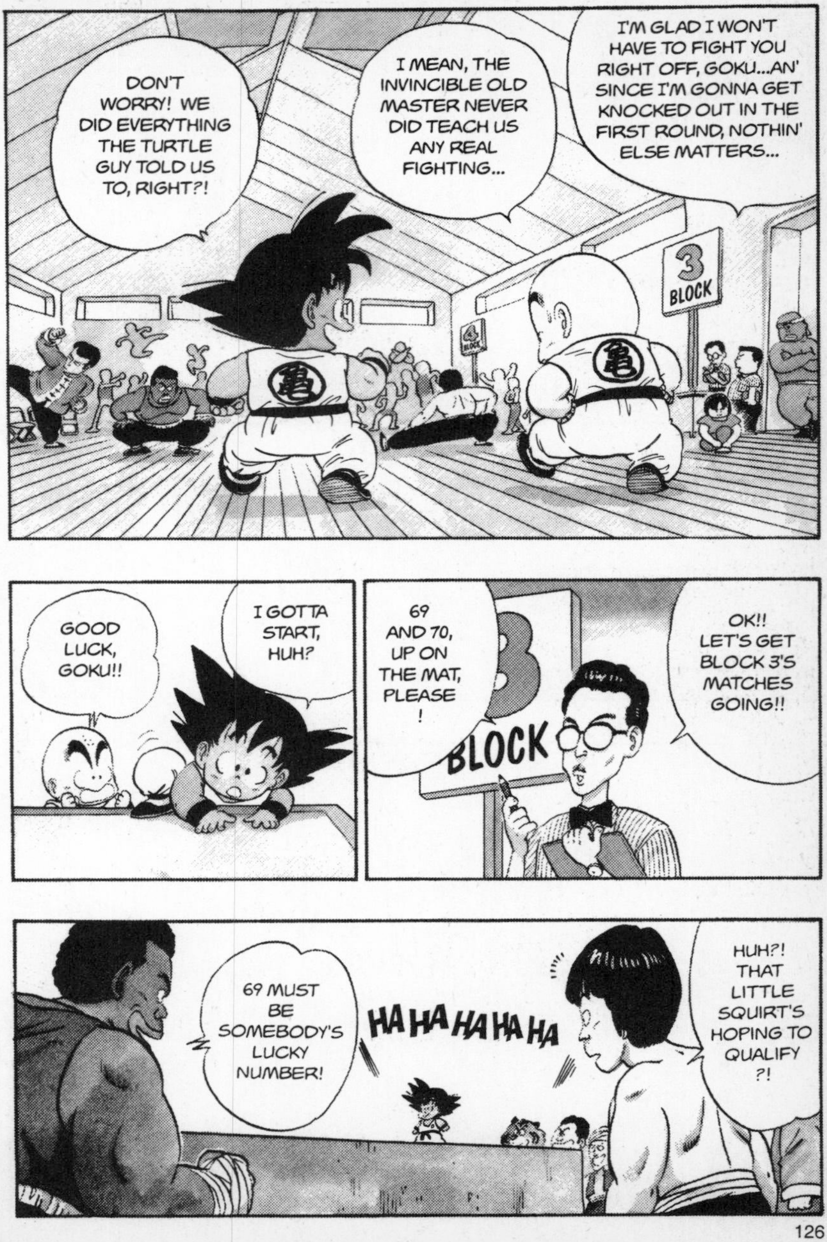
I'M GLAD I WON'T HAVE TO FIGHT YOU RIGHT OFF, GOKU...AN' SINCE I'M GONNA GET KNOCKED OUT IN THE FIRST ROUND, NOTHIN' ELSE MATTERS...
I MEAN, THE INVINCIBLE OLD MASTER NEVER DID TEACH US ANY REAL FIGHTING...
DON'T WORRY! WE DID EVERYTHING THE TURTLE GUY TOLD US TO, RIGHT?!
3 BLOCK
OK!! LET'S GET BLOCK 3'S MATCHES GOING!!
69 AND 70, UP ON THE MAT, PLEASE!
BLOCK
I GOTTA START, HUH?
GOOD LUCK, GOKU!!
HUH?! THAT LITTLE SQUIRT'S HOPING TO QUALIFY?!
HA HA HA HA HA HA
69 MUST BE SOMEBODY'S LUCKY NUMBER!

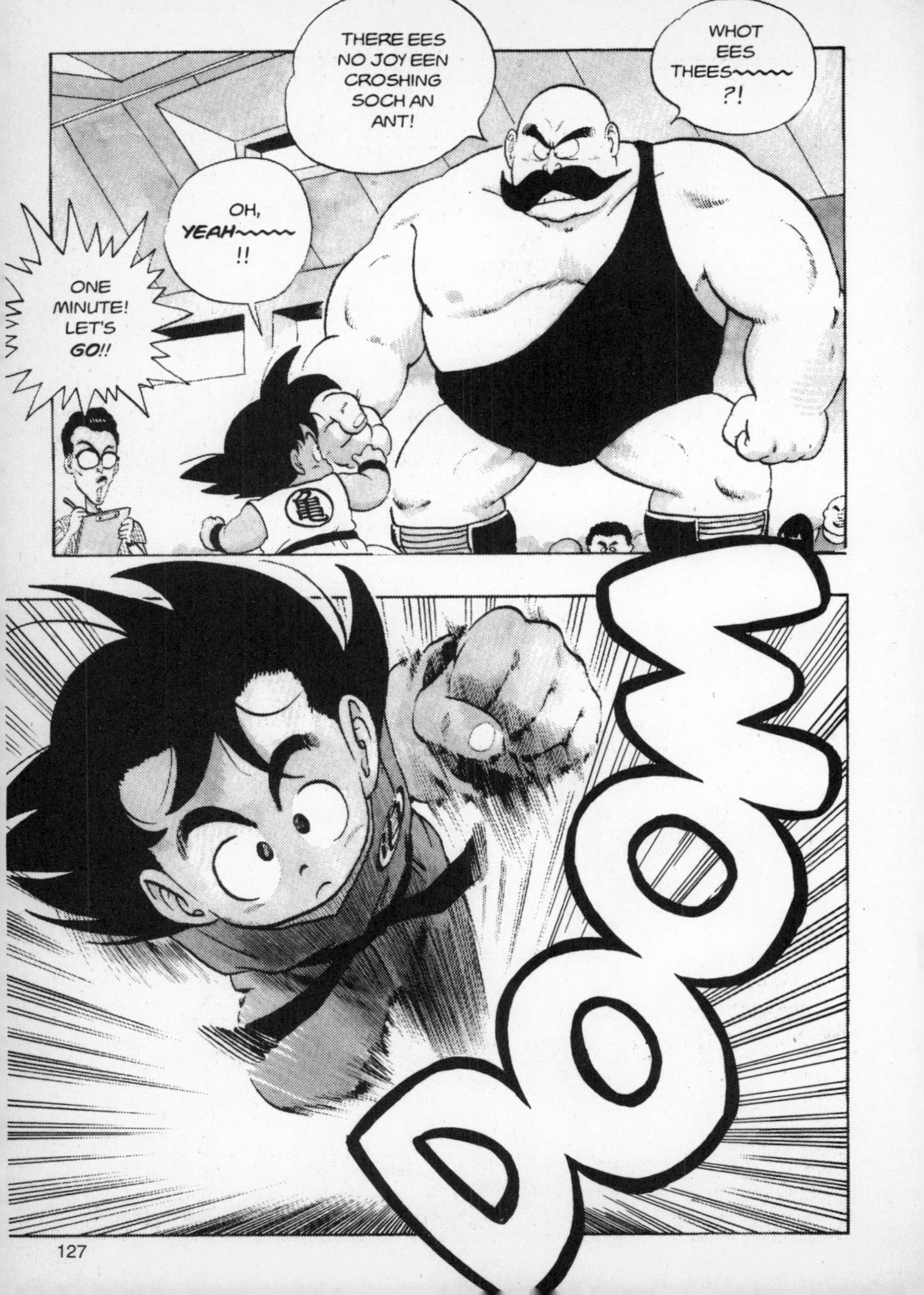
WHOT EES THEES~~~~ ?!
THERE EES NO JOY EEN CROSHING SOCH AN ANT!
OH, YEAH~~~~ !!
ONE MINUTE! LET'S GO!!
BOOM

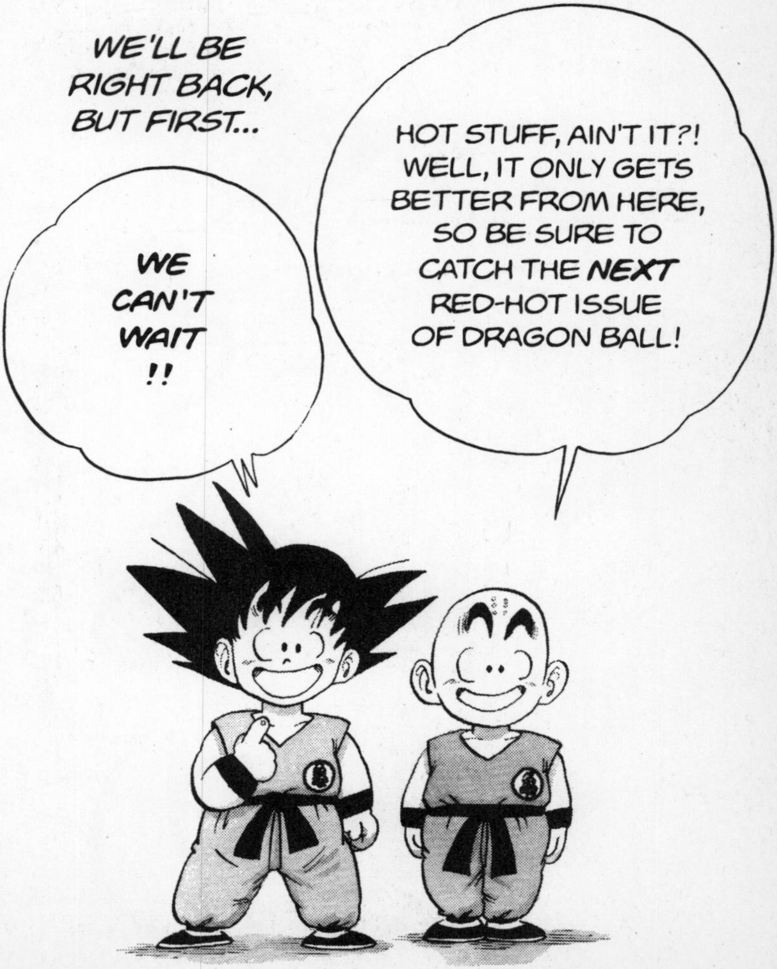
HOT STUFF, AIN'T IT?! WELL, IT ONLY GETS BETTER FROM HERE, SO BE SURE TO CATCH THE **NEXT** RED-HOT ISSUE OF DRAGON BALL!
WE'LL BE RIGHT BACK, BUT FIRST...
WE CAN'T WAIT !!

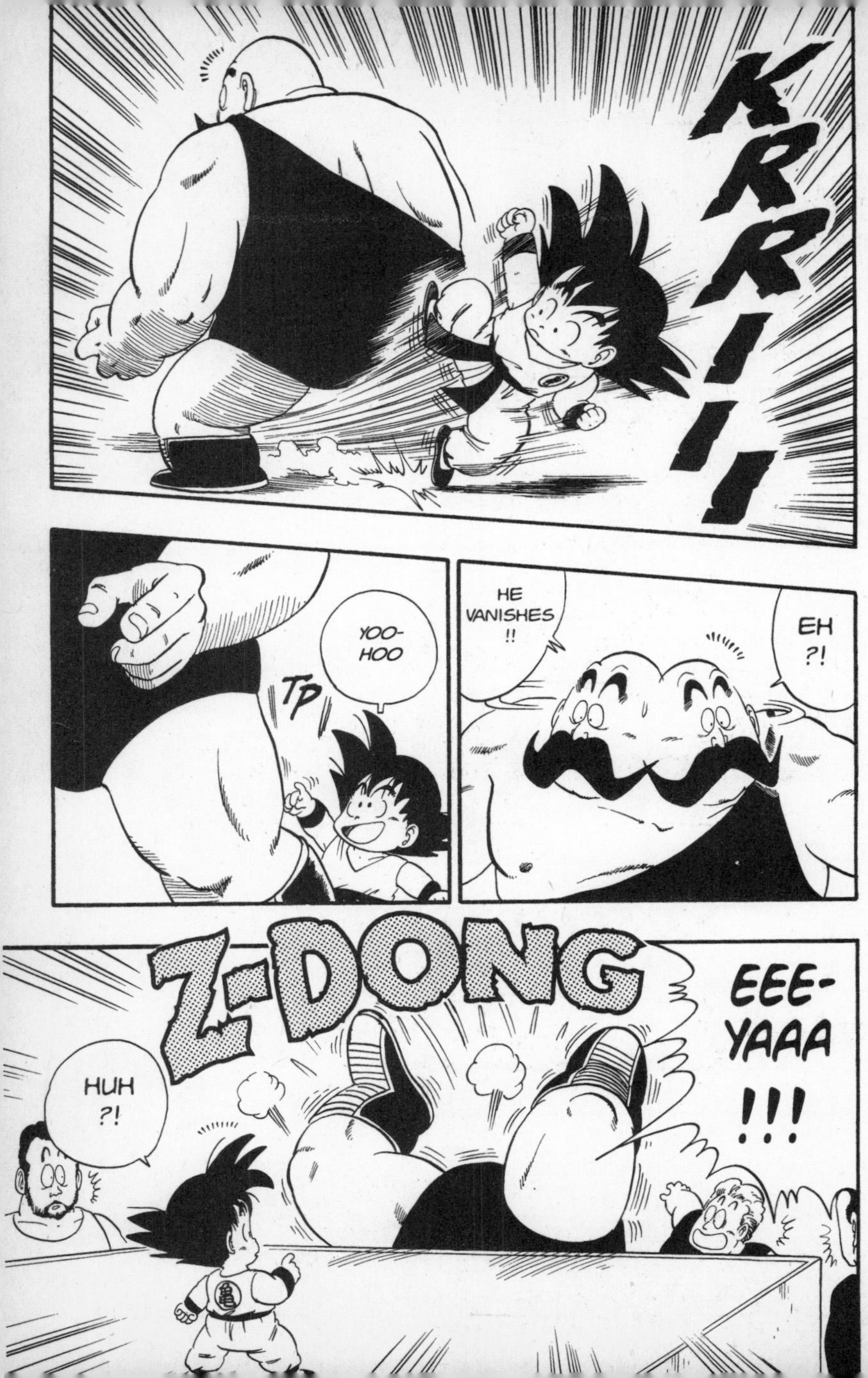
KRRIII
EH ?!
HE VANISHES !!
TP
YOO-HOO
EEE-YAAA !!!
Z-DONG
HUH ?!

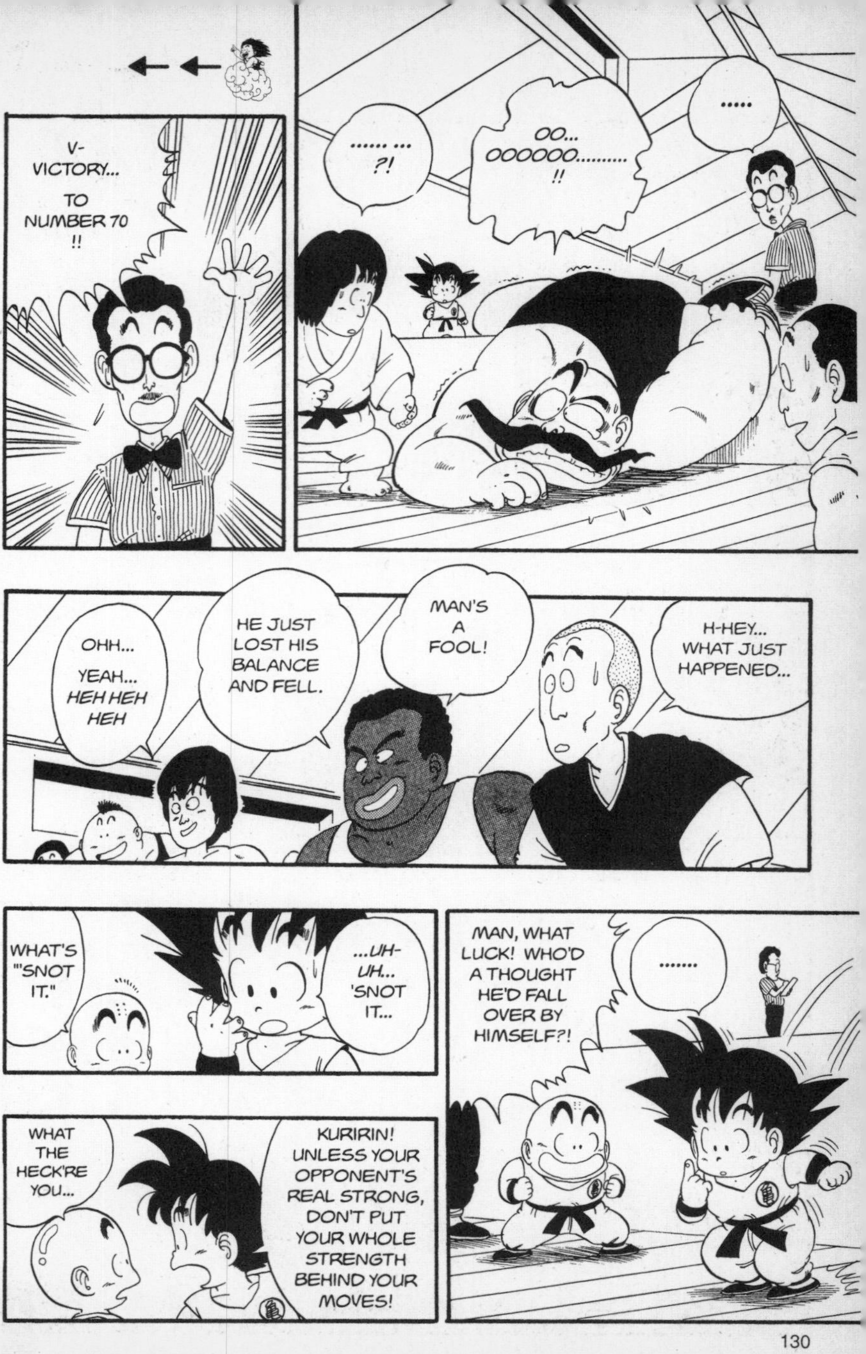
.....
OO... OOOOOO.......... !!
.... ?!
V-VICTORY... TO NUMBER 70 !!
H-HEY... WHAT JUST HAPPENED...
MAN'S A FOOL!
HE JUST LOST HIS BALANCE AND FELL.
OHH... YEAH... HEH HEH HEH
....
MAN, WHAT LUCK! WHO'D A THOUGHT HE'D FALL OVER BY HIMSELF?!
...UH-UH... 'SNOT IT...
WHAT'S "'SNOT IT."
KURIRIN! UNLESS YOUR OPPONENT'S REAL STRONG, DON'T PUT YOUR WHOLE STRENGTH BEHIND YOUR MOVES!
WHAT THE HECK'RE YOU...

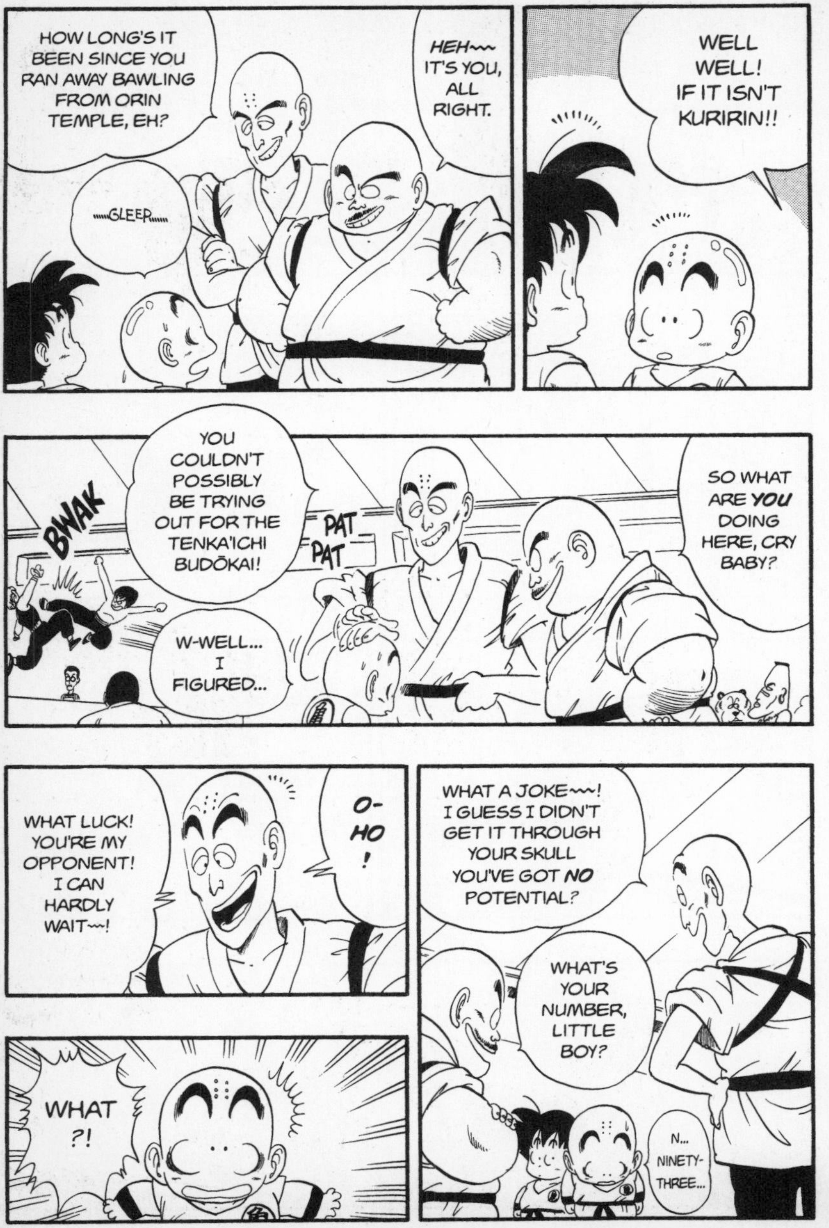
WELL WELL! IF IT ISN'T KURIRIN!!
HEH~~ IT'S YOU, ALL RIGHT.
HOW LONG'S IT BEEN SINCE YOU RAN AWAY BAWLING FROM ORIN TEMPLE, EH?
...GLEEP...
SO WHAT ARE YOU DOING HERE, CRY BABY?
PAT PAT
YOU COULDN'T POSSIBLY BE TRYING OUT FOR THE TENKA'ICHI BUDŌKAI!
W-WELL... I FIGURED...
BWAK
WHAT A JOKE~~! I GUESS I DIDN'T GET IT THROUGH YOUR SKULL YOU'VE GOT NO POTENTIAL?
WHAT'S YOUR NUMBER, LITTLE BOY?
N... NINETY-THREE...
O-HO!
WHAT LUCK! YOU'RE MY OPPONENT! I CAN HARDLY WAIT~~!
WHAT?!

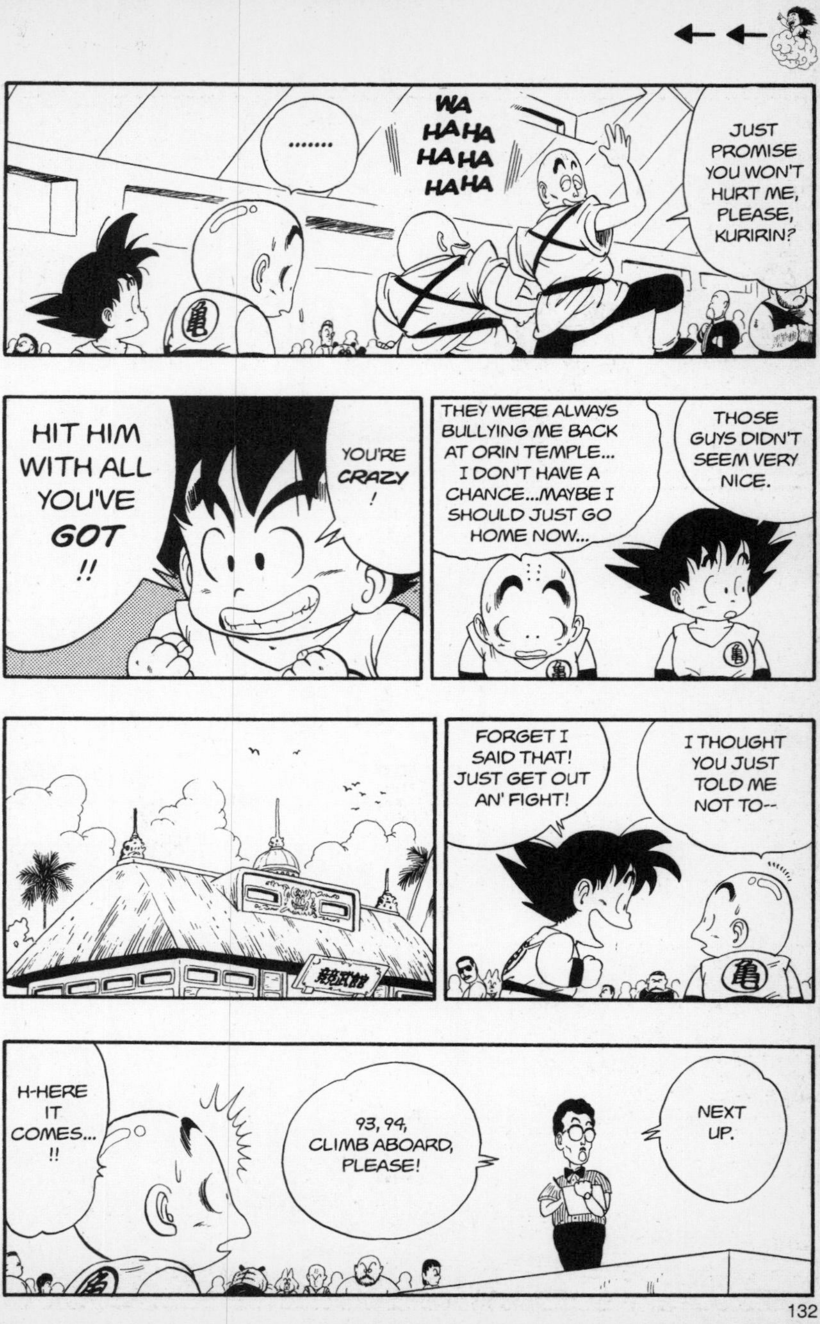
JUST PROMISE YOU WON'T HURT ME, PLEASE, KURIRIN?
WA HAHA HAHA HAHA
....
THOSE GUYS DIDN'T SEEM VERY NICE.
THEY WERE ALWAYS BULLYING ME BACK AT ORIN TEMPLE... I DON'T HAVE A CHANCE...MAYBE I SHOULD JUST GO HOME NOW...
YOU'RE CRAZY!
HIT HIM WITH ALL YOU'VE GOT!!
I THOUGHT YOU JUST TOLD ME NOT TO--
FORGET I SAID THAT! JUST GET OUT AN' FIGHT!
NEXT UP.
93, 94, CLIMB ABOARD, PLEASE!
H-HERE IT COMES...!!

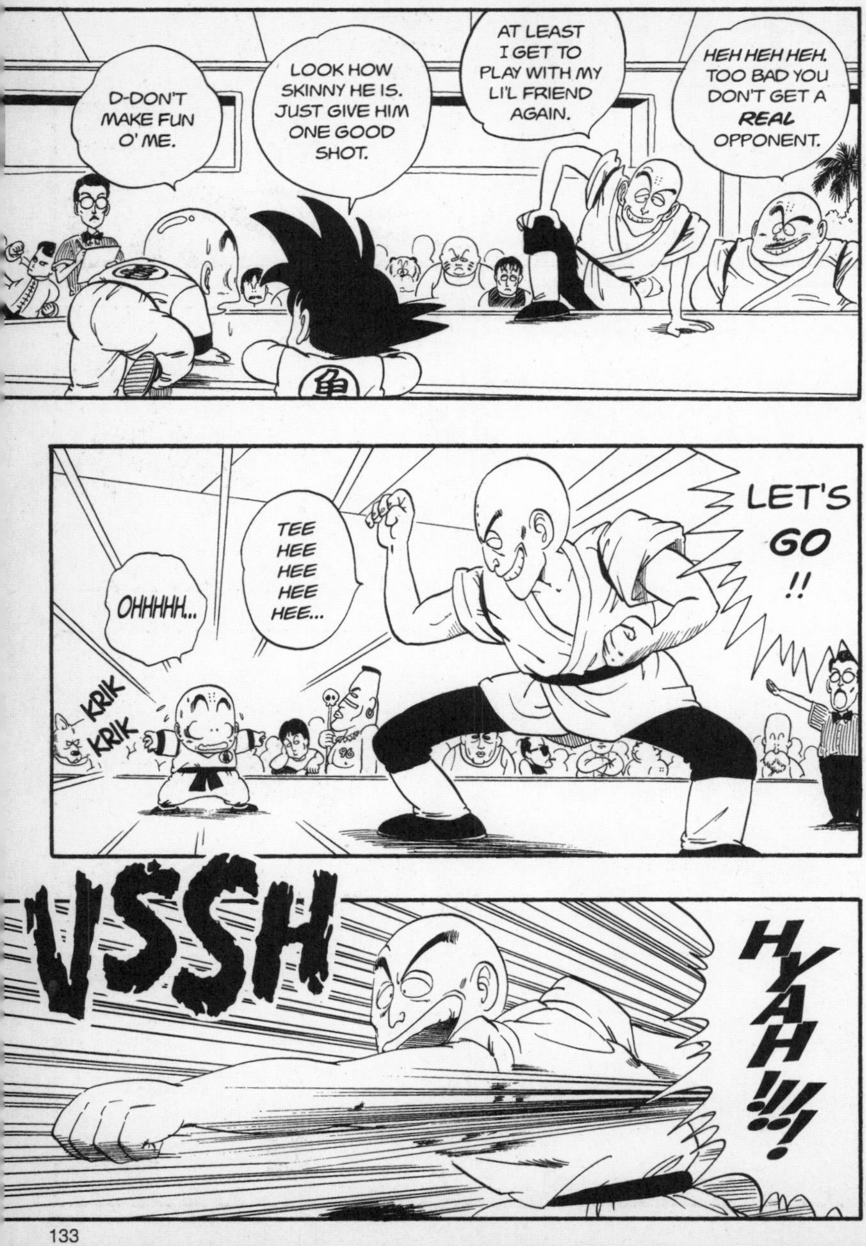
HEH HEH HEH. TOO BAD YOU DON'T GET A REAL OPPONENT.
AT LEAST I GET TO PLAY WITH MY LI'L FRIEND AGAIN.
LOOK HOW SKINNY HE IS. JUST GIVE HIM ONE GOOD SHOT.
D-DON'T MAKE FUN O' ME.
LET'S GO !!
TEE HEE HEE HEE HEE...
OHHHHH...
KRIK KRIK
HYAH!!!!
VSSH

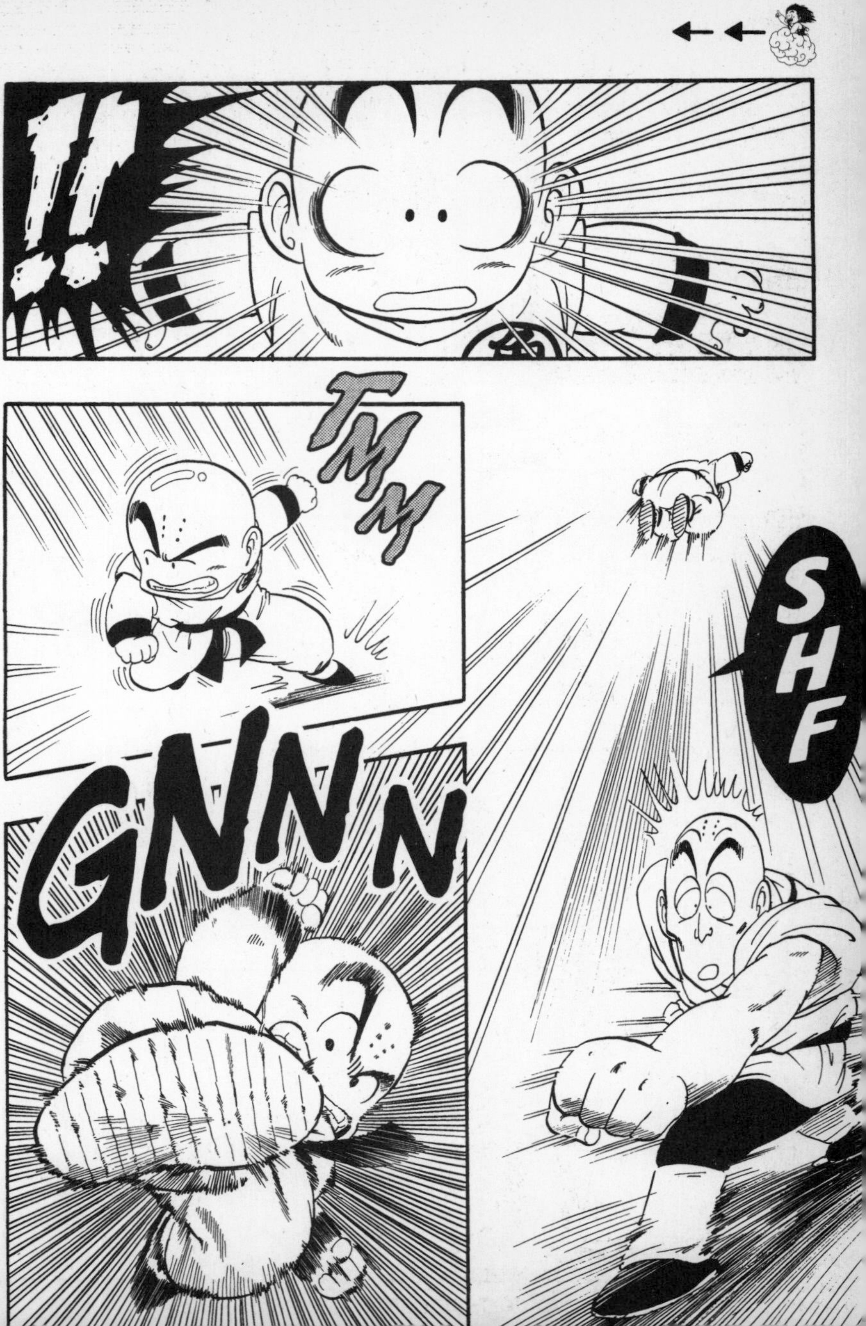
!!
SHF
TMM
GNNN

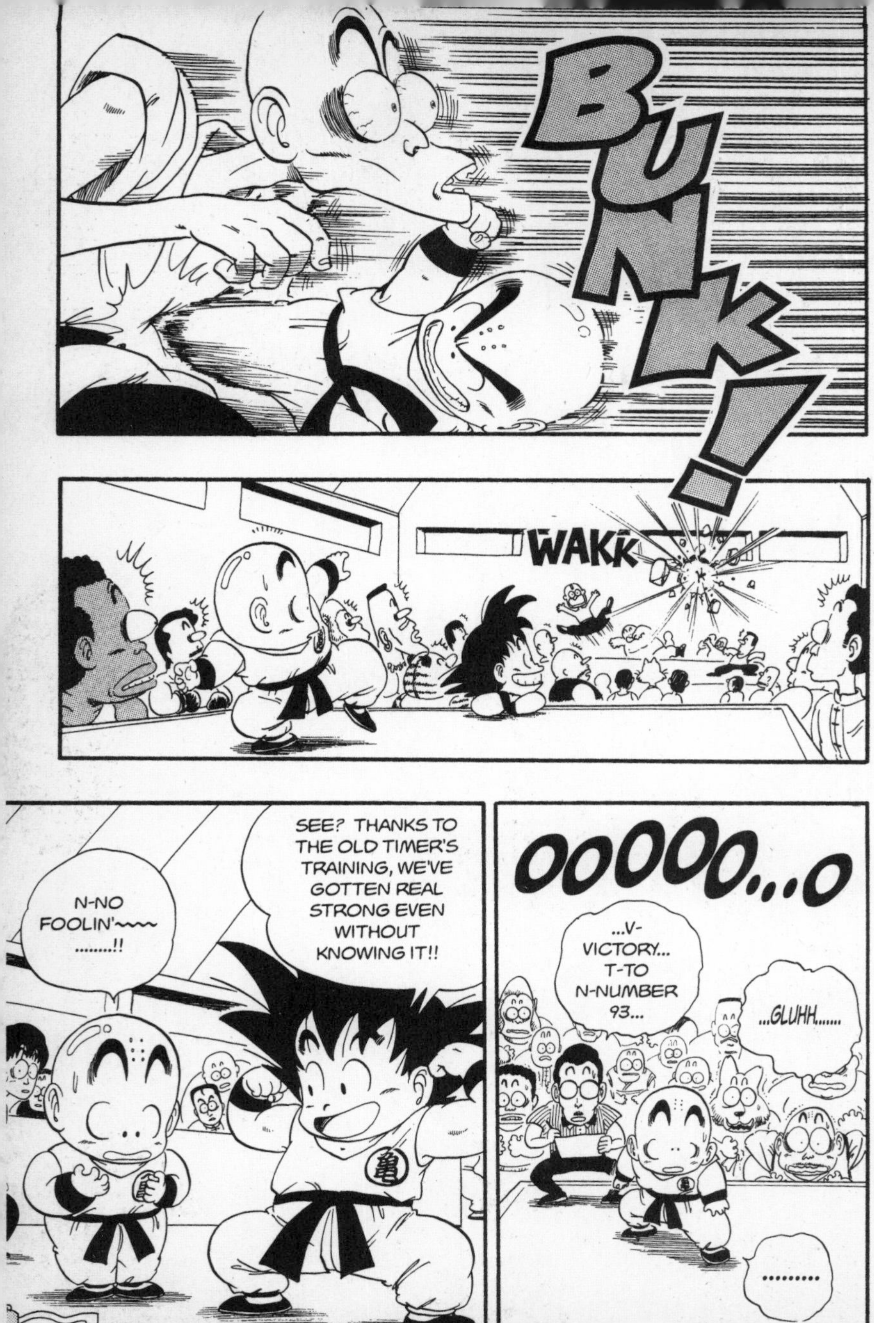
BUNK!
WAKK
OOOOO...O
...V- VICTORY... T-TO N-NUMBER 93...
...GLUHH......
....
SEE? THANKS TO THE OLD TIMER'S TRAINING, WE'VE GOTTEN REAL STRONG EVEN WITHOUT KNOWING IT!!
N-NO FOOLIN'~~~ ....!!

AND HOW! NEXT: Strongest Under the Heavens

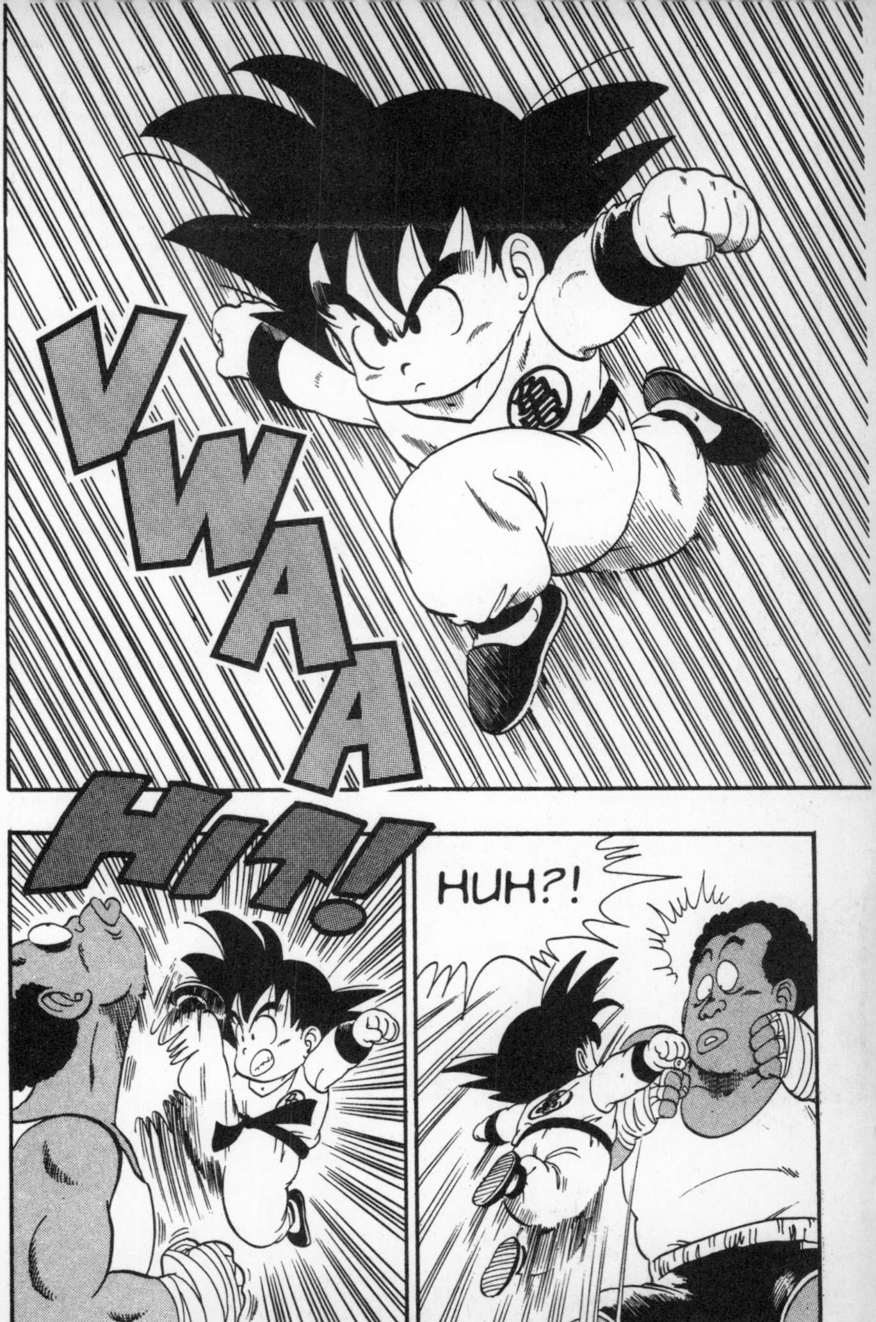
VWAA
HUH?!
HIT!

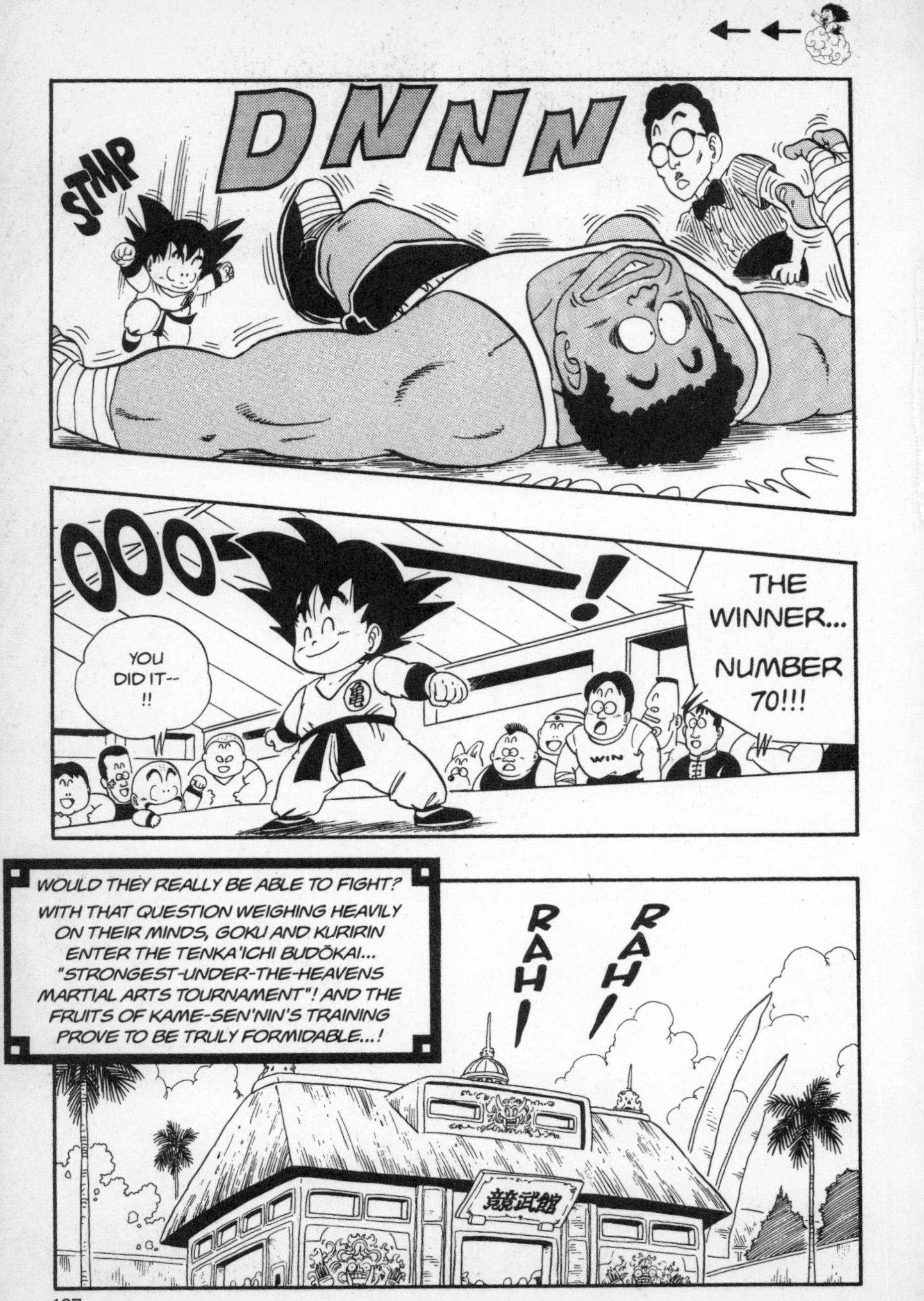
DNNN
STMP
THE WINNER... NUMBER 70!!!
OOO—!
YOU DID IT--!!
WIN
RAH!
RAH!
WOULD THEY REALLY BE ABLE TO FIGHT? WITH THAT QUESTION WEIGHING HEAVILY ON THEIR MINDS, GOKU AND KURIRIN ENTER THE TENKA'ICHI BUDŌKAI... "STRONGEST-UNDER-THE-HEAVENS MARTIAL ARTS TOURNAMENT"! AND THE FRUITS OF KAME-SEN'NIN'S TRAINING PROVE TO BE TRULY FORMIDABLE...!
競武館

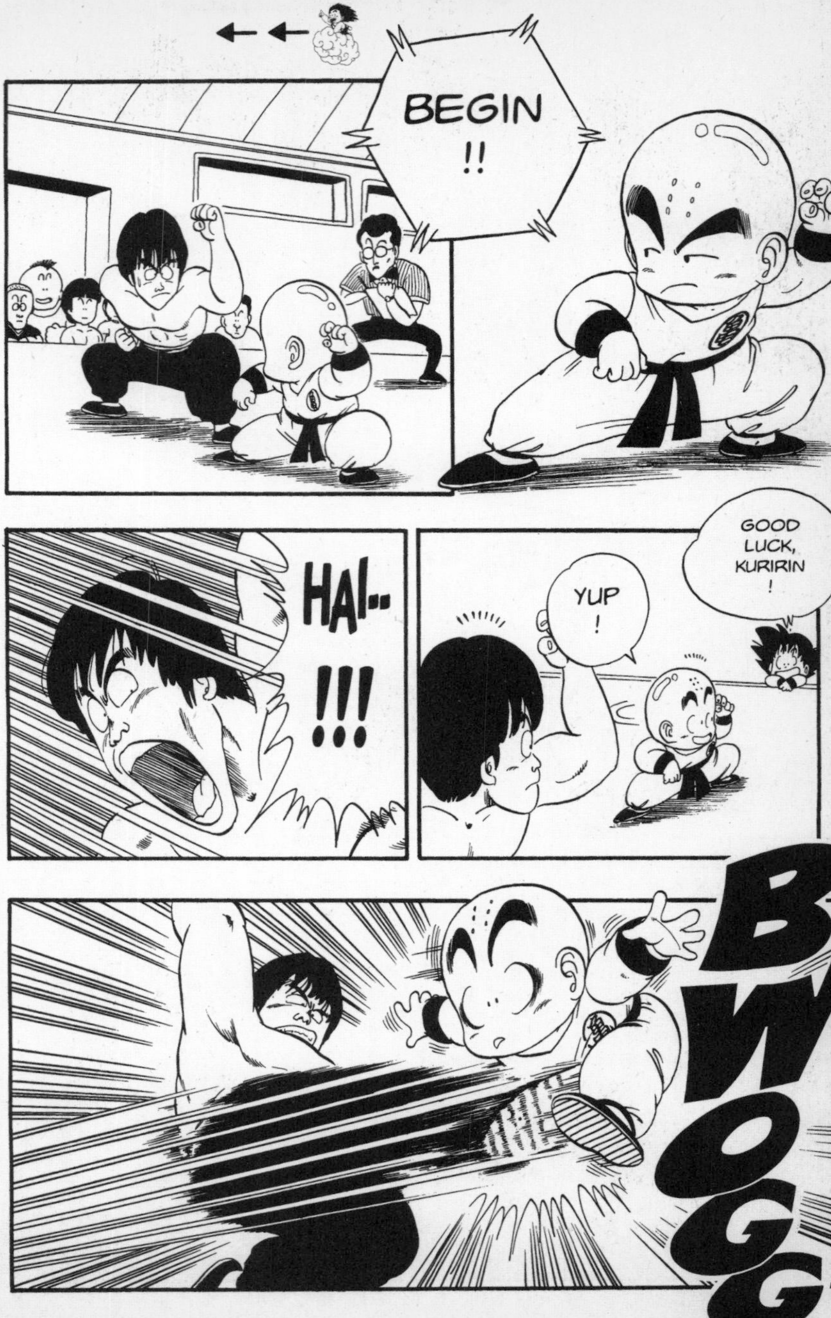
BEGIN !!
GOOD LUCK, KURIRIN !
YUP !
HAI.. !!!
BWOGG

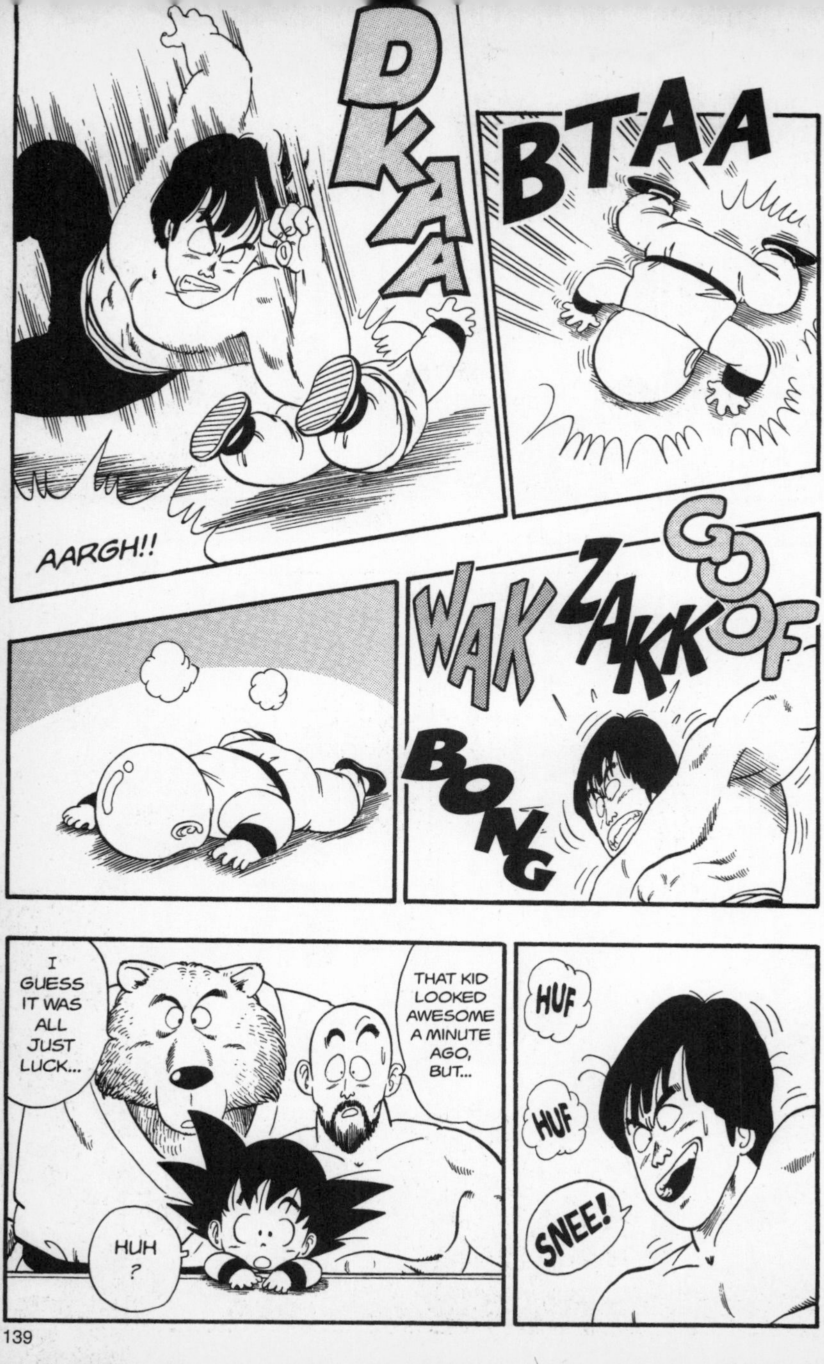
BTAA
DKAAA
AARGH!!
GOOF
ZAKK
WAK
BONG
HUF
HUF
SNEE!
THAT KID LOOKED AWESOME A MINUTE AGO, BUT...
I GUESS IT WAS ALL JUST LUCK...
HUH ?

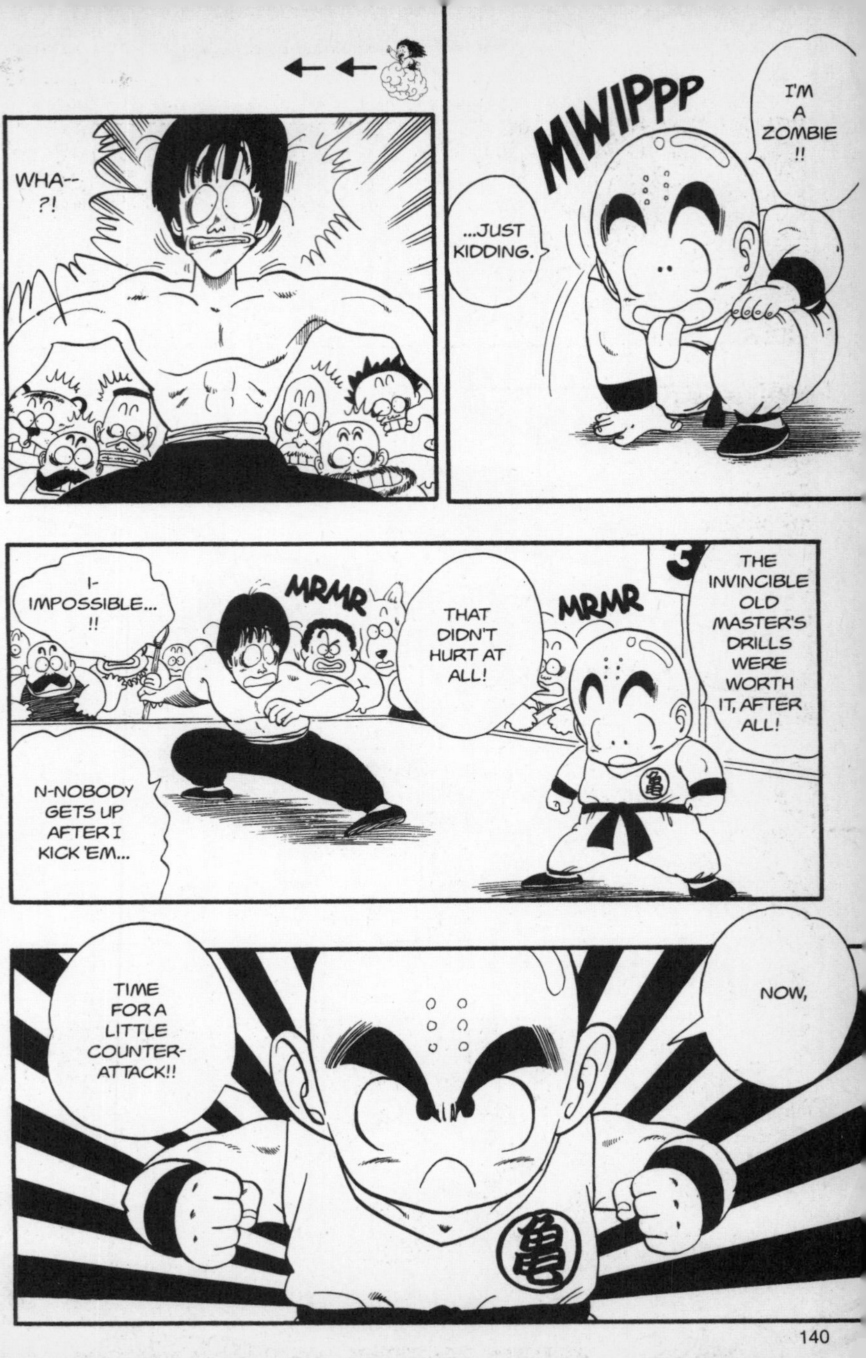
MWIPPP
I'M A ZOMBIE!!
...JUST KIDDING.
WHA--?!
THE INVINCIBLE OLD MASTER'S DRILLS WERE WORTH IT, AFTER ALL!
MRMR
THAT DIDN'T HURT AT ALL!
MRMR
I-IMPOSSIBLE...!!
N-NOBODY GETS UP AFTER I KICK 'EM...
NOW,
TIME FOR A LITTLE COUNTER-ATTACK!!

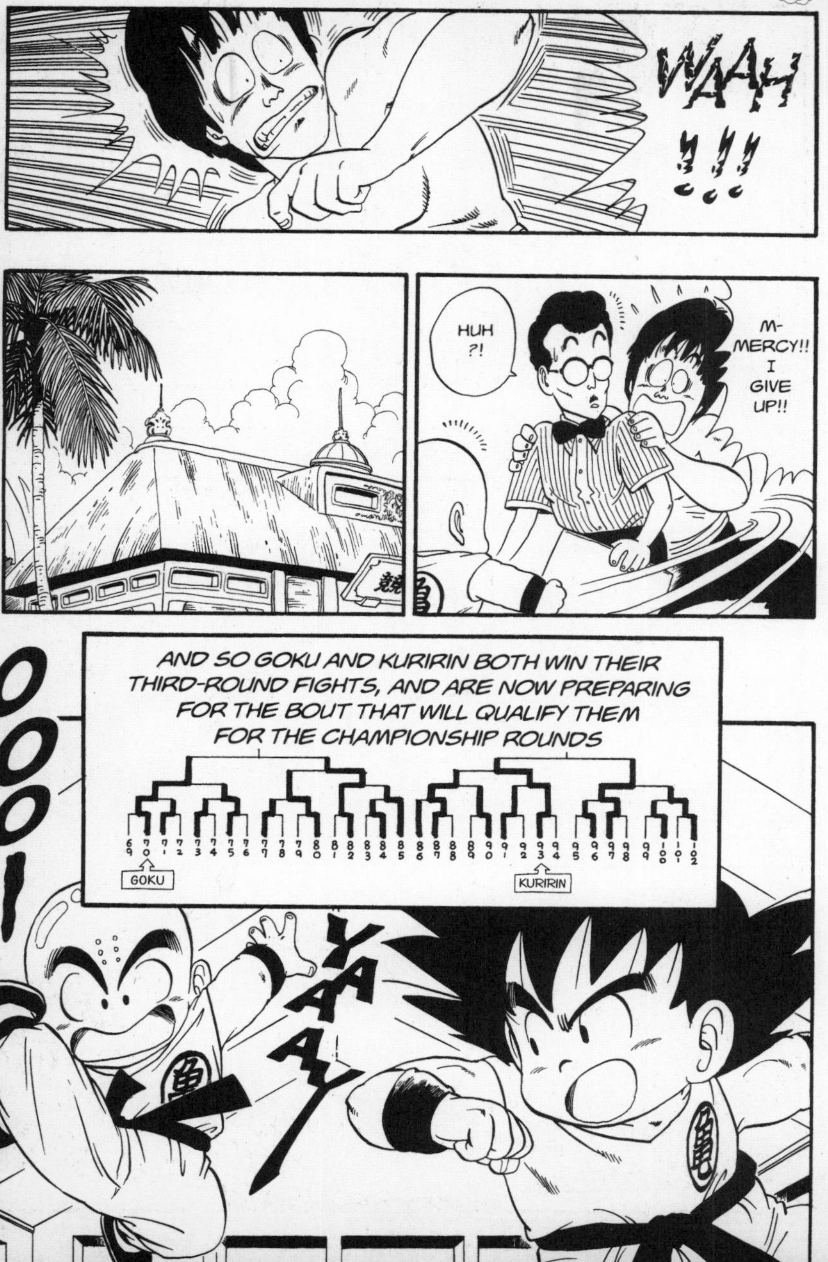
WAAH!!!
HUH?!
M-MERCY!! I GIVE UP!!
AND SO GOKU AND KURIRIN BOTH WIN THEIR THIRD-ROUND FIGHTS, AND ARE NOW PREPARING FOR THE BOUT THAT WILL QUALIFY THEM FOR THE CHAMPIONSHIP ROUNDS
GOKU
KURIRIN
OOOO!
YAAAY!

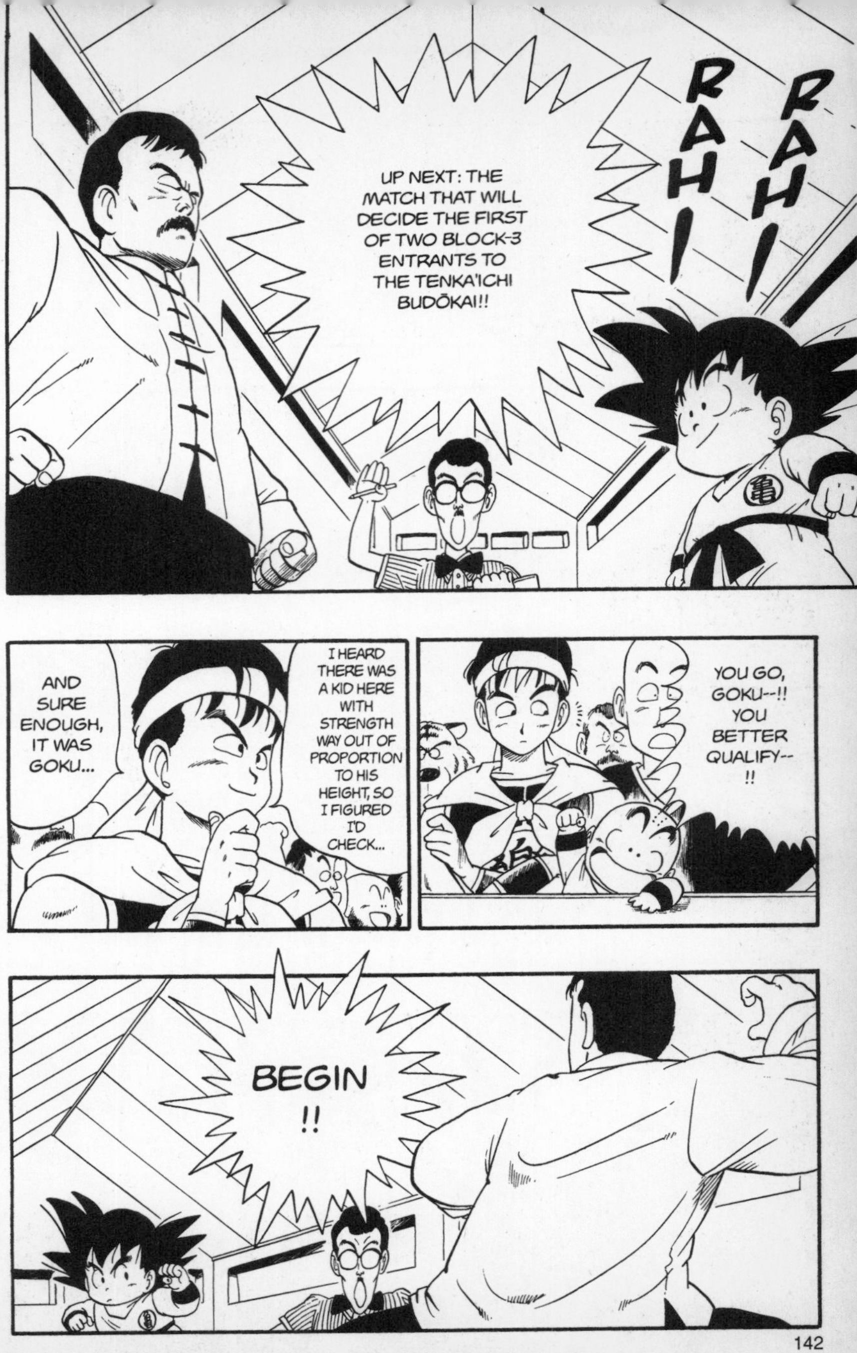
RAH!!
RAH!!
UP NEXT: THE MATCH THAT WILL DECIDE THE FIRST OF TWO BLOCK-3 ENTRANTS TO THE TENKA'ICHI BUDŌKAI!!
YOU GO, GOKU--!! YOU BETTER QUALIFY--!!
I HEARD THERE WAS A KID HERE WITH STRENGTH WAY OUT OF PROPORTION TO HIS HEIGHT, SO I FIGURED I'D CHECK...
AND SURE ENOUGH, IT WAS GOKU...
BEGIN!!

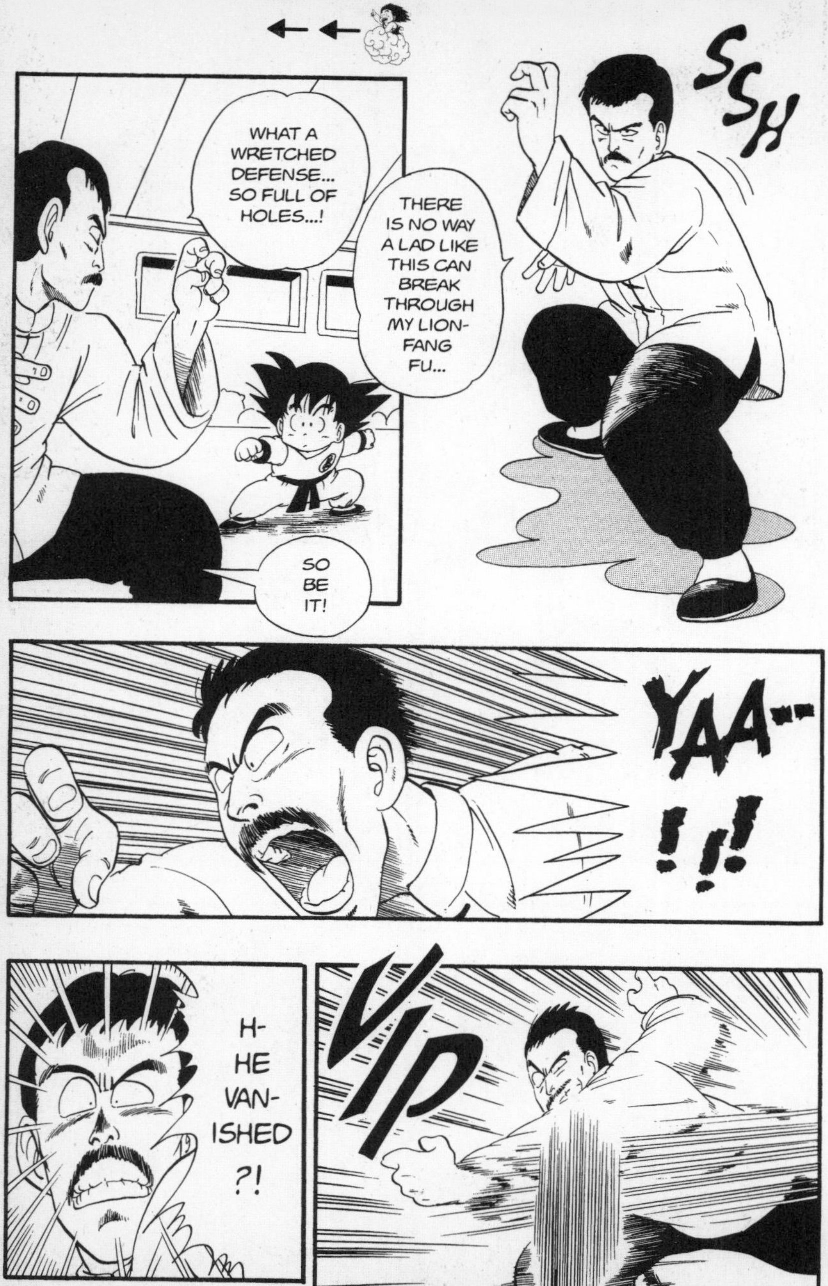
SSH
THERE IS NO WAY A LAD LIKE THIS CAN BREAK THROUGH MY LION-FANG FU...
WHAT A WRETCHED DEFENSE... SO FULL OF HOLES...!
SO BE IT!
YAA--!!!
VIP
H-HE VAN-ISHED?!

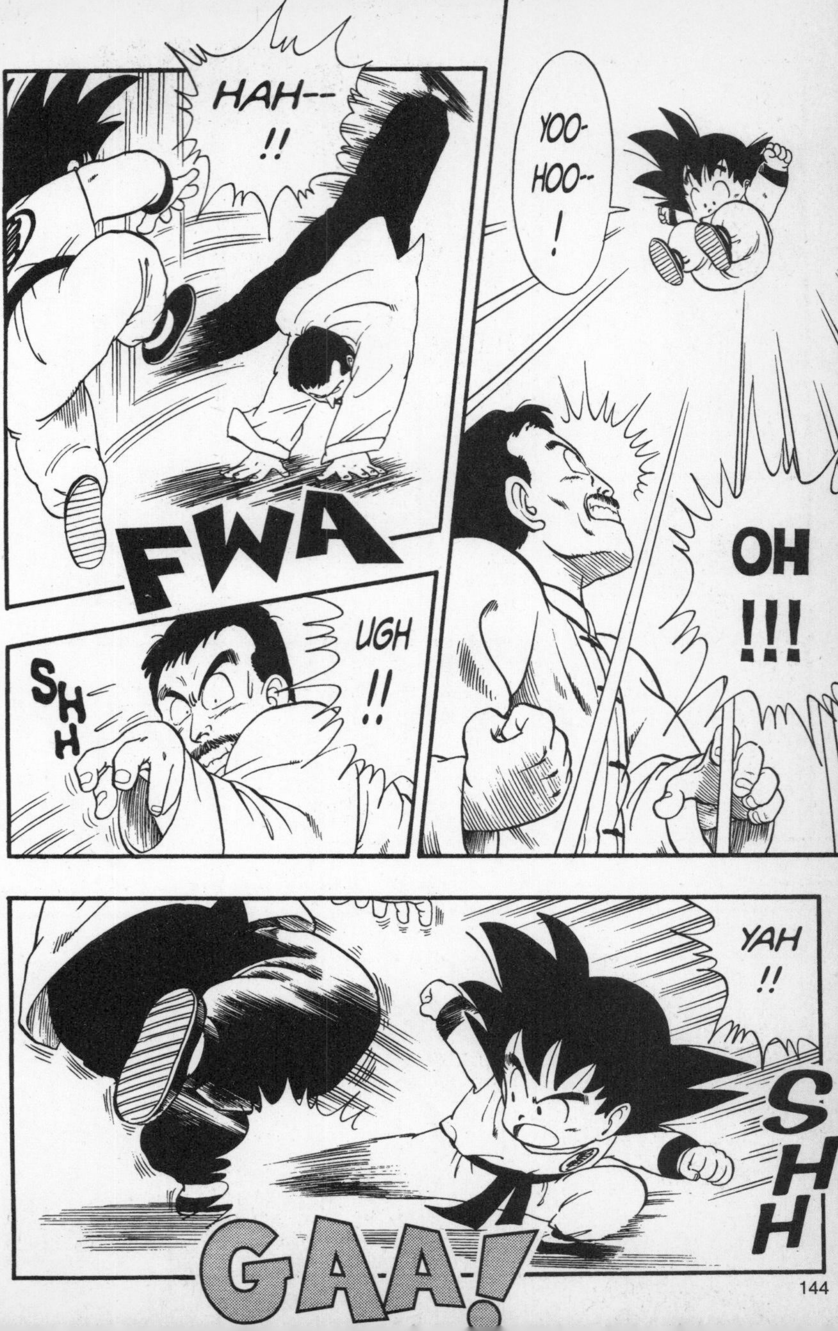

YOO-HOO--!
OH!!!
HAH--!!
FWA
UGH!!
SHH
YAH!!
SHH
GAA!

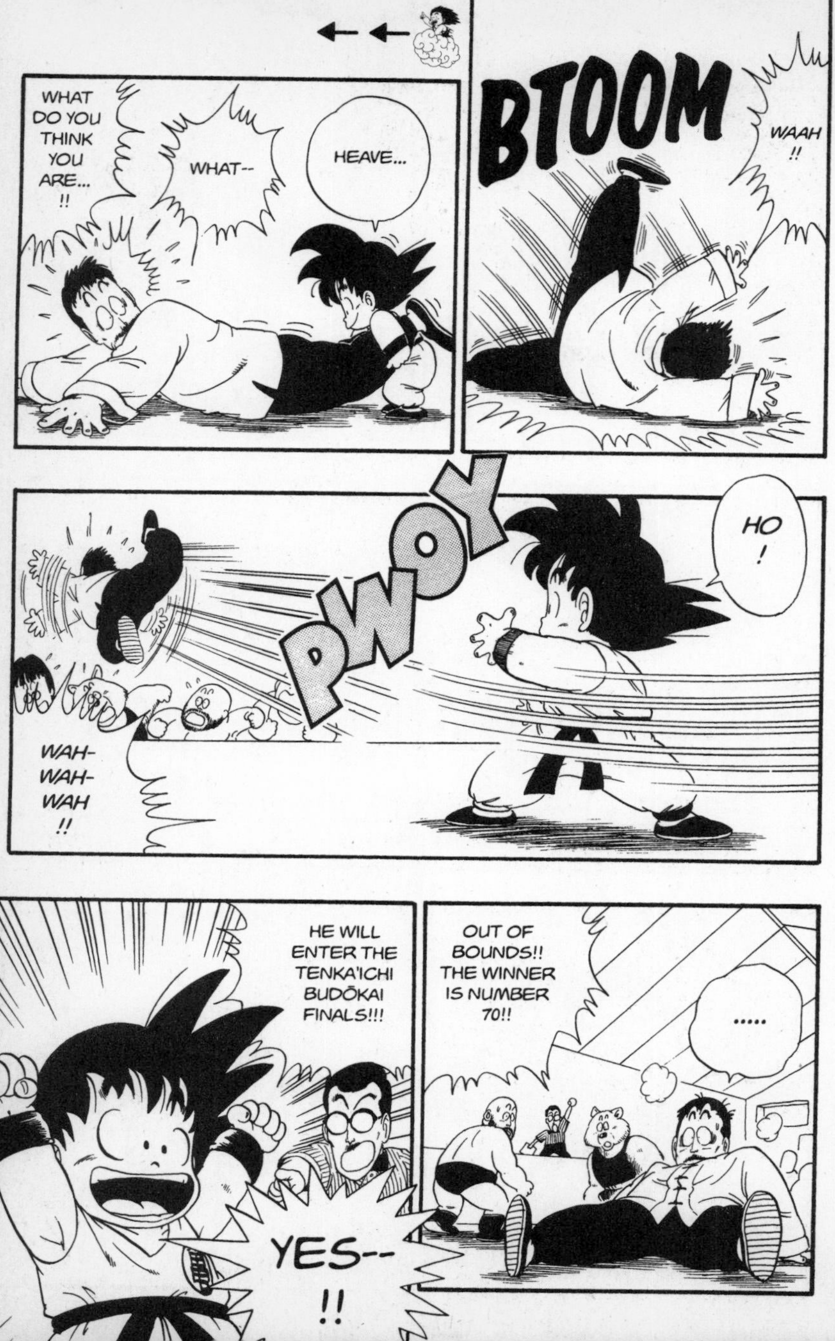
BTOOM
WAAH !!
HEAVE...
WHAT--
WHAT DO YOU THINK YOU ARE... !!
HO !
PWOY
WAH-WAH-WAH !!
OUT OF BOUNDS!! THE WINNER IS NUMBER 70!!
.....
HE WILL ENTER THE TENKA'ICHI BUDŌKAI FINALS!!!
YES-- !!

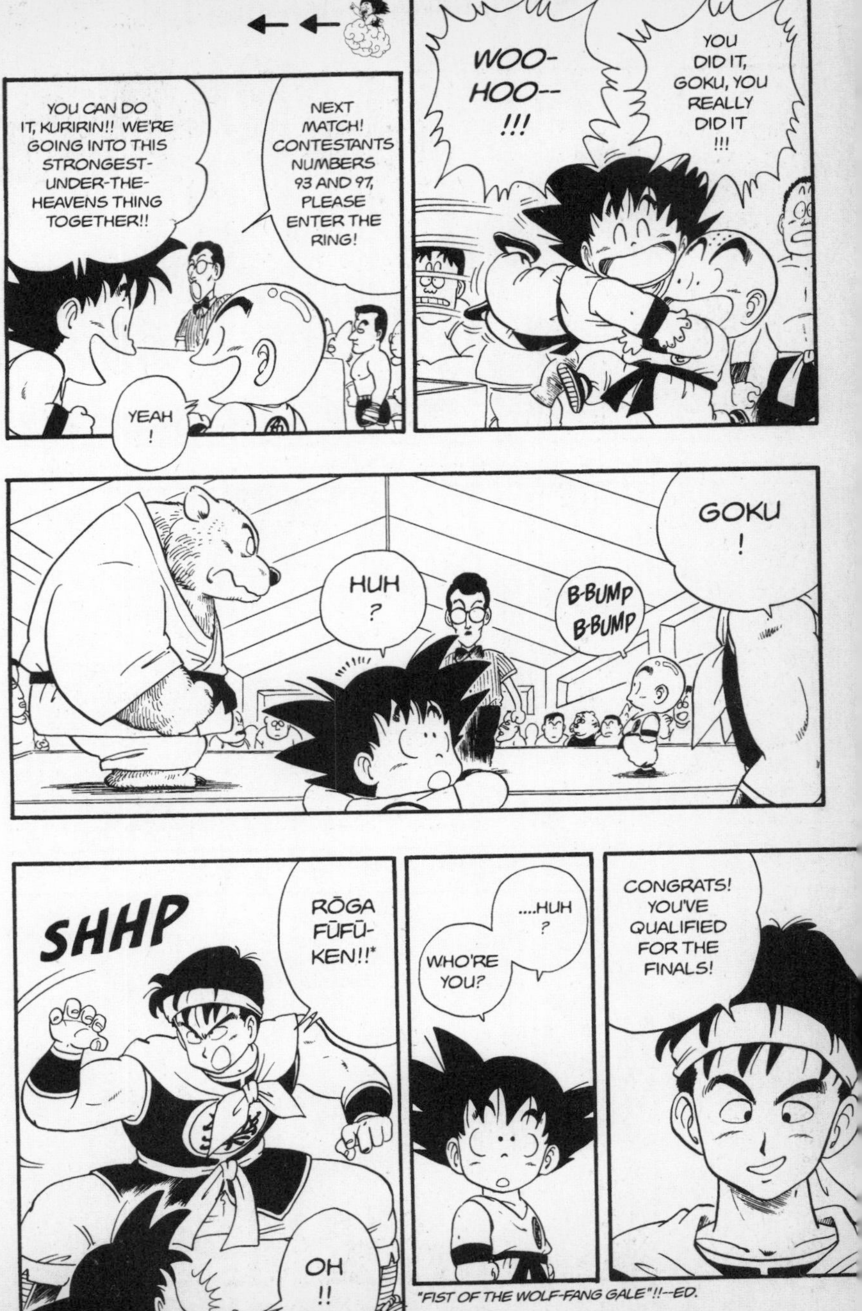
YOU DID IT, GOKU, YOU REALLY DID IT !!!
WOO-HOO-- !!!
NEXT MATCH! CONTESTANTS NUMBERS 93 AND 97, PLEASE ENTER THE RING!
YOU CAN DO IT, KURIRIN!! WE'RE GOING INTO THIS STRONGEST-UNDER-THE-HEAVENS THING TOGETHER!!
YEAH !
GOKU !
B-BUMP B-BUMP
HUH ?
CONGRATS! YOU'VE QUALIFIED FOR THE FINALS!
....HUH ?
WHO'RE YOU?
RŌGA FŪFŪ-KEN!!*
SHHP
OH !!
"FIST OF THE WOLF-FANG GALE"!!--ED.

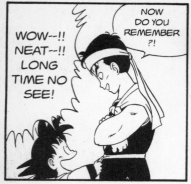

YAMCHA!!
NOW DO YOU REMEMBER?!
WOW--!! NEAT--!! LONG TIME NO SEE!
I DIDN'T RECOGNIZE YOU 'CAUSE YOUR HAIR'S DIFFERENT!!
BULMA KEPT ON BUGGING ME "'CUZ LONG HAIR IS SO TOTALLY *OUT* IN THE METROPOLIS," SO...
NEVER THOUGHT WE'D MEET AGAIN IN A PLACE LIKE THIS.
YOU CAME FOR THE STRONGEST-UNDER-THE-HEAVENS THINGIE, TOO, YAMCHA?! DID YOU QUALIFY?!
YUP! FOR A LONG TIME THAT'S ALL I'VE BEEN TRAINING FOR!
I DON'T THINK I HAVE A CHANCE AGAINST YOU, THOUGH, GOKU...
ALL THAT TRAINING YOU GOT FROM THE INVINCIBLE OLD MASTER'S PUT YOU AT A WHOLE DIFFERENT LEVEL.
OOOI!
AAAI!
I'M PRETTY SURPRISED, TOO!!

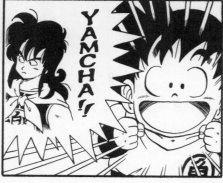

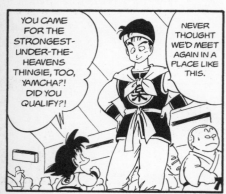

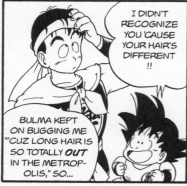

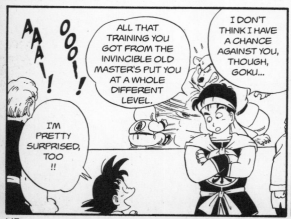

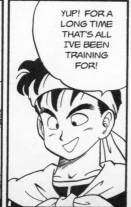

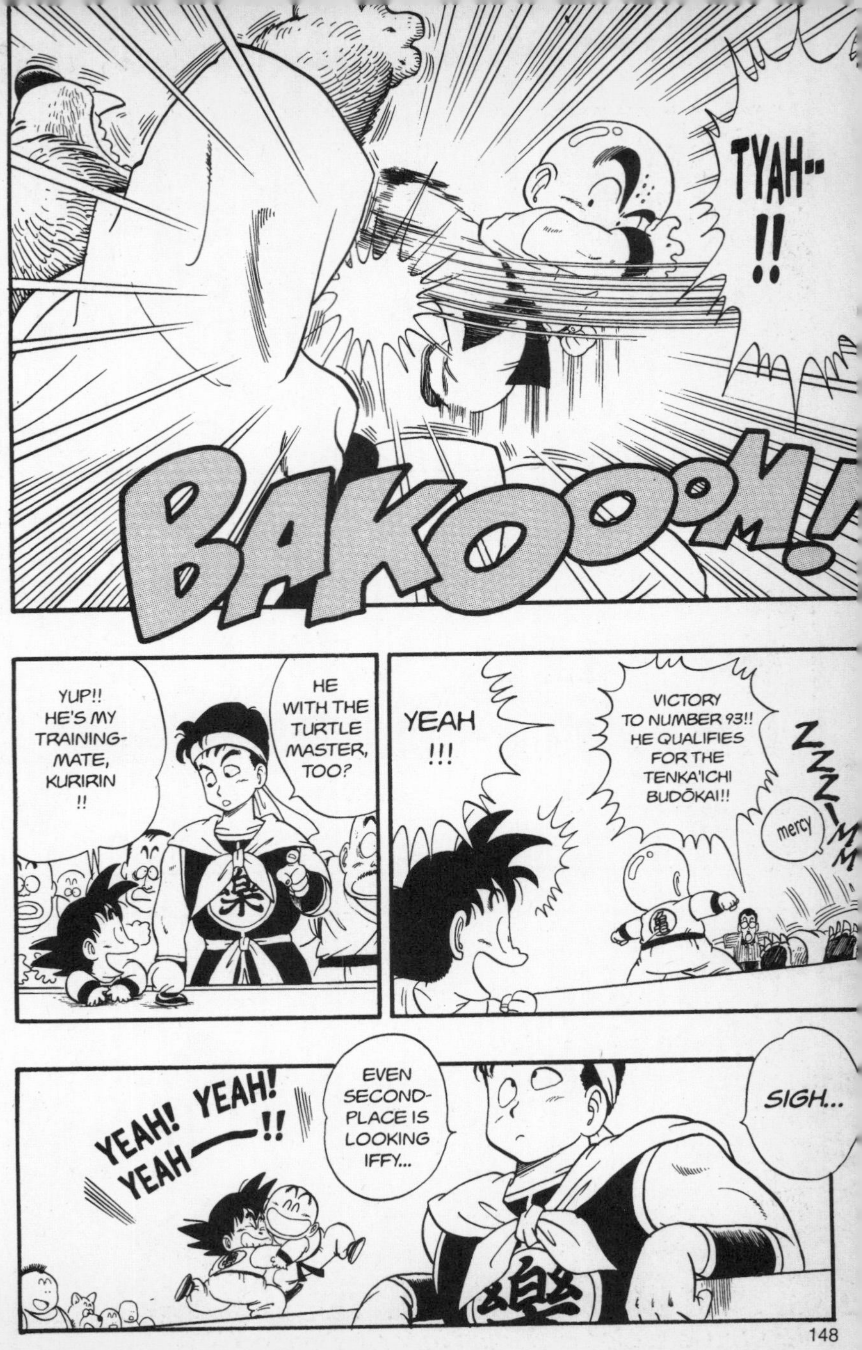
TYAH-- !!
BAKOOOM!!
ZZZ-MM
mercy
VICTORY TO NUMBER 93!! HE QUALIFIES FOR THE TENKA'ICHI BUDŌKAI!!
YEAH !!!
HE WITH THE TURTLE MASTER, TOO?
YUP!! HE'S MY TRAINING-MATE, KURIRIN !!
SIGH...
EVEN SECOND-PLACE IS LOOKING IFFY...
YEAH! YEAH! YEAH——!!

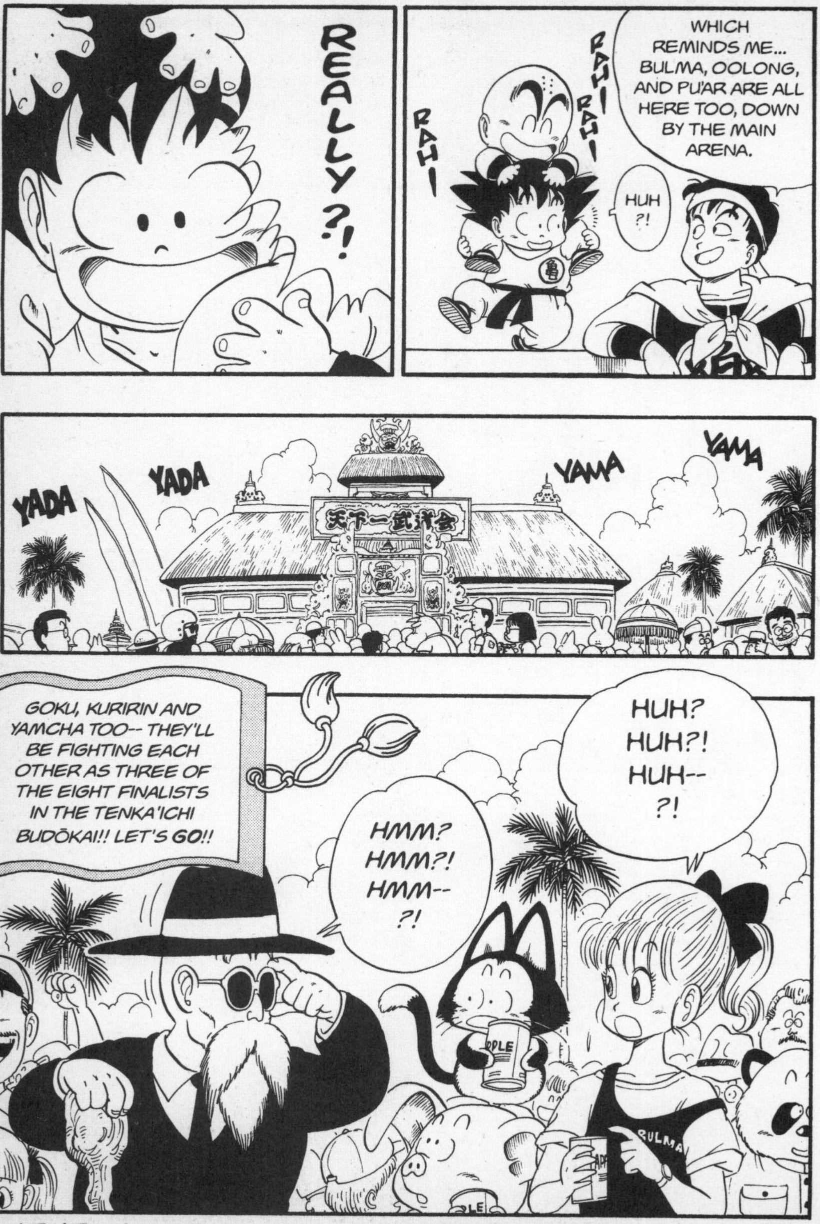
WHICH REMINDS ME... BULMA, OOLONG, AND PU'AR ARE ALL HERE TOO, DOWN BY THE MAIN ARENA.
RAH! RAH!
RAH!
HUH ?!
REALLY?!
YAMA
YAMA
YADA
YADA
天下一武道会
HUH? HUH?! HUH-- ?!
HMM? HMM?! HMM-- ?!
GOKU, KURIRIN AND YAMCHA TOO-- THEY'LL BE FIGHTING EACH OTHER AS THREE OF THE EIGHT FINALISTS IN THE TENKA'ICHI BUDŌKAI!! LET'S GO!!
BULMA

NEXT: Here Come Some New Challengers!!

Tale 35
The Battle is Set!!

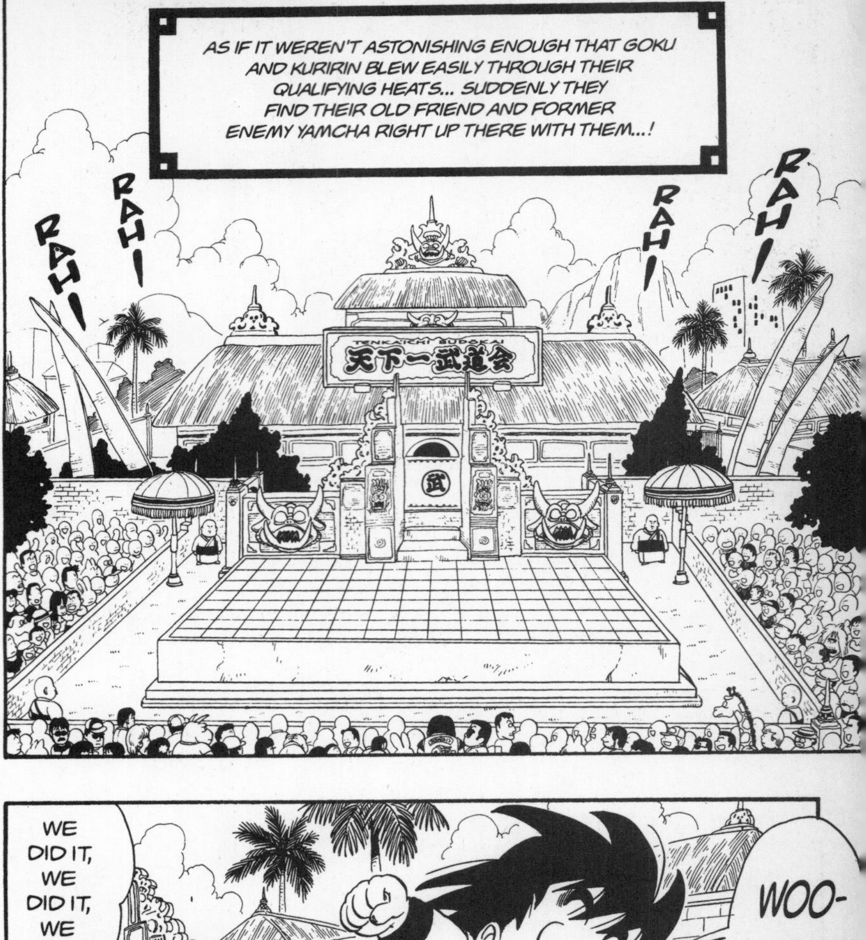
AS IF IT WEREN'T ASTONISHING ENOUGH THAT GOKU AND KURIRIN BLEW EASILY THROUGH THEIR QUALIFYING HEATS... SUDDENLY THEY FIND THEIR OLD FRIEND AND FORMER ENEMY YAMCHA RIGHT UP THERE WITH THEM...!
RAH!
RAH!
RAH!
RAH!
TENKAICHI BUDOKAI
天下一武道会
武

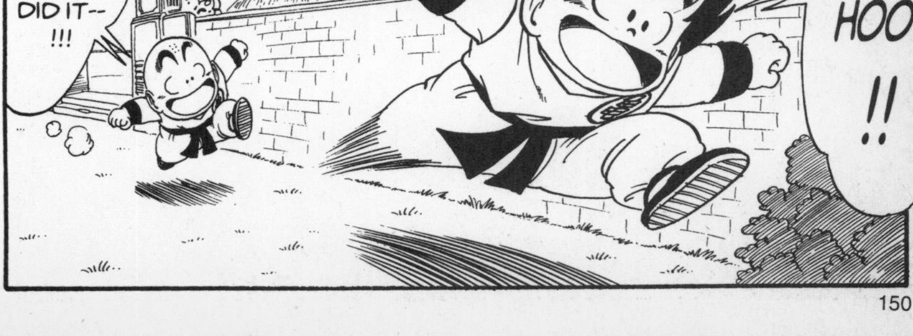
WOO-HOO--!!
WE DID IT, WE DID IT, WE DID IT--!!!

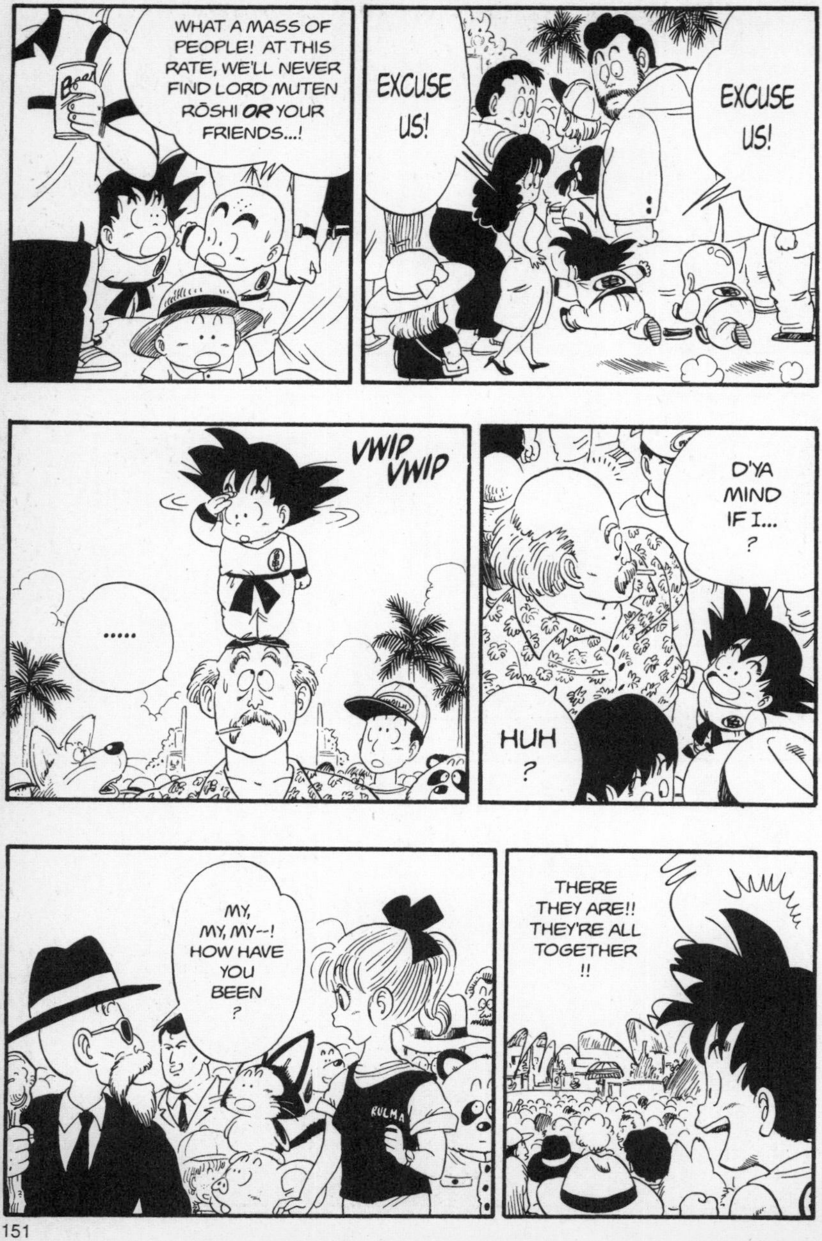
EXCUSE US!
EXCUSE US!
WHAT A MASS OF PEOPLE! AT THIS RATE, WE'LL NEVER FIND LORD MUTEN RŌSHI **OR** YOUR FRIENDS...!
D'YA MIND IF I... ?
HUH ?
VWIP VWIP
.....
THERE THEY ARE!! THEY'RE ALL TOGETHER !!
MY, MY, MY--! HOW HAVE YOU BEEN ?
BULMA

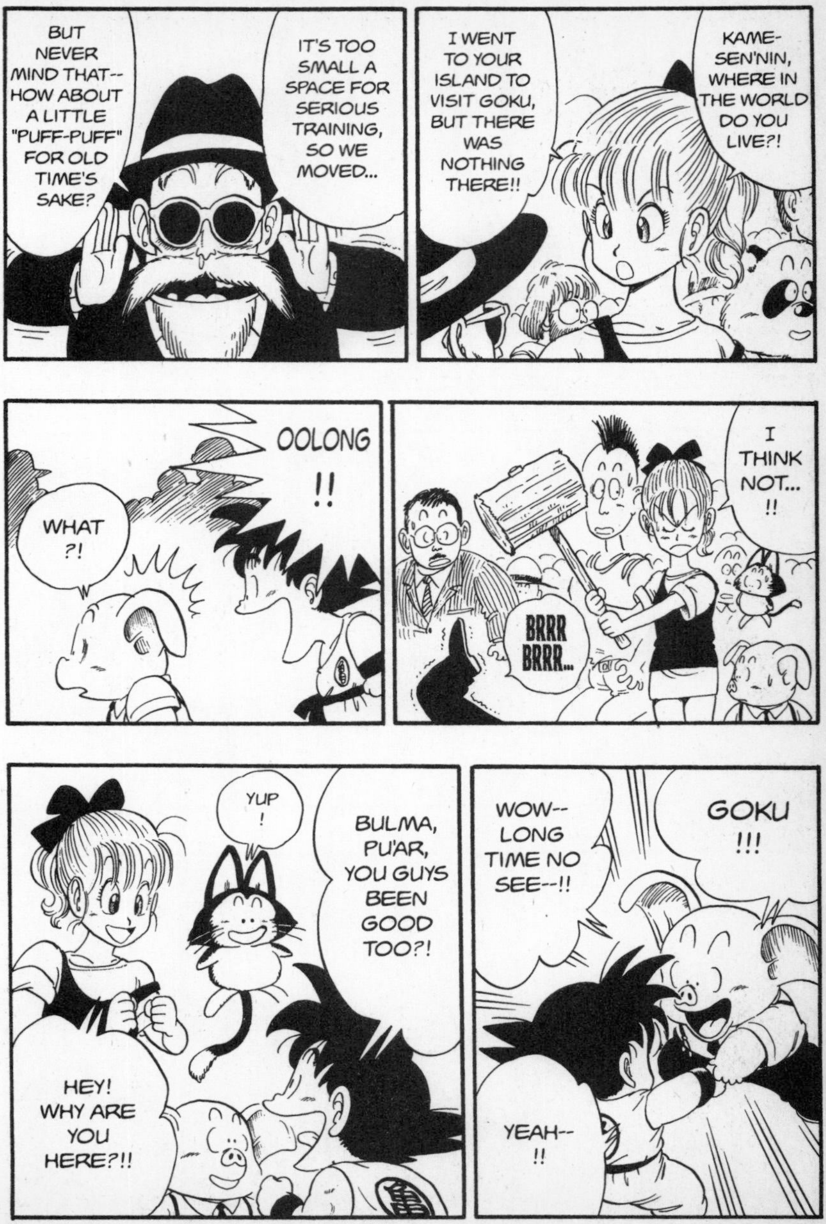
KAME-SEN'NIN, WHERE IN THE WORLD DO YOU LIVE?!
I WENT TO YOUR ISLAND TO VISIT GOKU, BUT THERE WAS NOTHING THERE!!
IT'S TOO SMALL A SPACE FOR SERIOUS TRAINING, SO WE MOVED...
BUT NEVER MIND THAT-- HOW ABOUT A LITTLE "PUFF-PUFF" FOR OLD TIME'S SAKE?
I THINK NOT... !!
BRRR BRRR...
OOLONG !!
WHAT ?!
GOKU !!!
WOW-- LONG TIME NO SEE--!!
YEAH-- !!
BULMA, PU'AR, YOU GUYS BEEN GOOD TOO?!
YUP !
HEY! WHY ARE YOU HERE?!!

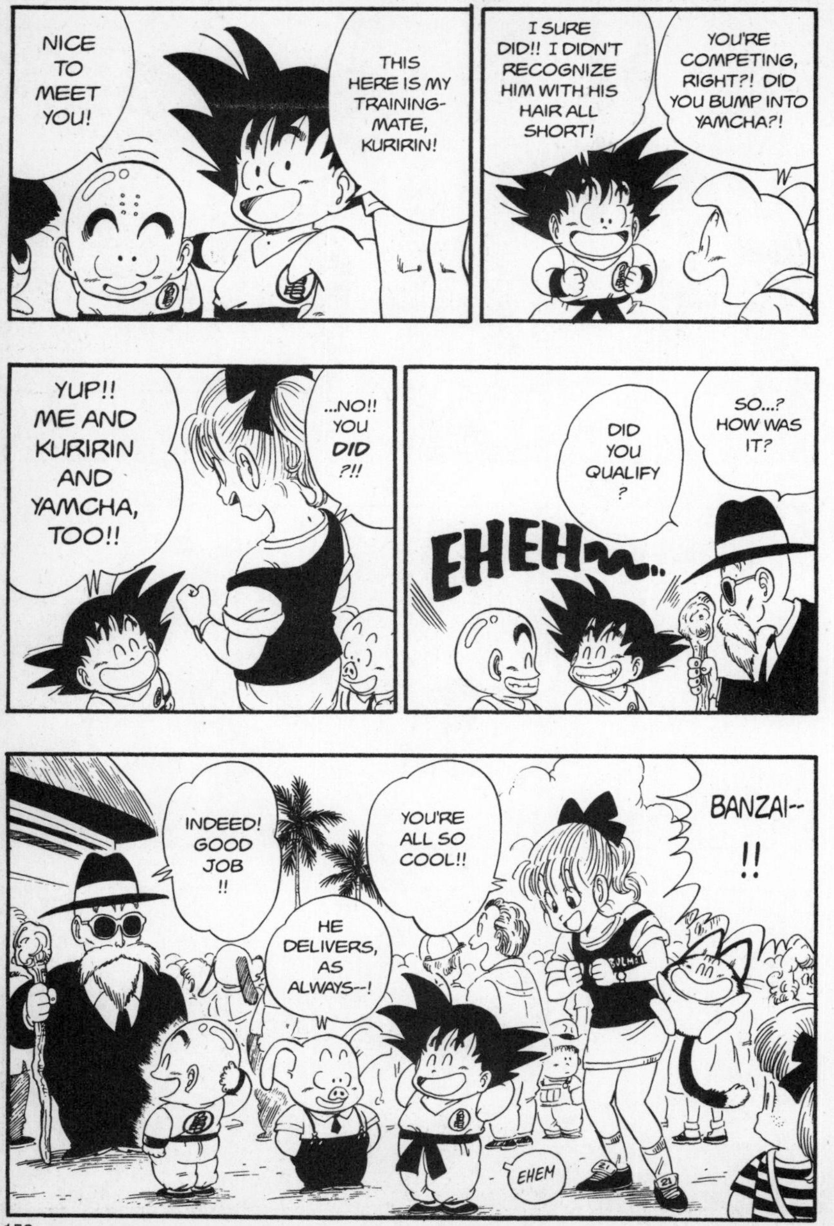
YOU'RE COMPETING, RIGHT?! DID YOU BUMP INTO YAMCHA?!
I SURE DID!! I DIDN'T RECOGNIZE HIM WITH HIS HAIR ALL SHORT!
THIS HERE IS MY TRAINING-MATE, KURIRIN!
NICE TO MEET YOU!
SO...? HOW WAS IT?
DID YOU QUALIFY?
EHEH~~..
YUP!! ME AND KURIRIN AND YAMCHA, TOO!!
...NO!! YOU DID?!!
BANZAI--!!
YOU'RE ALL SO COOL!!
INDEED! GOOD JOB!!
HE DELIVERS, AS ALWAYS--!
EHEM

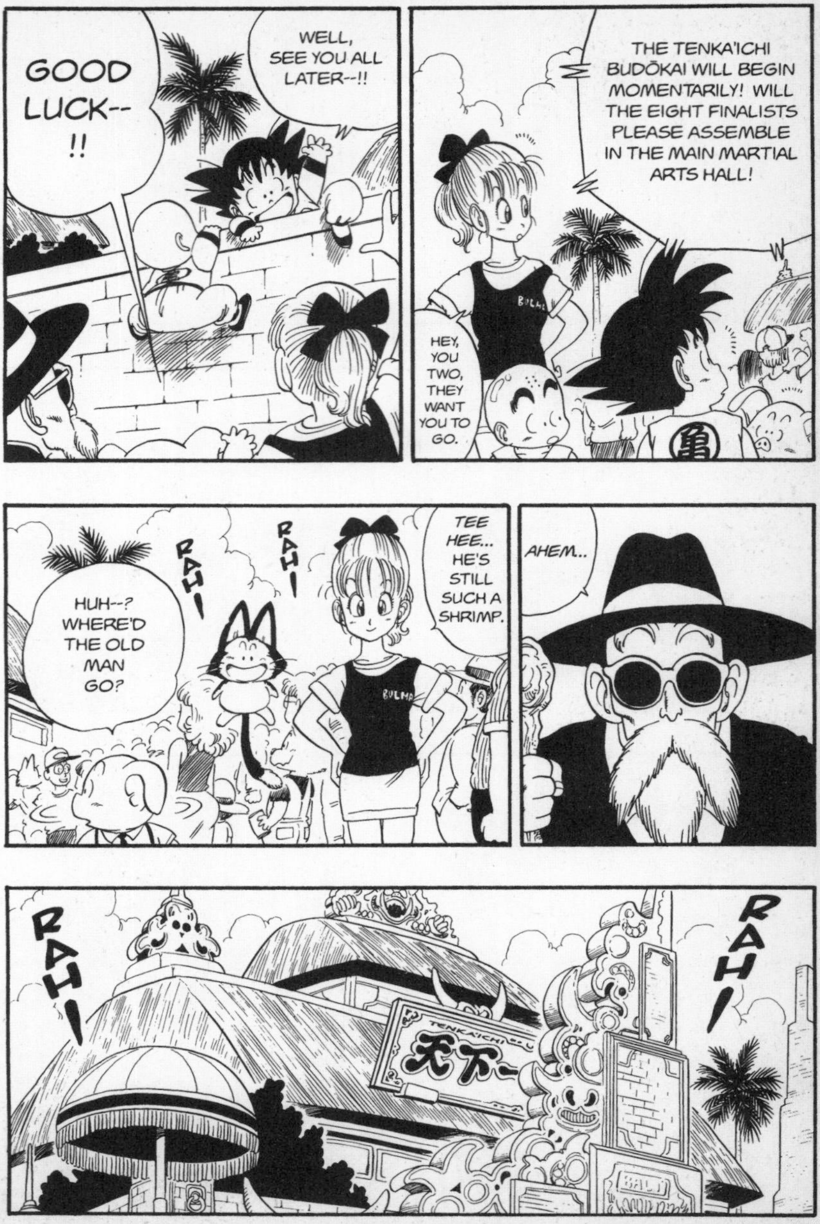
THE TENKA'ICHI BUDŌKAI WILL BEGIN MOMENTARILY! WILL THE EIGHT FINALISTS PLEASE ASSEMBLE IN THE MAIN MARTIAL ARTS HALL!
HEY, YOU TWO, THEY WANT YOU TO GO.
WELL, SEE YOU ALL LATER--!!
GOOD LUCK-- !!
AHEM...
TEE HEE... HE'S STILL SUCH A SHRIMP.
RAH!
RAH!
HUH--? WHERE'D THE OLD MAN GO?
RAH!
RAH!
TENKA'ICHI
天下一

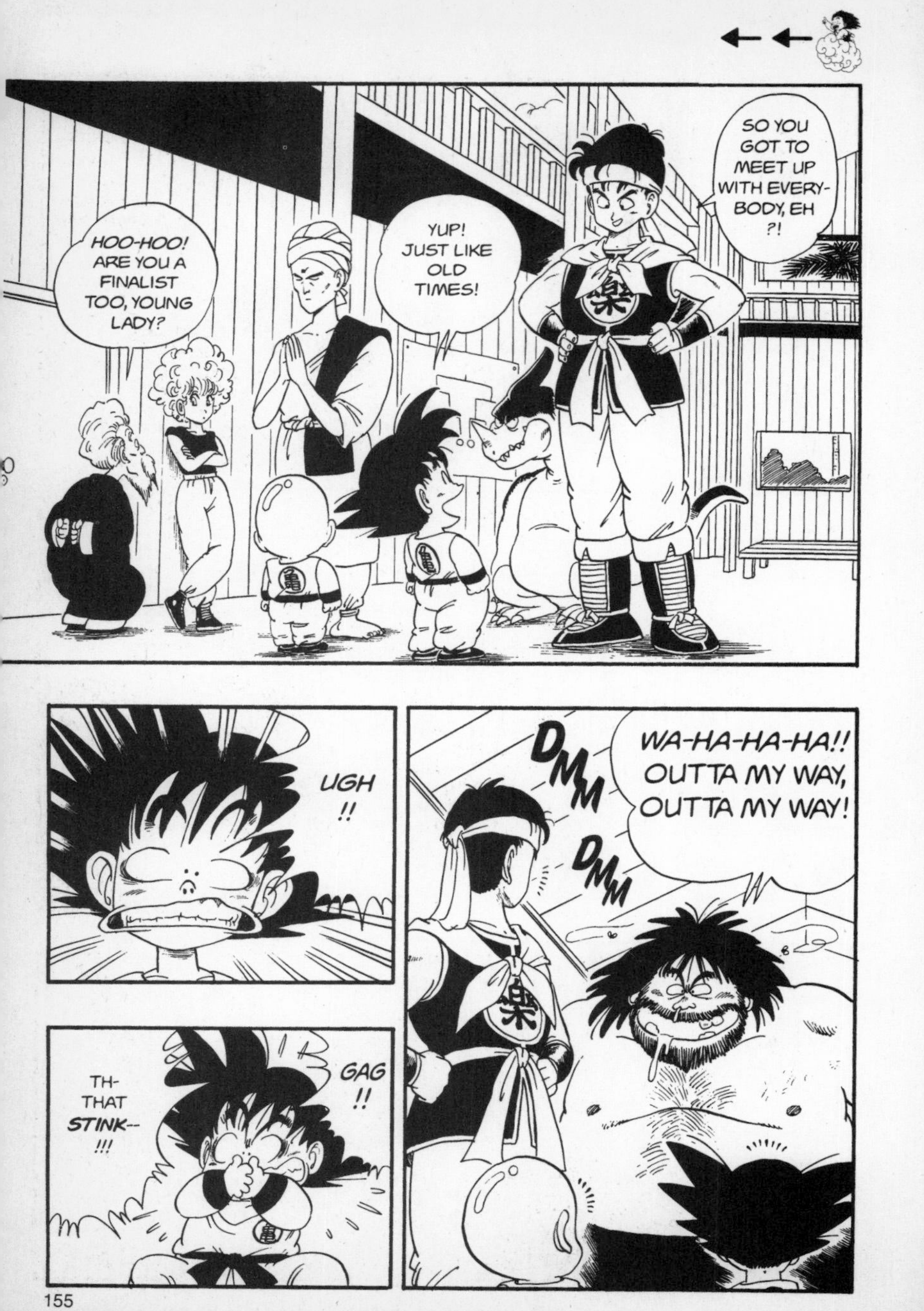
SO YOU GOT TO MEET UP WITH EVERY-BODY, EH ?!
YUP! JUST LIKE OLD TIMES!
HOO-HOO! ARE YOU A FINALIST TOO, YOUNG LADY?
DMM
DMM
WA-HA-HA-HA!! OUTTA MY WAY, OUTTA MY WAY!
UGH !!
GAG !!
TH-THAT STINK-- !!!

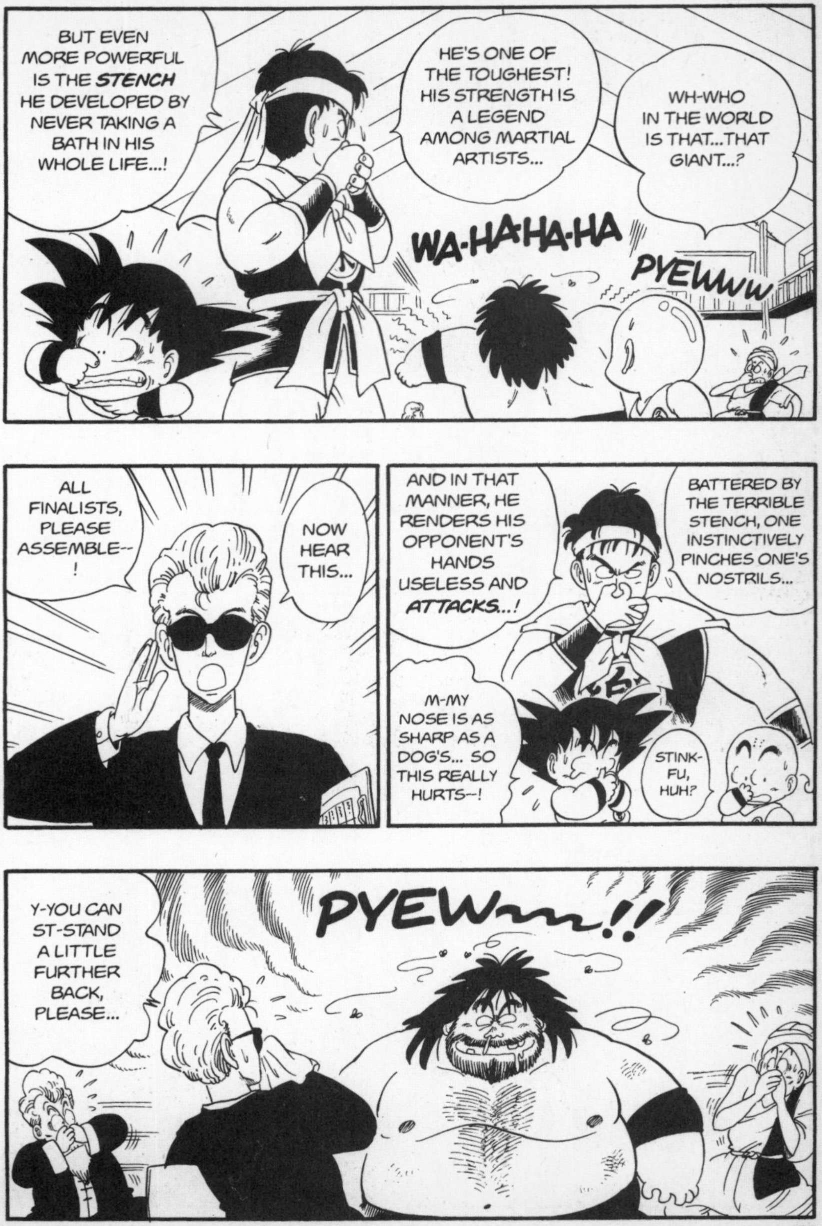

WH-WHO IN THE WORLD IS THAT...THAT GIANT...?
HE'S ONE OF THE TOUGHEST! HIS STRENGTH IS A LEGEND AMONG MARTIAL ARTISTS...
BUT EVEN MORE POWERFUL IS THE *STENCH* HE DEVELOPED BY NEVER TAKING A BATH IN HIS WHOLE LIFE...!
PYEWWW
WA-HA-HA-HA
BATTERED BY THE TERRIBLE STENCH, ONE INSTINCTIVELY PINCHES ONE'S NOSTRILS...
AND IN THAT MANNER, HE RENDERS HIS OPPONENT'S HANDS USELESS AND *ATTACKS*...!
STINK-FU, HUH?
M-MY NOSE IS AS SHARP AS A DOG'S... SO THIS REALLY HURTS--!
NOW HEAR THIS...
ALL FINALISTS, PLEASE ASSEMBLE--!
PYEW~!!
Y-YOU CAN ST-STAND A LITTLE FURTHER BACK, PLEASE...

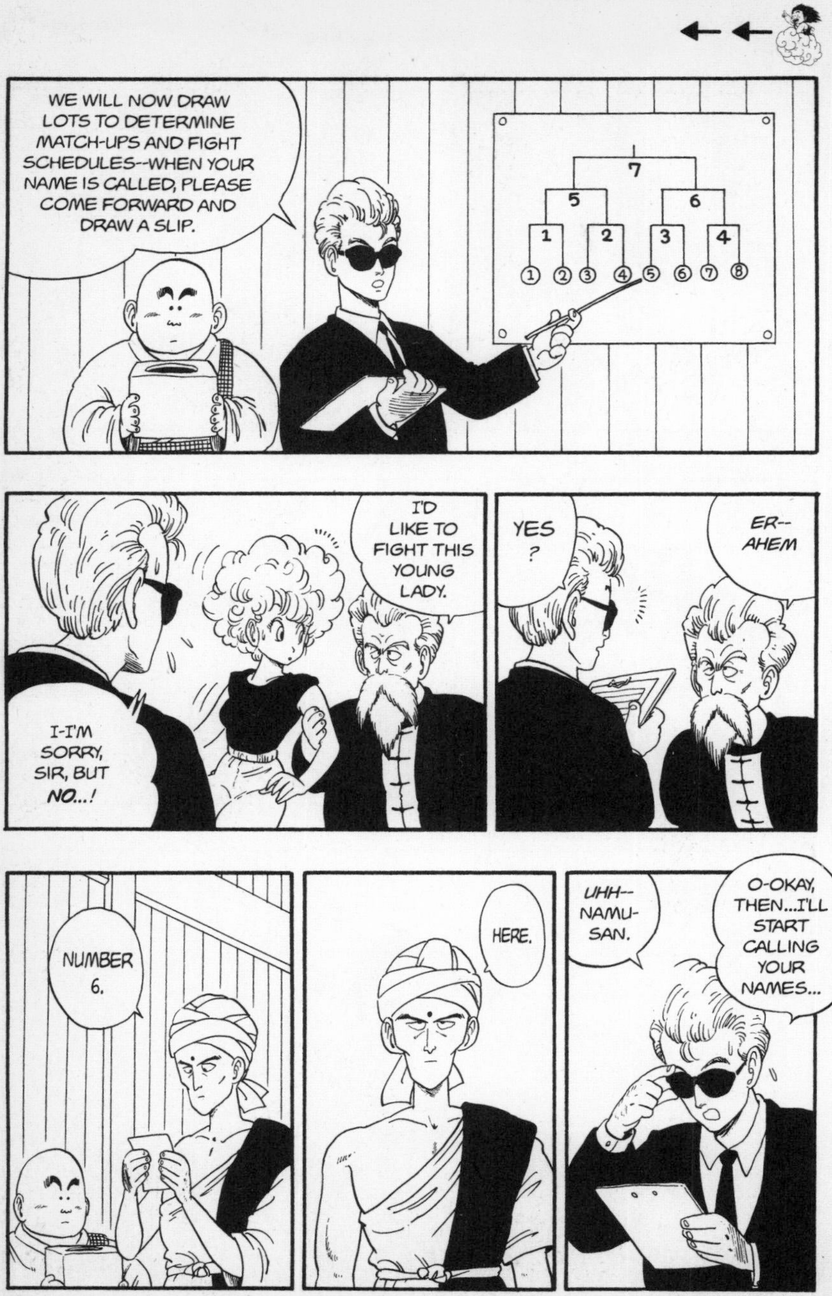
WE WILL NOW DRAW LOTS TO DETERMINE MATCH-UPS AND FIGHT SCHEDULES--WHEN YOUR NAME IS CALLED, PLEASE COME FORWARD AND DRAW A SLIP.
ER-- AHEM
YES ?
I'D LIKE TO FIGHT THIS YOUNG LADY.
I-I'M SORRY, SIR, BUT NO...!
O-OKAY, THEN...I'LL START CALLING YOUR NAMES...
UHH-- NAMU-SAN.
HERE.
NUMBER 6.

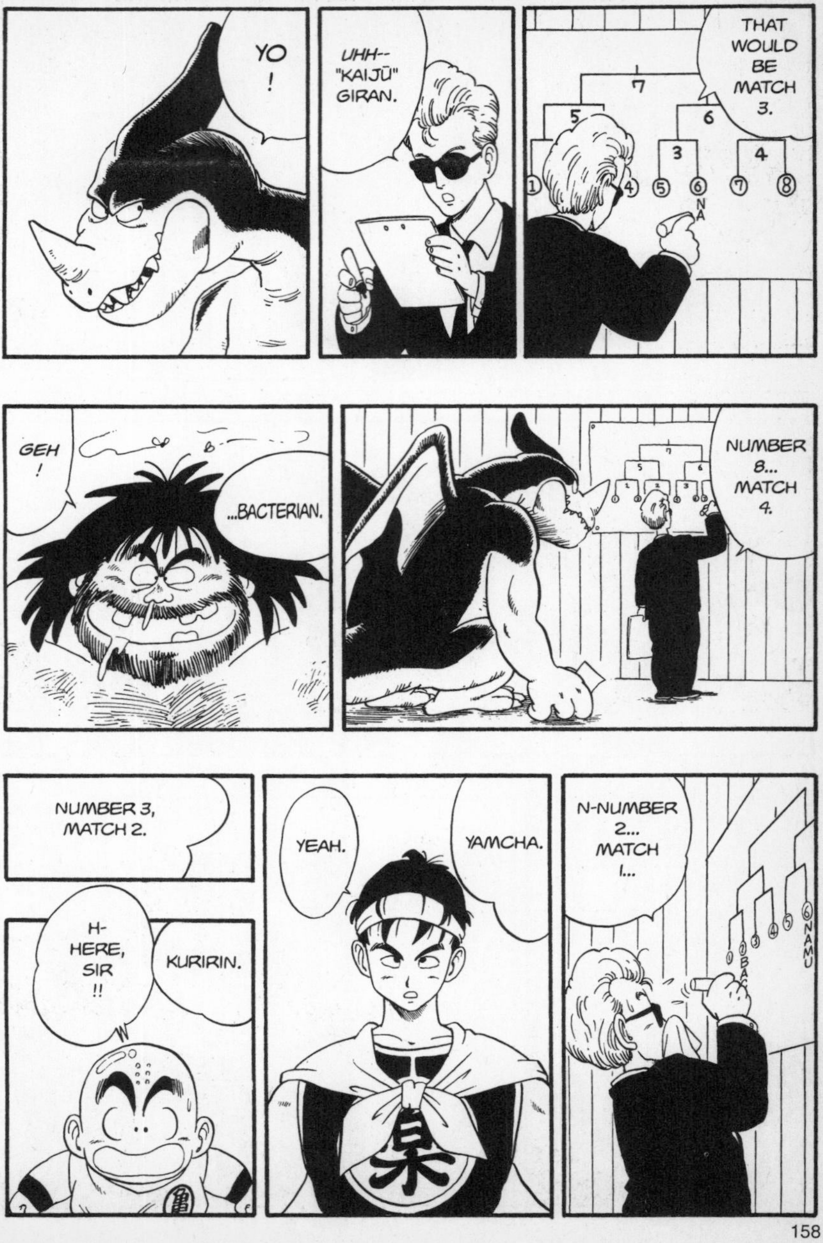
THAT WOULD BE MATCH 3.
NA
UHH-- "KAIJŪ" GIRAN.
YO !
NUMBER 8... MATCH 4.
...BACTERIAN.
GEH !
N-NUMBER 2... MATCH 1...
BAC
NAMU
YAMCHA.
YEAH.
NUMBER 3, MATCH 2.
KURIRIN.
H-HERE, SIR !!

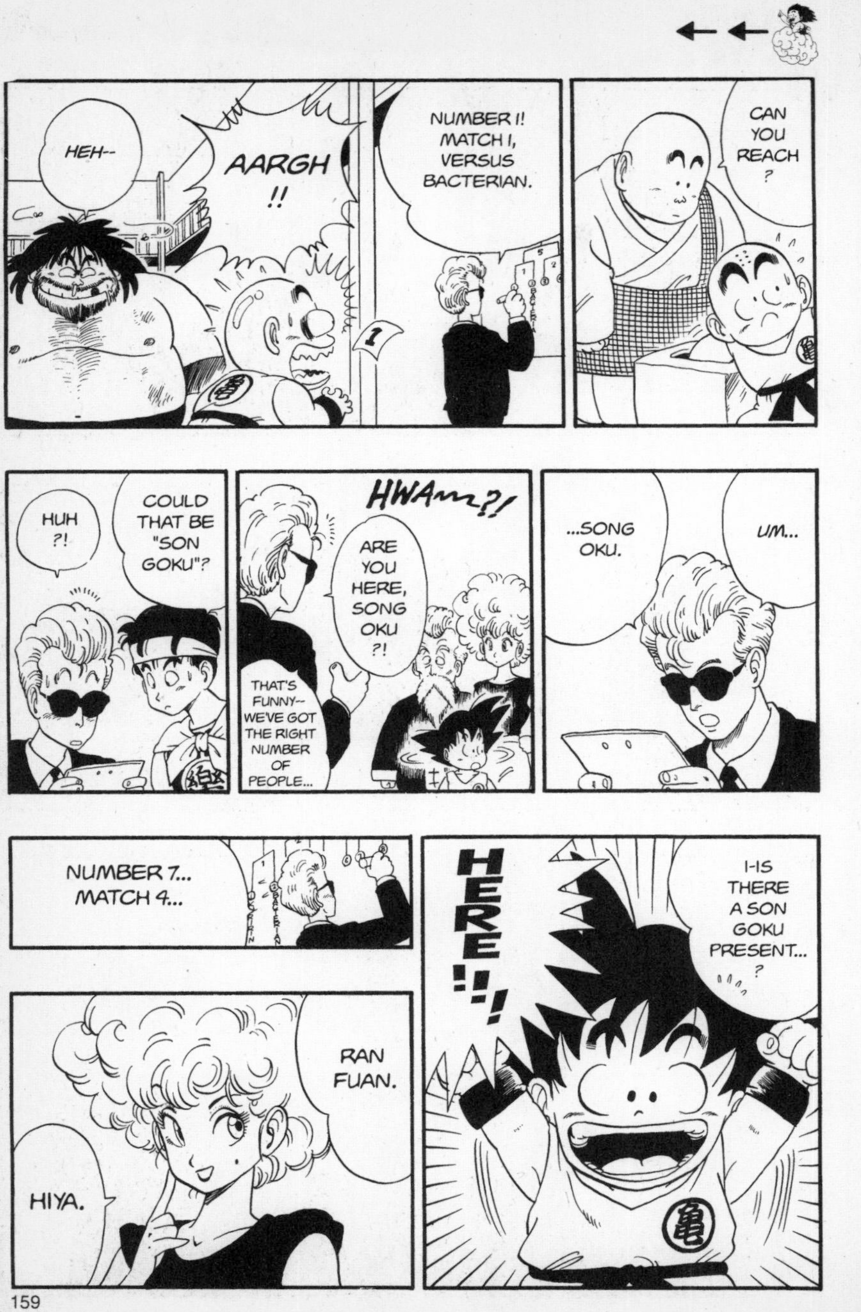
CAN YOU REACH ?
NUMBER 1! MATCH 1, VERSUS BACTERIAN.
AARGH !!
HEH--
UM...
...SONG OKU.
HWA?!
ARE YOU HERE, SONG OKU ?!
THAT'S FUNNY-- WE'VE GOT THE RIGHT NUMBER OF PEOPLE...
COULD THAT BE "SON GOKU"?
HUH ?!
I-IS THERE A SON GOKU PRESENT... ?
HERE!!!
NUMBER 7... MATCH 4...
RAN FUAN.
HIYA.

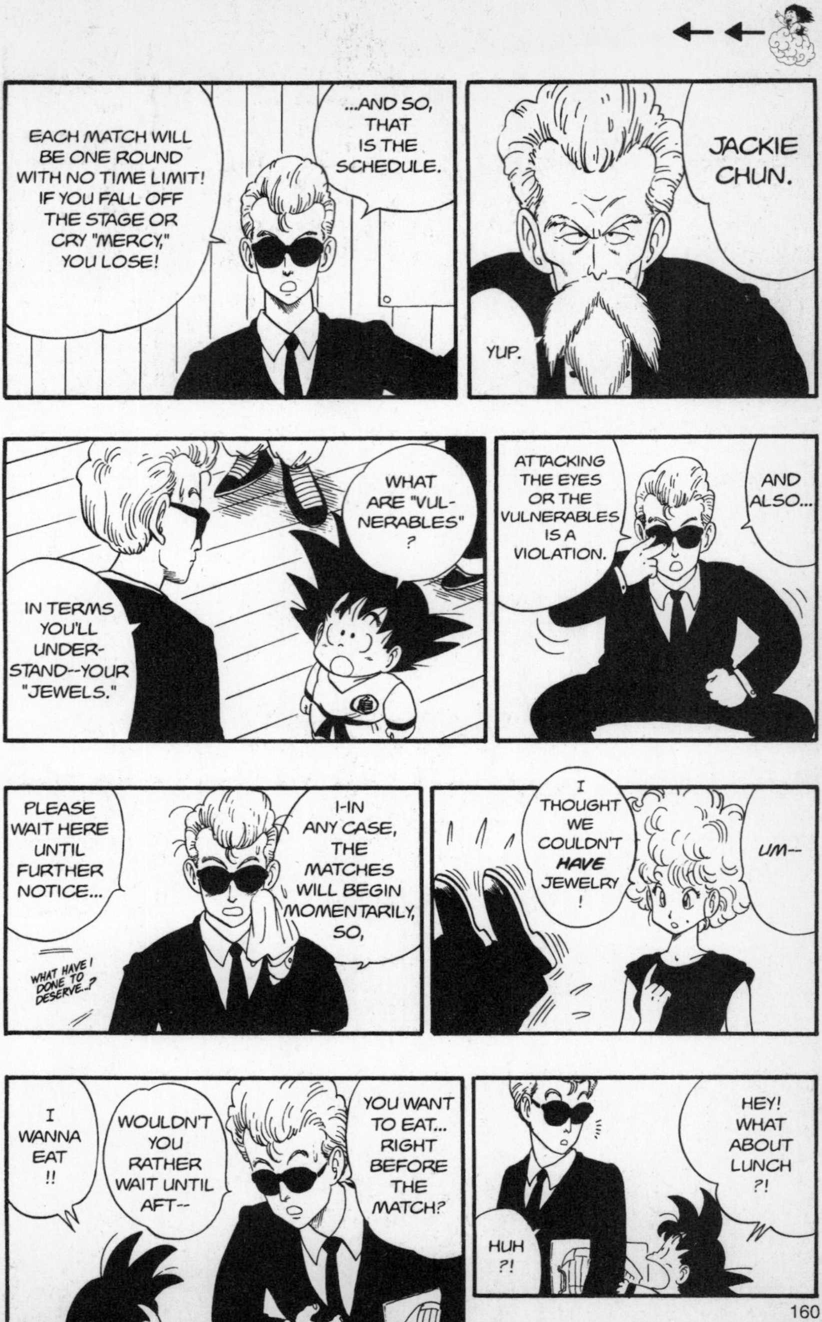
JACKIE CHUN.
YUP.
...AND SO, THAT IS THE SCHEDULE.
EACH MATCH WILL BE ONE ROUND WITH NO TIME LIMIT! IF YOU FALL OFF THE STAGE OR CRY "MERCY," YOU LOSE!
AND ALSO...
ATTACKING THE EYES OR THE VULNERABLES IS A VIOLATION.
WHAT ARE "VUL-NERABLES"?
IN TERMS YOU'LL UNDER-STAND--YOUR "JEWELS."
UM--
I THOUGHT WE COULDN'T ***HAVE*** JEWELRY!
I-IN ANY CASE, THE MATCHES WILL BEGIN MOMENTARILY, SO,
PLEASE WAIT HERE UNTIL FURTHER NOTICE...
WHAT HAVE I DONE TO DESERVE...?
HEY! WHAT ABOUT LUNCH?!
HUH?!
YOU WANT TO EAT... RIGHT BEFORE THE MATCH?
WOULDN'T YOU RATHER WAIT UNTIL AFT--
I WANNA EAT!!

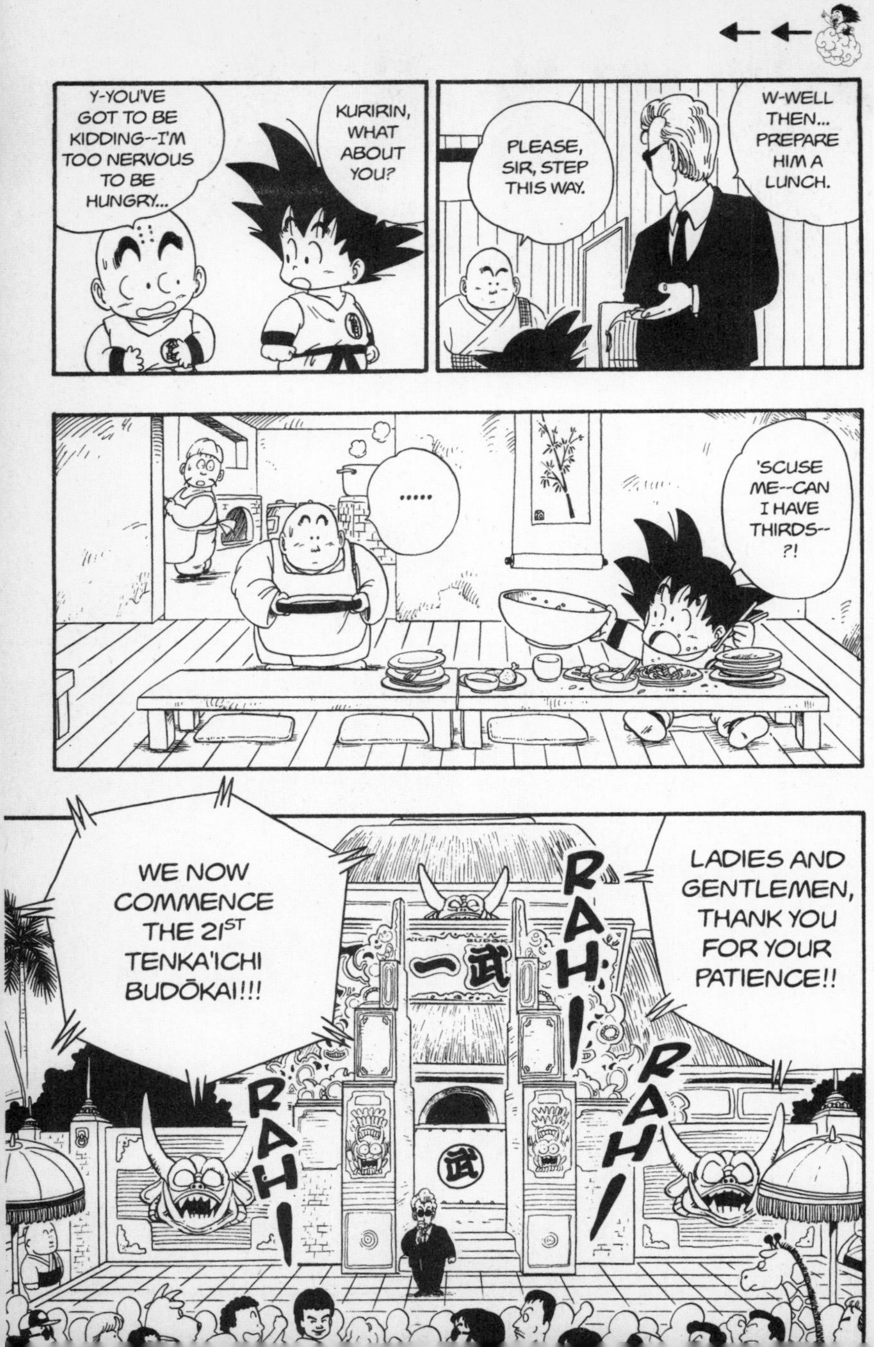
W-WELL THEN... PREPARE HIM A LUNCH.
PLEASE, SIR, STEP THIS WAY.
KURIRIN, WHAT ABOUT YOU?
Y-YOU'VE GOT TO BE KIDDING--I'M TOO NERVOUS TO BE HUNGRY...
'SCUSE ME--CAN I HAVE THIRDS--?!
......
LADIES AND GENTLEMEN, THANK YOU FOR YOUR PATIENCE!!
RAH!
RAH!
WE NOW COMMENCE THE 21ST TENKA'ICHI BUDŌKAI!!!
RAH!

ALL HAIL OUR 8 TENKA'ICHI BUDŌKAI CHALLENGERS!!!

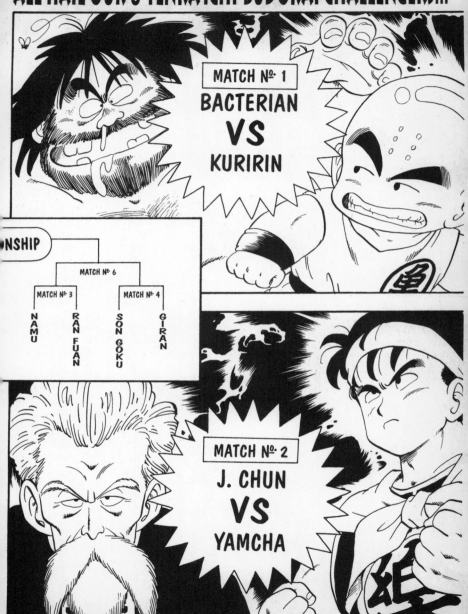

MATCH Nº· 1

BACTERIAN

VS

KURIRIN

NSHIP

MATCH Nº 6

MATCH Nº 3

MATCH Nº 4

NAMU

RAN FUAN

SON GOKU

GIRAN

MATCH Nº· 2

J. CHUN

VS

YAMCHA

THE BATTLES ARE ABOUT TO BEGIN!!!

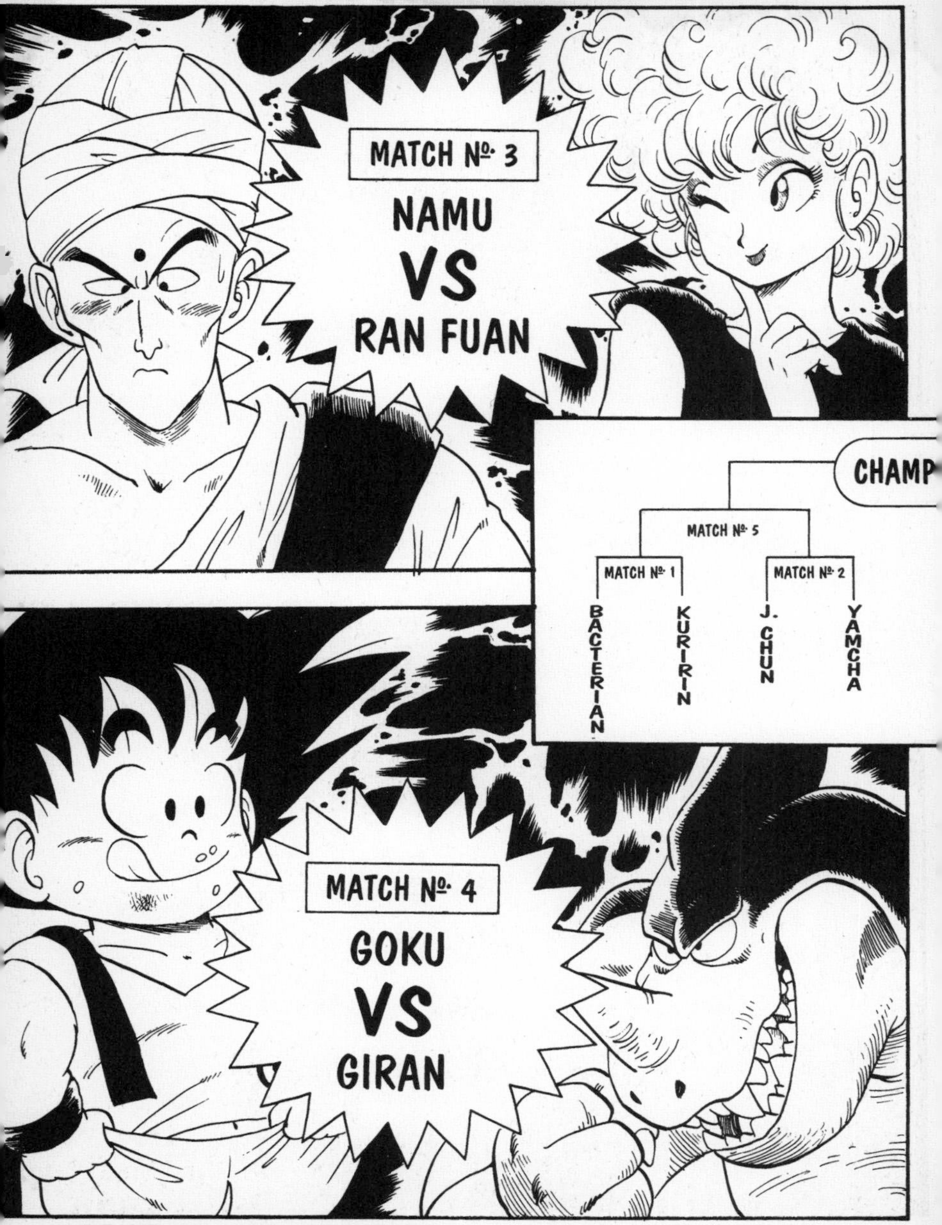
MATCH No. 3
NAMU
VS
RAN FUAN
CHAMP
MATCH No. 5
MATCH No. 1
MATCH No. 2
BACTERIAN
KURIRIN
J. CHUN
YAMCHA
MATCH No. 4
GOKU
VS
GIRAN

NEXT: The First Fight!

Tale 36 • Match No. 1

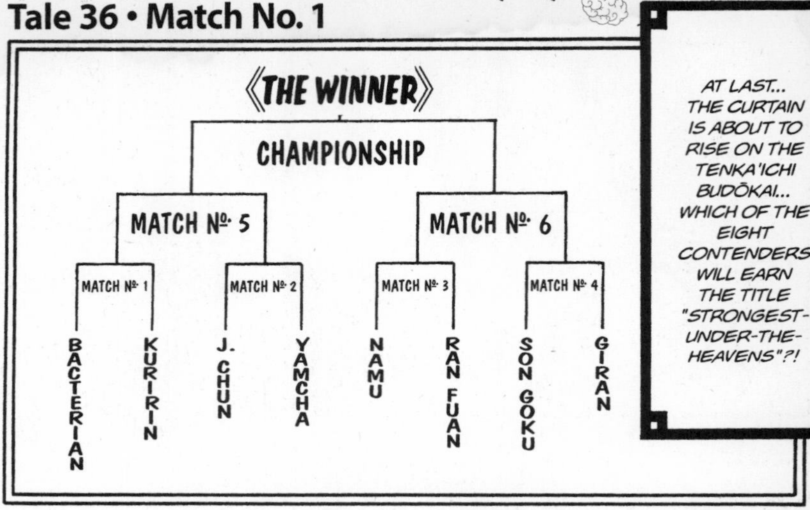
AT LAST... THE CURTAIN IS ABOUT TO RISE ON THE TENKA'ICHI BUDŌKAI... WHICH OF THE EIGHT CONTENDERS WILL EARN THE TITLE "STRONGEST-UNDER-THE-HEAVENS"?!
《THE WINNER》
CHAMPIONSHIP
MATCH №. 5
MATCH №. 6
MATCH №. 1
MATCH №. 2
MATCH №. 3
MATCH №. 4
BACTERIAN
KURIRIN
J. CHUN
YAMCHA
NAMU
RAN FUAN
SON GOKU
GIRAN

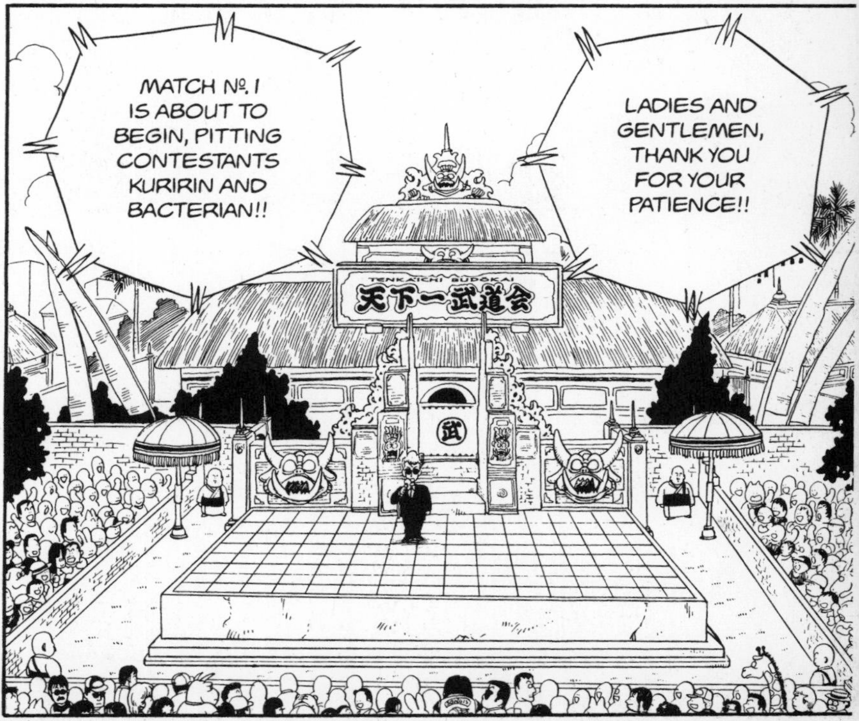
LADIES AND GENTLEMEN, THANK YOU FOR YOUR PATIENCE!!
MATCH №. 1 IS ABOUT TO BEGIN, PITTING CONTESTANTS KURIRIN AND BACTERIAN!!
TENKA'ICHI BUDŌKAI
天下一武道会

REMEMBER, THE CHAMPION OF THIS TOURNAMENT WILL BE AWARDED 500,000 ZENI IN PRIZE MONEY!

BUT BEFORE THE MATCH GETS UNDER WAY, LET'S HAVE A WORD FROM THE PRESIDING MONK OF THIS MARTIAL ARTS TEMPLE!

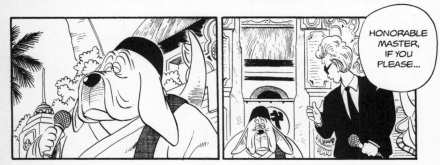

HONORABLE MASTER, IF YOU PLEASE...

THANK YOU VERY MUCH !!

WOOF

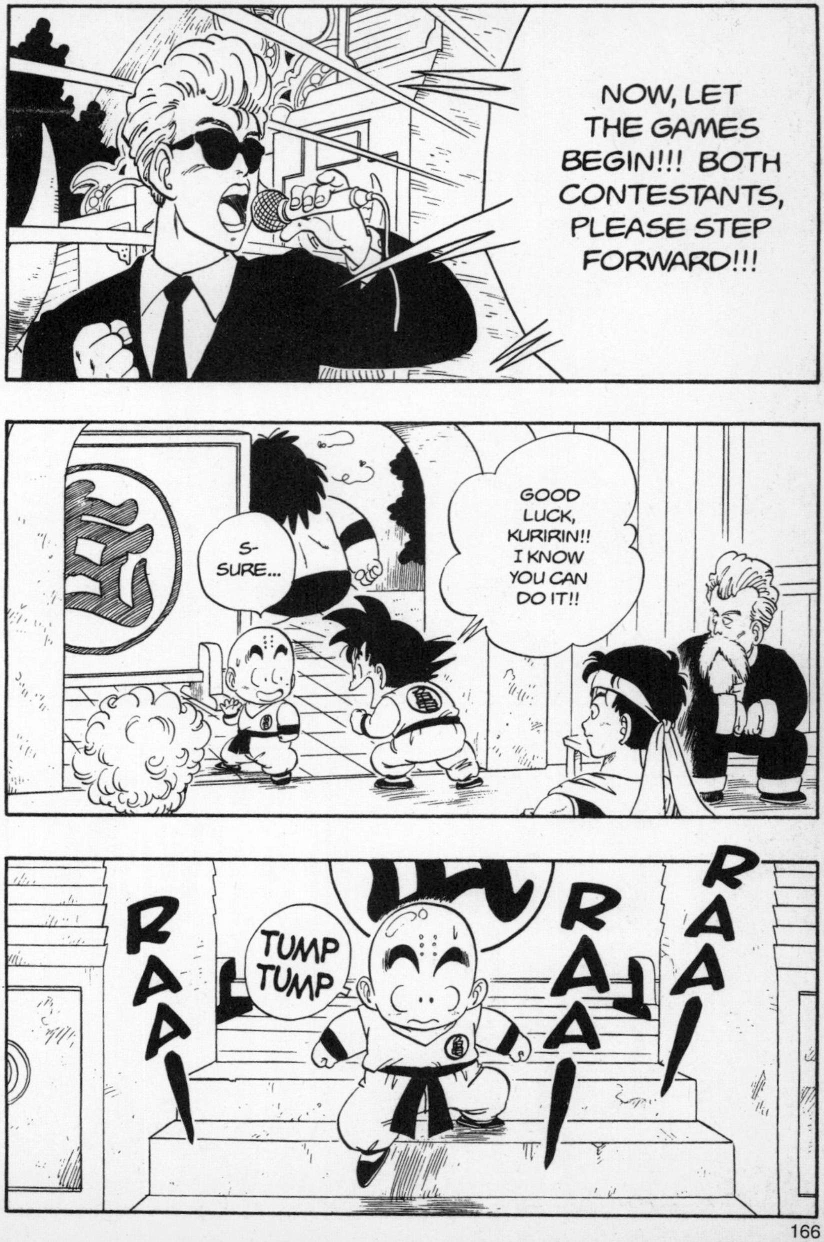
NOW, LET THE GAMES BEGIN!!! BOTH CONTESTANTS, PLEASE STEP FORWARD!!!
GOOD LUCK, KURIRIN!! I KNOW YOU CAN DO IT!!
S-SURE...
RAAA!
RAAA!
TUMP TUMP
RAAA!

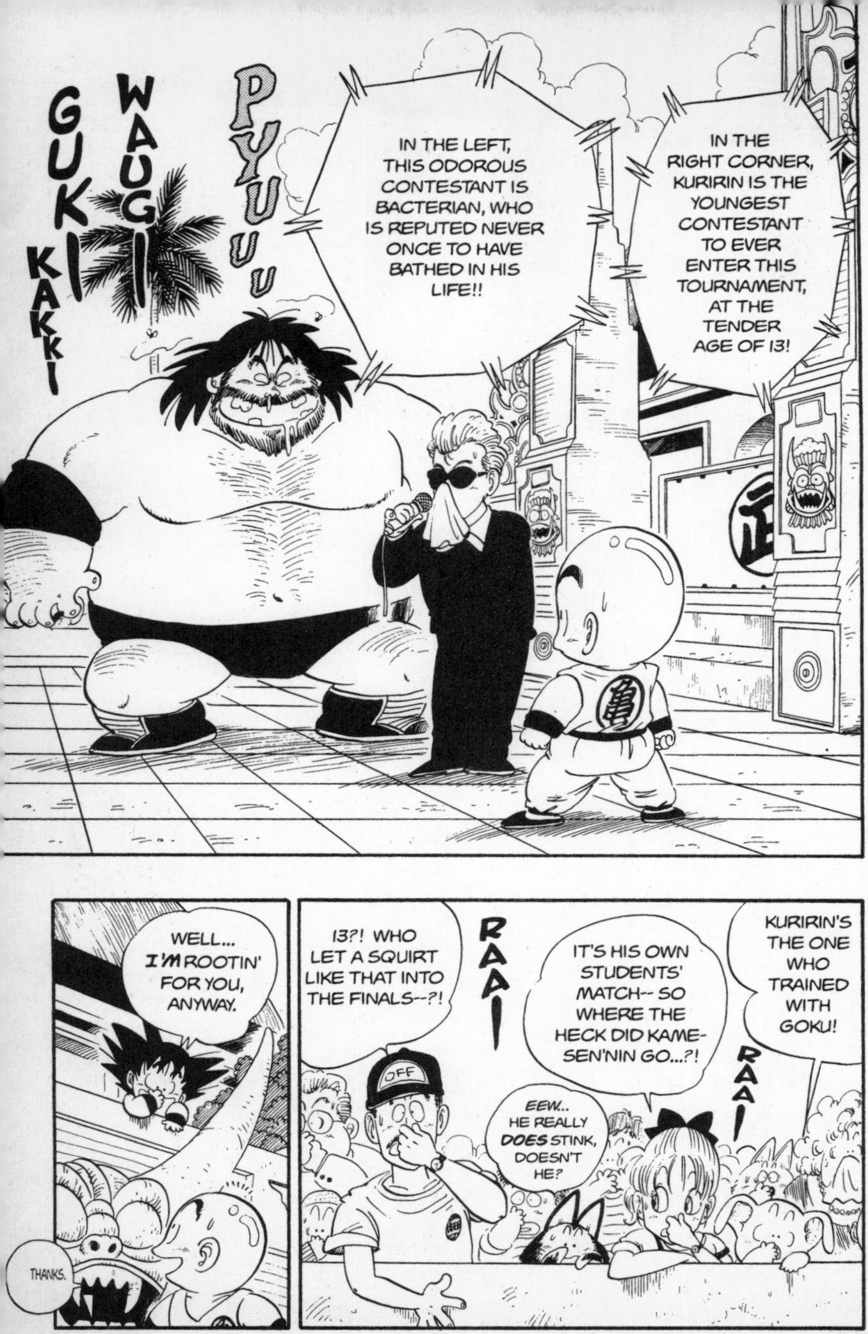
IN THE RIGHT CORNER, KURIRIN IS THE YOUNGEST CONTESTANT TO EVER ENTER THIS TOURNAMENT, AT THE TENDER AGE OF 13!
IN THE LEFT, THIS ODOROUS CONTESTANT IS BACTERIAN, WHO IS REPUTED NEVER ONCE TO HAVE BATHED IN HIS LIFE!!
PYUUU
WAUGI
GUKI
KAKKI
KURIRIN'S THE ONE WHO TRAINED WITH GOKU!
RAAI
IT'S HIS OWN STUDENTS' MATCH-- SO WHERE THE HECK DID KAME-SEN'NIN GO...?!
RAAI
13?! WHO LET A SQUIRT LIKE THAT INTO THE FINALS--?!
EEW... HE REALLY DOES STINK, DOESN'T HE?
OFF
WELL... I'M ROOTIN' FOR YOU, ANYWAY.
THANKS.

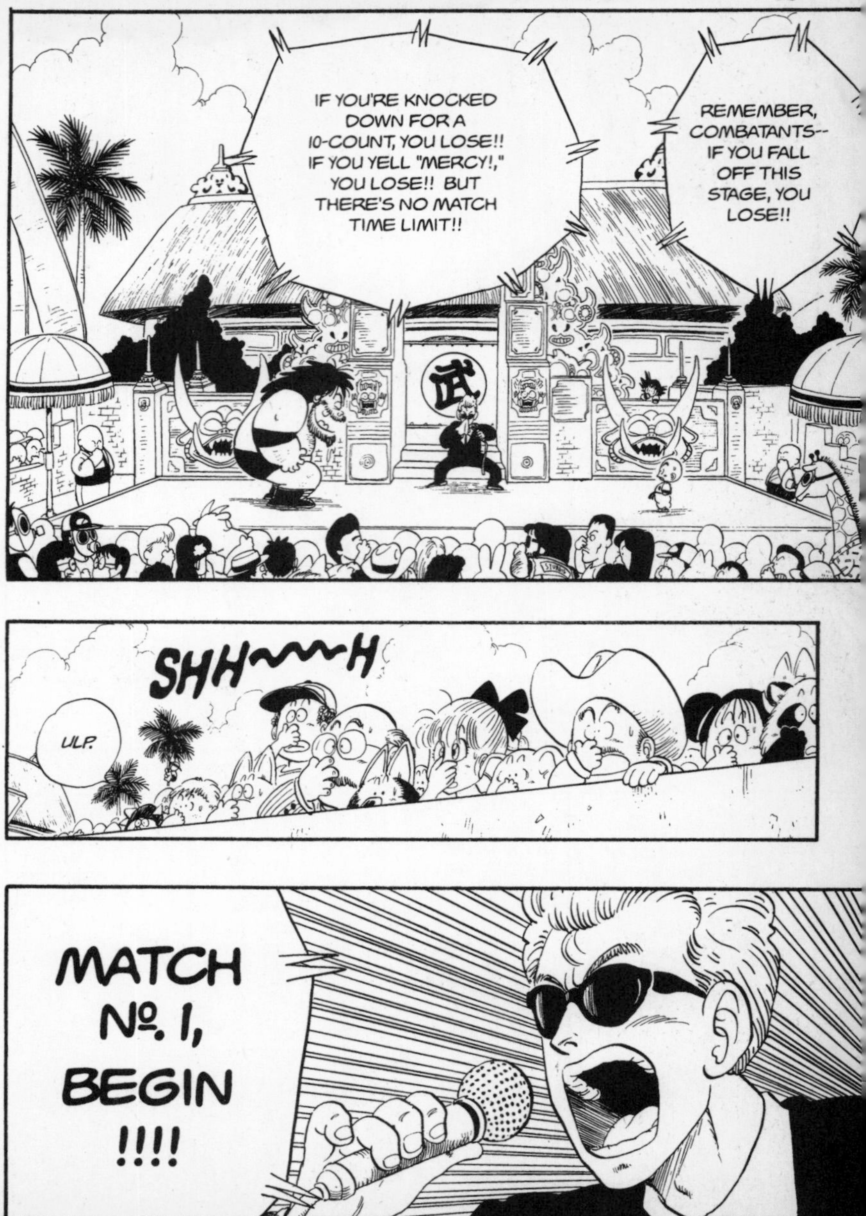
REMEMBER, COMBATANTS-- IF YOU FALL OFF THIS STAGE, YOU LOSE!!
IF YOU'RE KNOCKED DOWN FOR A 10-COUNT, YOU LOSE!! IF YOU YELL "MERCY!," YOU LOSE!! BUT THERE'S NO MATCH TIME LIMIT!!
SHH~~~H
ULP.
MATCH №. 1, BEGIN !!!!

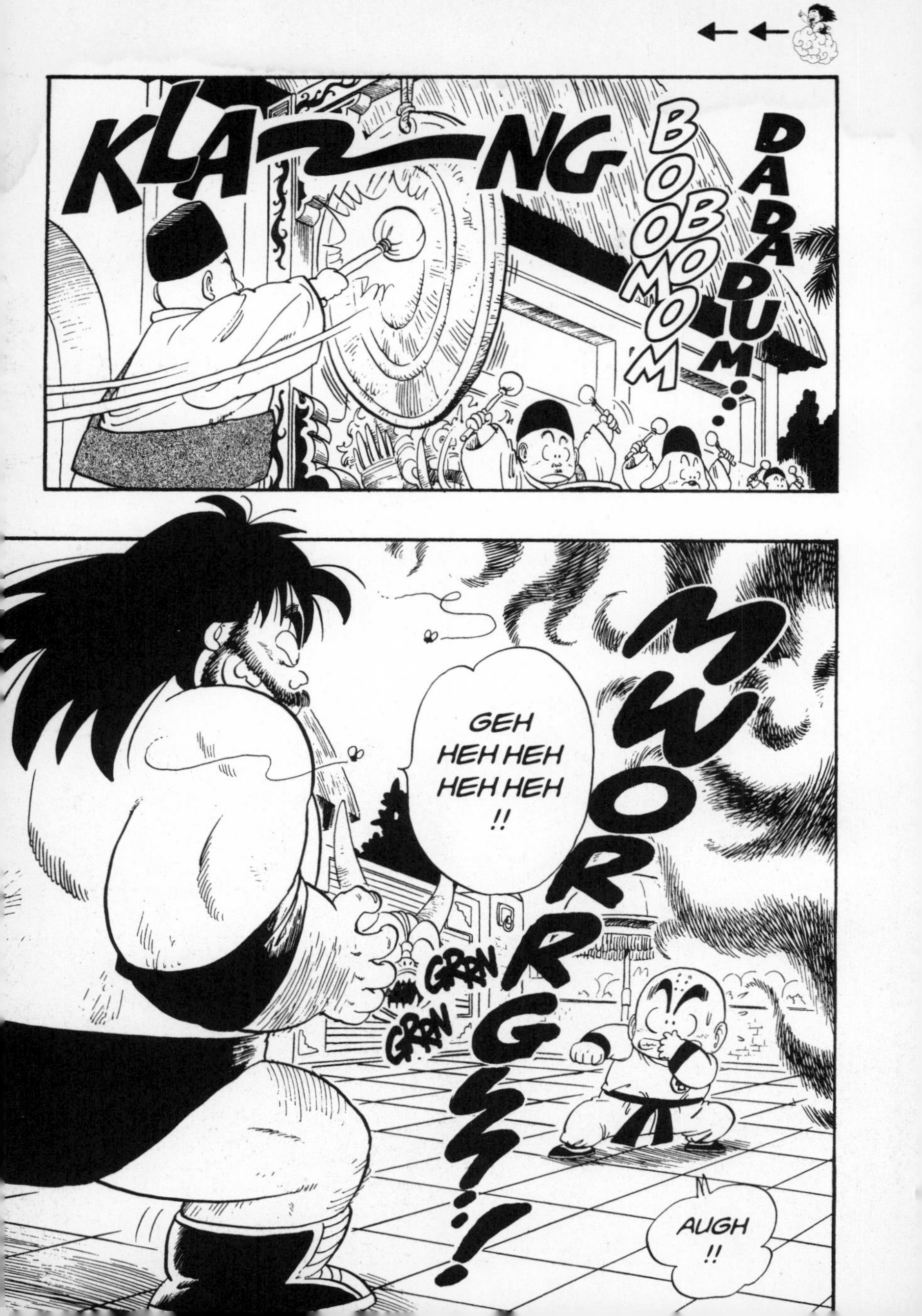
DADADUM!!
BOBOMOM
KLA—NG
MWORRRG!!
GEH HEH HEH HEH HEH !!
GRRN GRRN
AUGH !!

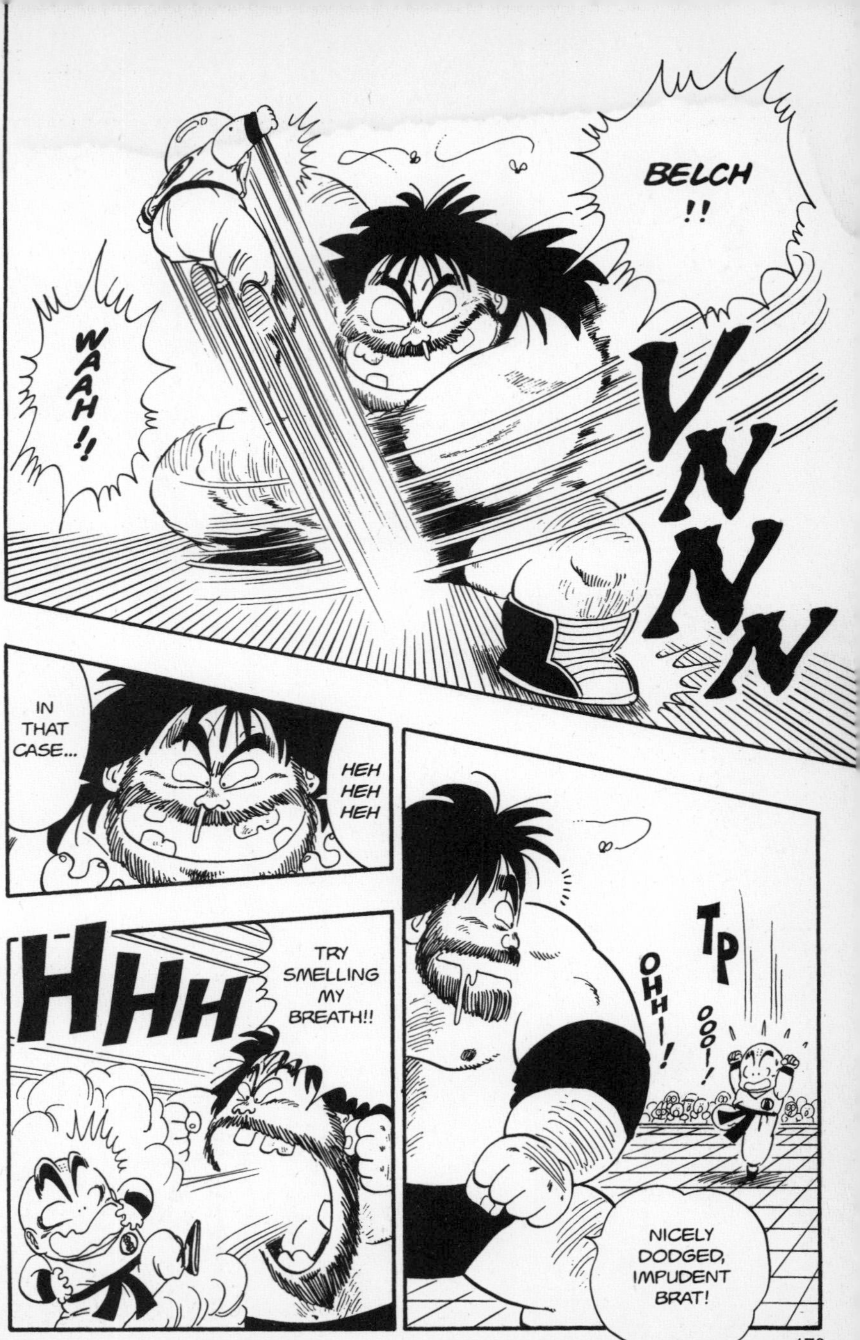
BELCH !!
VNNN
WAAH!!
TP
OHHH!!
OOO!!
NICELY DODGED, IMPUDENT BRAT!
IN THAT CASE...
HEH HEH HEH
TRY SMELLING MY BREATH!!
HHH

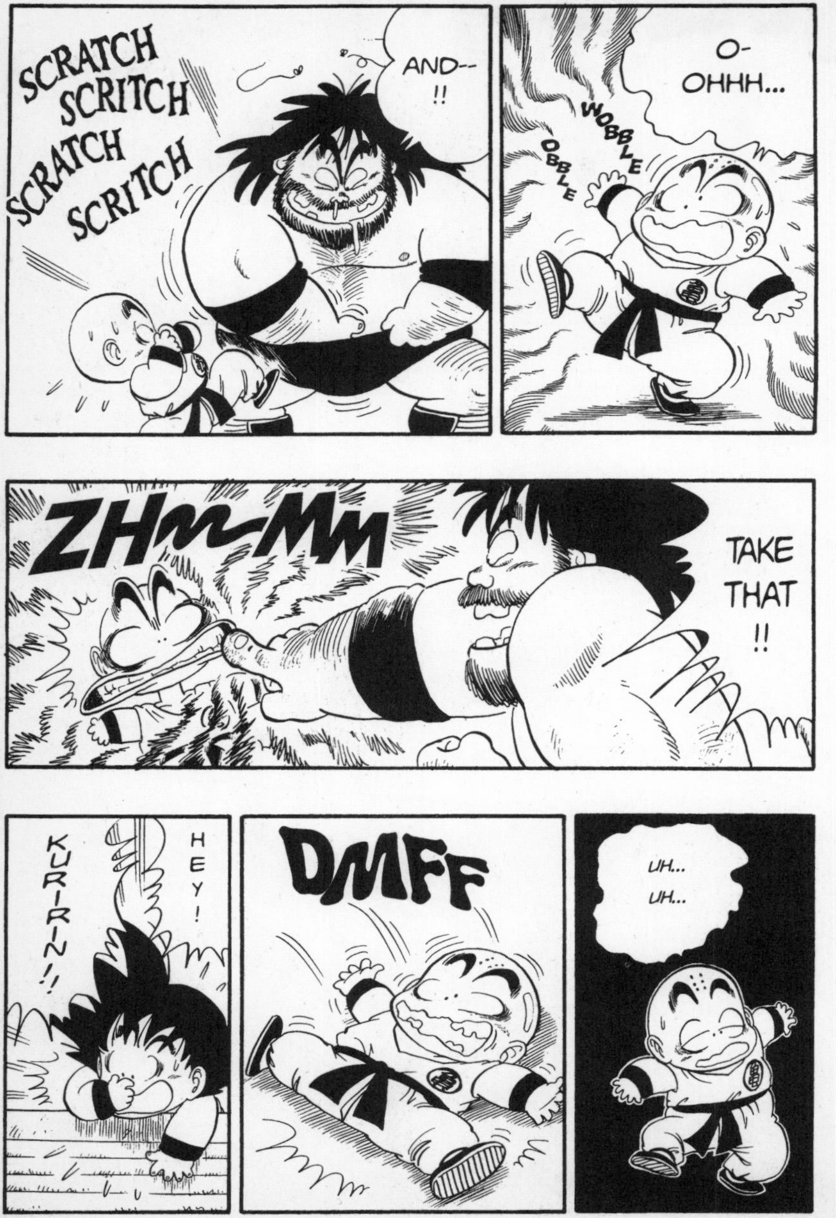
O-
OHHH...
WOBBLE
OBBLE
AND--
!!
SCRATCH
SCRITCH
SCRATCH
SCRITCH
TAKE THAT
!!
ZHM-MM
UH...
UH...
DMFF
HEY!
KURIRIN!!

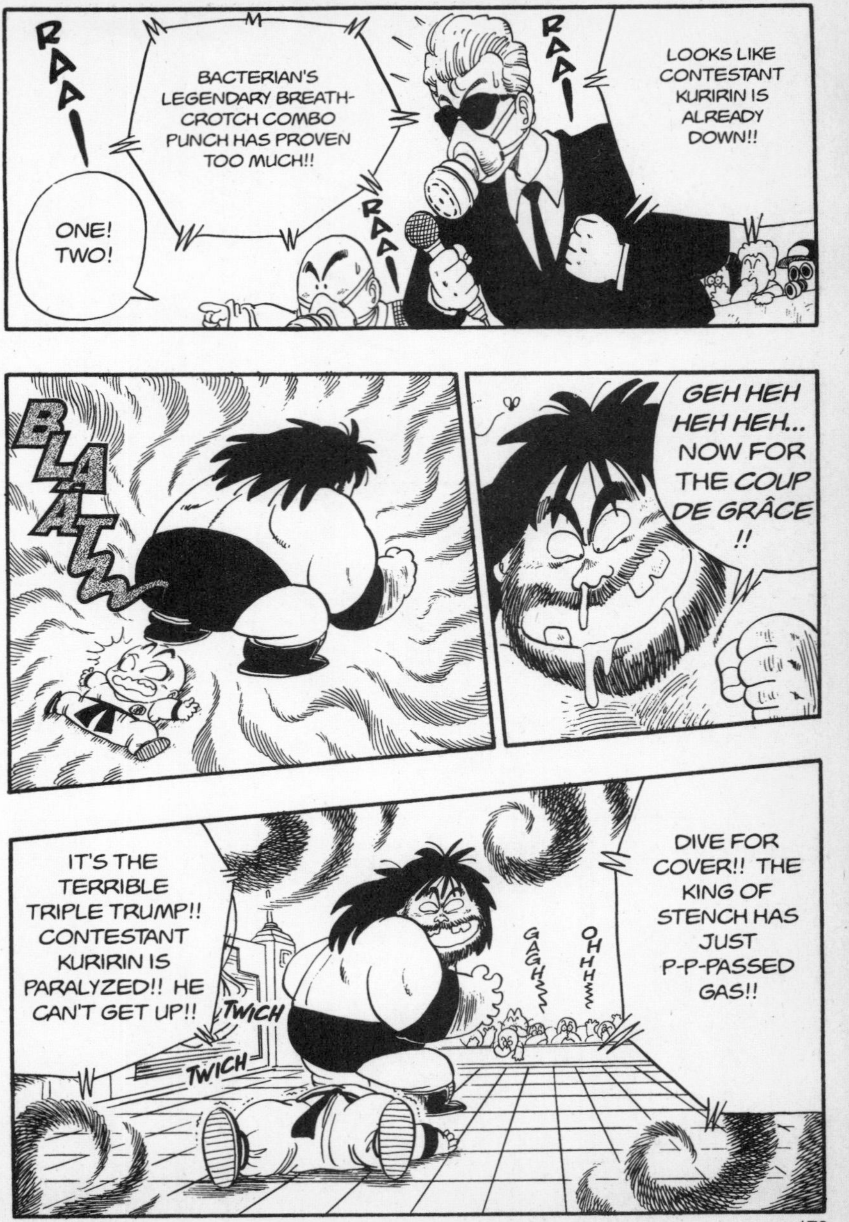

RAA!
LOOKS LIKE CONTESTANT KURIRIN IS ALREADY DOWN!!
RAA!
BACTERIAN'S LEGENDARY BREATH-CROTCH COMBO PUNCH HAS PROVEN TOO MUCH!!
RAA!
ONE! TWO!
GEH HEH HEH HEH... NOW FOR THE COUP DE GRÂCE !!
BLAAT
DIVE FOR COVER!! THE KING OF STENCH HAS JUST P-P-PASSED GAS!!
OHHH
GAGH
IT'S THE TERRIBLE TRIPLE TRUMP!! CONTESTANT KURIRIN IS PARALYZED!! HE CAN'T GET UP!!
TWICH
TWICH

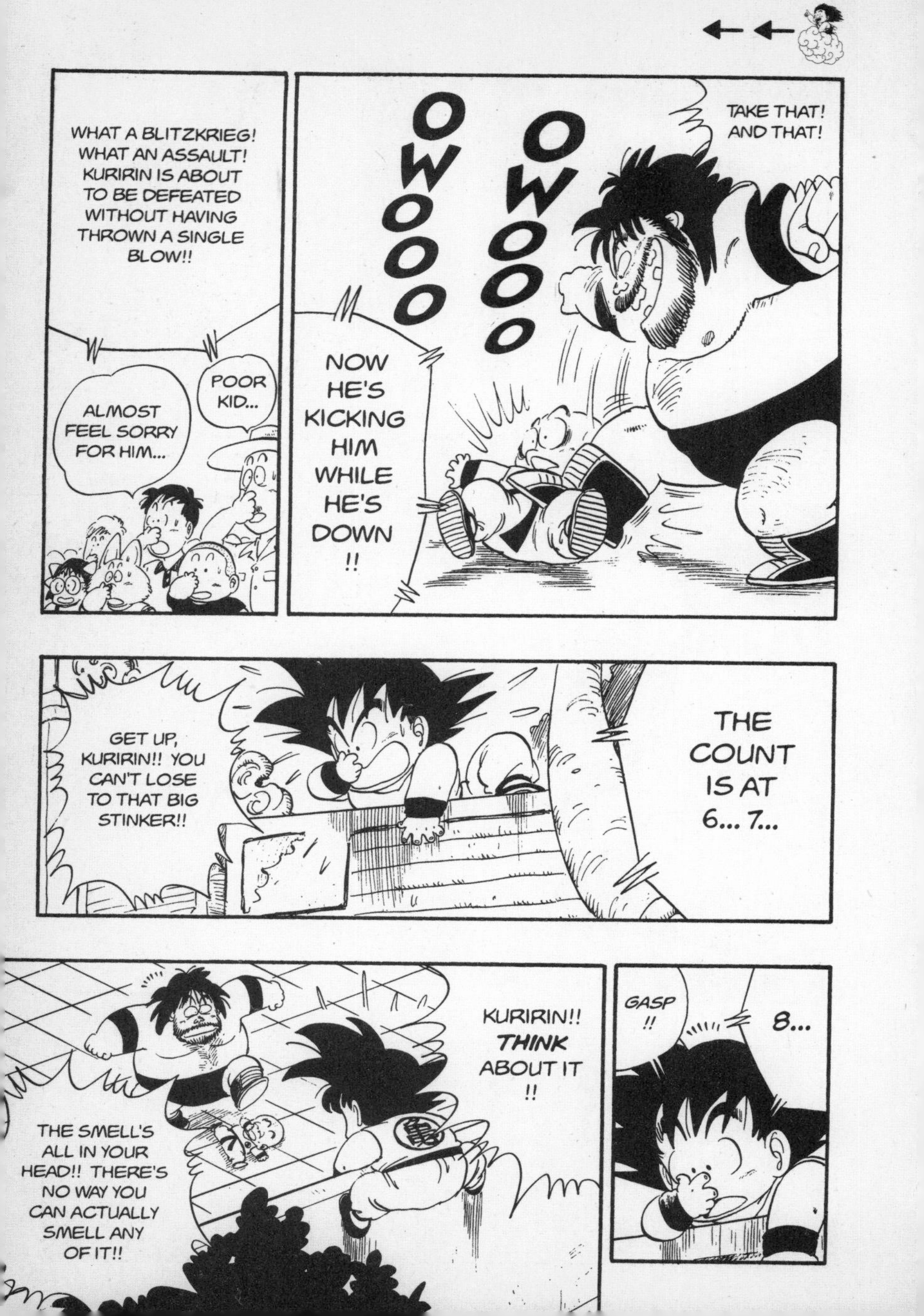

TAKE THAT! AND THAT!
OWOOO
OWOOO
NOW HE'S KICKING HIM WHILE HE'S DOWN !!
WHAT A BLITZKRIEG! WHAT AN ASSAULT! KURIRIN IS ABOUT TO BE DEFEATED WITHOUT HAVING THROWN A SINGLE BLOW!!
POOR KID...
ALMOST FEEL SORRY FOR HIM...
THE COUNT IS AT 6... 7...
GET UP, KURIRIN!! YOU CAN'T LOSE TO THAT BIG STINKER!!
8...
GASP !!
KURIRIN!! *THINK* ABOUT IT !!
THE SMELL'S ALL IN YOUR HEAD!! THERE'S NO WAY YOU CAN ACTUALLY SMELL ANY OF IT!!

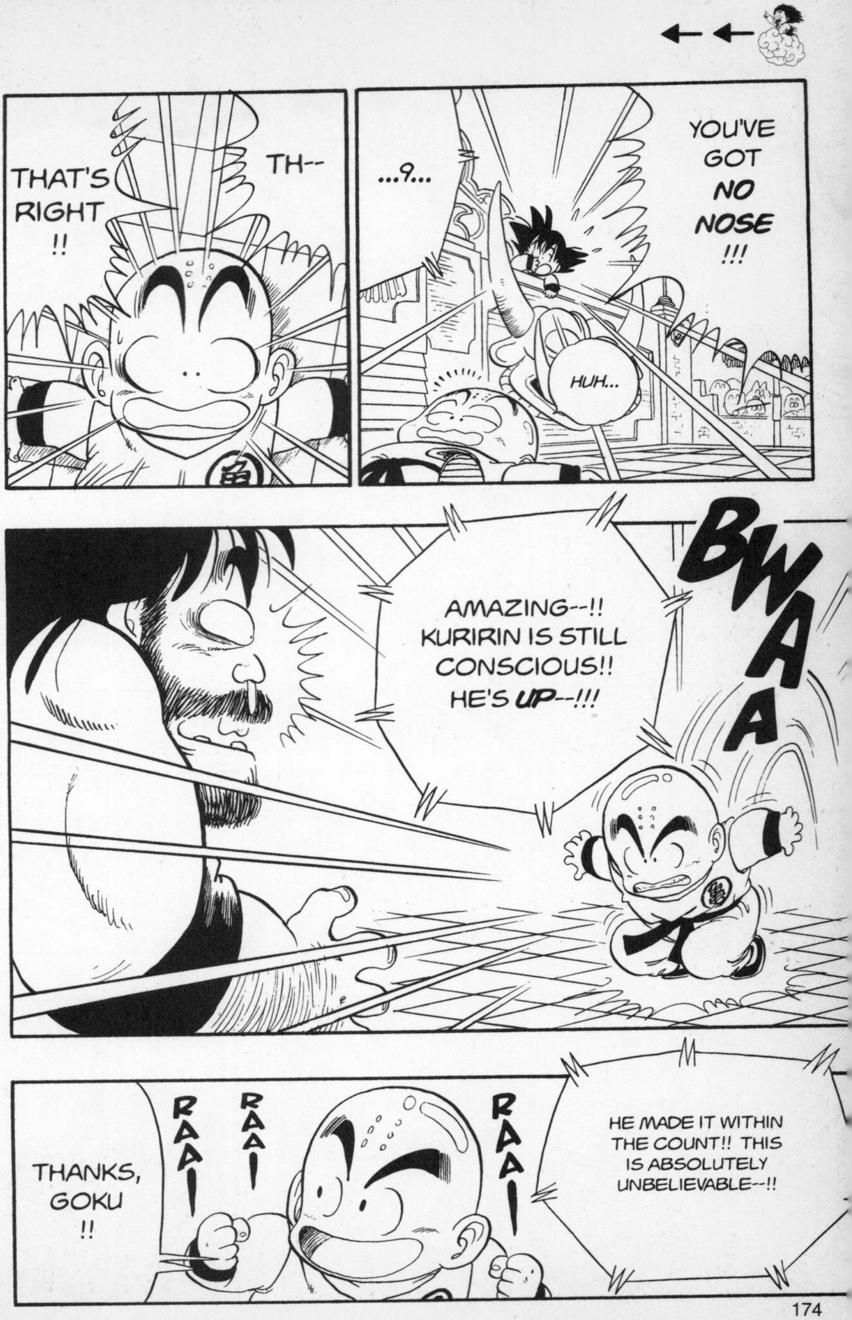
YOU'VE GOT NO NOSE!!!
...9...
HUH...
TH--
THAT'S RIGHT!!
AMAZING--!! KURIRIN IS STILL CONSCIOUS!! HE'S UP--!!!
BWAAA
HE MADE IT WITHIN THE COUNT!! THIS IS ABSOLUTELY UNBELIEVABLE--!!
RAAI
RAAI
RAAI
THANKS, GOKU!!

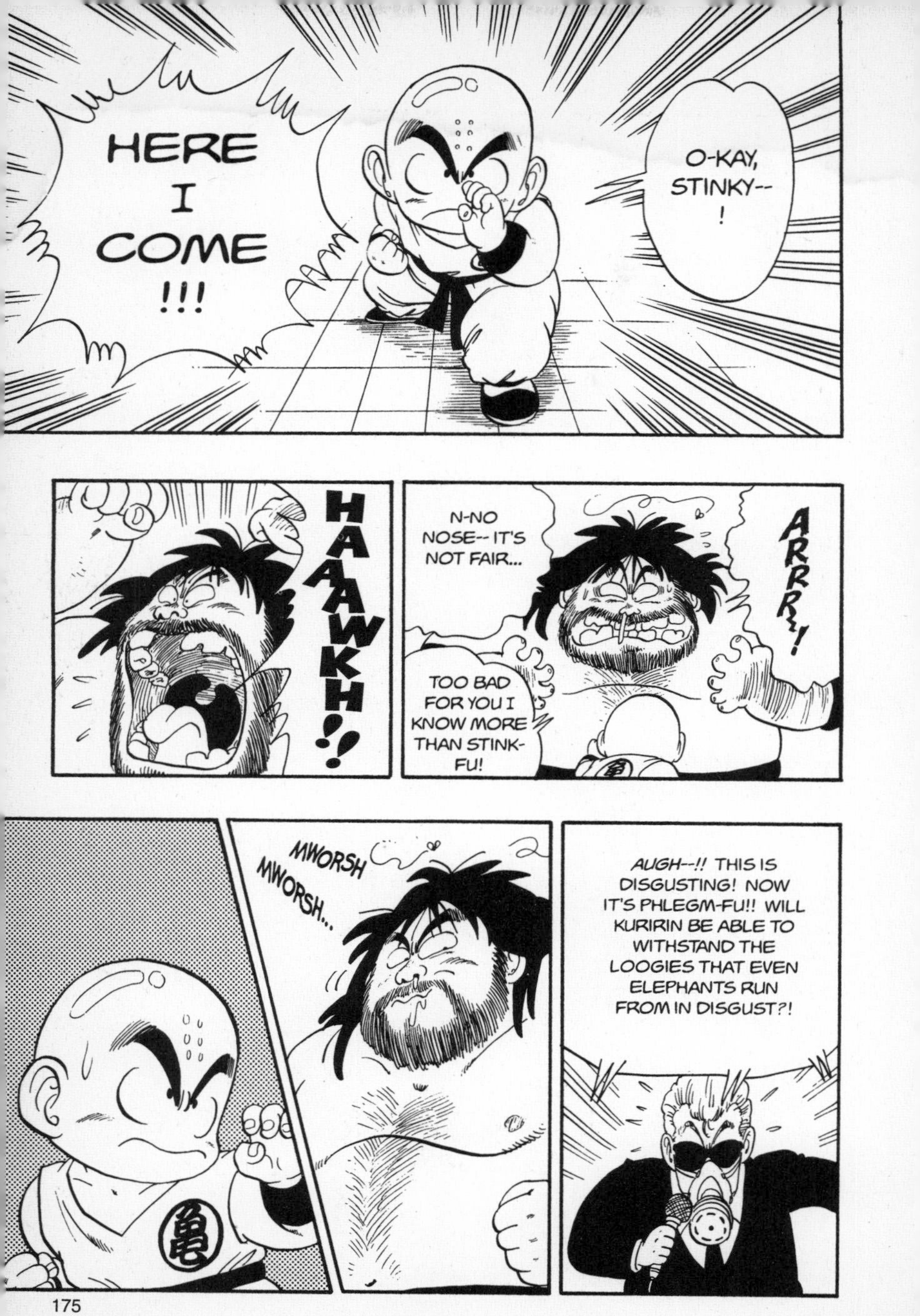
O-KAY, STINKY-- !
HERE I COME !!!
ARRRR!
N-NO NOSE-- IT'S NOT FAIR...
TOO BAD FOR YOU I KNOW MORE THAN STINK-FU!
HAAAWKH!!
AUGH--!! THIS IS DISGUSTING! NOW IT'S PHLEGM-FU!! WILL KURIRIN BE ABLE TO WITHSTAND THE LOOGIES THAT EVEN ELEPHANTS RUN FROM IN DISGUST?!
MWORSH MWORSH...

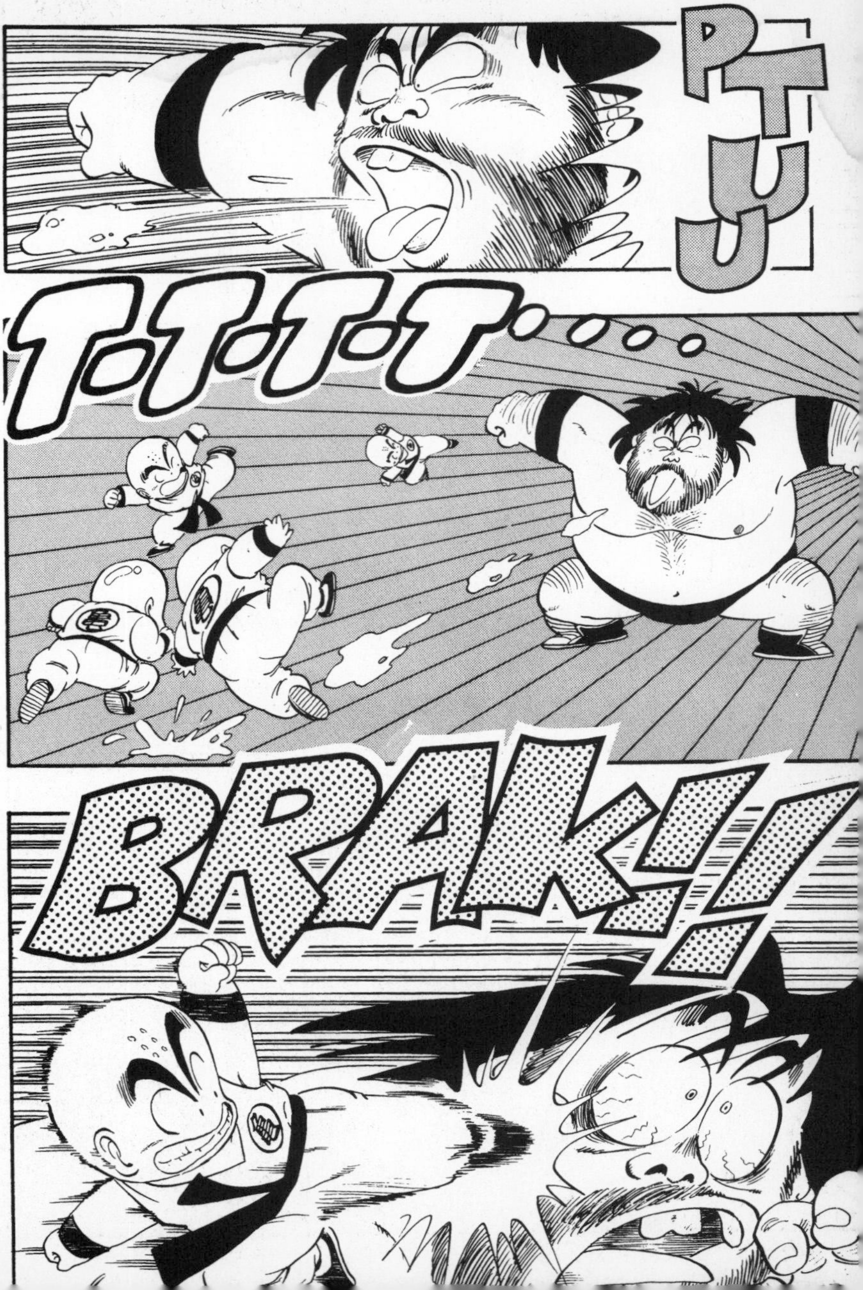
PTUJ
T-T-T-T...
BRAK!!

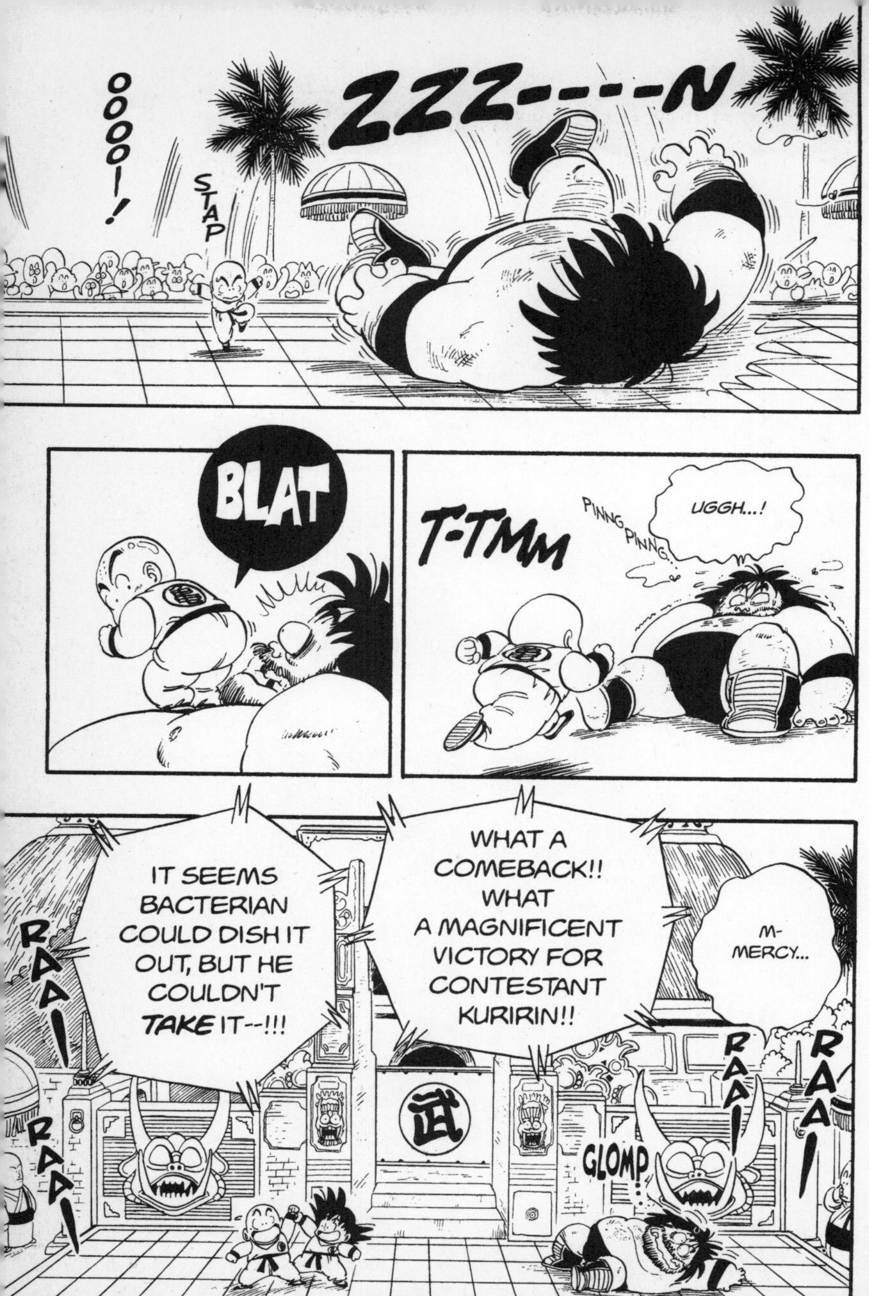
ZZZ---N
OOOO!!
STAP
UGGH...!
PINNG PINNG
T-TMM
BLAT
M-MERCY...
WHAT A COMEBACK!! WHAT A MAGNIFICENT VICTORY FOR CONTESTANT KURIRIN!!
IT SEEMS BACTERIAN COULD DISH IT OUT, BUT HE COULDN'T *TAKE* IT--!!!
RAA!
RAA!
GLOMP
RAA!
RAA!

NEXT: Jackie WHO?!

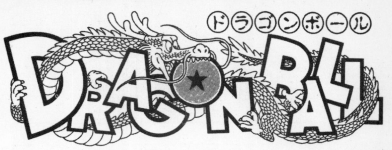

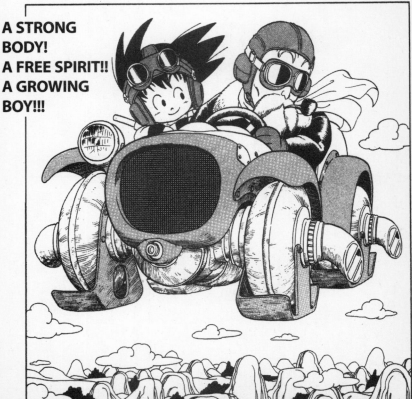

Title Page Gallery

Here are all the chapter title pages which were used when these chapters of **Dragon Ball** were originally published in Japan in 1985 in **Weekly Shonen Jump** magazine. Some were previously published in VIZ's **Dragon Ball** monthly comic series; some have never before been seen in America!

ドラゴンボール
DRAGON BALL
A STRONG BODY! A FREE SPIRIT!! A GROWING BOY!!!

Tale 28 • Let the Training Begin!!

Akira Toriyama
鳥山明
BIRD STUDIO

Tale 27 • Nothing to Sneeze At

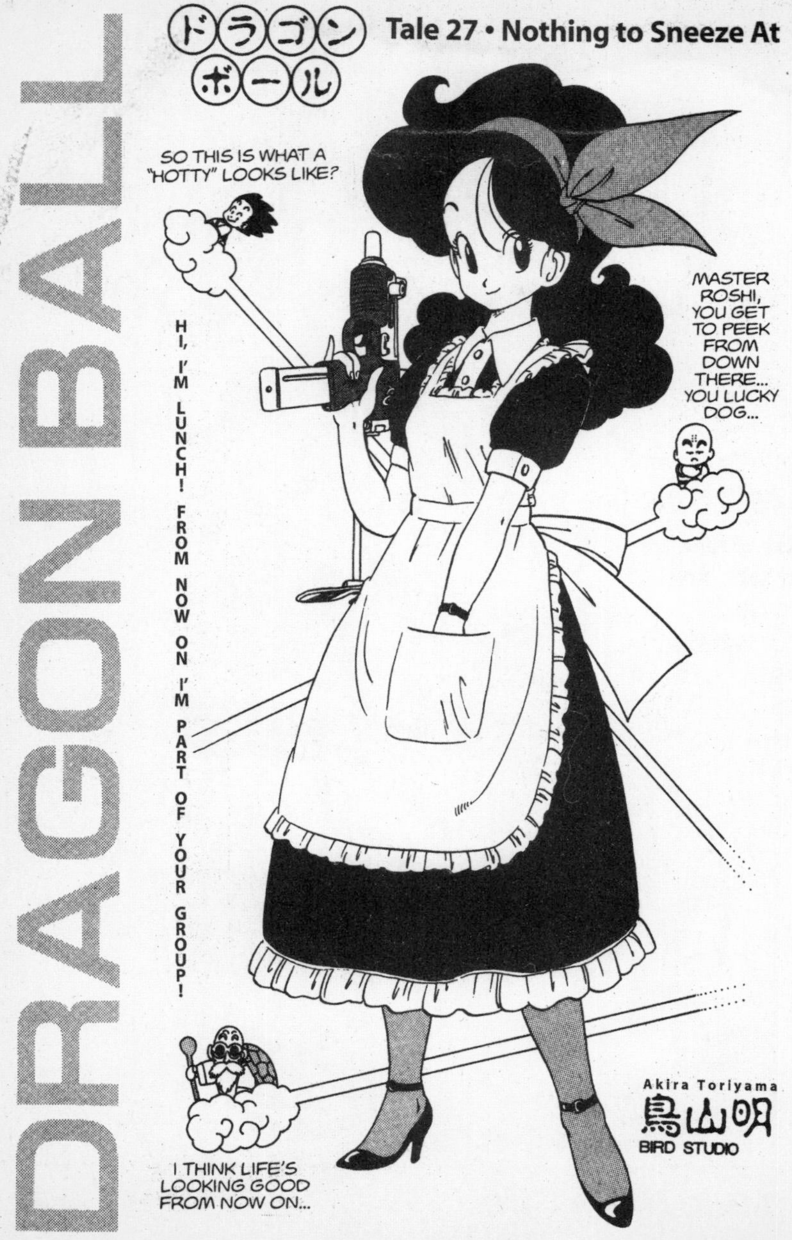

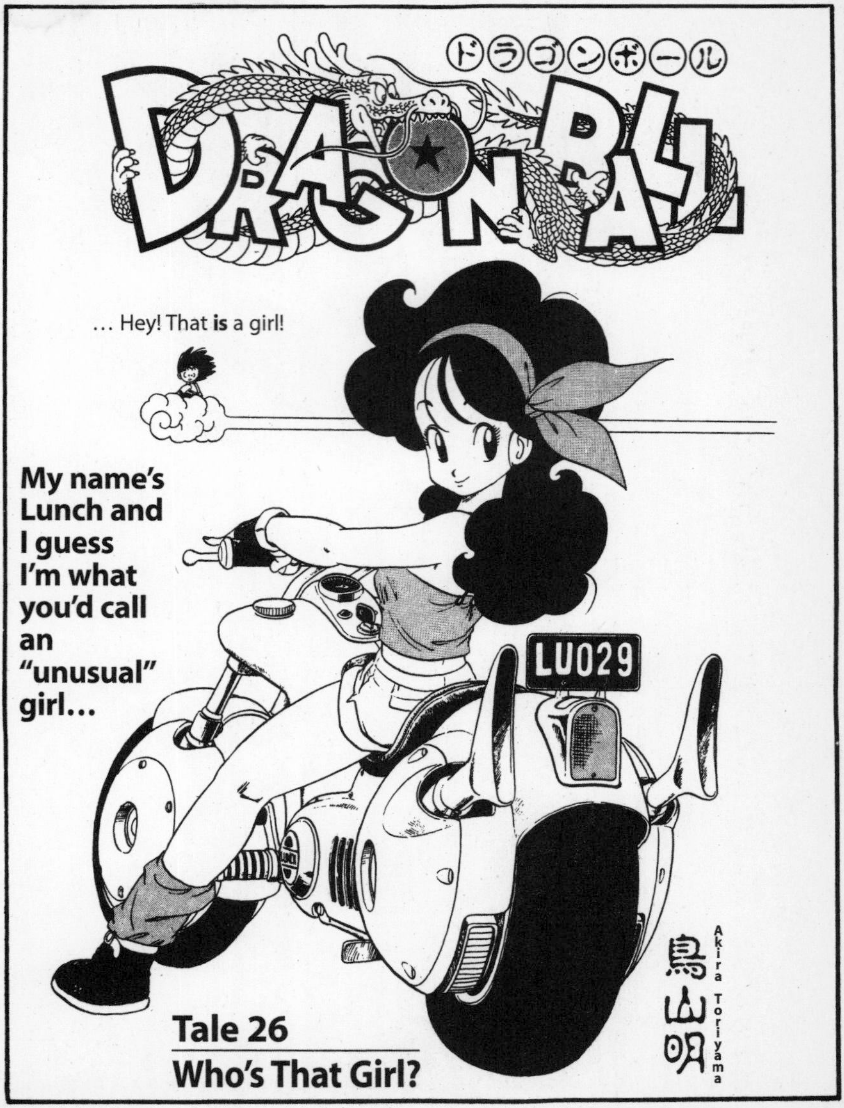
ドラゴンボール
DRAGON BALL
... Hey! That is a girl!
My name's Lunch and I guess I'm what you'd call an "unusual" girl...
LU029
鳥山明
Akira Toriyama
Tale 26
Who's That Girl?

ドラゴンボール

DRAGON BALL

I'M GONNA TRAIN AND TRAIN, FASTER AND STRONGER

Tale 29
Bad Day at Turtle Rock

Akira Toriyama
鳥山明

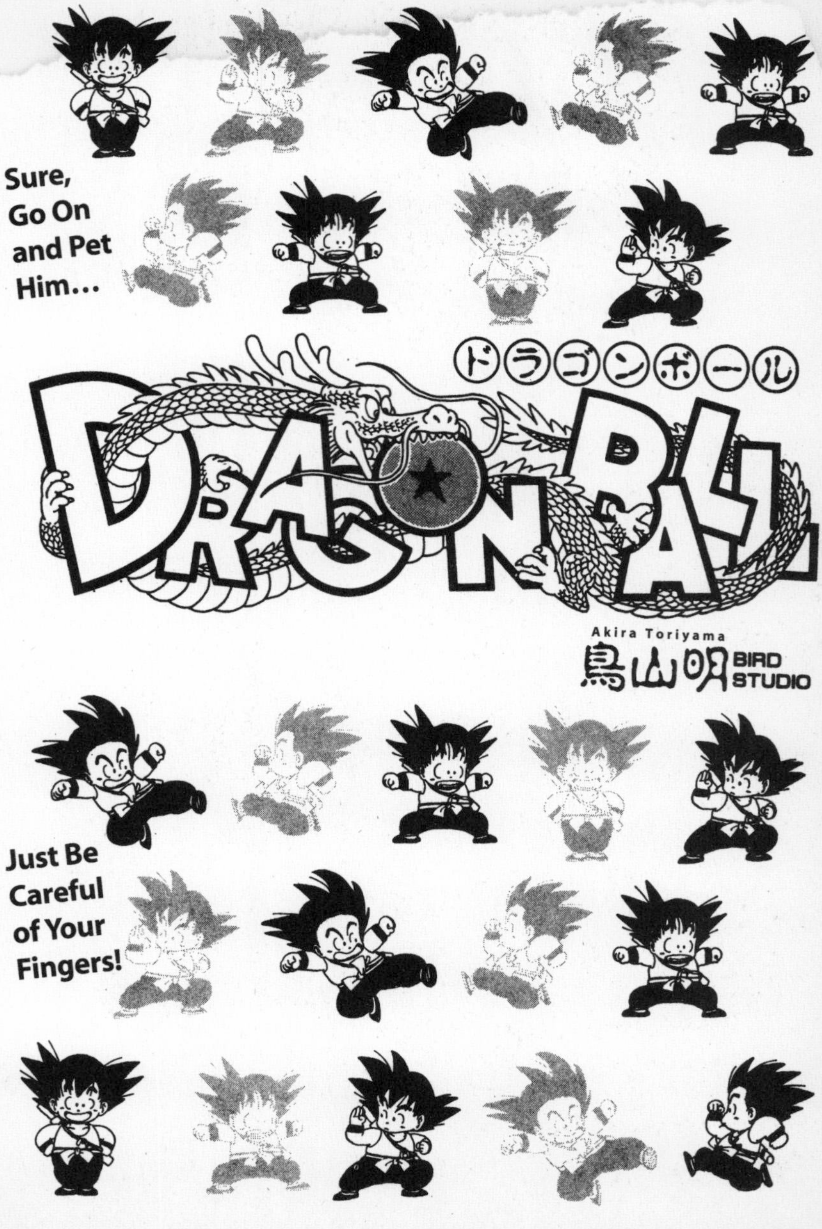
Sure, Go On and Pet Him…
ドラゴンボール
DRAGON BALL
Akira Toriyama
鳥山明 BIRD STUDIO
Just Be Careful of Your Fingers!

DRAGON BALL

ドラゴンボール

Tale 28

Let the Training Begin!!

Packing Up and Moving On...

THE BEST IS YET TO COME!

Akira Toriyama

鳥山明 BIRD STUDIO

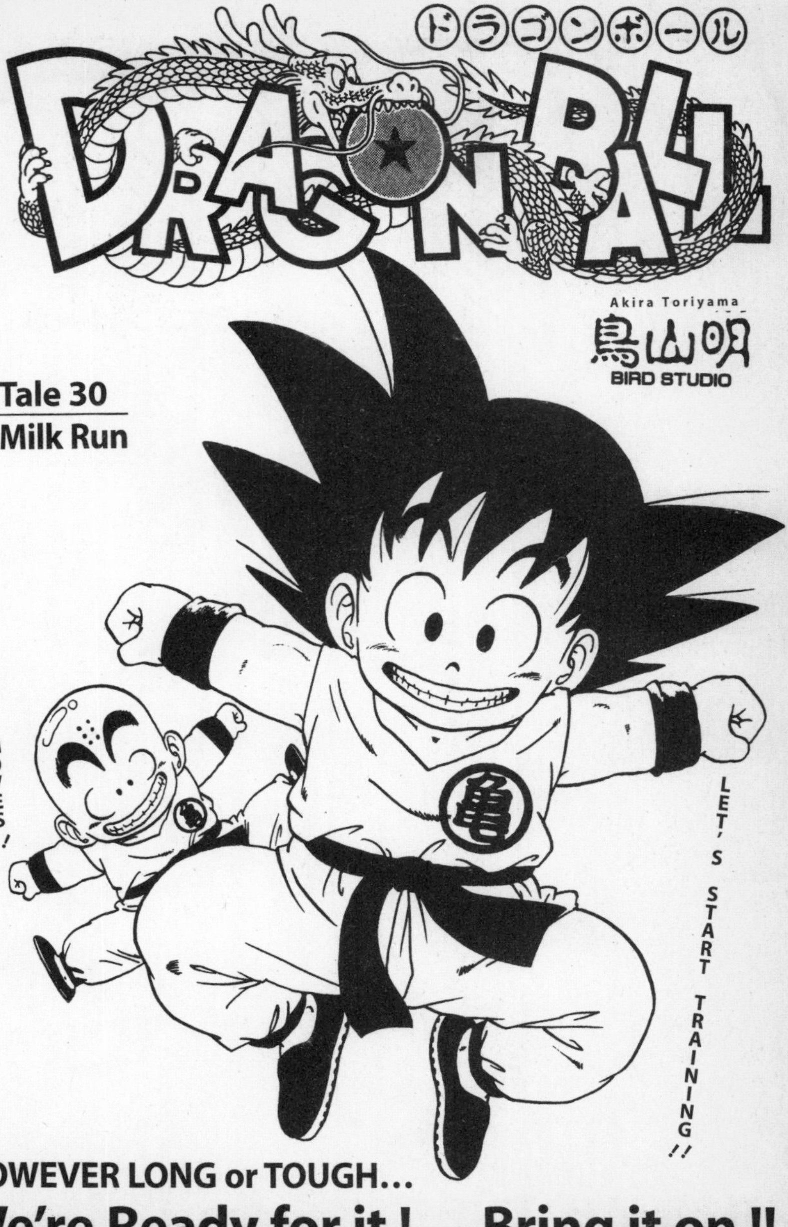
ドラゴンボール
DRAGON BALL
SHOW US SOME MOVES!!
LET'S START TRAINING!!

Akira Toriyama
鳥山明
BIRD STUDIO

Tale 30
Milk Run

HOWEVER LONG or TOUGH…

We're Ready for it! Bring it on!!

DRAGON BALL

ドラゴンボール

IF YOU CLIMB REAL HIGH CAN YOU SEE YOUR OWN FUTURE?

Tale 32
Let the Contest Begin!!

鳥山明

DRAGON BALL

ドラゴンボール

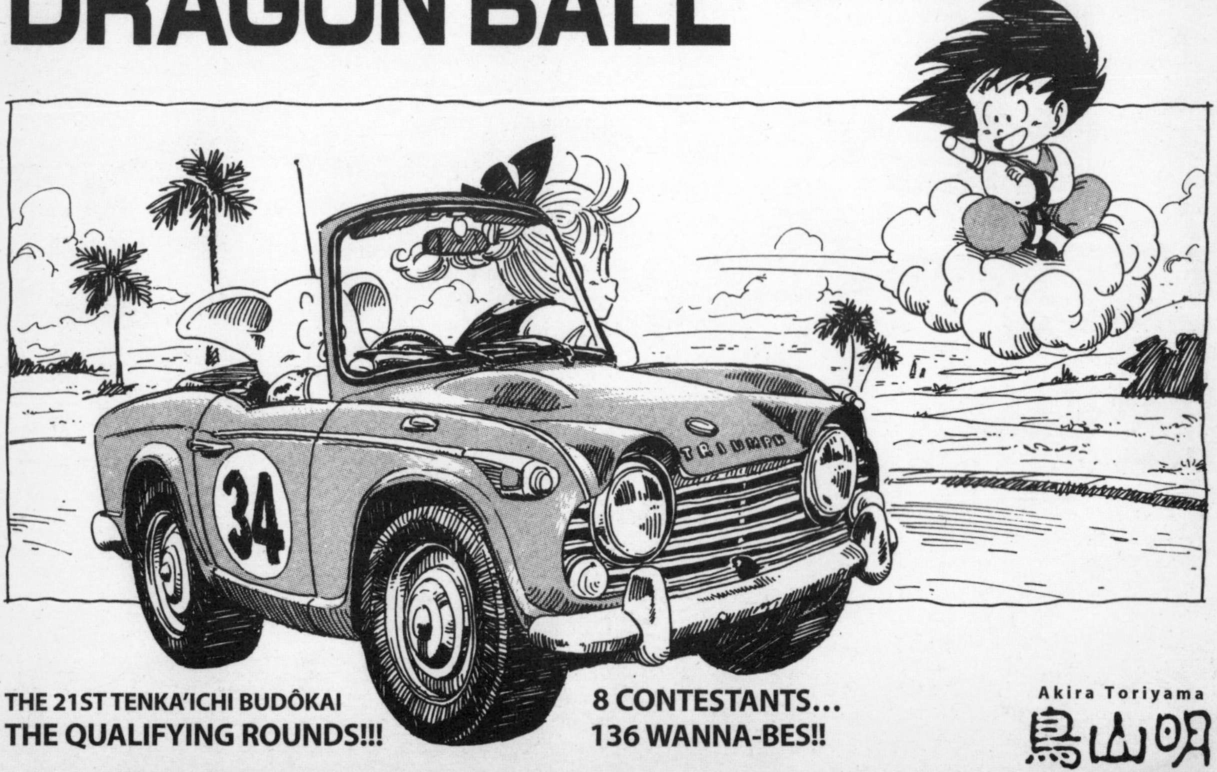
34
TRIUMPH

THE 21ST TENKA'ICHI BUDÔKAI
THE QUALIFYING ROUNDS!!!

8 CONTESTANTS...
136 WANNA-BES!!

Akira Toriyama
鳥山明

ドラゴンボール

DRAGON BALL

OKAY, WHO WANTS TO BE NEXT?!

Tale 34
Strongest Under the Heavens!

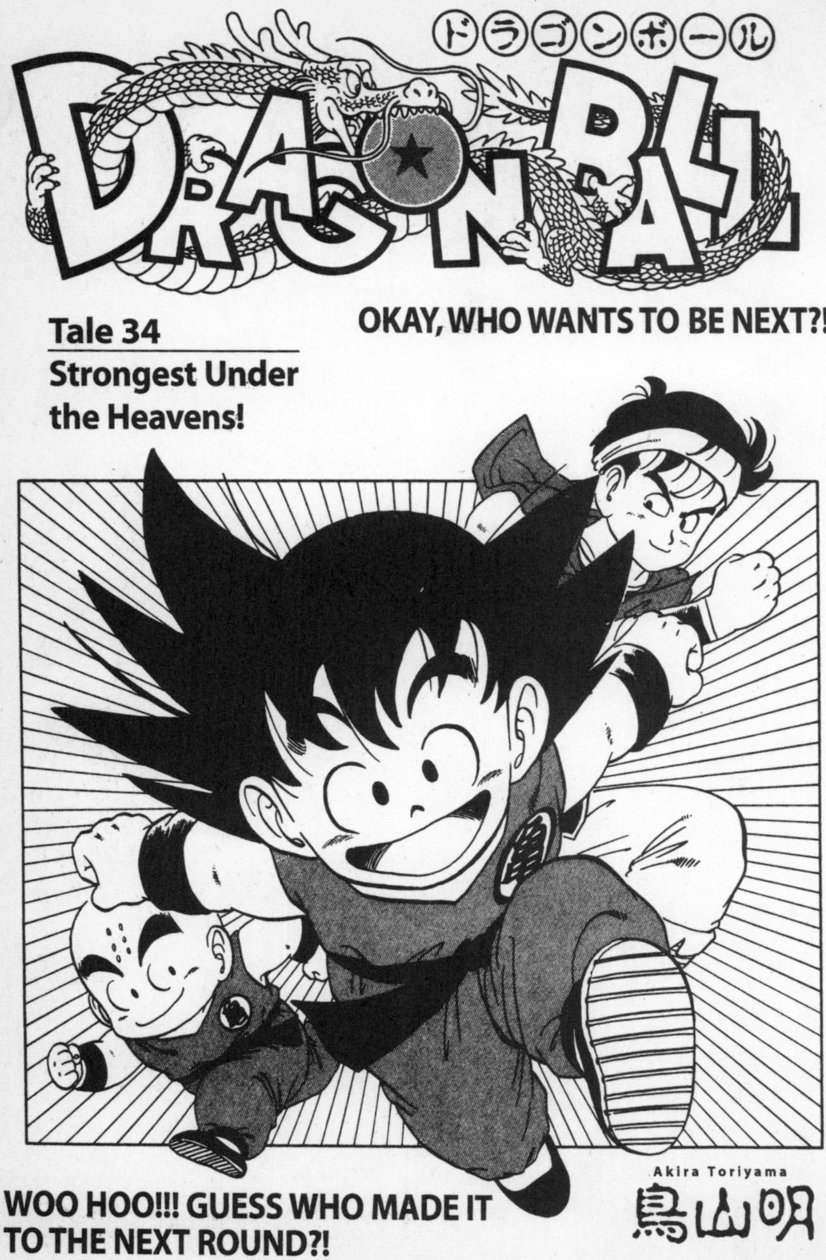

WOO HOO!!! GUESS WHO MADE IT TO THE NEXT ROUND?!

Akira Toriyama
鳥山明

ドラゴンボール

DRAGON BALL

Tale 36
Match No. 1

Akira Toriyama
鳥山明

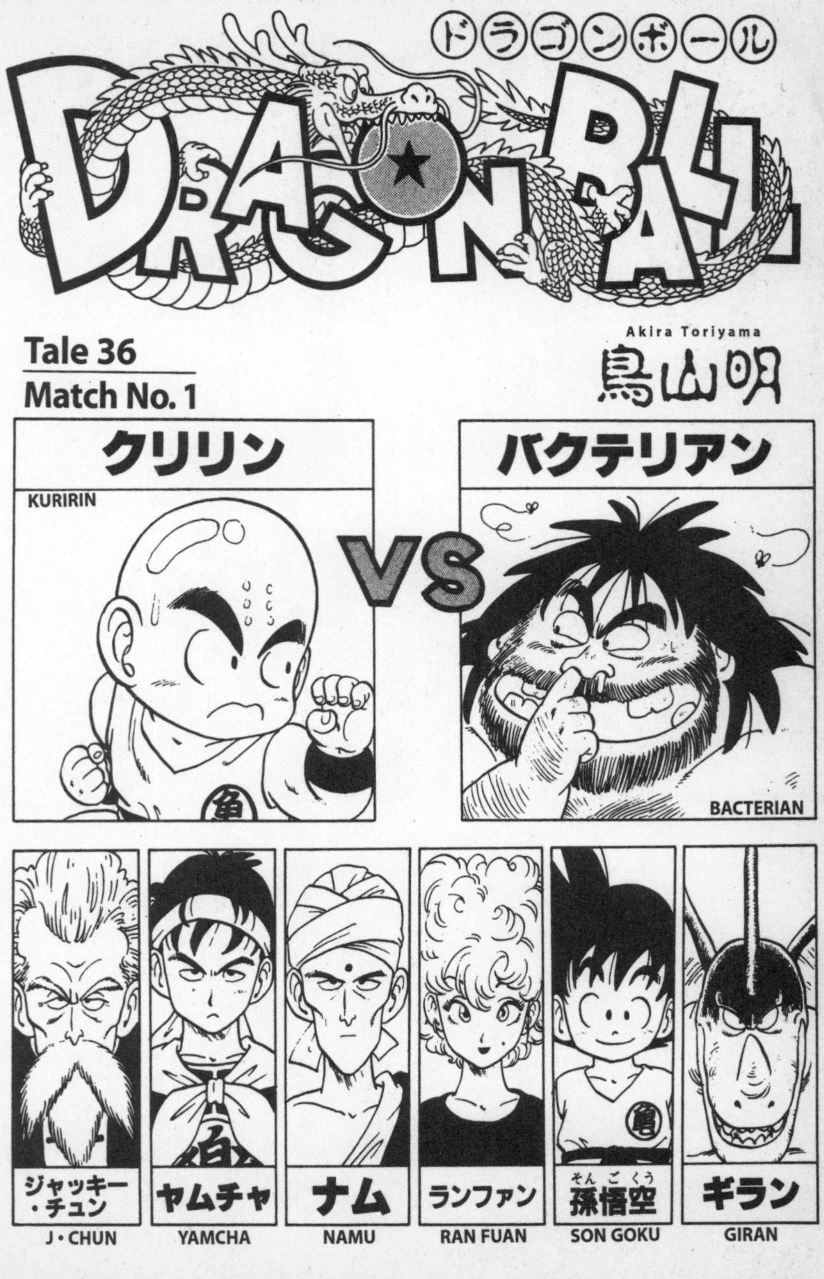

バクテリアン
BACTERIAN
VS
クリリン
KURIRIN
ギラン
GIRAN
そんごくう
孫悟空
SON GOKU
ランファン
RAN FUAN
ナム
NAMU
ヤムチャ
YAMCHA
ジャッキー・チュン
J・CHUN

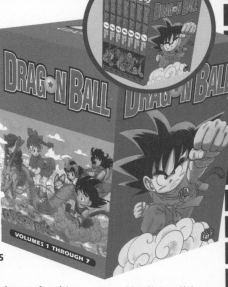

VALIDATION COUPON ③

DRAG☆N BALL™
DISPLAY BOX

To receive your Dragon Ball display box, complete the **Entry Form** from volume 1, collect the **Validation Coupons** from volumes 2 to 7, and mail them along with your payment of **$4.50** payable to:

DRAGON BALL DISPLAY BOX OFFER
P.O. Box 111238
Tacoma, WA 98411-1238

◀ **DETACH HERE**

COMPLETE OUR SURVEY AND LET US KNOW WHAT YOU THINK!

☐ Please check here if you DO NOT wish to receive information or future offers from VIZ

Name: _____

Address: _____

City: _____ **State:** _____ **Zip:** _____

E-mail: _____

☐ Male ☐ Female **Date of Birth** (mm/dd/yyyy): ___/___/_____ (Under 13? Parental consent required)

What race/ethnicity do you consider yourself? (please check one)

☐ Asian/Pacific Islander ☐ Black/African American ☐ Hispanic/Latino

☐ Native American/Alaskan Native ☐ White/Caucasian ☐ Other: _____

What VIZ product did you purchase? (check all that apply and indicate title purchased)

☐ DVD/VHS _____

☐ Graphic Novel _____

☐ Magazines _____

☐ Merchandise _____

Reason for purchase: (check all that apply)

☐ Special offer ☐ Favorite title ☐ Gift

☐ Recommendation ☐ Other _____

Where did you make your purchase? (please check one)

☐ Comic store ☐ Bookstore ☐ Mass/Grocery Store

☐ Newsstand ☐ Video/Video Game Store ☐ Other: _____

☐ Online (site: _____)

What other VIZ properties have you purchased/own? _____

_____

How many anime and/or manga titles have you purchased in the last year? How many were VIZ titles? **(please check one from each column)**

ANIME	MANGA	VIZ
☐ None	☐ None	☐ None
☐ 1-4	☐ 1-4	☐ 1-4
☐ 5-10	☐ 5-10	☐ 5-10
☐ 11+	☐ 11+	☐ 11+

I find the pricing of VIZ products to be: **(please check one)**

☐ Cheap ☐ Reasonable ☐ Expensive

What genre of manga and anime would you like to see from VIZ? **(please check two)**

☐ Adventure ☐ Comic Strip ☐ Detective ☐ Fighting
☐ Horror ☐ Romance ☐ Sci-Fi/Fantasy ☐ Sports

What do you think of VIZ's new look?

☐ Love It ☐ It's OK ☐ Hate It ☐ Didn't Notice ☐ No Opinion

THANK YOU! Please send the completed form to:

NJW Research
42 Catharine St.
Poughkeepsie, NY 12601

All information provided will be used for internal purposes only. We promise not to sell or otherwise divulge your information.

DRAGON BALL VOL. 3
The SHONEN JUMP Graphic Novel Edition

This graphic novel is number 3 in a series of 42.

STORY AND ART BY
AKIRA TORIYAMA

ENGLISH ADAPTATION BY
GERARD JONES

Translation/Mari Morimoto
Touch-Up Art & Lettering/Wayne Truman
Cover Design/Izumi Evers & Dan Ziegler
Graphics & Design/Sean Lee
Original Editor/Trish Ledoux
Graphic Novel Editor/Jason Thompson

Managing Editor/Annette Roman
Editor in Chief/Hyoe Narita
V.P. of Sales and Marketing/Liza Coppola
V.P. of Strategic Development/Yumi Hoashi
Publisher/Seiji Horibuchi

PARENTAL ADVISORY
Dragon Ball is rated "T" for Teen. It may contain violence,
language, alcohol or tobacco use, or suggestive situations. It
is recommended for ages 13 and up.

In the original Japanese edition, DRAGON BALL and DRAGON
BALL Z are known collectively as the 42-volume series DRAGON
BALL. The English DRAGON BALL Z was originally volumes 17-42
of the Japanese DRAGON BALL.

Published by VIZ, LLC
P.O. Box 77010 • San Francisco, CA 94107

SHONEN JUMP Graphic Novel Edition
10 9 8 7 6 5 4 3 2 1
First printing, March 2003

www.viz.com

THE WORLD'S MOST
POPULAR MANGA

SHONEN JUMP
GRAPHIC NOVEL
www.shonenjump.com

鳥 山 明

About half a year ago, during the night, I ended up taking in a stray cat. It was a rainy night, so I took pity on it and figured that I would let it stay in the house until the rain let up. But it was a really friendly, cute cat, so we decided to make it an addition to the household. It's a completely black cat, so we named it "Koge" (char). As a result my assistant Matsuyama, who's deathly afraid of cats, is in a constant state of terror every time he comes over to work.

—*Akira Toriyama, 1986*

Artist/writer Akira Toriyama burst onto the manga scene in 1980 with the wildly popular **Dr. Slump**, a science fiction comedy about the adventures of a mad scientist and his android "daughter." In 1984 he created his hit series **Dragon Ball**, which ran until 1995 in Shueisha's best-selling magazine **Weekly Shonen Jump**, and was translated into foreign languages around the world. Since **Dragon Ball**, he has worked on a variety of short series, including **Cowa!**, **Kajika**, **SandLand**, and **Neko Majin**, as well as a children's book, **Toccio the Angel**. He is also known for his design work on video games, particularly the **Dragon Warrior** RPG series. He lives with his family in Japan.